BIR UMM FAWAKHIR 3

Frontispiece. Building 93 under excavation by team of workers near end of 1999 season.
Dump 2 (left) and Dump 1 (right) flank the building. Bir Umm Fawakhir. Photo by Henry Cowherd

BIR UMM FAWAKHIR 3

EXCAVATIONS 1999–2001

by

Carol Meyer

with contributions by

Lisa A. Heidorn

Salima Ikram

Richard L. Jaeschke

Thomas C. Roby

and

Wendy Smith

ORIENTAL INSTITUTE PUBLICATIONS • VOLUME 141
THE ORIENTAL INSTITUTE OF THE UNIVERSITY OF CHICAGO
CHICAGO • ILLINOIS

Library of Congress Control Number: 2014940903
ISBN-10: 1-61491-020-0
ISBN-13: 978-1-61491-020-6
ISSN: 0069-3367

The Oriental Institute, Chicago

Published 2014. Printed in the United States of America.

Oriental Institute Publications, Volume 141

Series Editors

Leslie Schramer

and

Thomas G. Urban

with the assistance of

Rebecca Cain

Spine Illustration

Copper/bronze weight (fig. 41c, pl. 35b)

Printed by Thomson-Shore, Inc., Dexter, Michigan U.S.A.

The paper used in this publication meets the minimum requirements of American National Standard for Information Services — Permanence of Paper for Printed Library Materials, ANSI Z39.48-1984.

∞

To my friend CNB for all her support

Table of Contents

List of Abbreviations

ARS	African Red Slip ware
ca.	*circa*, approximately
cf.	*confer*, compare
cm	centimeter(s)
dia.	diameter
EDW	Eastern Desert Ware
et al.	*et alii*, and others
e.g.	*exempli gratia*, for example
ERS	Egyptian Red Slip ware
ERSA	Egyptian Red Slip A
ERSB	Egyptian Red Slip B
esp.	especially
etc.	*et cetera*, and so forth
fig(s).	figure(s)
ibid.	*ibidem*, in the same place
i.e.	*id est*, that is
km	kilometer(s)
L	liter(s)
m	meter(s)
max.	maximum
misc.	miscellaneous
ml	milliliter(s)
μm	micrometer(s)
n(n).	note(s)
no(s).	number(s)
n.p.	no publisher
p(p).	page(s)
pers. comm.	personal communication
pers. obs.	personal observation
pl(s).	plate(s)
sp.	species
vol(s).	volume(s)

List of Figures

List of Plates

List of Tablcs

Acknowledgments

The 1999 excavations were supported mainly by the National Geographic Society grant no. NGS-6355-98. We are especially grateful for the Society's flexibility in reallocating the funds when plans changed at the last minute. The construction of a barricade for site preservation was supported by the American Research Center in Egypt's (ARCE) Egyptian Antiquities Project (EAP), itself under USAID grant no. 263-G-00-93-00089-00. Further support for the 1999 excavations and the 2001 study season was contributed by Catherine Novotny-Brehm, Leila Foster, Albert Haas, Diana Grodzins, Mr. and Mrs. Henry I. Meyer, Pennzoil Corporation, Robert K. Smither, and Worldwide Chain Store Systems. Essential logistical and quartermastery support came from Chicago House in Luxor, for which we would like to thank Dr. W. Raymond Johnson, Sue Lezon, Yarko Kobylecky, and especially Tina Di Cerbo. Dr. Donald Whitcomb and Dr. Janet Johnson granted us looting privileges among their dig supplies left from the Quseir al-Qadim excavations. A National Endowment for the Humanities (NEH)/ARCE grant in 2003–2004 was used mainly to write portions of the final report on the Bir Umm Fawakhir 1996–1997 survey seasons, but also to finish and field-check the master site map included in this volume (fig. 3).

Many thanks are due to Dr. Gaballa Ali Gaballa, Secretary General of the Supreme Council of Antiquities (SCA; now the Ministry of State for Antiquities), Dr. Mohammed Sughair and Mohammed Nasr in Luxor, Chief Inspector Hussein Afyouni of the Qena office, and the site inspectors listed below with the field teams. We could never have done so much work in the desert without the help and resources of the Egyptian Geological Survey and Mining Authority (EGSMA), so we would like to render special thanks to Mr. Mohammed el-Hinnawi, Dr. Abd el-Aziz, and Dr. Gaber Naim.

In Cairo we were further assisted by the American Research Center in Egypt, especially Robert K. Vincent, Cynthia Schartzer, and Jaroslaw Dobrowolski of the Egyptian Antiquities Project. Mme. Amira Khattab was, as ever, effective and helpful in too many ways to enumerate.

Henry Cowherd shot the photographs on the cover and plates 1–19, 20b, 21, 25c, 26b, 27a, 31–34, 35b, and 36. Richard Jaeschke contributed figure 45 and color plates 24c, 35a, and 37–42, and Tom Roby, figure 46. All the survey team members contributed to the basic site map in figures 3 and 4; the final version was prepared by Mohamed Omar and the author. Unattributed illustrations are the handiwork of the author. The reconstructions (in *Chapter 9*) are a kind of visual hypothesis, how various archaeological finds might have worked together, finds that are usually pulled apart and pinned down on plates in different chapters if not different volumes.

Above all, we would like to thank the hard-working field teams that made the excavation and study seasons not merely possible but highly productive. Another team might have done things differently, but none could have done more. The 1999 team included me as field director; Clare Leader, archaeologist; Mohamed Badr el-Din Omar of EGSMA, geologist; Henry Cowherd, photographer; Richard Jaeschke, objects conservator; Thomas Roby, architectural conservator; Ayman Hindawa and Wail Karam, inspectors; Seif Shared Mahmud, raʾis; Abd el-Jalil Mohamed Samir, driver; and nine Qufti workmen. Girges Samwel of El Mohandes for Construction, Luxor, carried out the construction of the barricade. The 2001 team consisted of myself as field director and draftsman; Henry Cowherd, photographer; Dr. Salima Ikram, archaeozoologist; Dr. Wendy Smith, archaeobotanist; and Abd el-Regal Abu Bakr, inspector. Many thanks are due once again to raʾis Seif Shared Mahmud and his family for assistance and deeply appreciated hospitality.

Carol Meyer
Chicago, October 2013

Bibliography

Adams, William Y.

1986 *Ceramic Industries of Medieval Nubia*. 2 volumes. Memoirs of the UNESCO Archaeological Survey of Sudanese Nubia 1. Lexington: University Press of Kentucky.

Almásy, Adrienn

2010 "6.3. Greek Dockets." In *Biʾr Minayh: Report on the Survey 1998–2004*, edited by Ulrich Luft, pp. 194–96. Studia Aegyptiaca Series Maior 3. Budapest: Archaeolingua Alapítvány.

Aston, David A.

2007 "Amphorae, Storage Jars and Kegs from Elephantine." *Cahiers de la Céramique Égyptienne* 8/2: 419–45.

Bailey, Donald

1996 "The Pottery from the South Church at el-Ashmunein." *Cahiers de la Céramique Égyptienne* 4: 47–111.

Ballet, Pascale, and Delphine Dixneuf

2004 "Ateliers d'amphores de la chôra égyptienne aux époques romaine et byzantine." In *Transport Amphorae and Trade in the Eastern Mediterranean*, edited by Jonas Eiring and John Lund, pp. 67–72. Monographs of the Danish Institute at Athens 5. Athens: Danish Institute.

Ballet, Pascale, and Thomas von der Way

1993 "Exploration archéologique de Bouto et de sa région (époques romaine et byzantine)." *Mitteilungen des Deutsches Archäologisches Institut, Abteilung Kairo* 49: 1–22.

Barnard, Hans

2008a "Eastern Desert Ware from Marsa Nakari and Wadi Sikait." *Journal of the American Research Center in Egypt* 42 (2005–2006): 131–46.

2008b *Eastern Desert Ware*. British Archaeological Reports, International Series 1824. Oxford: British Archaeological Reports.

Barnard, Hans, and P. J. Rose

2007 "Eastern Desert Ware from Berenike and Kab Marfuʾa." In *Berenike 1999/2000: Report on the Excavations at Berenike, Including Excavations in Wadi Kalalat and Siket, and the Survey of the Mons Smaragdus Region*, edited by Steven E. Sidebotham and Willeke Wendrich, pp. 183–99. Los Angeles: Cotsen Institute of Archaeology.

Bellinger, Alfred R.

1966 *Catalogue of the Byzantine Coins in the Dumbarton Oaks Collection*, Vol. I: *Anastasius to Maurice (491–602)*. Washington, D.C.: Dumbarton Oaks Center for Byzantine Studies.

Bernand, André

1984 *Les portes du désert*. Paris: Éditions du Centre national de la recherche scientifique.

Boessneck, J.

1969 "Osteological Differences between Sheep (*Ovis aries* Linné) and Goat (*Capra hircus* Linné)." In *Science in Archaeology*, edited by D. Brothwell and E. S. Higgs, pp. 331–58. London: Thames & Hudson.

Breasted, James Henry

1906 *Ancient Records of Egypt*, Vol. 1: *The First through the Seventeenth Dynasties*. Chicago: University of Chicago Press. Reprint, Urbana: University of Illinois Press, 2001.

Brun, Jean-Pierre

2003a "Méthodes et conditions de fouille des fortins et des dépotoirs." In *La route de Myos Hormos*, edited by Hélène Cuvigny, pp. 61–71. Fouilles de l'Institut Français d'Archéologie Orientale 48, Vols. 1 and 2. Cairo: Institut Français d'Archéologie Orientale.

2003b "Chronologie de l'équipement de la route à l'époque greco-romaine." In *La route de Myos Hormos*. edited by Hélène Cuvigny, pp. 187–205. Fouilles de l'Institut Français d'Archéologie Orientale 48, Vols. 1 and 2, Cairo: Institut Français d'Archéologie Orientale.

Brun, Jean-Pierre, and M. Reddé

2011 "Le fort." In *Didymoi*, Vol. 1: *Les fouilles et le matériel*, edited by Hélène Cuvigny, pp. 17–113. Fouilles de l'Institut Français d'Archéologie Orientale 64. Cairo: Institut Français d'Archéologie Orientale.

Bülow-Jacobsen, Adam

2003 "The Traffic on the Road and the Provisioning of the Stations." In *La route de Myos Hormos*, edited by Hélène Cuvigny. Fouilles de l'Institut Français d'Archéologie Orientale 48, Vol. 2, pp. 399–426. Cairo: Institut Français d'Archéologie Orientale.

Burstein, Stanley M., trans.

1989 *Agatharcides of Cnidus*. London: The Hakluyt Society.

Cannuyer, Christian

2001 *Coptic Egypt: The Christians of the Nile*. New York: Harry N. Abrams.

Cappers, René T. J.

1996 "Archaeobotanical Remains." In *Berenike 1995: Preliminary Report of the 1995 Excavations at Berenike (Egyptian Red Sea Coast) and the Survey of the Eastern Desert*, edited by Steven E. Sidebotham and Willemina Z. Wendrich, pp. 319–36. Leiden: Research School Center for Non-Western Studies.

1998a "Archaeobotanical Remains." In *Berenike 1996: Report of the 1996 Excavations at Berenike (Egyptian Red Sea Coast) and the Survey of the Eastern Desert*, edited by Steven E. Sidebotham and Willemina Z. Wendrich, pp. 289–330. Leiden: Research School Center for Non-Western Studies.

1998b "Botanical Contribution to the Analysis of Subsistence at Berenike." In *Life on the Fringe: Living in the Southern Egyptian Deserts during the Roman and Early-Byzantine Period*, edited by Olaf E. Kaper, pp. 75–85. Leiden: Research School Center for Non-Western Studies.

1999a "The Archaeobotanical Remains." In *Berenike 1997: Report of the 1997 Excavations at Berenike and the Survey of the Egyptian Desert, including Excavations at Shenshef*, edited by Steven E. Sidebotham and Willemina Z. Wendrich, pp. 299–305. Leiden: Research School CNWS, School of Asian, African, and Amerindian Studies.

1999b "Archaeobotanical Remains from Shenshef." In *Berenike 1997: Report of the 1997 Excavations at Berenike and the Survey of the Egyptian Desert, including Excavations at Shenshef*, edited by Steven E. Sidebotham and Willemina Z. Wendrich, pp. 419–26. Leiden: Research School CNWS, School of Asian, African, and Amerindian Studies.

2000 "Archaeobotanical Remains." In *Berenike '98: Report of the 1998 Excavations at Berenike and the Survey of the Egyptian Eastern Desert, including Excavations in the Wadi Kalalat*, edited by Steven E. Sidebotham and Willemina Z. Wendrich, pp. 305–10. Leiden: Research School CNWS, School of Asian, African, and Amerindian Studies.

2006 *Roman Foodprints at Berenike*. Berenike Reports 6. Cotsen Institute of Archaeology Monograph 55. Los Angeles: Cotsen Institute of Archaeology.

Casson, Lionel

1989 *The Periplus Maris Erythraei*. Princeton: University Press.

Castiglioni, Alfredo; Angelo Castiglioni; and Jean Vercoutter

1995 *Das Goldland der Pharaonen*. Mainz: Philipp von Zabern.

Castrizio, Daniele

2010 *Le monete della necropoli nord di Antinoupolis (1937–2007)*. Istituto Papirologico "G. Vitelli": Scavi e Materiali 2. Florence: Istituto Papirologico "G. Vitelli."

Couyat, M. Jules, and Pierre Montet

1912 *Les inscriptions hiéroglyphiques et hiératiques du Ouâdi Hammâmât*. Mémoires de l'Institut Français d'Archéologie Orientale 34. Cairo: Imprimerie de l'Institut français.

Crum, W. E., and H. I. Bell

1922 *Wadi Sarga: Coptic and Greek Texts*. Coptica 3. Hauniae: Gyldendalske Boghandel-Nordisk Forlag.

Curtis, R. I.

1991 *Garum and Salsamenta: Production and Commerce in Materia Medica*. Leiden: E. J. Brill.

Cuvigny, Hélène

1996 "The Amount of Wages Paid to the Quarry-workers at Mons Claudianus." *Journal of Roman Studies* 86: 139–45.

2012 "Introduction." In *Didymoi*, Vol. 2: *Les texts*, edited by Hélène Cuvigny, pp. 1–37. Fouilles de l'Institut Français d'Archéologie Orientale 67. Cairo: Institut Français d'Archéologie Orientale.

Cuvigny, Hélène, editor

2003 *La route de Myos Hormos*. Fouilles de l'Institut Français d'Archéologie Orientale 48. 2 Vols. Cairo: Institut Français d'Archéologie Orientale.

2005 *Ostraca de Krokodilo: la correspondance militaire et sa circulation O. Krok. 1–151: Praesidia du désert de Berenice* II. Fouilles de l'Institut Français d'Archéologie Orientale 51. Cairo: Institut Français d'Archéologie Orientale.

2011 *Didymoi: Une garnison romaine dans le désert oriental d'Égypt*, Vol. 1: *Les fouilles et le matériel*. Fouilles de l'Institut Français d'Archéologie Orientale 64. Cairo: Institut Français d'Archéologie Orientale.

2012 *Didymoi: Une garnison romaine dans le désert oriental d'Égypt*, Vol. 2: *Les textes*. Fouilles de l'Institut Français d'Archéologie Orientale 67. Cairo: Institut Français d'Archéologie Orientale.

Dixneuf, Delphine

2011a "La diffusion des céramiques d'Assouan et du désert Occidental dans le nord du

Sinaï." *Cahiers de la Céramique Égyptienne* 9: 141–65.

2011b *Amphores égyptiennes: production, typologie, contenu et diffusion.* Études Alexandrines 22. Alexandria: Centre d'études Alexandrines.

Dunham, Dows

1957 *The Royal Cemeteries of Kush*, Vol. 4: *Royal Tombs at Meroë and Barkal.* Boston: Museum of Fine Arts.

Dussart, Odile

1998 *Le verre en Jordanie et en Syrie du sud.* Bibliothèque archéologique et historique 152. Beirut: Institut français d'archéologie du Proche-Orient.

Egloff, Michel

1977 *Kellia: La poterie copte, quatre siècles d'artisanat et d'échanges en basse-Égypte.* Recherches Suisses d'archéologie copte 3. Geneva: Georg, Librarie de l'université.

Entwistle, Christopher

2002 "Byzantine Weights." In *The Economic History of Byzantium from the Seventh through the Fifteenth Century*, edited by Angeliki E. Laiou, Vol. 2, pp. 610–14. Dumbarton Oaks Studies 39. Washington, D.C.: Dumbarton Oaks.

Faiers, Jane

2005 *Late Roman Pottery at Amarna and Related Studies.* Excavation Memoir 72. London: Egypt Exploration Society.

Fenwick, H.

2004 "Ancient Roads and GPS Survey: Modelling the Amarna Plain." *Antiquity* 78: 880–85.

2005 "Tel el-Amarna, 2005: Desert Survey." *Journal of Egyptian Archaeology* 91: 20–21.

Floyer, E. A.

1893 *Étude sur le Nord-Etbai.* Cairo: Imprimerie nationale.

Fournet, Jean-Luc, and Dominique Pieri

2008 "Les dipinti amphoriques d'Antinoopolis." In *Antinoupolis* I, edited by Rosario Pintaudi, pp. 175–216. Istituto Papirologico "G. Vitelli": Scavi e Materiali 1. Florence: Istituto Papirologico "G. Vitelli."

Foy, Danièle

2000 "Un atelier de verrier à Beyrouth au début de la conquête Islamique." *Syria* 77: 239–88.

Frankfurter, David

1998 *Religion in Roman Egypt: Assimilation and Resistance.* Princeton: Princeton University Press.

Fulford, Michael G.

1984 "The Red-Slipped Wares." In *Excavations at Carthage: The British Mission*, Vol. 1, Part 2: *The Avenue du Président Habib Bourguiba, Salammbo: The Pottery and Other Ceramic Objects from the Site*, edited by Michael G. Fulford and David P. S. Peacock, pp. 48–115. Sheffield: British Academy, University of Sheffield, Department of Prehistory and Archaeology.

Gascou, Jean

1978 "Amphores byzantines à dipinti grecs de Saqqara." *Bulletin de liaison du Grupe International d'Étude de la Céramique Égyptienne* 3: 24–27.

Gazda, Elaine K.

1983 *Karanis: An Egyptian Town in Roman Times; Discoveries of the University of Michigan Expedition to Egypt (1924–1935).* Ann Arbor: University of Michigan.

Gempeler, Robert D.

1992 *Elephantine X: Die Keramik römisher bis frühharabisher Zeit.* Deutsches archäologisches Institut Abteilung Kairo, Archäologischer Veröffentlichungen 43. Mainz: Philipp von Zabern.

Goodacre, Hugh

1957 *A Handbook of the Coinage of the Byzantine Empire.* London: Spink & Son.

Grant, A.

1982 "The Use of Tooth Wear as a Guide to the Age of Domestic Ungulates." In *Ageing and Sexing Animal Bones from Archaeological Sites*, edited by B. Wilson, C. Grigson, and S. Payne. British Archaeological Reports, British Series 109. Oxford: British Archaeological Reports.

Guéraud, Octave

1942 *Ostraca Grecs et Latins de l'Wâdi Fawâkhir.* Bulletin de l'Institut Français d'Archéologie Orientale 41. Cairo: Institut Français d'Archéologie Orientale.

Guerrini, Lucia

1974 "Materiali ceramici." In *Antinoe (1965–1968)*, pp. 69–113. Serie archeologica 21. Rome: Istituto de studi del Vicino Oriente, Università.

Guidotti, Maria Cristina

2008 "La ceramica del Kom II A ad Antinoe." In *Antinoupolis*, Vol. 1, edited by Rosario Pintaudi, pp. 293-417. Istituto Papirologico "G. Vitelli" Scavi e Materiali 1. Florence: Istituto Papirologico "G. Vitelli."

Hamilton-Dyer, Sheila

2001 "The Faunal Remains." In *Mons Claudianus: Survey and Excavation*, Vol. 2: *The Excavations*, by Valerie A. Maxfield and David P. S. Peacock, pp. 251–301. Fouilles de l'Institut Français d'Archéologie

Orientale 43. Cairo: Institut Français d'Archéologie Orientale.

2011 "Faunal Remains." In *Myos Hormos – Quseir al-Qadim: Roman and Islamic Ports on the Red Sea*, Vol. 2: *Finds from the Excavations 1999–2003*, edited by David P. S. Peacock and Lucy Blue, pp. 245–88. British Archaeological Reports, International Series 2286. University of Southampton Series in Archaeology 6. Oxford: Archaeopress.

Harden, Donald B.

1936 *Roman Glass from Karanis found by the University of Michigan Archaeological Expedition in Egypt, 1924–29*. University of Michigan Studies, Humanistic Series 41. Ann Arbor: University of Michigan Press.

1940 "The Glass." In *Temples of Armant: The Text and Plates*, by Robert Mond, pp. 117–23. Egypt Exploration Society 47 and 48. London: Egypt Exploration Society.

1969 "Ancient Glass, II: Roman." *Archaeological Journal* 126: 44–77.

Harrell, James A.

2010 "Archaeological Geology of Hosh el-Guruf, Fourth Nile Cataract, Sudan." In *Proceedings of the International Conference "The Fourth Cataract Archaeological Salvage Project, 1996–2009"* (Gdańsk, 2–4 July, 2009), edited by Henryk Paner, Stefan Jakobielski, and Julie R. Anderson, pp. 71–84. Gdańsk Archaeological Museum and Heritage Protection Fund African Reports 7. Gdansk: n.p.

Harrell, James A., and V. Max Brown

1992 "The World's Oldest Surviving Geological Map: The 1150 B.C. Turin Papyrus from Egypt." *Journal of Geology* 100: 3–18.

Hayes, J. W.

1972 *Late Roman Pottery: A Catalogue of Roman Fine Wares*. London: British School at Rome.

1977 "North African Flanged Bowls: A Problem in Fifth Century Chronology." In *Roman Pottery Studies in Britain and Beyond*, edited by John Dore and Kevin Greene, pp. 279–87. British Archaeological Reports Supplementary Series 30. Oxford: Oxford University Press.

1980 *A Supplement to Late Roman Pottery*. London: British School at Rome.

1995 "Summary of Pottery and Glass Finds." In *Berenike 1994: Preliminary Report of the 1994 Excavations at Berenike (Egyptian Red Sea Coast) and Survey of the Eastern Desert*, edited by Steven E. Sidebotham and Willemina Wendrich, pp. 33–40. Leiden: Research School CNWS, School of Asian, African, and Amerindian Studies.

1996 "The Pottery." In *Berenike 1995: Preliminary Report of the 1995 Excavations at Berenike (Egyptian Red Sea Coast) and Survey of the Eastern Desert*, edited by Steven E. Sidebotham and Willemina Wendrich, pp. 147–78. Leiden: Research School CNWS, School of Asian, African, and Amerindian Studies.

1997 "Ceramics of the Byzantine Period." In *The Oxford Encyclopedia of Archaeology in the Near East*, edited by Eric M. Meyers, Vol. 1, pp. 471–75. New York: Oxford University Press.

Heidorn, Lisa A.

1995 "The Pottery," pp. 58–61, in "Gold, Granite, and Water: The Bir Umm Fawakhir Survey Project 1992," by Carol Meyer. In *Preliminary Excavation Reports: Sardis, Bir Umm Fawakhir, Tell el-ʿUmeiri, the Combined Caesarea Expeditions, and Tell Dothan*, edited by William G. Dever. Annual of the American Schools of Oriental Research 52. New Haven: American Schools of Oriental Research.

2000 "Pottery from the 1993 Survey." In *Bir Umm Fawakhir Survey Project 1993: A Byzantine Gold-mining Town in Egypt*, by Carol Meyer, Lisa A. Heidorn, Walter E. Kaegi, and Terry Wilfong, pp. 27–42. Oriental Institute Communications 28. Chicago: The Oriental Institute.

Herbert, Sharon

1999 "Quft/Qift (Coptos)." In *Encyclopedia of the Archaeology of Ancient Egypt*, edited by Kathryn A. Bard, pp. 656–57. New York: Routledge.

Herbert, S. C., and A. Berlin

2003 "The Excavation: Occupation History and Ceramic Assemblages." In *Excavations at Coptos (Qift) in Upper Egypt 1987–1992*, pp. 13–135. Journal of Roman Archaeology Supplementary Series 53. Portsmouth: Journal of Roman Archaeology.

Hobbs, Joseph J.

1990 *Bedouin Life in the Egyptian Wilderness*. 2nd ed. Cairo: American University in Cairo Press.

Hölscher, Uvo

1954 *The Excavations at Medinet Habu*, Vol. 5: *Post-Ramessid Remains*. Oriental Institute Publications 66. Chicago: University of Chicago Press.

Hurlbut, Cornelius S.

1959 *Dana's Manual of Mineralogy*. 17th ed., revised by C. S. Hurlbut. New York: John Wiley & Sons.

Ikram, Salima

1995 *Choice Cuts: Meat Production in Ancient Egypt*. Leuven: Peeters.

Jacquet-Gordon, Helen

1972 *Les ermitages chrétiens du désert d'Esna*, Vol. 3: *Céramique et objets*. Fouilles de l'Institut Français d'Archéologie Orientale du Caire 29/3. Cairo: Institut Français d'Archéologie Orientale.

Jennings, Sarah

2006 *Vessel Glass from Beirut: BEY 006, 007, and 045*. Archaeology of the Beirut Souks 2, Berytus 48–49. Beirut: American University of Beirut.

Kaegi, Walter E.

2000 "Observations on the Historical Context of Bir Umm Fawakhir." In *Bir Umm Fawakhir Survey Project 1993: A Byzantine Gold Mining Town in Egypt*, by Carol Meyer, Lisa A. Heidorn, Walter E. Kaegi, and Terry Wilfong, pp. 3–4. Oriental Institute Communications 28. Chicago: The Oriental Institute.

Kaiser, Werner; Günter Dreyer; Günter Grimm; Gerhard Haeny; Horst Jaritz; and Christa Müller

1975 "Stadt und Tempel von Elephantine: Fünfter Grabungsbericht." *Mitteilungen des Deutschen Archäologische Instituts Abteilung Kairo* 31: 39–84.

Kasser, Rodolphe

1972 *Kellia: Topographie*. Recherches Suisse d'Archéologie Copte 2. Geneva: George, Librairie de l'Université.

Kawanishi, Hiroyki, and Sumiyo Tsujimura, editors

1988 *Preliminary Report: Sixth Season of the Excavations at the Site of Akoris, Egypt 1986*. Kyoto: Paleological Association of Japan.

Keay, Simon J.

1984 *Late Roman Amphorae in the Western Mediterranean*. British Archaeological Reports, International Series 196. Oxford: British Archaeological Reports.

Kemp, Barry J., editor

1984 *Amarna Reports* 1. London: Egypt Exploration Society.

Klemm, Dietrich; Rosemarie Klemm; and Andreas Murr

2002 "Ancient Gold Mining in the Eastern Desert of Egypt and the Nubian Desert of Sudan." In *Egypt and Nubia: Gifts of the Desert*, edited by Renée Friedman, pp. 215–31. London: The British Museum.

Kromer, Karl

1967 *Römische Weinstube in Sayala (Unternubien)*. Berichte des Österreichischen Nationalkomitees der UNESCO-Aktion für die Rettung der Nubischen Altertümer 4. Vienna: Hermann Böhlaus Nachf.

Lassányi, Gábor

2010a "7.3. Test Excavations it the Settlement." In *Biʾr Minayh: Report on the Survey 1998–2004*, edited by Ulrich Luft, pp. 255–57. Studia Aegyptiaca Series Maior 3. Budapest: Archaeolingua Alapítvány.

2010b "8.1. Pottery." In *Biʾr Minayh: Report on the Survey 1998–2004*, edited by Ulrich Luft, pp. 271–90. Studia Aegyptiaca Series Maior 3. Budapest: Archaeolingua Alapítvány.

2010c "8.4. Various Small Finds." In *Biʾir Minayh: Report on the Survey 1998–2004*, edited by Ulrich Luft, pp. 295–96. Studia Aegyptiaca Series Maior 3. Budapest: Archaeolingua Alapítvány.

Lawrence, Susan

1998 "Gender and Community Structure on Australian Colonial Goldfields." In *Social Approaches to an Industrial Past*, edited by A. Bernard Knapp, Vincent C. Piggott, and Eugenia W. Herbert, pp. 39–58. New York: Routledge.

Lecuyot, Guy, and Geneviève Pierrat

1992 "À propos des lieux de production de quelques céramiques trouvées à Tôd et dans la Vallée des Reines." *Cahiers de la Céramique Égyptienne* 3: 173–80.

Leguilloux, Martine

2003 "Les animaux et l'alimentation d'après la faune: Les restes de l'alimentation carnée des fortins de Krokodilô et Maximianon." In *La route de Myos Hormos*, edited by Hélène Cuvigny. Fouilles de l'Institut Français d'Archéologie Orientale 48, Vol. 2, pp. 549–88. Cairo: Institut Français d'Archéologie Orientale.

2006 *Les objets en cuir de Didymoi, Praesidium de la route caravanière Coptos-Berenice: Praesidia du désert de Berenice III*. Fouilles de l'Institut Français d'Archéologie Orientale 53. Cairo: Institut Français d'Archéologie Orientale.

2011 "Les animaux à Didymoi d'après les restes faunique du dépotoir extérieur." In *Didymoi*, Vol. 1: *Les fouilles et le matériel*, edited by Hélène Cuvigny, pp. 167–204. Fouilles de l'Institut Français d'Archéologie Orientale 64. Cairo: Institut Français d'Archéologie Orientale.

Luft, Ulrich, editor

2010 *Biʾr Minayh: Report on the Survey 1998–2004*. Studia Aegyptiaca Series Maior 3. Budapest: Archaeolingua Alapítvány.

Mason, Brian, and L. G. Berry

1968 *Elements of Mineralogy*. San Francisco: W. H. Freeman.

Maxfield, Valerie A.

2001 "Stone Quarrying in the Eastern Desert with Particular Reference to Mons Claudianus and Mons Porphyrites." In *Economies beyond Agriculture in the Classical World*, edited by David J. Mattingly and John Salmon, pp. 143–70. New York: Routledge.

Melkawi, Ansam; Khairieh ʿAmr; and Donald S. Whitcomb

1994 "The Excavation of Two Seventh Century Pottery Kilns at Aqaba." *Annual of the Department of Antiquities of Jordan* 38: 447–68.

Meyer, Carol

1987 "Glass from the North Theater, Byzantine Church, and Soundings at Jerash, Jordan, 1982-1983." *Bulletin of the American Schools of Oriental Research Supplement* 25: 175–222.

1992 *Glass from Quseir al-Qadim and the Indian Ocean Trade*. Studies in Ancient Oriental Civilization 53. Chicago: The Oriental Institute.

1995 "Gold, Granite, and Water: The Bir Umm Fawakhir Survey Project 1992." *Annual of the American Schools of Oriental Research* 52: 37–92.

2011 *Bir Umm Fawakhir 2: Report on the 1996–1997 Survey Seasons*. Oriental Institute Communications 30. Chicago: The Oriental Institute.

Meyer, Carol, and Lisa A. Heidorn

1998 "Three Seasons at Bir Umm Fawakhir in the Central Eastern Desert." In *Life on the Fringe*, edited by Olaf E. Kaper, pp. 197–212. Leiden: Research School CNWS, School of Asian, African, and Amerindian Studies.

2011 "Pottery from the 1996 and 1997 Surveys." In *Bir Umm Fawakhir 2: Report on the 1996–1997 Survey Seasons*, by Carol Meyer, pp. 115–51. Oriental Institute Communications 30. Chicago: The Oriental Institute.

Meyer, Carol; Lisa A. Heidorn, Walter E. Kaegi; and Terry Wilfong

2000 *Bir Umm Fawakhir Survey Project 1993: A Byzantine Gold-Mining Town in Egypt*. Oriental Institute Communications 28. Chicago: The Oriental Institute.

Meyer, Carol; Bryan Earl; Mohamed Omar; and Robert K. Smither

2005 "Ancient Gold Extraction at Bir Umm Fawakhir." *Journal of the American Research Center in Egypt* 40: 13–53.

Myśliwiec, Karol

1987 *Keramik und Kleinfunde aus der Grabung im Tempel Sethos' I. in Gurna*. Deutsches Archäologisches Institut, Abteilung Kairo, Archäologischer Veröffentlichungen 57. Mainz: Philipp von Zabern.

Op de Beeck, Lies, and Stan Hendrickx

2011 "Deir al-Barsha 2002 Pottery Survey." *Cahiers de la Céramique Égyptienne* 9: 311–44.

Osborne, Dale J.

1998 *The Mammals of Ancient Egypt*. Warminster: Aris & Phillips.

Osborne, Dale J., and Ibrahim Helmy

1980 *The Contemporary Land Mammals of Egypt (including Sinai)*. Fieldiana Zoology, n.s., 5. Chicago: Field Museum of Natural History.

Osypińska, Marta

2011 "Faunal Remains." In *Berenike 2008–2009*, edited by Steven E. Sidebotham and Iwona Zych, pp. 67–76. PCMA Excavation Series. Warsaw: Polish Centre of Mediterranean Archaeology.

Payne, S.

1973 "Kill-off Patterns in Sheep and Goats: The Mandibles from Asvan Kale." *Anatolian Studies* 23: 281–303.

Peacock, David P. S.

1984 "The Amphorae." In *Excavations at Carthage: The British Mission*, by M. G. Fulford and David P. S. Peacock, Vol. 1, Part 2, pp. 116–40. Sheffield: University of Sheffield Department of Prehistory and Archaeology.

1997 "The Quarries." *Survey and Excavation at Mons Claudianus*, Vol. 1, by Valerie A. Maxfield and David P. S. Peacock, pp. 175–255. Cairo: Institut Français d'Archéologie Orientale.

Peacock, David P. S., and Lucy Blue

2006 *Myos Hormos – Quseir al-Qadim: Roman and Islamic Ports on the Red Sea*, Vol. 1: *Survey and Excavations 1999–2003*. Oxford: Oxbow Books.

Peacock, David P. S., and Lucy Blue, editors

2011 *Myos Hormos – Quseir al-Qadim: Roman and Islamic Ports on the Red Sea*, Vol. 2: *Finds from the Excavations 1999–2003*. British Archaeological Reports, International Series 2286. University of Southampton Series in Archaeology 6. Oxford: Archaeopress.

Peña, J. Theodore

2007 *Roman Pottery in the Archaeological Record*. Cambridge: Cambridge University Press.

Petrie, W. M. Flinders

1891 *Illahun, Kahun, and Gurob*. London: Egypt Exploration Society.

1896 *Koptos*. London: Egypt Exploration Society.

1914 *Amulets*. London: Egypt Exploration Society.

Pieri, Dominique

2005 *Le commerce du vin oriental à l'époque byzantine (Ve–VIIe siècles)*. Bibliothèque Archéologique et Historique 174. Beirut: Institut Français du Proche-Orient.

Pierrat, Geneviève

1996 "Évolution de la céramique de Tôd." *Cahiers de la céramique égyptienne* 4: 189–214.

Pierrat-Bonnefois, Geneviève

2000 "La ceramique dynastique et ptolémaïc des fouilles du Louvre à Tôd, 1989-1991." *Cahiers de la céramique égyptienne* 6: 299–332.

Pintaudi, Rosario, editor

2008 *Antinoupolis*, Vol. 1. Istituto Papirologico "G. Vitelli" Scavi e Materiali 1. Florence: Istituto Papirologico "G. Vitelli."

Priese, Karl-Heinz

1997 "The Kingdom of Napata and Meroe." In *Sudan: Ancient Kingdoms of the Nile*, edited by Dietrich Wildung, pp. 206–42. New York: Flammarion.

Pyke, Gillian

2005 "Later Roman Egyptian Amphorae from Squares U and V at Kom el-Nana." In *Late Roman Pottery at Amarna and Related Studies*, by Jane Faiers, pp 213–43. Excavation Memoir 72. London: Egypt Exploration Society.

Ratto, Rodolfo

1974 *Monnaies byzantines et d'autres pays contemporaines à l'époque byzantine*. Amsterdam: J. Schulman. [reprint of 1930 catalog]

Ricke, Herbert

1967 *Ausgrabungen von Khor-Dehmit bis Bet el-Wali*. Oriental Institute Nubian Expedition 2. Chicago: University of Chicago Press.

Russo, Simona

2008 "Campagne di scaro 2005–2007: le calzature." In *Antinoupolis*, Vol. 1, edited by Rosario Pintaudi, pp. 439–70. Florence: Instituto Papirologico "G. Vitelli."

Sauneron, Serge, and Jean Jacquet

1972 *Les ermitages chrétiens du désert d'Esna*, Vol. 2: *Descriptions et plans*. Fouilles de l'Institut Français d'Archéologie Orientale du Caire 29/2. Cairo: Institut Français d'Archéologie Orientale.

Schmid, E.

1972 *Atlas of Animal Bones*. London: Elsevier.

Sear, David

1987 *Byzantine Coins and Their Values*. 2nd rev. ed. London: Seaby.

Sells, David, trans.

1989 *Desert Tracings: Six Classic Arabian Odes by 'Alqama, Shafara, Labid, 'Antara, Al-A'sha, and Dhu al-Rumma*. Middletown: Wesleyan University Press.

Shaw, Ian

1998 "Exploiting the Desert Frontier: The Logistics and Politics of Ancient Egyptian Mining Expeditions." In *Social Approaches to an Industrial Past*, edited by A. Bernard Knapp, Vincent C. Piggott, and Eugenia Herbert, pp. 242–58. New York: Routledge.

1999 "Sikait Zubara." In *Encyclopedia of the Archaeology of Ancient Egypt*, edited by Kathryn A. Bard, pp. 731–33. New York: Routledge.

Shea, Michael O'Dwyer

1983 "The Small Cuboid Incense Burner of the Ancient Near East." *Levant* 15: 76–109.

Sidebotham, Steven E.

2011 *Berenike and the Ancient Maritime Spice Route*. Berkeley: University of California Press.

Sidebotham, Steven E.; Hans Barnard; and Gillian Pyke

2002 "Five Enigmatic Late Roman Settlements in the Eastern Desert." *Journal of Egyptian Archaeology* 88: 187–225.

Sidebotham, Steven E.; Martin Hense; and Hendrikje M. Nouwens

2008 *The Red Land: The Illustrated Archaeology of Egypt's Eastern Desert*. New York: The American University of Cairo Press.

Sidebotham, Steven E.; Hendrikje M. Nouwens; A. Martin Hense; and James A. Harrell

2004 "Preliminary Report on Archaeological Fieldwork at Sikait (Eastern Desert of Egypt), and Environs: 2002–2003." *Sahara* 15: 7–30.

Sidebotham, Steven E., and Willemina Wendrich, editors

1995 *Berenike 1994: Preliminary Report of the 1994 Excavations at Berenike (Egyptian Red Sea Coast) and Survey of the Eastern Desert*. Leiden: Research School CNWS, School of Asian, African, and Amerindian Studies.

1996 *Berenike 1995: Preliminary Report of the 1995 Excavations at Berenike (Egyptian Red Sea Coast) and Survey of the Eastern Desert*. Leiden: Research School CNWS, School of Asian, African, and Amerindian Studies.

1999 *Berenike 1997: Report of the 1997 Excavations at Berenike (Egyptian Red Sea Coast) and the Survey of the Eastern Desert, including Excavations at Shenshef*. Leiden: Research School CNWS, School of Asian, African, and Amerindian Studies.

2000 *Berenike 1998: Report of the 1997 Excavations at Berenike and the Survey of the Eastern Desert, including Excavations in Wadi Kalalat*. Leiden: Research School CNWS, School of Asian, African, and Amerindian Studies.

2007 *Berenike 1999/2000: Report on the Excavations at Berenike Including Excavations in Wadi Kalalat and Siket, and the Survey of the Mons Smaragdus Region*. Los Angeles: Cotsen Institute of Archaeology.

Sidebotham, Steven E.; Ronald E. Zitterkopf; and John A. Riley

1991 "Survey of the 'Abu Sha'ar – Nile Road." *American Journal of Archaeology* 95: 571–622.

Sidebotham, Steven E., and Iwona Zych, editors

2011 *Berenike 2008-2009: Report on the Excavations at Berenike, Including a Survey in the Eastern Desert*. PCMA Excavation Series 1. Warsaw: Polish Centre of Mediterranean Archaeology.

Silver, I. A.

1963 "The Ageing of Domestic Animals." In *Science in Archaeology*, edited by D. Brothwell and E. S. Higgs, pp. 282–302. London: Thames & Hudson.

Smith, Wendy

1998 "Fuel for Thought: Archaeobotanical Evidence for the Use of Alternatives to Wood Fuel in Late Antique North Africa." *Journal of Mediterranean Archaeology* 11/2: 191–205.

Spencer, A. Jeffrey, and Donald M. Bailey

1986 *British Museum Expedition to Middle Egypt: Ashmunein (1985)*. British Museum Occasional Paper 67. London: The British Museum.

Spencer, A. Jeffrey; Donald M. Bailey; and A. Burnett

1983 *British Museum Expedition to Middle Egypt: Ashmunein (1982)*. British Museum Occasional Paper 46. London: The British Museum.

Spencer, A. Jeffrey; Donald M. Bailey; and W. Vivian Davies

1984 *British Museum Expedition to Middle Egypt: Ashmunein 1984*. British Museum Occasional Paper 53. London: The British Museum.

Strouhal, Eugen

1984 *Wadi Qitna and Kalabsha South: Late Roman-Early Byzantine Tumuli Cemeteries in Egyptian Nubia*. Czechoslovak Institute of Egyptology Publications 1. Prague: Charles University.

Täckholm, V.

1974 *Students' Flora of Egypt*. 2nd ed. Cairo: Cairo University.

Tatton-Brown, V. A.

1984 "The Glass." In *Excavations at Carthage: The British Mission* , Vol. 1, Part 1: *The Site and Finds Other than Pottery*, by H. R. Hurst and S. P. Roskams, pp. 194–212. Sheffield: University of Sheffield.

Tengberg, Margareta

2011 "Analyse archéobotanique." In *Didymoi: Une garnison romaine dans le désert Oriental d'Égypt*, Vol. 1: *Les fouilles et le matériel*, edited by Hélène Cuvigny, pp. 205–14. Fouilles de l'Institut Français d'Archéologie Orientale 64. Cairo: Institut Français d'Archéologie Orientale.

Then-Obluska, Joanna

In press "Beads and Pendants." In *Berenike 2010-2011: Report on the Excavations at Berenike*, edited by Steven E. Sidebotham and Iwona Zych. PCMA Excavation Series. Warsaw: Polish Centre of Mediterranean Archaeology.

Thompson, Reginald Campbell

1922 "Introduction. 1. The Excavations at Wadi Sarga." In *Wadi Sarga: Coptic and Greek Texts*, by W. E. Crum and H. I. Bell, pp. 1–5. Coptica 3. Hauniae: Gyldendalske Boghandel-Nordisk Forlag.

Tolstoï, Jean

1968 *Monnaies Byzantines*. Amsterdam: Adolf M. Hakkert.

Tomber, Roberta S.

1998 "The Pottery." In *Berenike 1996: Report of the 1996 Excavations at Berenike (Egyptian Red Sea Coast) and Survey of the Eastern Desert*, edited by Steven E. Sidebotham and Willemina Wendrich, pp. 163–80. Leiden: Research School CNWS, School of Asian, African, and Amerindian Studies.

1999 "The Pottery." In *Berenike 1997: Report of the 1997 Excavations at Berenike and the Survey of the Egyptian Eastern Desert, including Excavations at Shenshef*, edited by Steven E. Sidebotham and Willemina Z. Wendrich, pp. 123–59. Leiden: Research School CNWS, School of Asian, African, and Amerindian Studies.

2001 "The Pottery." In *The Roman Imperial Quarries: Survey and Excavation at Mons Porphyrites 1994–1998*, Vol. 1: *Topography and Quarries*, by Valerie A. Maxfield and David P. S. Peacock, pp. 242–303. Excavation Memoir 67. London: Egypt Exploration Society.

2007 "Pottery from the Excavated Deposits." In *The Roman Imperial Quarries: Survey and Excavation at Mons Porphyrites 1994–1998*, Vol. 2: *The Excavations*, by David P. S. Peacock, Evan Peacock, and Valerie A. Maxfield, pp. 177–208. Excavation Memoir 82. London: Egypt Exploration Society.

van der Veen, Marijke

1996 "The Plant Remains from Mons Claudianus, a Roman Quarry Settlement in the Eastern Desert of Egypt – An Interim

Report." *Vegetation History and Archaeobotany* 5: 137–41.

1998 "Gardens in the Desert." In *Life on the Fringe: Living in the Southern Egyptian Deserts during the Roman and Early-Byzantine Periods*, edited by O. E. Kaper, pp. 221–42. Leiden: Research Center for Non-Western Studies.

2001 "The Botanical Evidence." In *Mons Claudianus: Survey and Excavation*, Vol. 2: *The Excavations*, by Valerie A. Maxfield and David P. S. Peacock, pp. 171–247. Fouilles de l'Institut Français d'Archéologie Orientale 43. Cairo: Institut Français d'Archéologie Orientale.

2011 *Consumption, Trade and Innovation: Exploring the Botanical Remains from the Roman and Islamic Ports at Quseir al-Qadim*. Egypt. Journal of African Archaeology Monograph Series 6. Frankfurt am Main: Africa Magna.

van der Veen, Marijke; Alison Cox; and Jacob Morales

2011 "Plant Remains – Evidence for Trade and Cuisine." In *Myos Hormos – Quseir al-Qadim: Roman and Islamic Ports on the Red Sea*, Vol. 2: *Finds from the Excavations 1999–2003*, edited by David P. S. Peacock and Lucy Blue, pp. 227–34. British Archaeological Reports, International Series 2286. University of Southampton Series in Archaeology 6. Oxford: Archaeopress.

van der Veen, Marijke, and Sheila Hamilton-Dyer

1998 "A Life of Luxury in the Desert: The Food and Fodder Supply to Mons Claudianus." *Journal of Roman Archaeology* 11: 101–16.

van der Veen, Marijke, and Helen Tabinor

2007 "Food, Fodder and Fuel at Mons Porphyrites: The Botanical Evidence." In *The Roman Imperial Quarries: Survey and Excavation at Mons Porphyrites 1994–1998*, Vol. 2: *The Excavations*, by David P. S. Peacock and Valerie A. Maxfield, pp. 83–142. Excavation Memoir 82. London: Egypt Exploration Society.

van Neer, N., and A. M. H. Ervynck

1998 "The Faunal Remains." In *Berenike 1996: Report of the 1996 Excavations at Berenike (Egyptian Red Sea Coast) and the Survey of the Eastern Desert*, edited by Steven E. Sidebotham and Willemina Z. Wendrich, pp. 349–88. Leiden: Research School Center for Non-Western Studies.

1999 "The Faunal Remains." In *Berenike 1997: Report of the 1997 Excavations at Berenike (Egyptian Red Sea Coast) and the Survey of the Eastern Desert, including Excavations at Shenshef*, edited by Steven E. Sidebotham and Willemina Z. Wendrich, pp. 325–42. Leiden: Research School CNWS, School of Asian, African, and Amerindian Studies.

van Neer, N., and A. Lentacker

1996 "The Faunal Remains." In *Berenike 1995: Preliminary Report of the 1995 Excavations at Berenike (Egyptian Red Sea Coast) and Survey of the Eastern Desert*, edited by Steven E. Sidebotham and Willemina Wendrich, pp. 337–56. Leiden: Research School CNWS, School of Asian, African, and Amerindian Studies.

Vasáros, Zsolt

2010 "7. Architectural Remains, 7.1. Introduction." In *Biʾr Minayh: Report on the Survey 1998–2004*, edited by Ulrich Luft, pp. 197–213. Studia Aegyptiaca Series Maior 3. Budapest: Archaeolingua Alapítvány.

Vidman, Ladislav

1984 "Inscriptions." In *Wadi Qitna and Kalabsha South: Late Roman–Early Byzantine Tumuli Cemeteries in Egyptian Nubia*, by Eugen Strouhal, pp. 215–22. Czechoslovak Institute of Egyptology Publications 1. Prague: Charles University.

Wattenmaker, P.

1982 "Fauna." In *Quseir al-Qadim 1980 Preliminary Report*, edited by Donald S. Whitcomb and Janet H. Johnson, pp. 347–53. Malibu: Undena Publications.

Weill, M. Raymond

1911 "Koptos." *Annales du Service des antiquités de l'Égypte* 11: 97–141.

Weinberg, Gladys Davidson, editor

1988 *Excavations at Jalame*. Columbia: University of Missouri Press.

Wetterstrom, Wilma

1982 "Plant Remains." In *Quseir al-Qadim 1980: Preliminary Report*, edited by Donald S. Whitcomb and Janet H. Johnson, pp. 355–77. Malibu: Undena Publications.

Wilfong, Terry G.

1995 "The Graffiti." In "Gold, Granite, and Water: The Bir Umm Fawakhir Survey Project 1992," by Carol Meyer, pp. 47–49. In *Preliminary Excavation Reports: Sardis, Bir Umm Fawakhir, Tell el-ʿUmeiri, the Combined Caesarea Expeditions, and Tell Dothan*, edited by William G. Dever. Annual of the American Schools of Oriental Research 52. New Haven: American Schools of Oriental Research.

2000 "Textual Remains." In *Bir Umm Fawakhir Survey Project 1993: A Byzantine Gold Mining Town in Egypt*, by Carol Meyer, Lisa A. Heidorn, Walter E. Kaegi, and Terry Wilfong, pp. 25–26. Oriental Institute Communications 28. Chicago: The Oriental Institute.

Winlock, Herbert E., and W. E. Crum

1926 *The Monastery of Epiphanius at Thebes*, Part 1. New York: Metropolitan Museum of Art.

Winterbottom, S.

2001 "Leather." In *Mons Claudianus: Survey and Excavation*, Vol. 2: *The Excavations*, by Valerie A. Maxfield and David P. S. Peacock, pp. 313–56. Fouilles de l'Institut Français d'Archéologie Orientale 43. Cairo: Institut Français d'Archéologie Orientale.

Zieliński, Jarosław

2011 "Archaeobotanical Remains." In *Berenike 2008–2009: Report on the Excavations at Berenike, Including a Survey in the Eastern Desert*, edited by Steven E. Sidebotham and Iwona Zych, pp. 59–66. PCMA Excavation Series 1. Warsaw: Polish Centre of Mediterranean Archaeology.

Zitterkopf, Ronald E., and Steven E. Sidebotham

1989 "Stations and Towers on the Quseir-Nile Road." *Journal of Egyptian Archaeology* 75: 155–89.

Zohary, D., and M. Hopf

1993 *Domestication of Plants in the Old World: The Origin and Spread of Cultivated Plants in West Asia, Europe, and the Nile Valley*. 2nd ed. Oxford: Clarendon Press.

Chapter 1

Introduction

Carol Meyer

The site of Bir Umm Fawakhir lies in the central Eastern Desert of Egypt at the midpoint of the modern road running from Quft on the Nile, through the Wadi Hammamat, and on to Quseir on the Red Sea coast (fig. 1). Bir Umm Fawakhir is about 5 kilometers northeast of the famous rock inscriptions at the ancient *bekhen*-stone and "breccia" quarries in the Wadi Hammamat. The route that passes through the Wadi Hammamat is also the shortest road from the Nile valley to the Red Sea, and as such has been used for millennia by traders to East Africa, the Arabian peninsula, India, and beyond. The Wadi Hammamat zone also preserves traces of human exploitation of the desert from predynastic hunters to pharaonic and Roman-period quarrymen hewing out *bekhen*-stone (graywacke) and other valuable, beautiful stones, to miners seeking gold or other metallic ores, up to the present day. The site of Bir Umm Fawakhir (26°00′05″ N, 33°36′30″ E), although located close to the Wadi Hammamat and the ancient Roman track, is not easily visible from the modern road. The main settlement and its outlying clusters of ruins lie in some long, deep wadis cut in Precambrian granite (ca. 590 million years ago), itself injected into still older dark gray ultramafic rocks that now rise in rugged ridges immediately west of the site. The contact zone between the Fawakhir granite stock and the ultramafic rocks is enriched in metallic ores such as iron pyrite, or fool's gold, but also true gold and silver. Further, the granite has been fractured, jointed, and fissured over the eons so it carries water in its cracks, until the underground flow is blocked by the dense ultramafic rocks on the west. Here the wells, all-important in a hyperarid desert, are sunk and probably always have been.

The central Eastern Desert of Egypt was long overlooked by archaeologists overwhelmed by the great pharaonic pyramids, tombs, and temples along the Nile valley. At times the Eastern Desert has been off limits to foreign archaeologists and others for security reasons. Thus it was not until 1978 that the first major, multi-season archaeological excavations were initiated at Quseir al-Qadim (ancient Myos Hormos) on the Red Sea coast, under the direction of Donald Whitcomb and Janet Johnson. Their pioneering work was followed by excavations from the 1980s to date at Abu Shaʾar, at the *praesidia* along the ancient Roman road from ancient Coptos (modern Quft) to Myos Hormos, at the Roman granodiorite quarries of Mons Claudianus and the imperial porphyry quarries of Mons Porphyrites, and at a number of smaller sites. The most stunning recent discovery is the Middle Kingdom landing site and shrines at Wadi Gawasis that served the Red Sea trade to Punt. All the major sites in the Eastern Desert can be explained as supporting quarries, mines, sea routes, or ports for shipping on the Red Sea and beyond. (There are also numerous small, short-lived settlements of uncertain function in the fifth and sixth centuries; everything from mine prospecting to monastic *laura*, military training to semi-settled Bedouin camps has been suggested as their raison d'être; Sidebotham, Barnard, and Pyke 2002; Sidebotham and Wendrich 2007, p. 298.) Far the most important and long-lived site, however, was the port and town of Berenice, founded by the Ptolemies and not abandoned until the sixth century. It was the largest town in the Eastern Desert, and it boasted port facilities, well-built houses, streets, workshops, notable public architecture such as the Serapis temple, small shrines, a church or ecclesiastical structure, and a ring of small forts and outlying settlements. Berenice lies over 300 kilometers southeast of Bir Umm Fawakhir as the crow flies, farther still by the various desert and mountain tracks, but both sites faced many of the same supply sources and difficulties. In addition, a number of wide-ranging, multi-year surveys have mapped the whole Via Hadriana along the Red Sea coast, located sources of metallic ore and valuable stones, and documented collections of rock inscriptions in the southern Eastern Desert. As for Bir Umm Fawakhir, the four previously published survey seasons (Meyer et al. 2000; Meyer 1995, 2011) and the

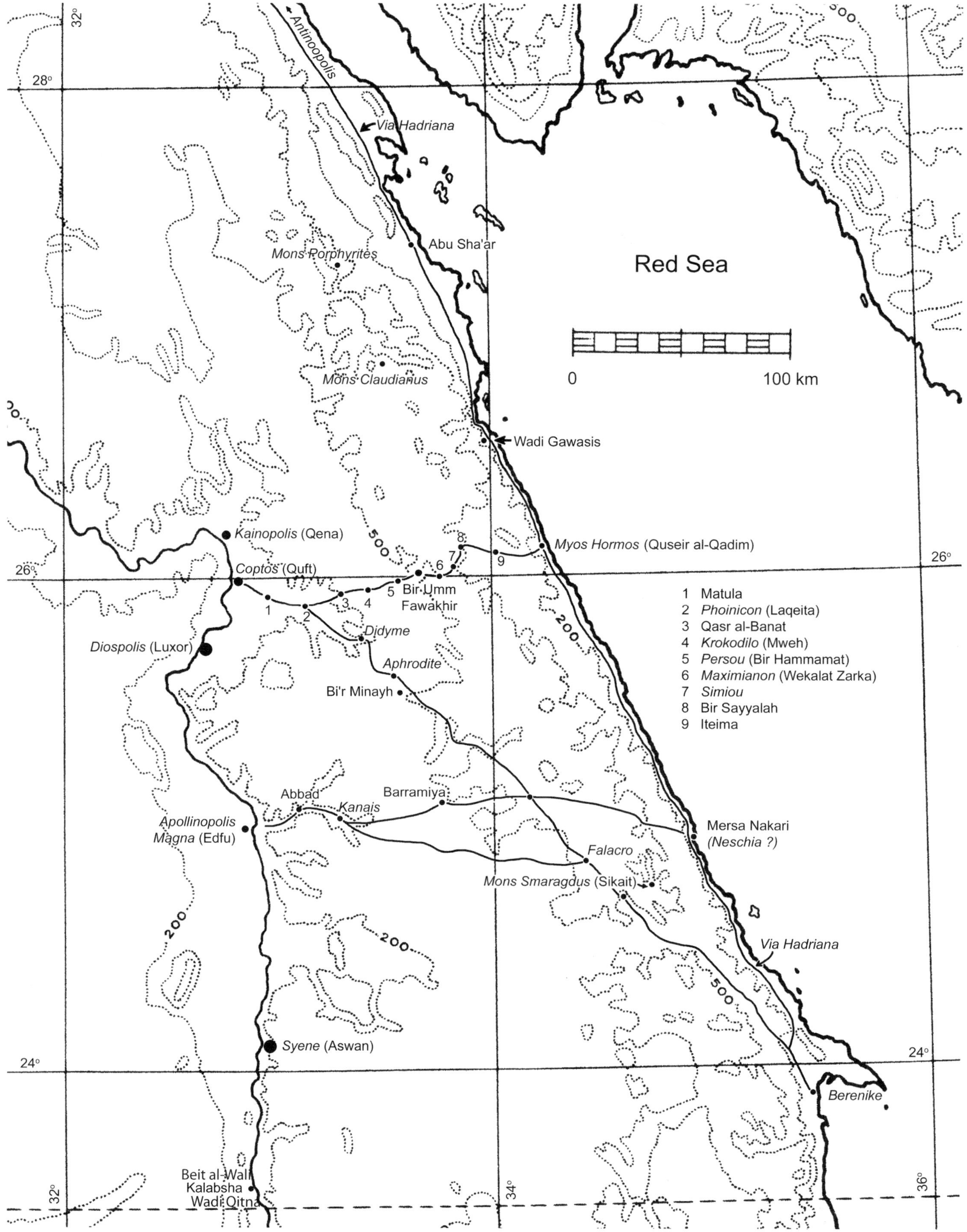

Figure 1. Map of relevant Eastern Desert sites

1999 excavations reported here should be seen in relation to the many other recent archaeological projects in the desert. In short, far from being bleak, barren, and utterly hostile, it is now clear that the Eastern Desert, the "Red Land" of the ancient Egyptians, was at times traversed, exploited, and even settled.

At the site of Bir Umm Fawakhir itself, no archaeological work had been undertaken prior to 1992. That said, a number of geologists, travelers, and archaeologists had passed by the site, and some of them published their notes about it. The occasional early travelers' and archaeologists' notes are summarized in the report on the 1992 season (Meyer 1995, pp. 40–44), and the geologists' notes are included in the study of ancient mines and mining (Meyer et al. 2005, pp. 28–31). Most of the old accounts, which go back to 1900, remark on the very large number of ancient workmen's huts and the ancient quarries and mines, the Ptolemy III temple (destroyed sometime before 1953), the well, and the heaps and piles of mining debris, which was reworked before World War II to extract the residual gold. Many of the previous accounts also remark on the *bekhen*-stone and "breccia" quarries in the Wadi Hammamat, ancient workings in the Wadi Atallah, and ancient gold mining in the Wadi el-Sid, the site of a large British gold mine, mill, and smelter in the 1950s.

The author first encountered Bir Umm Fawakhir while working with the Quseir al-Qadim excavations in 1982. One weekend she and Steve Sidebotham were sent to Luxor on the weekly mail and supply run and dithered their way back through the Wadi Hammamat tallying as many as possible of the intervisible Roman watch towers high on the mountain peaks, marveling at the preservation of the dozen or so Roman-period *praesidia* (then believed to be *hydreumata*), and stopping for tea at the modern one-donkey settlement at Bir Umm Fawakhir. They strolled down what is now referred to as Outlier 2 on the ancient Roman road, which bends northeast away from the modern asphalt road at this point. A young guide said "there's more" and led them up and over a high ridge for a first astonishing view of what is now called the main settlement of Bir Umm Fawakhir, a whole wadi full of little houses. It was not in any guide book. Some years later when the author was a member of the Epigraphic Survey — usually referred to as Chicago House — in Luxor, the staff often used weekends to visit other sites and even to visit the Eastern Desert, including the Wadi Hammamat. Trying to find out more about the ruins at Bir Umm Fawakhir was unsatisfactory; almost nothing but a few notes was published, and what there was called the site "Roman." The pottery was nothing like the first- and second-century A.D. material from Quseir al-Qadim, and the sprawling ruins looked nothing like the neat, quadrilateral, towered, and gated Roman-period *praesidia* on the old Roman Coptos (Quft)-to-Myos Hormos-(Quseir al-Qadim) route.

Summary and Goals of Previous Seasons

In January 1992, with the assistance of Peter Dorman, then director of Chicago House; the Oriental Institute of the University of Chicago; the Egyptian Geological Survey and Mining Authority (EGSMA); and the American Research Center in Egypt (ARCE) in Cairo, the author assembled a small expedition to spend two weeks at Bir Umm Fawakhir to map the site, collect pottery, and determine the date and function of the site (fig. 2). The project failed to complete so ambitious an agenda, but failed in such a manner that twenty years later the author is still writing about the site. The 1992 expedition did, however, succeed in mapping fifty-five buildings at the far southeast end of the site, studying a preliminary pottery corpus, which gave us a fifth- and sixth-century Coptic/Byzantine-period[1] date, determining that the site was a gold-mining town, and estimating what it would take to finish mapping the ancient town completely (Meyer 1995) — for it is a remarkably well-preserved town. So little has happened there since it was abandoned sometime in the sixth century that the houses and one-room outbuildings can be mapped room for room and generally

[1] For an early identification of the site as fifth–seventh century in date, see Zitterkopf and Sidebotham 1989, p. 166. Here we use the term "Coptic/Byzantine period" to refer to the time span from the founding of Constantinople in 324 to the Islamic conquest in 640. This period has also been called "Roman," "Late Roman," or "Late Antiquity." We use "Coptic/Byzantine" because "Coptic" is the name used in many publications for this time span in Egypt, but the country was also part of the Byzantine empire, and a very important part, too. "Coptic/Byzantine period" as used here is not intended to refer to religion, ethnicity, style of government, or anything apart from a time span.

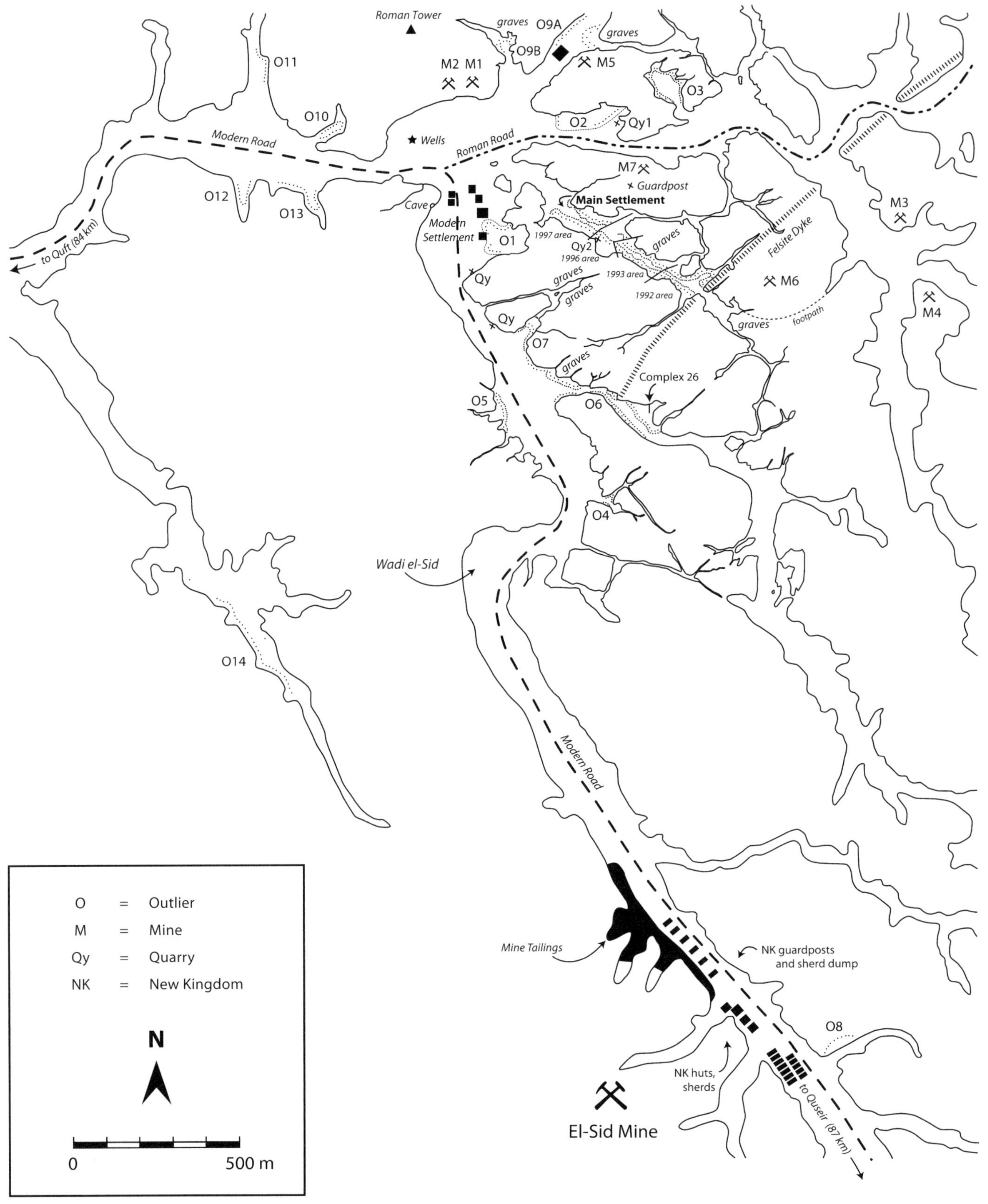

Figure 2. Bir Umm Fawakhir and vicinity

door for door, without excavation. Some walls stand over a meter high and preserve features such as built-in niches. The basic house pattern became clear, usually two or three adjoining rooms. Often several little houses were joined by party walls into larger agglomerated buildings. Scattered around them were many one-room outbuildings. We established that the main function of Bir Umm Fawakhir was as a gold-mining town (*pace* Klemm, Klemm, and Murr 2002). The ridges and mountains around are trenched and tunneled with ancient opencast and underground mines, and grinding and crushing stones are the second most common artifact after potsherds. There are no stables to shelter the large number of draft animals needed to haul quarried granite to the Nile, nor are there any animal lines or wheel ruts on the ancient track from Bir Umm Fawakhir to the Nile.[2] We also concluded that, contrary to what Agatharcides and Diodorus said, the miners were not criminals or prisoners of war. The ancient settlement sprawls along both sides of a deep wadi and has nothing of a central plan, there are no defenses to keep anyone in or out, the silos in Outlier 2 look more like household granaries than rations doled out daily to prisoners, and ostraca from the somewhat earlier Roman-period granodiorite quarries at Mons Claudianus indicate fairly generous salaries for all workmen there (Cuvigny 1996). Another short season in 1993 (Meyer et al. 2000) succeeded in mapping fifty more buildings, investigating some of the outlying clusters of ruins or "outliers," and calculating the population of the ancient town. The main settlement at maximum could have housed about a thousand people, far larger than any settlement on the Quft-to-Quseir road until quite recently, this without including any of the outliers, some of which seem to be residential rather than day shelters for outlying mines. The 1996 project was one of the most difficult. It had the smallest field team and only ten working days, but it nonetheless mapped forty-eight more buildings in the main settlement, located Outlier 8, and found evidence of New Kingdom mining activity near the modern mill in the Wadi el-Sid. The 1997 season, however, had a full team of eleven people and four weeks in the field. The goals were to complete the map of the main settlement; map well-preserved Outlier 2; study the ancient mines, mining, and ore-reduction techniques; investigate the cemeteries if possible; and continue exploration and documentation of the other outliers and the New Kingdom remains. The team geologist, Mohamed Omar, and a British mining engineer, Bryan Earl, carried out a study of the ancient (and modern) mines in and around Bir Umm Fawakhir and Wadi el-Sid and experimented with ore reduction and panning. The ores are gold bearing, as further proven by a mass spectrometry experiment at Argonne National Laboratory, but they are hard to work. The gold occurs in enriched quartz veins in granite, which requires a large labor force to hack out the quartz, crush it, grind it to powder to free the finely disseminated gold, wash out a heavy and dark residue or "head," and finally smelt it in a complicated, multi-step operation with cupellation. In short, hard-rock mining like that at Bir Umm Fawakhir requires a large labor force, adequate and reliable support in the desert, a heavy capital investment, and organization, and at least parts of the operation require highly skilled labor. The report on the mining study appears in Meyer et al. 2005, and the final report on the 1996 and 1997 seasons is published in Meyer 2011.

Summary and Goals of the 1999 and 2001 Seasons

Four seasons of surface survey and mapping were extremely rewarding, but there were questions that could only be addressed by excavation, and these were the focus of the 1999 project. It was unclear from surface remains whether ancient Bir Umm Fawakhir was occupied continuously for a hundred and fifty years or so, occupied for long stretches of time but abandoned in between, or occupied only fitfully as demand for gold compelled the Byzantine government to spend wealth in the form of men and grain to support a large mining operation in a remote desert. We also wanted to find out more about the ancient miners and their families, if any. When we started, there were only two other excavated town sites of this period in Egypt, Jême at Medinet Habu, on the west bank of Luxor, and Oxyrhynchus, south of the Fayyum, so Bir Umm Fawakhir was an opportunity to check, supplement, and fill out those data. We hoped to find ostraca, but none was recovered. The only textual material is a number of cursive, cryptic dipinti on wine amphoras. We

[2] Zitterkopf and Sidebotham 1989, pp. 160, 168.

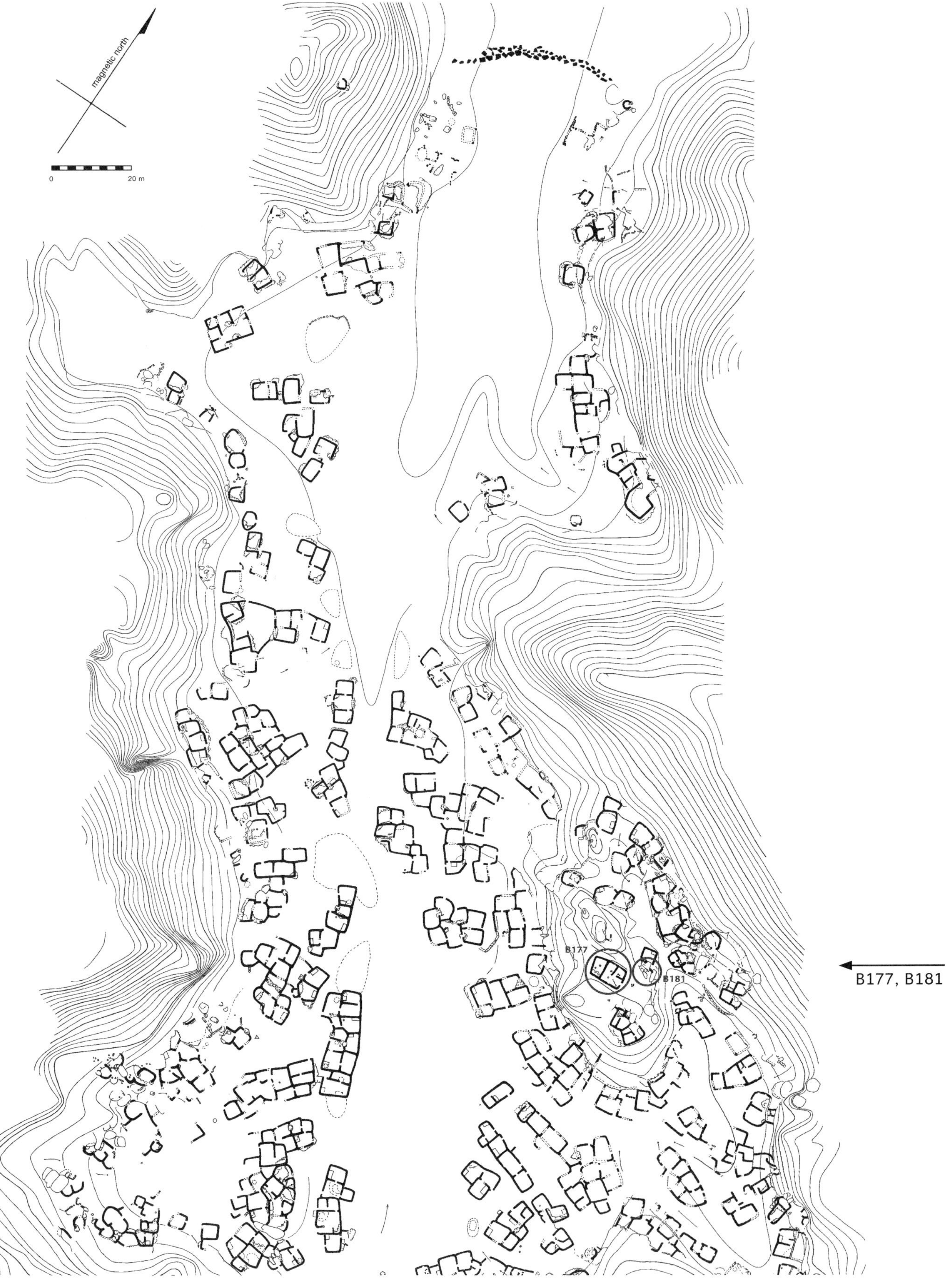

Figure 3a. Bir Umm Fawakhir main settlement (top)

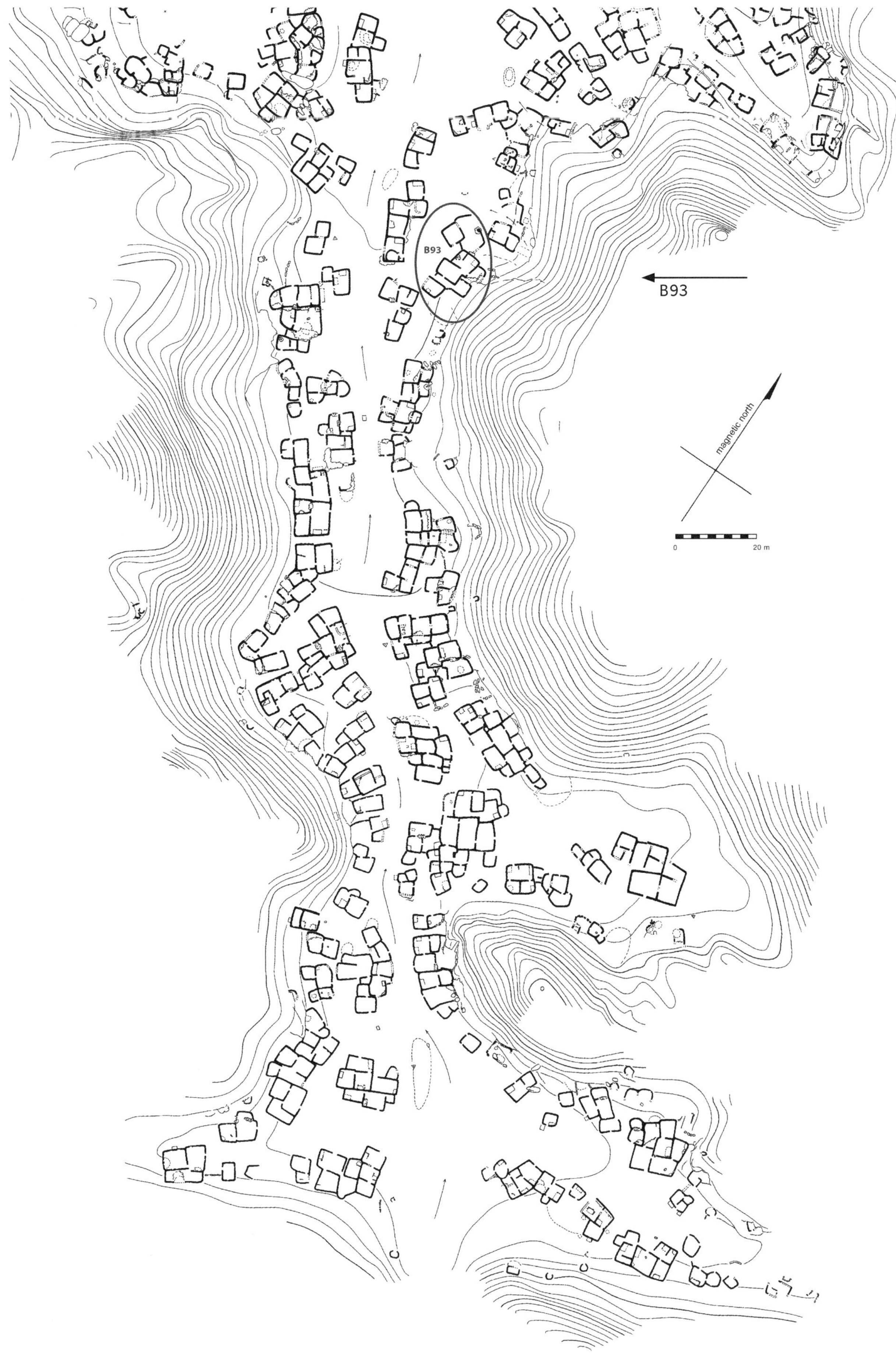

Figure 3b. Bir Umm Fawakhir main settlement (bottom)

hoped to finish the nearly complete map of Outlier 2 and at least photograph Outlier 1. This was done, but these results were published with the 1997 season for the sake of consistency (Meyer 2011). Finally, we were concerned about the preservation of the site. It is out of sight from the modern road, but it was nonetheless all too easy to drive up and down the wadi bottom that formed its main street. Since the houses are just drystone masonry, they are easily tumbled. Therefore we wanted to erect a barricade to prevent vehicles from driving around a fragile site.

We were in the field from February 5 to March 5, 1999, but we were very short-handed. Due to last-minute cancellations, we lacked two archaeologists, a draftsman/registrar, and our invaluable ceramicist. Plans to excavate some of the New Kingdom remains in the Wadi el-Sid could not be carried out, there was only one archaeological supervisor rather than two per trench, and in the end many partly documented finds had to be registered and stored in the Supreme Council of Antiquities (SCA) magazine in Quft. In order to complete the documentation of the small finds, bones, floral material, and pottery, we therefore had to add on a short study season in Quft from March 17 to 27, 2001.

The excavations were intended to sample a variety of structures and features at Bir Umm Fawakhir, but with two archaeologists, one raʾis, nine workmen, and 237 buildings in the main settlement alone, this was a small sample indeed. We selected Building 93 in the main settlement because it was quite well preserved but otherwise utterly typical (fig. 3b). It consisted of two house units joined by a party wall and had trash dumps on either side. The middens at Bir Umm Fawakhir are located close to a house or group of houses, and apart from a little modern looting, they have not been extensively reworked, redeposited, pitted, or trenched. Our working assumption therefore was that most of the debris came from the closest houses. Archaeologically, this is a rather a special opportunity, and one we took advantage of by excavating part of both dumps. We selected Building 177 (fig. 3a) for excavation partly for its unusual location high on the granite knob dubbed the "Hillock," and partly because it seemed to have more dipinti from wine jars and more of the polished and stamped orange plates than usual (fig. 4). Although Bir Umm Fawakhir is a large, sprawling, and well-preserved site, all the buildings seem to be domestic. So far, no defensive, administrative, warehousing, or other non-domestic structures have been identified. The only known religious building was the tiny Ptolemy III shrine dedicated to Min, which survived until the 1950s. Our expectation, then, was that Building 177 might have had a different function from the mass of houses in the main settlement, even though it was too small to have been an important administrative structure. Finally, we excavated Building 181 near Building 177 in order to test at least one outbuilding. As for site conservation, we were able to construct a boulder barricade across the entrance to the site in 1999 in order to keep vehicles out, as reported in *Chapter 8*. Documentation, drawing, and photography of small finds and pottery were completed during the 2001 study season, and the specialist studies of fauna and flora were carried out then as well, as reported in *Chapters* 5 and 6.

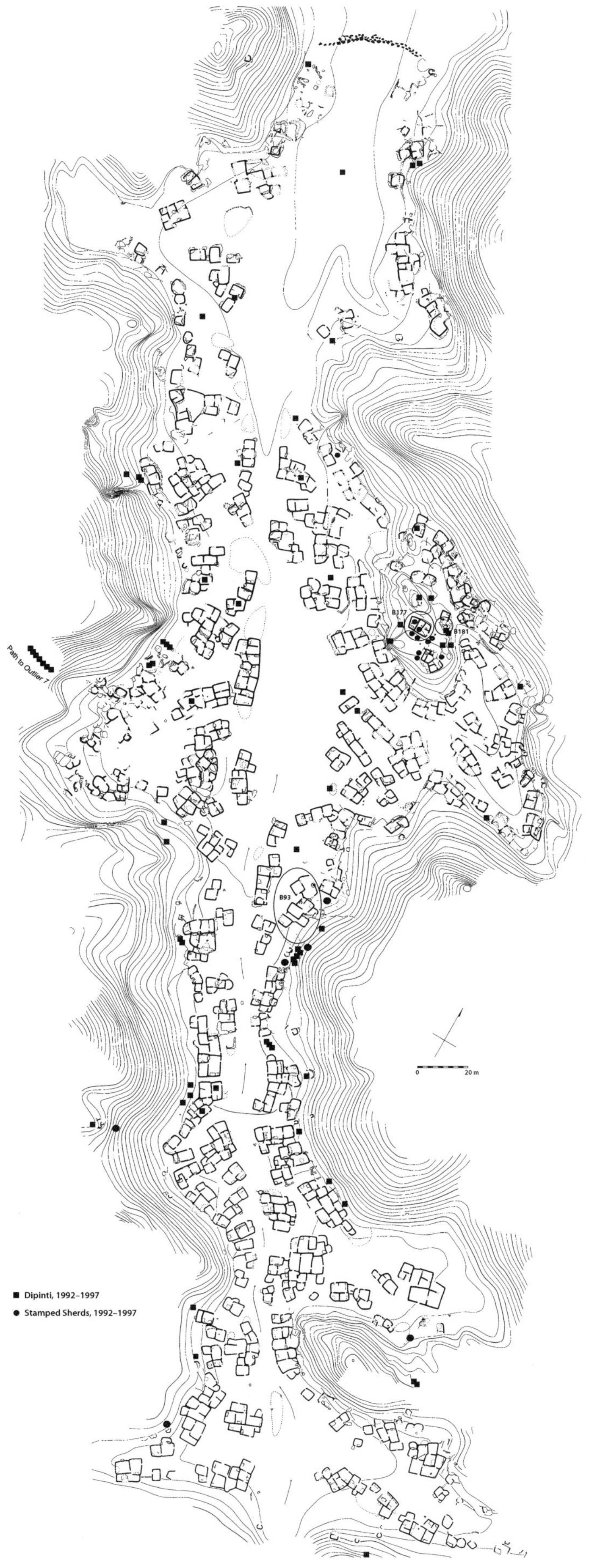

Figure 4. Distribution of dipinti and stamped sherds from previous seasons

Chapter 2

Excavations

Carol Meyer

Out of 237 buildings and outbuildings mapped in the main settlement at Bir Umm Fawakhir, two houses, Buildings 93 and 177, and one outbuilding, Building 181, were selected for excavation. The project chose Building 93 (fig. 3b) because it appeared to be better preserved than many other multi-room houses and because it seemed otherwise utterly ordinary. Building 177, on the other hand, was chosen because it was somewhat atypical, if only for its location up on the granite Hillock (fig. 3a) and for its apparent concentration of dipinti and stamped sherds (fig. 4). This could have been an accident of our surface sherd collections, but with so little to differentiate one building from another, we wanted to investigate the possibility that Building 177 had some special function. Outbuilding 181, also on the Hillock, was a little unusual in being situated between and under boulders, but many outbuildings do seem rather ad hoc. It was excavated in order to sample at least one of the many one-room outbuildings at the site. Two thick trash dumps on either side of Building 93 were excavated as well. One of the rather special features of the Bir Umm Fawakhir site is the thick middens near the houses, dumps that appear never to have been scraped aside, redeposited, or reworked, except to a very limited extent by modern looters. The expectation, then, was that the contents of the trash dumps most likely came from the adjacent houses, an unusual archaeological opportunity.

Clare Leader excavated Rooms A, B, C, and D in Building 93, Rooms B, C, and D in Building 177, and Building 181. Carol Meyer excavated Room E in Building 93; Room A in Building 177; and both dumps. Building 93 and Dumps 1 and 2 were excavated from February 8 to 18 and 24 to 27, 1999. Building 177 was excavated from February 20 to 23, and Building 181 on February 22 and 23. Detailed locus lists may be found in *Appendix A*. Note that the colors in the sections (pls. 22–30) are artificial; they do not relate to Munsell soil colors. The use of color is intended solely to make the sections more legible than the usual hatching, stippling, or cross-hatching.

Building 93

Building 93 (fig. 5, pls. 1a, 40b) was plotted during the 1993 survey season (Meyer et al. 2000, p. 13). It was described as a large, rambling, six-room house consisting of four interconnected rooms plus two non-interconnecting rooms and an irregular, partly walled space to the north. The southern room appeared to be a much-ruined single room (F) with a bench and presumably a door on the west. The walls of the room/corridor (A), cliffside room (B), and the rest of Building 93 were, however, preserved to considerable height, as much as 192 cm above the surface sand. The cliffside Room B also had some especially well-preserved niches.[3] Room D was described as containing a bench, a thin partition wall, and perhaps a second one, and a concave grinding stone. Heavy wall fall in other rooms obscured other possible features. A semi-detached room to the north (E) was linked to the core of the house by a now-ruined low wall. Room E had one door looking southeast and perhaps another near the north corner. The large space delineated by some low walls connected to Rooms D and E might not even have been covered, and the rough space (G) between Room D

[3] Clockwise from the door, the niches measure: damaged; 32 cm wide × 31 high × 27 deep; 30 cm wide × 27 high × 38 deep.

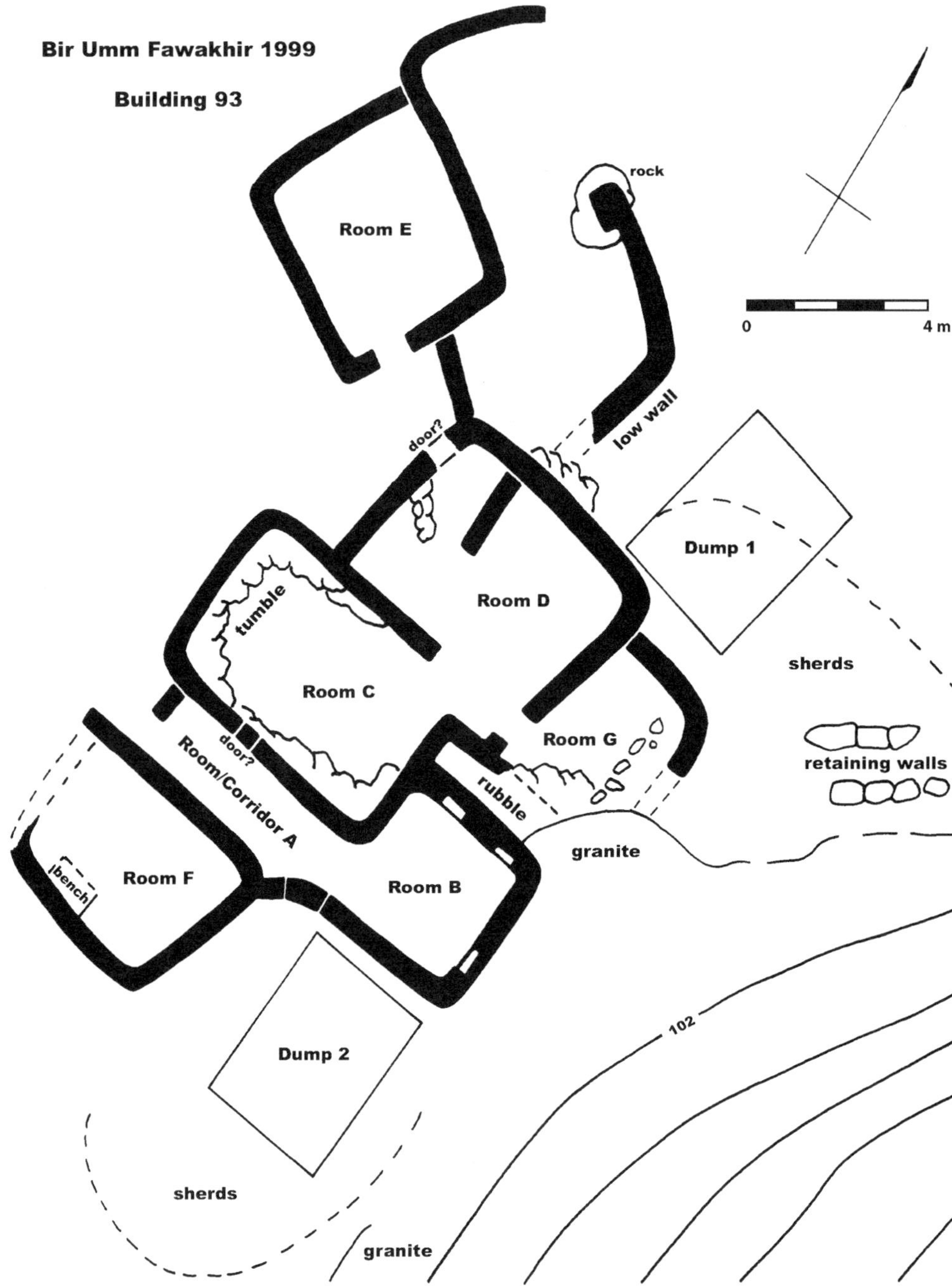

Figure 5. Top plan of Building 93

and the granite cliff was too full of rock debris to determine how or whether it functioned as a room. Two rows of boulders upslope from Building 93 seem to have served as retaining walls. There was a large trash heap (Dump 1) just below them, between Buildings 93 and 97, that yielded a Late Roman 1 amphora sherd with dipinto (RN 93/37; Meyer et al. 2000, p. 48) and a sherd with a stamped cross (RN 93/41; Heidorn 2000, p. 32, fig. 56:36). Dump 2 lay to the south of Building 93.

In the course of excavation, we revised our interpretation of the house somewhat. Room A did indeed lead to Room B at the back, but a threshold between them suggests that Room A was as much a room as a corridor. What looked at first like a door between Rooms A and C on excavation looked more like tumble or perhaps a blocked door. On the other hand, the north corner of Room D seems to have traces of a door facing the sole opening into room E, which has one, not two, entrances. Thus Building 93 would constitute two agglomerated house units, a common layout at Bir Umm Fawakhir. Rooms C, D, and E would have constituted one unit, and A, B, and F the second. The (possible) door between Rooms A and C may have been blocked when Rooms A and B were constructed, perhaps in stages; certainly their south wall was built in segments. Such piecemeal construction is attested elsewhere at the site.

What these revisions in the location of doors means, obviously, is that some of the doorways plotted over the course of four seasons of survey could be misleading. Some doors survive sturdily framed by large, neatly set stones, but many are represented by only one jamb or corner of a jamb. We did not plot a door on the map, at least not without a question mark beside it, unless there was evidence of a doorframe on both faces of the wall, but badly tumbled drystone masonry can be misinterpreted.

Finds in Building 93 were surprisingly rich for a building selected partly for its apparent ordinariness. The copper/gold-alloy bracelet was surely something not lightly discarded, even if broken. An iron wedge and an iron ladle must also have been valuable items. Room C was especially rich: an intact, upside-down deep bowl or krater, two coins, a polished oval agate gemstone, a copper-alloy Bes amulet, and many raw emeralds (green beryls) were excavated.

Room A

Room A (fig. 6, pls. 1b, 22a) was labeled a "corridor" in 1993 because it is so long and thin (5.0 × 1.4 m), but it does have a short bit of wall and a door at the west end and a neatly laid threshold at the east end (fig. 7, pl. 2a), leading to Room B. Only 3.4 m of the approximately 5 m length of the room was excavated to bedrock; the west end was left intact in order to permit excavation of Room C. Room A had one clear level of occupation, loci 4 and 5 on the north and south sides of the trench, excavated separately because of tumbled rock. On section a–b (pl. 22a), the bottom of loci 4/5 shows up as a thin layer of ash. Loci 4/5 yielded not only the expected sherds, bone, ash, charcoal, and glass, but also a pestle (RN 99/207; pl. 17b), an articulated leg bone and hoof, and bits of woven material and matting.[4] The bottom of locus 3, on top of loci 4/5, may have been another occupation level; it had a relatively flat floor, much cultural debris, and even some matting. The loose silty sand of locus 2 is post-occupation fill, presumably windblown, and locus 6 on the bottom appears to be fill, perhaps from a midden, leveled out to make a floor for Room A. Note the large amount of organic matter in locus 6, including articulated vertebrae of a fairly large

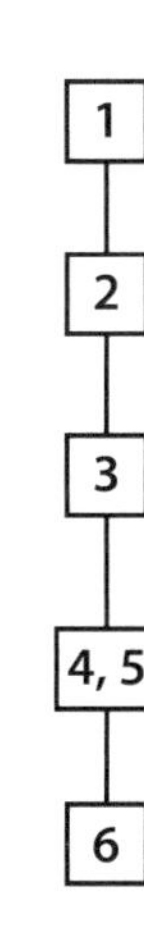

Building 93, Room A matrix

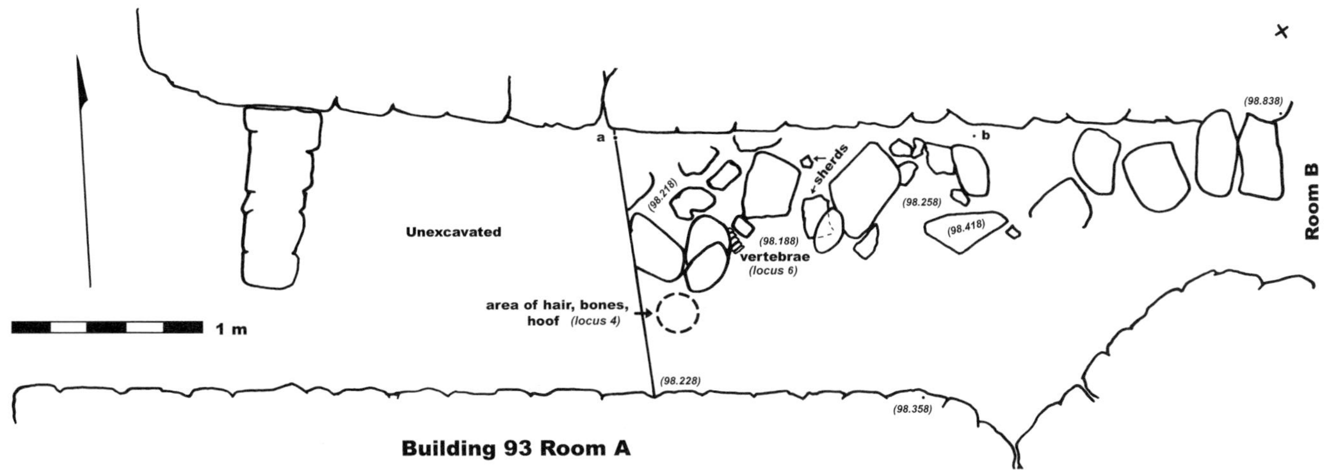

Figure 6. Top plan of Building 93, Room A

[4] Matting of many materials and weaves is abundant and thoroughly studied at Berenice (Sidebotham and Wendrich 2007, pp. 228–50), including some very well-preserved grass mats that seem to have been found in situ (ibid., pp. 104–05).

animal, more bone, some hair, charcoal, and shell. The copper/gold-alloy bracelet (RN 99/230; fig. 41a, pl. 33b) was found here as well.

Room B

Room B (fig. 7, pls. 1b–2, 22b–23) was a fairly large (2.9 × 2.5 m) and well-preserved room with two niches on the north side and one on the east, presumably for storage. The room was excavated in two halves, the eastern side first, so loci 4 and 5 are merely the western parts of loci 1 and 2 on the east. Excavation in the eastern half quickly reached granite bedrock, which shelved down abruptly in the western half, as may be seen on the section of the north baulk (pl. 23b). Loci 1 and 4 are loose, silty, windblown surface sand; a pink granite mano-like grinding stone, about half of a pink granite upper rotary grinding stone, and three cobble pounders (quartz or unidentified stone) were recovered from the surface.[5] The bottom of loci 2 and 5, even though the floor dips a good 20 cm, seems to be the main occupation level. Locus 2 near the east wall contained many lenses of fine, silty, water- or wind-laid sand and also an ash pit in the bedrock filled with rocky debris and ash. Locus 5 contained more sherds, bone, ash, charcoal, and other cultural material, including an iron spike or wedge (RN 99/241; pl. 35a) and the rim of a potstand (RN 99/206) cut from the

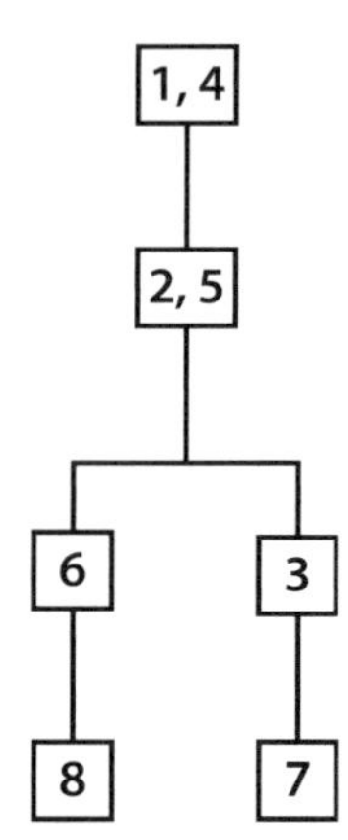

Building 93, Room B matrix

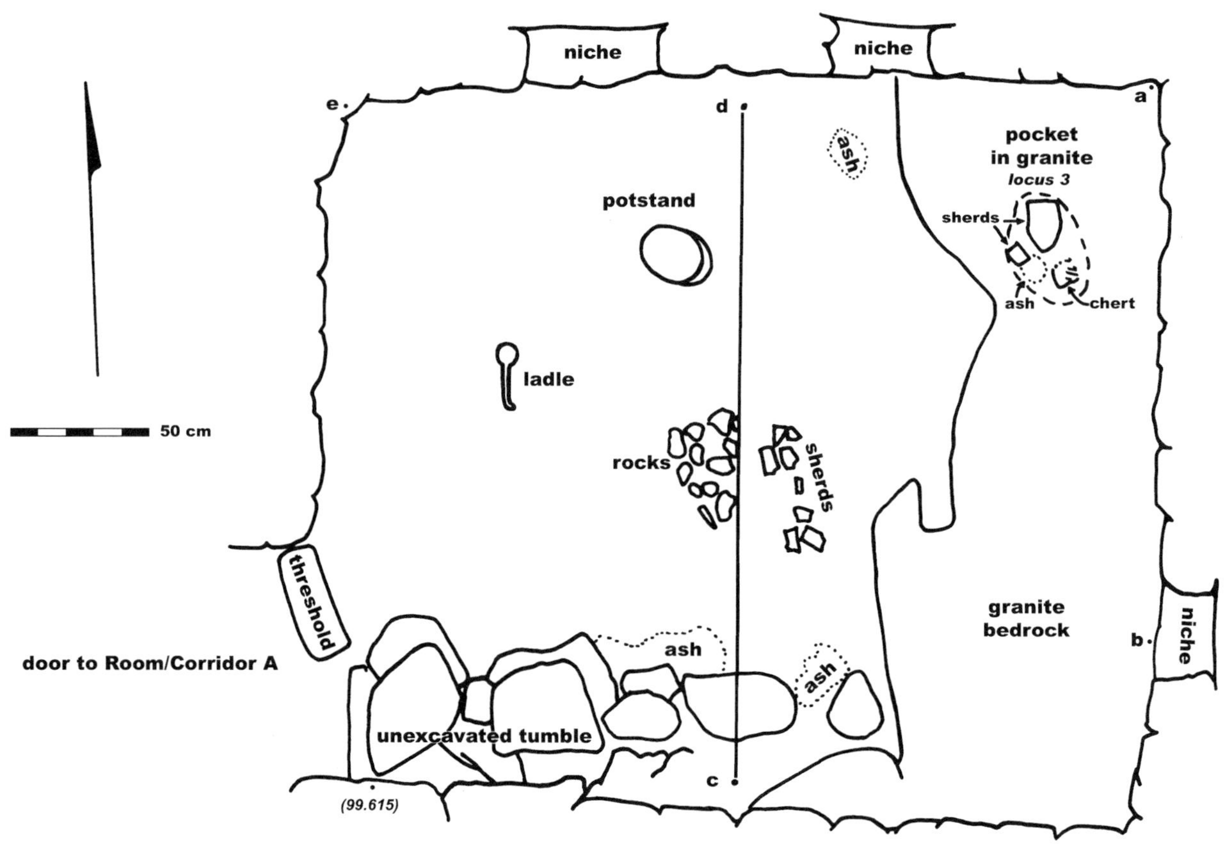

Figure 7. Top plan of Building 93, Room B

[5] For a discussion of the kinds of grinding stones found at Bir Umm Fawakhir and its vicinity, see Meyer 2011, p. 153.

middle section of a large ridged amphora (fig. 7).[6] The iron ladle (RN 99/228; pls. 34e, 36) lay face down on the floor, on top of locus 6. Locus 6, below 2/5, was a more compact sandy to silty to gravelly fill in the dip on the west. It yielded animal teeth and bones, sherds, charcoal, eggshell, a tiny amount of blue glazed faience and glass, a rectangular piece of talc chlorite schist, and a small, crude serpentinite bowl (RN 99/205; pl. 17a). Locus 3 is the fill in a pocket in the granite, and locus 7 below that is mostly scrapings of rotten granite, as is locus 8 in the western half of the room.

The iron wedge is one of the few possibly mining-related tools found at Bir Umm Fawakhir. Iron tools are also curiously rare at the major granodiorite quarry at Mons Claudianus (Peacock 1997, p. 190, fig. 6:9). Either they were worn and smithed to useless slivers, or they were so valuable the workmen took them when they left the site, or they were among the first things scavenged by post-occupation visitors.

The potstand was followed down through locus 6 but seems to have rested in a small depression in the granite rather than in cultural fill. It was packed around with rock chips and rotten granite. Traces of ash and burnt earth near the rim suggest a heating function. The iron ladle and perhaps the small serpentinite bowl also suggest domestic uses of Room B.

Room C

Room C (fig. 8, pls. 3–4, 24) was the largest room in Building 93 (5.3 × 3.5 m) and its stratigraphy among the most complicated and important of the units excavated. Excavation in Room C was hampered by a great deal of wall fall that could not be removed without endangering the trenches and excavators and by a thin partition wall (section c–d on top plan, pl. 24b) at the upper level that effectively split the trench into northeast and northwest halves. There seem to be three occupation stages in Room C, though the floors were gouged, filled, and re-filled to a certain extent.

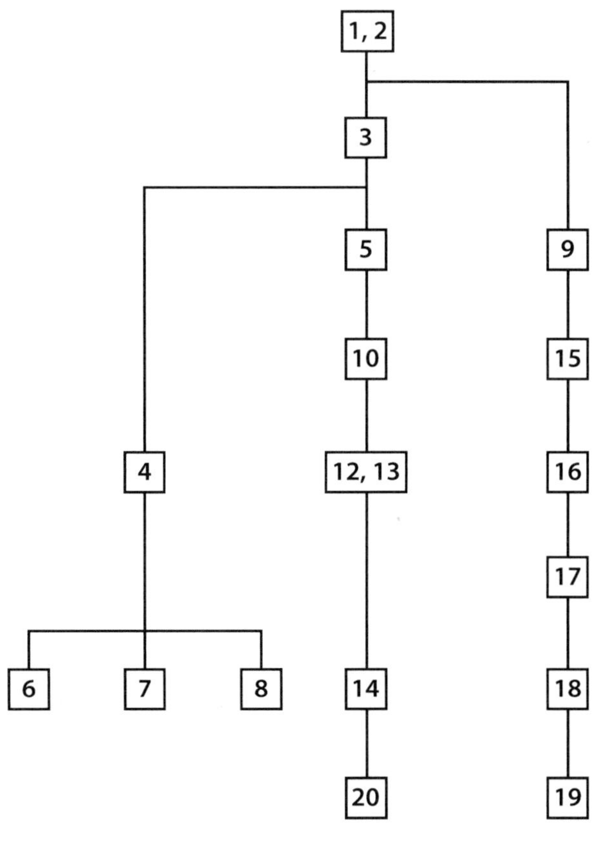

Building 93, Room C matrix

The bottommost level reached was locus 19 in the northwest quadrant and locus 20, a sandy fill in the northeast. An intact, upside-down krater (RN 99/222; fig. 28:109, pls. 13a, 24c) in locus 18 rested on the locus 19 floor. It looked as if it had been washed and left to dry; the sample collected from underneath it appeared to contain insect eggs and webs. Loci 18 in the northwest and 14 in the northeast quadrant were fill layers over the floor; the east end of locus 14 reached granite bedrock. In addition to the upside-down krater, locus 18 yielded sherds, much ash, charcoal, bone, two coins (RN 99/237, fig. 40a–b), a polished oval agate gemstone (RN 99/203; pl. 33c), and a copper-alloy Bes amulet (RN 99/240; fig. 41b, pl. 34a). Next to the east and west walls, the tops of loci 14 and 18 seem to have been scooped into and refilled at least twice (see section a–b, pl. 24a). The next occupational stage is marked by the bottom of loci 16 and 12, both of which were rich in sherds and other cultural relics, bones and other organic remains. The east end of locus 12, toward the east wall, seems to have been scooped out, filled, and re-filled several times, and the northwest quadrant had a large ash pocket on locus 17, a possible floor or surface. Locus 13 in the north half of the northeast quadrant is a continuation of locus 12 so

[6] Potstands and cooking or heating installations made out of segments of amphoras are well attested at Berenice (Sidebotham and Wendrich 2007, p. 153; 2011, p. 104). For a general discussion of amphora segments used as supports or hearths, see Peña 2007, pp. 149–50.

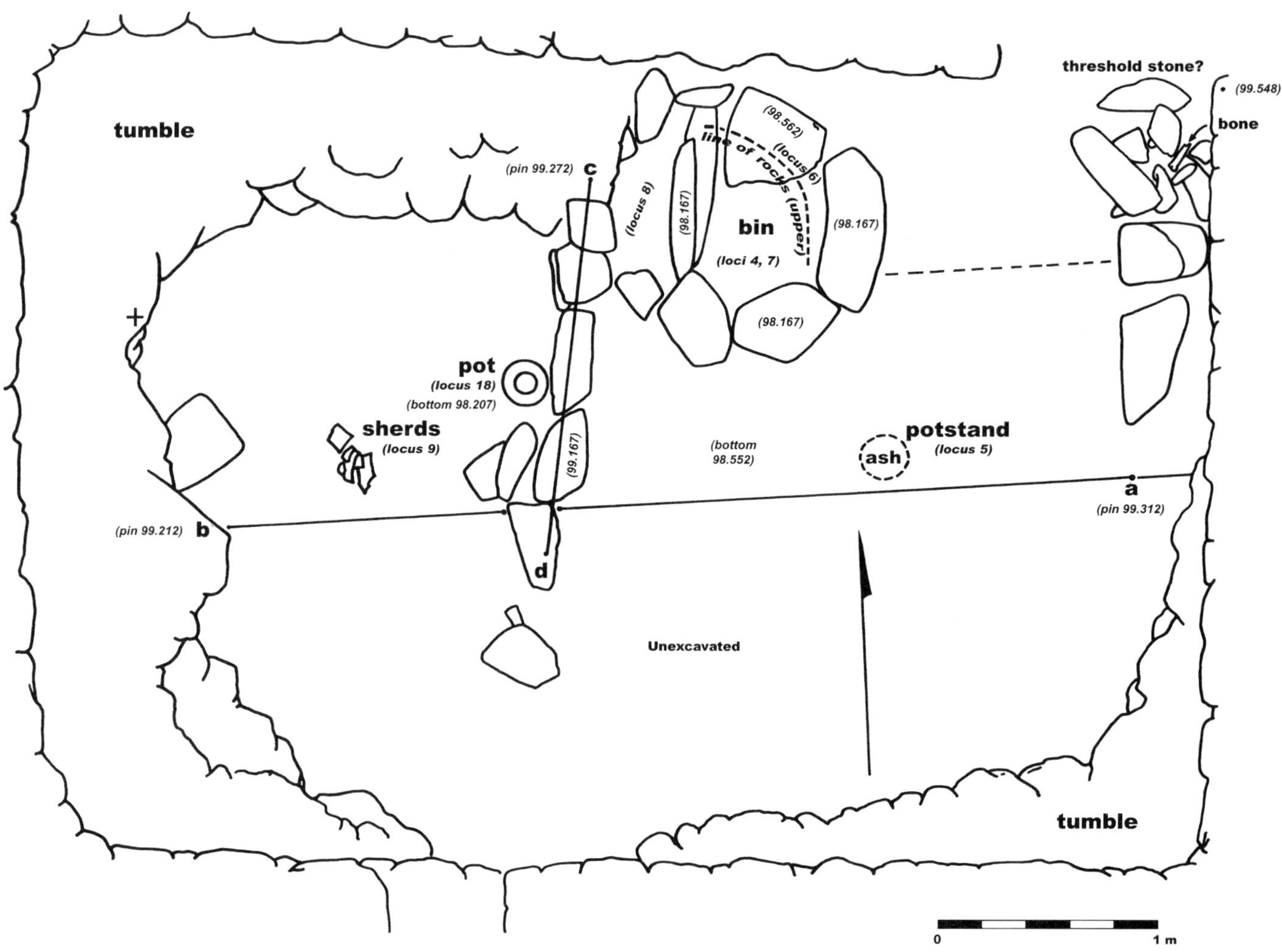

Figure 8. Top plan of Building 93, Room C

they can be lumped. One of the raw emeralds/green beryls (RN 99/232) was recovered here.[7] Note the thick ash lenses, loci 10 and 15. Locus 15 in the northwest quadrant yielded more raw emeralds (RN 99/232; pl. 34d). The bin must have been in use at this time (see fig. 8 center top).

Locus 4 was the upper layer inside the bin. The walls of the bin were a single thickness of fairly large but thin stones (pl. 4). The bin appears to have been rebuilt or repartitioned. A rim of smaller stones, including a reused, dimpled crushing stone of red porphyry, was added inside the bin. The space inside the rim was excavated as locus 7, the space outside, at the mouth of the bin, as locus 6. Locus 6 was a fine, laminated, flaky fill, and locus 7 was a similar silty, powdery sand, so finely laminated it flaked. It contained a little ash, charcoal, and bone but also a raw emerald/green beryl (RN 99/232). The bin may also have been partitioned by a vertical slab; the small pocket to the west, locus 8, was too restricted by wall fall to determine much except that its fill consisted of granular sand with bits of felsite. The flat-lying stone labeled with elevation 98.562 sits on the bottom of the bin at its mouth.

Locus 5 was the clearest surviving floor level in Room C (pl. 3b). It was marked by two groups of flat-lying sherds and another potstand cut from an amphora and filled with ash.[8] Part of the top of locus 5 was covered with ash as well. The thin north–south partition wall (c–d on top plan) was added at this level. Locus 3 in the northeast quadrant and locus 9 in the northwest are the fill layers over the top floor. Locus 3 was a

[7] The varieties of the mineral beryl, including the green variety generally known as "emerald," are discussed more fully in *Chapter 4*.

[8] A similar installation is reported from Berenice (Sidebotham and Wendrich 2011, p. 104).

fairly compact, somewhat granular, silty sand. The top of the bin emerged here (stone labeled with elevation 99.167 on the top plan, fig. 8).

Locus 1 in the northwest quadrant was a thin, loose surface layer 14 to 20 cm deep. Locus 2 in the northeast was similar but richer in finds, not only sherds, bone, charcoal, and organic matter but also a raw emerald (RN 99/232), and two dimpled crushing stones from near the north wall. The Room C excavations were backfilled and the southern half of the room remained unexcavated.

Judging from the potstand in the upper level, the upside-down krater on the lowest floor, and the bin, Room C had domestic functions, but judging from the surprising abundance of items of personal wealth or adornment, especially in the northwest corner, valuables were kept here as well. Room C is some of the best evidence for at least three stages of occupation, and if this is the case, then it supports the idea that the Bir Umm Fawakhir mines were worked intermittently, when the need for gold was urgent and when capital in the form of labor and supplies could be dispatched to the desert.

Room D

Room D (fig. 9, pls. 5a, 25), at 4.8 × 3.6 m, was the second largest in Building 93. An exceptionally wide door leads to Room C on the south and to "Room G," the rock-filled walled space beside the cliff. Room D was sampled at the very end of the 1999 season, so work was restricted to surface clearance over the whole room and deeper excavation in the southwest corner, delimited by the wall between Rooms C and D, a large rock, and a possible partition wall.

Locus 1 was a thick layer of loose surface silt covering the whole room. Locus 2 below was a more compact, fine, silty sand with many sherds, a little glass, bone, shell, and seeds, and lenses of ash and charcoal. The bottom of locus 2 probably represents the latest floor of the room. Locus 3 was a compact, granular, silty

Figure 9. Top plan of Building 93, Room D

layer with a few rootlets. A bottle plug (RN 99/202) was retrieved here. This locus runs over the top of a circular stone-rimmed feature (pl. 25c) in the corner of the room, and locus 5 is a hard, reddish, silty fill around the back and side of the circular feature. Since both time and the trench size were so restricted, the floor associated with the feature was not defined, though it might be the bottom of locus 3. Locus 4 was the fill of the circular feature, fine silt and sand at the top grading to fine gravel at the lowest level reached, which was not the bottom of the feature. The fill contained many sherds, some charcoal, bone, ash, bits of wood, and insect exoskeletons. Note also the animal holes in loci 3 and 5.

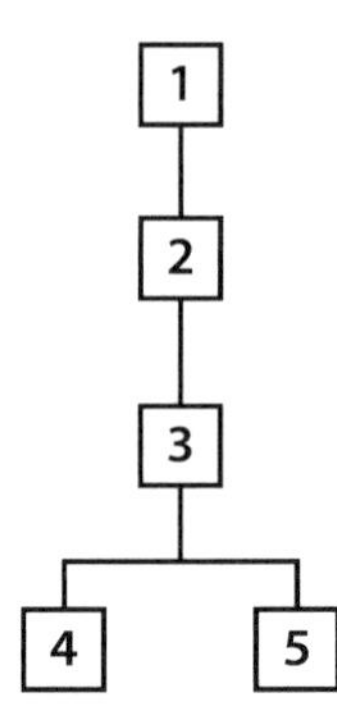

Building 93, Room D matrix

Clearance of the thick surface silt and some of the rock tumble revealed a probable door at the northwest corner, though this area was not excavated in order to permit access to the rest of the room. Room D appears to be the outer room of the C-D house unit, and the thin north–south partition wall would have made the room a little more private. The large rock (see top plan) and perhaps another thin partition wall, now represented by the line of tumble, partly marked off the circular feature in the corner. Since the excavation did not reach the bottom of the feature, we do not know what it was, though there is no indication that it was a fireplace. The rootlets and numerous animal holes suggest that there was some moisture and perhaps food or weeds here immediately post-occupation. A skeleton of a silky jird, a midden-loving rodent, was recovered from Dump 1 outside Room D, as discussed below and in *Chapter 5*.

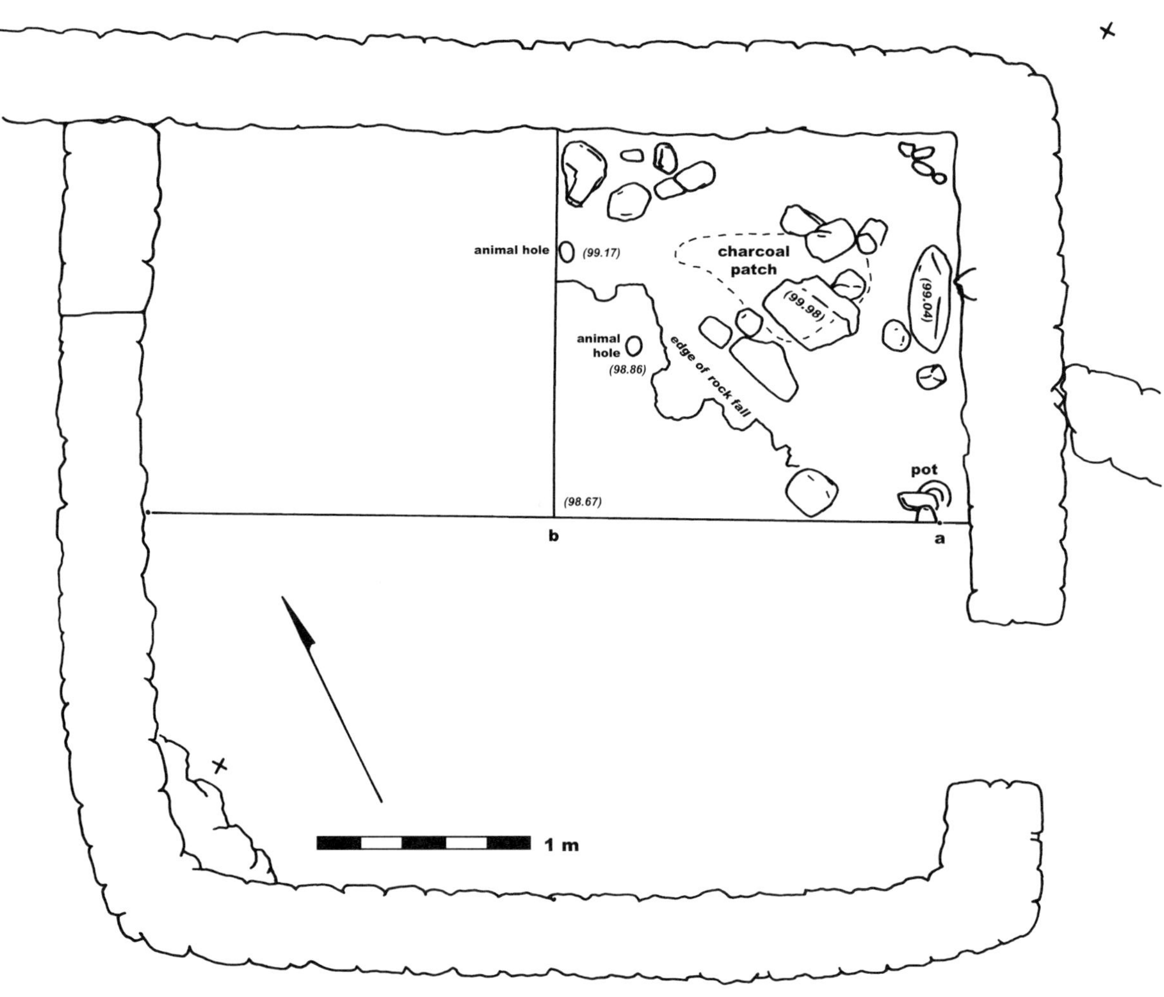

Figure 10. Top plan of Building 93, Room E

Room E

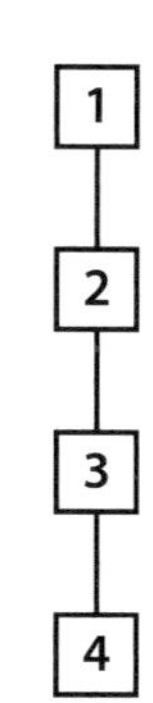

Building 93,
Room E matrix

Only the northeast quadrant of Room E (fig. 10, pls. 5b, 26) (3.50 × 3.64–3.33 m) could be sampled at the very end of the 1999 season. The west wall was built in two segments and abuts the north wall. Two grinding stones were reused in the north wall construction, one of which was deeply ground and striated, and the other may have been part of an upper rotary quern stone. The surface, locus 1, was a very fine windblown silt with virtually no finds. Locus 2 underneath was a thick bed of sandy and silty laminated layers with a couple of beads but few other finds. Note the animal holes. Below this, another fine silty layer (locus 3) with charcoal and ash patches continued down to a layer of rocky tumble dipping toward the middle of the room, presumably fallen from the walls. The fill around the stones (locus 4) was a brownish laminated silt that contained more cultural debris, including a pot. Since the vessel was partly buried under rocks projecting from the south baulk, it was left in place (pl. 26b). Thus locus 4 and the rock tumble may overlie a floor level, though excavation ceased at this point.

What is most encouraging about the Room E excavation is the depth of fill, a good 70 cm just to rock fall and cultural remains. On the surface the walls of Room E look low and very ruined, but in fact they are deeply buried in silt and sand. In antiquity the wadi bottom, the ancient main street, must have lain significantly lower than it does now. By contrast, units such as the back of Room B rise up against the granite cliff face and reach bedrock in a few centimeters. Thus Building 93, and many others, stepped downhill more or less steeply. Also, many of the house units that appear most ruined in the middle of the wadi and toward the northwest end of the site may in fact be rather well preserved, just buried by a millennium and a half of sandstorms and rare but heavy flash floods.

Building 93 Overview

Rooms C and D and perhaps G seem to be the core of Building 93. Certainly the excavations in Room C indicate several floors and hence intervals of occupation and infilling. Rooms E and F might originally have been independent or semi-independent one-room buildings. Room E was linked to Room D at some point by a wall, though there is no suggestion that the space between Rooms E, D, and C was ever enclosed, much less covered. The area north of Rooms D and E was partly enclosed by low walls and may have functioned as some sort of work area. Dump 1, discussed below, contained several cooking installations and thick layers of refuse. Rooms A and B appear to have been enclosed after Rooms C and F were constructed. The stub of a wall closing off the west end of Room A abuts Room C, but unfortunately we cannot be sure whether the Room B walls abut Rooms C and F. The south wall of Room B was built in segments, or perhaps the wall segment where Room A narrows to make the door to Room B was once an exterior door, if a rather wide one. If there was in fact a door between Rooms C and A, it must have been blocked off at this time. Dump 2 also contained cooking installations and refuse and may represent debris from the Rooms A, B, F house unit.

Dump 1

We excavated two trash dumps on either side of Building 93, Dumps 1 and 2. Our working assumption was that a lived-in dwelling will be kept relatively clean, and only sudden abandonment will leave many artifacts on a living floor, such as the iron ladle in Room B and the upside-down krater in Room C of Building 93. Debris would presumably be dumped outside a house, and at Bir Umm Fawakhir at least, at no great distance. One of the features of the site is ancient dump heaps close to a house or cluster of houses, not a remote or central dump. Furthermore, apart from incidental looting, the ancient trash heaps were relatively undisturbed; they had never been shoved aside, re-piled, or dug into for later structures, moats, city walls, or anything else. We hoped to find ostraca that could illuminate aspects of life at the ancient site, but neither dump yielded any written material.[9] Instead, they proved to be not only middens but also kitchens.

Dump 1 (figs. 11, 12, pls. 6–7, 27–28) was a 3 × 4 m trench perpendicular to the north wall of Room D of Building 93. Another and probably quite thick part of the dump lies east of the trench, where the ground starts to slope up steeply to the cliffside. Thus much of the thick layer of surface sherds was probably washed down from the east. Locus 1 was the top 10 to 30 cm of sandy to powdery soil with a little ash and very dense sherds, including four dipinti (RN 99/225; three illustrated in figs. 37b–c, 38c). Two quartzite pounding stones, a cowrie shell cut to make an ornament (RN 99/201; pl. 18a), a very coarse plate with an "XP" stamp (st-1; RN 99/226), and a thick basalt stone disk were recovered as well. Locus 2 was a thin ashy layer most evident at the west side of the trench. It had more bone and organic material, including a horn, cloth fibers, twine, many date pits, wood, twigs, and dung, but also some decorated glass.

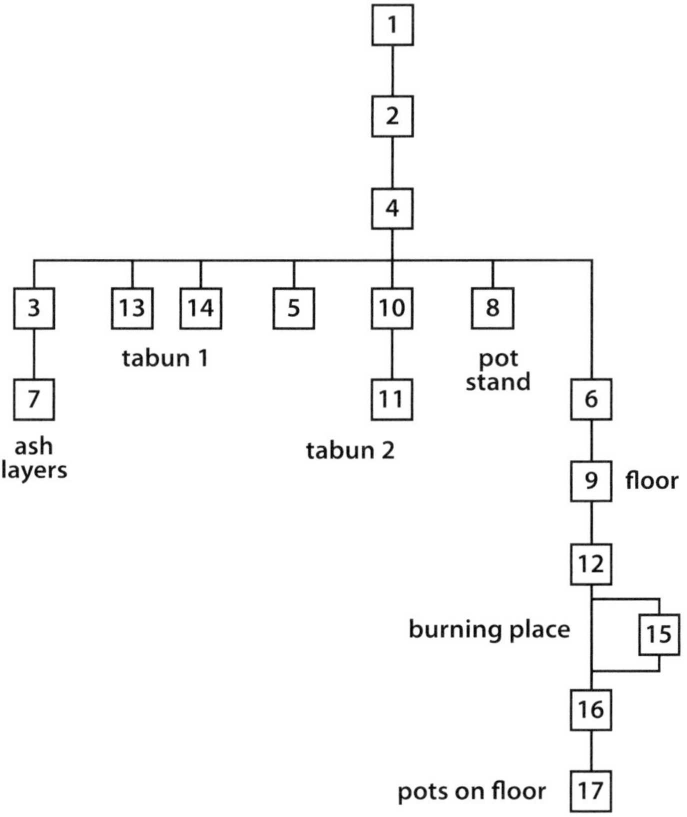

Dump 1 matrix

At this point the tops of the first of a series of cooking features started to appear (fig. 11, pl. 6). Basically, loci 3 and 7 are thick layers of fine ash presumably scraped out of hearths or ovens and dumped in the southeast corner. Locus 4 is the thick layers of sandy fill around the "tabuns," and loci 5, 8, 10, 11, 13, and 14 are fill in and around them. "Tabun" 1 was a truncated clay cone 33 to 37 cm in diameter at the surviving rim, 55 cm at the bottom, and standing at least 49 cm high. It was surrounded by a low stone circle that survived 28 cm high. At first we thought it was a bread oven, but it has almost no ash inside, only a thin layer under the lowest floor, so it might be a storage facility like the "*dolia*" at Berenice. Locus 14 was the fill between the tabun/*dolium*[10] and its stone wall, and locus 13 was the fill inside, which at the bottom had a series of four thin clay floors over a thin layer of ash. The clay oven or *dolium* was fairly fragile so it was excavated, documented, and consolidated by the objects conservator (see *Chapter 7* and pl. 37a). The soil sample from locus 13 is treated in *Chapter 7*. Tabun 2 was more damaged; pieces of its wall had broken off and fallen into it. The tabun itself appears to have been built up of belts or horizontal slabs of clay joined along the edges and smeared together with wet clay. It was surrounded by a very hard clay rim that was left in situ. Locus 5 was a pocket of black ash around the tabun. Locus 10 was the upper layer of fill inside the tabun. It was sandy with a little charcoal and some burnt bone, but locus 11 below consisted of dark, fine ash and a great deal of dung, most of which was collected for later analysis (see *Chapter 7*).[11] "Tabun" 3 was just a circle of stone with little evidence of cooking; it seems to have been a potstand and is labeled as

---

[9] So far there are no ostraca from any of the other Eastern Desert Coptic/Byzantine-period sites, either. The thousands of ostraca from sites such as Wadi Mweh and Wekalat Zarka were retrieved from the dump heaps outside the gates of the Roman-period forts. Unlike sprawling, unwalled Bir Umm Fawakhir, the *praesidia* were walled, towered, and accessed by a main gate, and rubbish was periodically dumped outside on a large and growing trash heap. This meant that all or virtually all the discarded ostraca were deposited in one spot (Brun 2003a, p. 61).

[10] A *dolium*, strictly speaking, is a large, thick-walled, rounded storage jar that is immovable or nearly so. The possible *dolia* at Bir Umm Fawakhir are cruder vessels, constructed in place, and protected by low stone walls.

[11] We experimented with a dung fire. Cowherd collected about a kilo of dung, mostly goat but also some larger sheep droppings, placed them between two large flat stones, and fired them at 9:08 a.m. The flames died down by 9:25, and the dung was still glowing ten to fifteen minutes later. It shrinks but retains its shape as it burns and smells like wood smoke. It also leaves a lot of soot on the bottom of a teakettle, which raises the issue of why so few Bir Umm Fawakhir sherds are sooted. Perhaps cooking was not done until the flames died down and only charcoal was left (Cappers 2006, p. 47, describing wood fires of modern nomads).

such in figure 11. Its interior fill, locus 8, was sandy with a little bone. "Tabun" 4 was ruined to a rim (ca. 60 cm dia.) by the time the other tabuns were in use; it may have been the remains of another *dolium*, but we excavated no lower at this point.

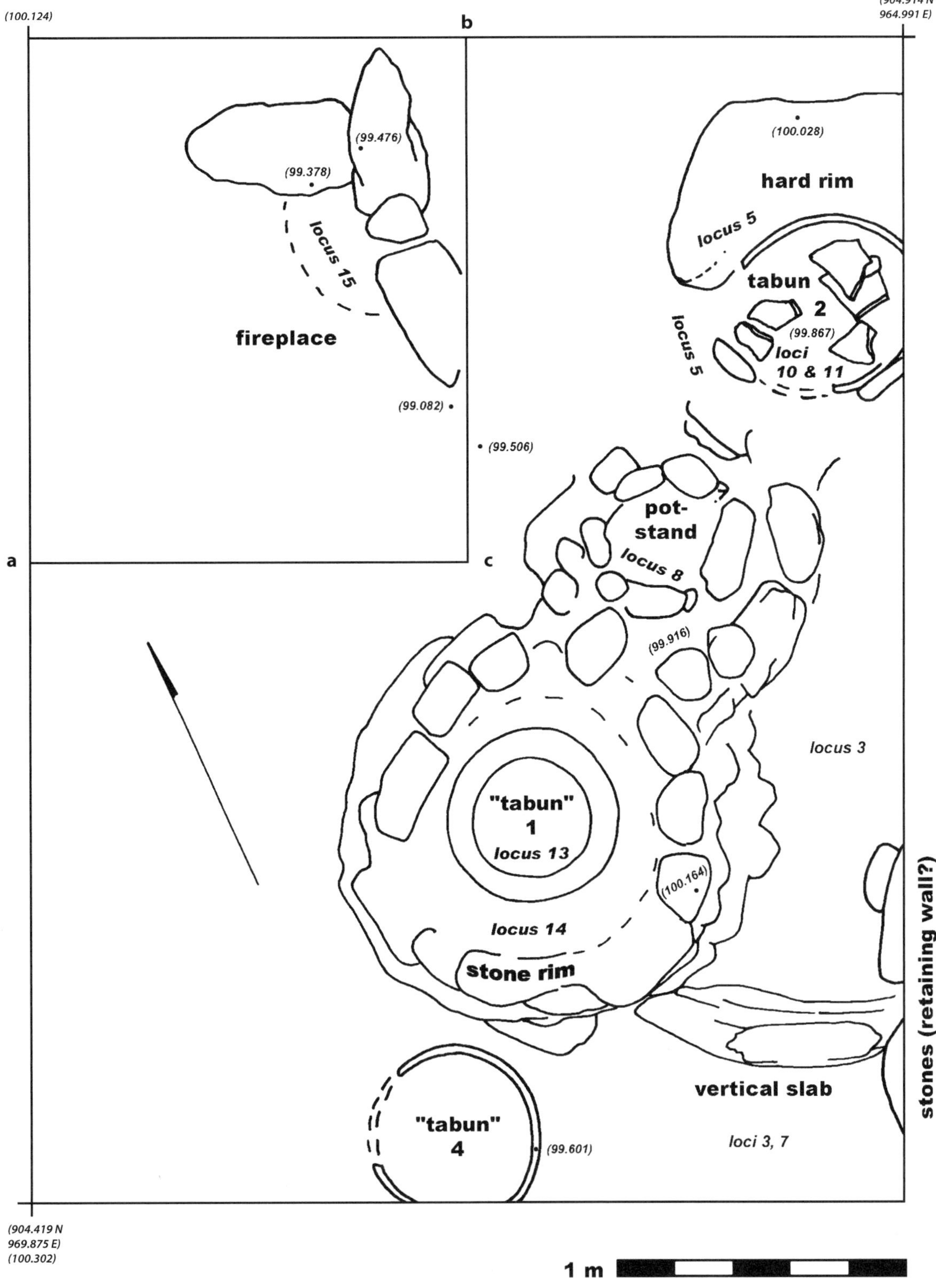

Figure 11. Top plan of Dump 1, upper levels

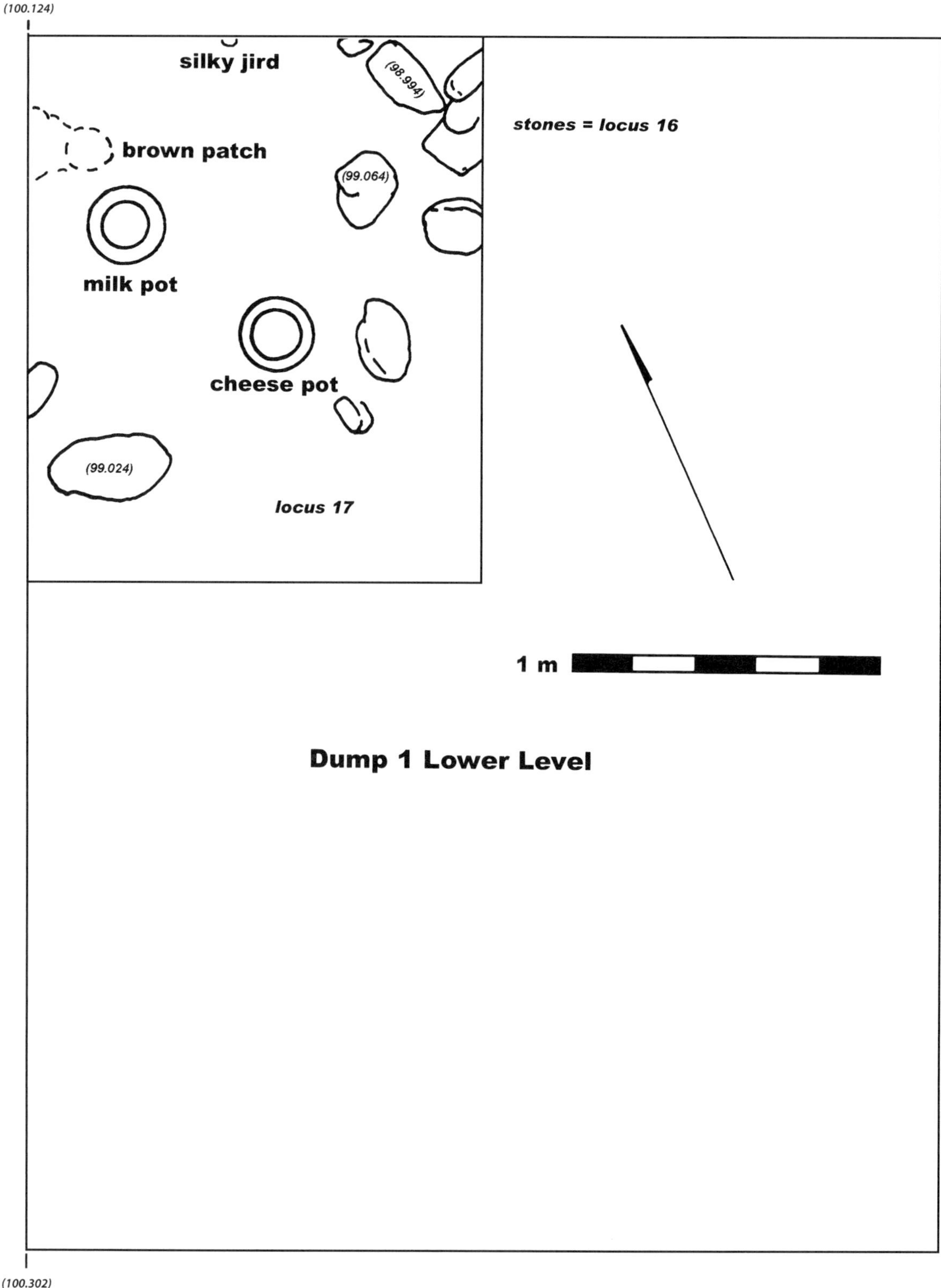

Figure 12. Top plan of Dump 1, lower level

Some better-preserved kitchens from other sites support our interpretation of the upper level of Dump 1 as a kitchen area. Some good examples have been reported from Berenice, especially building BE00-34, a well-constructed house. The excavated part was a room or partly covered court with stairs leading up to a second floor, a door with a wooden threshold opening onto a street, and a series of food containers or preparation facilities. The earlier phase had a large (84 cm dia.) *dolium* in the corner by the stairs. The second, slightly higher level had three features. The first was a potstand or storage container consisting of the top of a Late Roman 1 amphora set neck down and surrounded by a low wall of coral lumps. The second was another ceramic vessel set in a ring of coral stones, and the third, in the southwest corner by the door, was a *dolium* ca. 50 cm in diameter, again surrounded by a rim of coral chunks. In all three cases the gap between the ceramic vessel and the wall was filled with ash, perhaps as insulation or as a repellent against insects or rodents (Sidebotham and Wendrich 2007, pp. 114–20). An oven with an "insulating shell" very similar to our "tabun" 1 has been published from Karanis in the Fayyum (Gazda 1983, p. 28). Some of the indoor kitchens at the hermitages at Kellia and Esna are quite well preserved. A kitchen from Kellia has a hearth or stove in the southeast corner of the room; the fire box is below and the flat top could have been used for cooking. The southwest corner of the kitchen was occupied by a large jar heavily plastered in place; it seems to have been an ash receptacle. Crammed in between it and the rectangular stove is a small horseshoe-shaped brasero or grill almost at floor level (Kasser 1972, p. 134, fig. 137). The well-preserved kitchens at the Esna hermitages are likewise roofed rooms with low, built-in stoves, ovens, chimneys, and other features useful for food preparation (Sauneron and Jacquet 1972).

Locus 3, the pocket between the east side of "tabun" 1 and the side of the trench, was almost pure ash. The three stones shown projecting out of the east baulk (fig. 11) may have been part of a retaining wall that we could not trace without extending the trench, and the south baulk of the trench almost touches the north wall of Building 93, so the pocket in the southeast corner of the trench from "tabun" 4 to tabun 2 is actually tightly confined. Locus 3 was as much as 70 cm deep and very rich in animal bones. A single loose brick (70 × 54 × 58 cm) was burnt red but was too damaged to determine its original dimensions or shape. The only other notable find was an unburned wooden peg (RN 99/208; pl. 18b) about 14 cm long. The vertical stone slab near the southeast corner closed off at least the lower part of locus 3. This space was excavated as locus 7 and consisted of extremely fine ash.

Locus 4 is a thick sandy fill with many ash lenses. Since it overlaps a little of the locus 3 ash where it seems to have spilled out of the ash box(es) at the southeast corner (pl. 27b, east baulk), it looks as if the ash was deposited first, and not too carefully at that, and then locus 4 filled in the area when it went out of use as a kitchen.

Locus 9 was the floor or working surface of the tabun level. It is a hard-packed sandy soil with some organic matter, bone (including the knobs of some large joints), another horn, one of the few excavated dipinti (RN/225; fig. 38d), and a bit of iron.

Since we wanted to reach bedrock if possible but did not want to remove the kitchen installations, we laid out a small 1.5 × 1.8 m trench in the northwest corner. This immediately cut through locus 12, a thick layer with many lenses of ash and organic material. A great deal of pottery and bone was recovered, including semi-articulated animal vertebrae and feet, and also cloth, seeds, wood, charcoal, twine, bits of fiber, leather (including a strap cut like the top of a tuning fork), a dung beetle, and a copper/bronze strip. It looks like a series of rubbish tips. The only construction was a simple fireplace in the angle of some rough boulders. Locus 15 is the ash from this burning place, and locus 16 is a packed sandy silt below loci 12 and 15, perhaps a sort of work space right in front of the fire (fig. 11, pl. 28a, north baulk and section b–c).

Below this lay locus 17, a 15 cm thick layer of fine, fairly soft, silty sand, probably windblown. Here we recovered the entire skeleton of a small animal we thought was a mouse or rat but that is actually a silky jird (RN 99/235; see *Chapter 5*), a desert native that also seeks out human trash heaps. At the bottom of locus 17 were two nearly intact vessels sitting upright on an earthen floor (pl. 7), one a round, wide-mouth pot (RN 99/219; fig. 32:129, pl. 13b) and the other a tall jar with five holes in the bottom (RN 99/220; fig. 33:135, pl. 14). The round pot had some large, ribbed amphora sherds resting on top like a partial cover. The workmen immediately identified the pots as cheese-making vessels. We tend to agree, but since we had no means whatsoever of carrying out any tests for residues, if any, we cannot prove the point. We can only suggest that the round, wide-mouth pot (no. 129) could have been used for milk and the one with holes (no. 135) for straining out whey. Making cheese is, however, a good solution to the problem of keeping milk in a hot desert climate. At a depth of 140 cm, we still had not reached bedrock, but the trench was too deep and restricted to excavate any farther.

Thus Dump 1 provided another good stratigraphic sequence with evidence of three stages of occupation: the lowest level with the cheese-making pots, the fireplace buried in layers of rubbish, and the kitchen level with several kinds of features: a cooking oven (tabun 2), a potstand, a large tabun or *dolium* ("tabun" 1), and the ruined rim of another, presumably earlier feature ("tabun" 4).

Dump 2

Dump 2 (fig. 13, pls. 8a, 29), in the angle between Rooms B and F of Building 93, was another 3 × 4 m square. It too covered a kitchen area, though the overlying fill layers are probably disturbed and hence less useful for stratigraphic analysis.

Granite bedrock emerged almost immediately below the surface at the east side of the trench and then stepped down abruptly toward the west, as may be seen most easily in the north baulk (pl. 29a). The kitchen installations (pl. 8a) sat on the lowest level excavated on the western side. Although we did not reach bedrock on the western side, digging deeper would have required removal of the kitchen installations and/or extending the trench farther west, up to the back wall of Room F. The kitchen consisted of a clay tabun or *dolium* in the southwest corner, two reused amphora segments, and a "bin." The tabun/*dolium* was shaped like a truncated cone, but the clay was very crumbled. It was surrounded by ash (locus 10) and a partial rim of stones. Because of the very fragile textile remains on top, the tabun interior was excavated by the conservator and is reported in more detail in *Chapter 7*. "Pot 2" (see top plan, fig. 13) lay to the north in its own rim of stones; it was excavated as locus 11. The pot was so shattered it was originally thought to be a pot smash, but on removal it proved to be the upside-down upper half of a Late Roman 1 amphora, complete with dipinto (RN 99/224; fig. 37a).[12] It was packed with other sherds outside and some sherds and stones inside, and it looks as much like a miniature tabun as a potstand. The other installation ("pot 1" in fig. 13) consists of a segment of a ridged Late Roman 7 amphora. It was surrounded by a complete rim of stones excavated as locus 9 (see pl. 38a). The fill consisted mainly of fine ash. Between the two pot features was a small but well-defined "bin" (locus 7) with a black, ashy fill; it is possible that this was the actual cooking hearth. A thick ash layer (locus 5) may be seen on the south baulk sloping upward with the granite bedrock; in the west baulk it appears as a series of thinner lenses. Locus 8 at the bottom of the trench may be seen in the west baulk (pl. 29b). It runs up against the line of cooking installations, up to the northwest and southwest corners. It consisted of sand and ash lenses with sherds, cloth, and other organic matter. Both the northwest and southwest corners of the trench were marked by very hard-packed surfaces that were probably associated with the kitchen features, like the very hard surface next to tabun 2 in Dump 1.

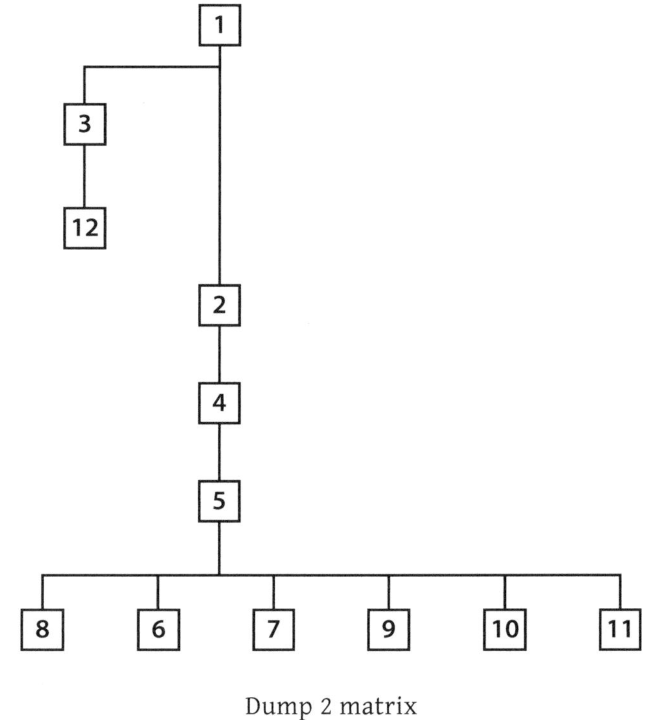

Dump 2 matrix

Over and around the tops of the kitchen installation were layers of rubbish, loci 4 and 2. Locus 4 is a soft sandy layer with much organic debris, especially in the northwest corner, including cloth, fiber, twine, charcoal, and dung. Locus 2, over the whole trench, is also sandy but harder. Abundant sherds were recovered, but also some important glass fragments, including the handle of a jug (fig. 42n) and a rim fragment

[12] Potstands made of broken amphoras set in the ground are well attested at Berenice (Sidebotham and Wendrich 2007, pp. 114, 116, 153).

of a red Roman-period bowl (fig. 42o, pl. 35c). The surface layer, locus 1, is the top 4 to 25 cm of sandy wash from the cliff. It yielded dense sherds, some bone, and a little ash. The problem is that a shallow, ill-defined pit was scooped into the loci 2 and 4 layers. It can be seen on plate 8a, behind the menu board. The top of the pit, locus 3, had much ash and organic debris, and the bottom, locus 12, had even more. In addition to animal bone, there was a hoof, hide, cloth, fiber, and dung.

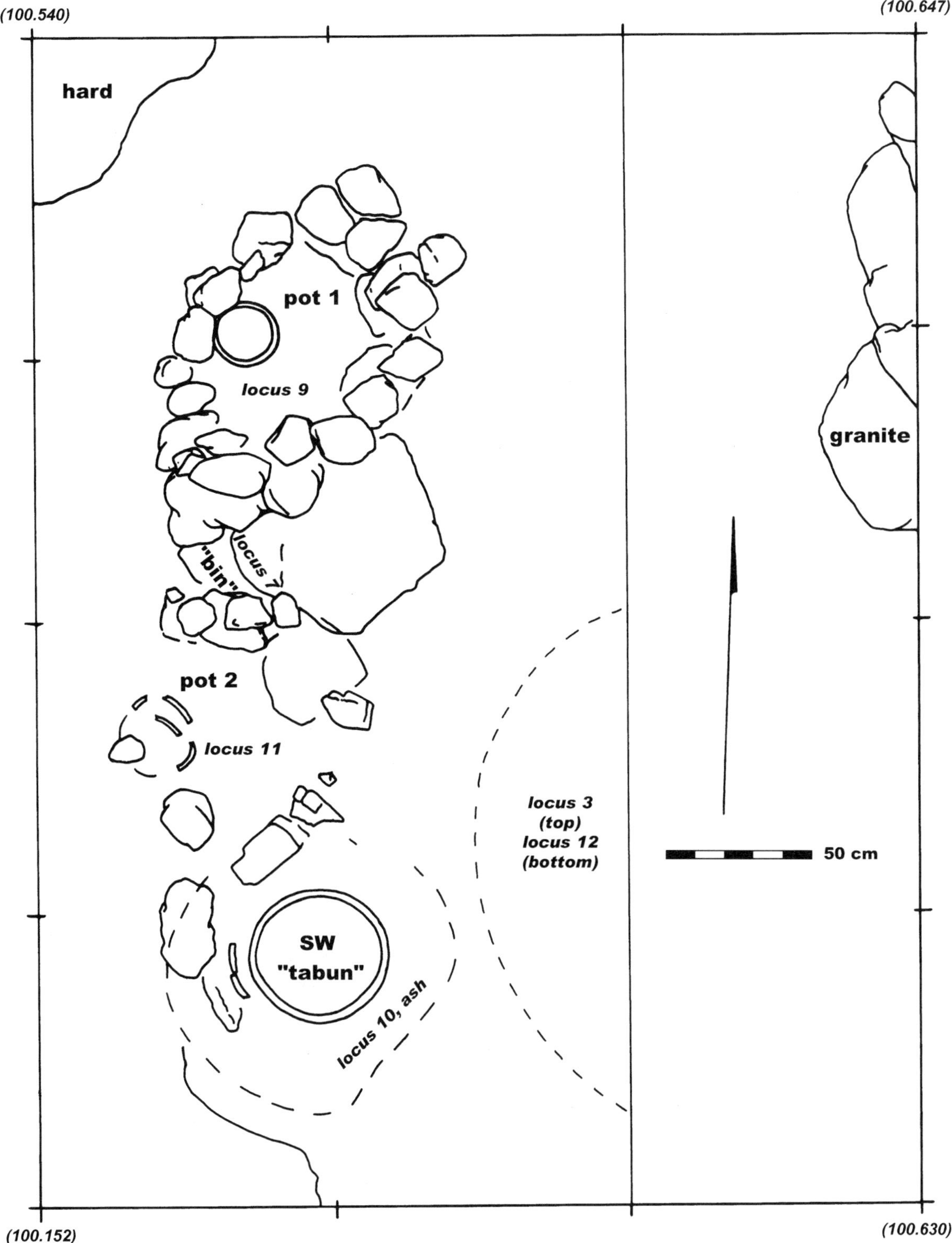

Figure 13. Top plan of Dump 2

The upper layers of the trench are mixed, but the lower loci in and around the tabun or *dolium*, pot features, "bin," and hardened patches are clearly a second cooking area or kitchen, presumably serving the house unit made up of Rooms A, B, and F of Building 93.

Building 177

Building 177 (figs. 14–15, pls. 8b–11, 30) was selected for excavation partly because of its good preservation and partly because it seemed a little different from most of the other houses at ancient Bir Umm Fawakhir. From one end of the main settlement to the other, the houses are quite similar. Some are larger and more rambling, but all have the same sort of drystone masonry, and all seem to be rather modest dwellings. As noted in earlier publications, we have not yet identified any important, formally laid-out administrative buildings or even churches or temples (barring the much earlier tiny Ptolemy III shrine). Buildings 176 and 177, however, were constructed on top of a granite knob called the "Hillock" in the middle of the site (pl. 8b) and hence were somewhat separated from the other houses on either side of the wadi bottom. Building 176 was too full of boulders and cobbles to be easily excavated. Also, there appeared to be an unusual concentration of dipinti, and hence presumably wine, as well as fancy plates with stamped decoration in and around Building 177 (see fig. 4). In addition to the sherds collected in 1997, seven more dipinti from wine amphoras

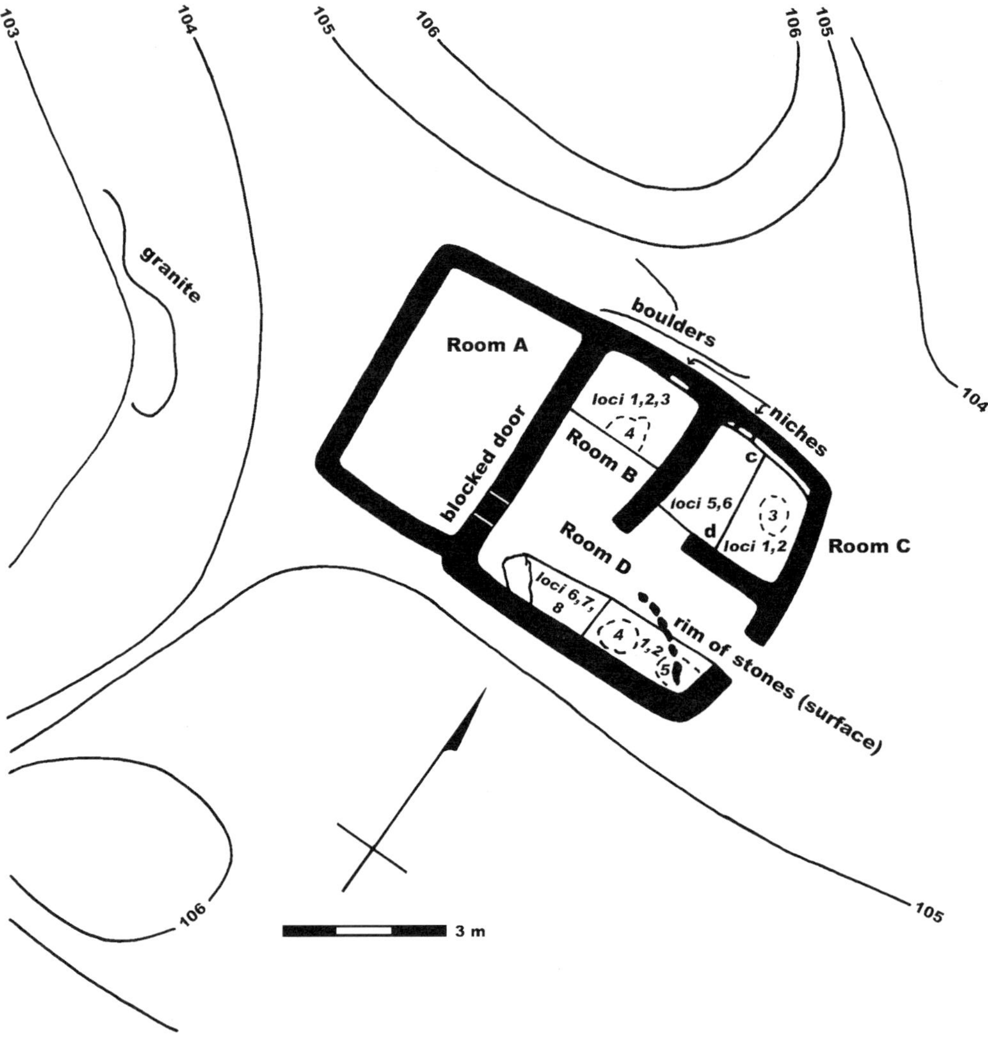

Figure 14. Top plan of Building 177

(e.g., fig. 38h; see *Chapter 4*) and at least ten sherds of stamped plates (*Chapter* 3, fig. 18) were retrieved from the surface around Building 177 in 1999.

Building 177 was mapped during the 1997 survey season (Meyer 2011, p. 65, figs. 21b, 37b, 40b). It was described as a very solidly built four-room house. The entrance room (D) has a line of stones forming a partition in the south corner. The north wall of Room C consists partly of some large boulders and utilizes a hollow in the native granite as a niche. Room B opens onto Room D, and it, too, has a niche in its north wall. The door to Room A, at the back, was deliberately blocked off. Tumble at the south wall was thought to cover a mastaba, but excavation revealed no such feature. A remarkable number of crushing and grinding stones was found in and around Building 177, namely, a dimpled crushing stone and the lower half of a rotary quern in Room A, three dimpled crushing stones in Rooms D and C, a concave grinding stone in Room B, and a cluster of concave grinding stones just outside and east of the building. In addition to surface picking, we took a systematic sherd sample from the dump downslope (west) from B177. Among other finds, a fine painted juglet fragment, ten plates with stamped decoration, and a dipinto were collected (Meyer and Heidorn 2011, pp. 126–27; and *Appendix A*).

Room A

Room A (fig. 15, pls. 9b–10a, 30a) at 4.0 × 2.5 m was the largest in Building 177. Since the building and Room A can easily be accessed only from the northeast, the room was excavated in two halves, the western part first and the eastern half later, hence some of the oddities on the matrix, such as locus 15 apparently over locus 1.

Building 177 was constructed toward one side of the Hillock, so bedrock under Room A slopes steeply and irregularly from the northeast corner to the southwest, and the base of the south wall is much deeper than that of the north wall (pl. 9b). Loci 14 and 12 are interpreted as fill under the first floor. Both are sandy with sherds and much bone, including what looked like an articulated hoof of a sheep or goat in locus 12, and abundant small, round dung pellets. The layers are separated by an ash lens but not necessarily by any great lapse of time. More importantly, locus 12 also yielded three dipinti (RN 99/225; one illustrated in fig. 39i) and a piece of a plate with stamped decoration (RN 99/236; fig. 18:15). Although the latter are not uncommon surface finds, this is the only example we excavated. If the top of locus 12 represents an occupation floor, then it would have been quite uneven, partly packed sandy fill and partly granite bedrock with a short step down (pl. 30a). The fill over the possible floor, locus 9, certainly is rich in cultural materials such as bone, sherds, and many small finds including a soapstone pendant (RN 99/199; fig. 40s), a raw emerald/green beryl (RN 99/232; see pl. 34d), a dipinto (fig. 37d), a bit of metal, and two carved stone "incense burners" with feet (99/227; figs. 41e–f, pls. 15c–16a). Locus 8 is a very sherdy patch in locus 9.

The floor at the bottom of locus 3 is the clearest occupation level in the room; it is marked, inter alia, by flat-lying sherds on the bottom. The small square hearth (pl. 10a) in the west corner was in use at this level (and if the room did step down, perhaps earlier). The hearth (locus 13) was filled not with burnt dung[13] like the clay oven in the kitchen area of Dump 1, but with ash, charred wood and twigs, and a few splintery potsherds. Loci 4 and 5 are merely brown patches around the hearth, and locus 16 is a shallow pit with more burning debris. A small date pit-shaped bead (fig. 40q) was retrieved from locus 4. Locus 3, the fill over the floor level,

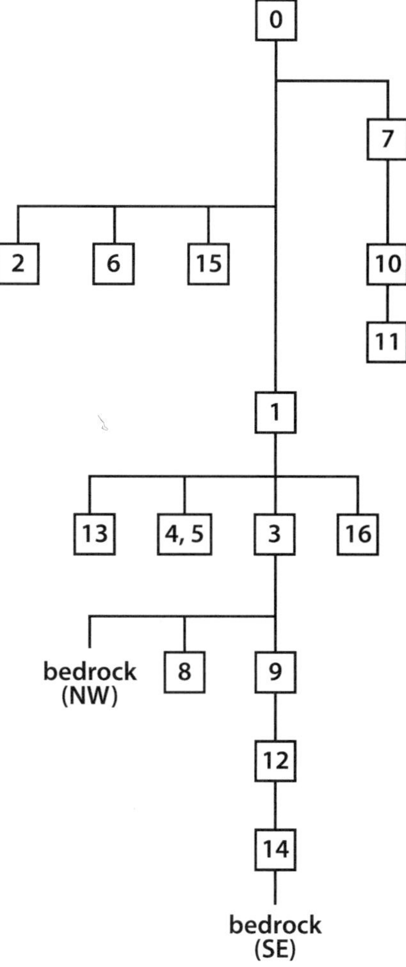

Building 177, Room A matrix

[13] There were, however, some small, round dung pellets west of the hearth, perhaps from goats.

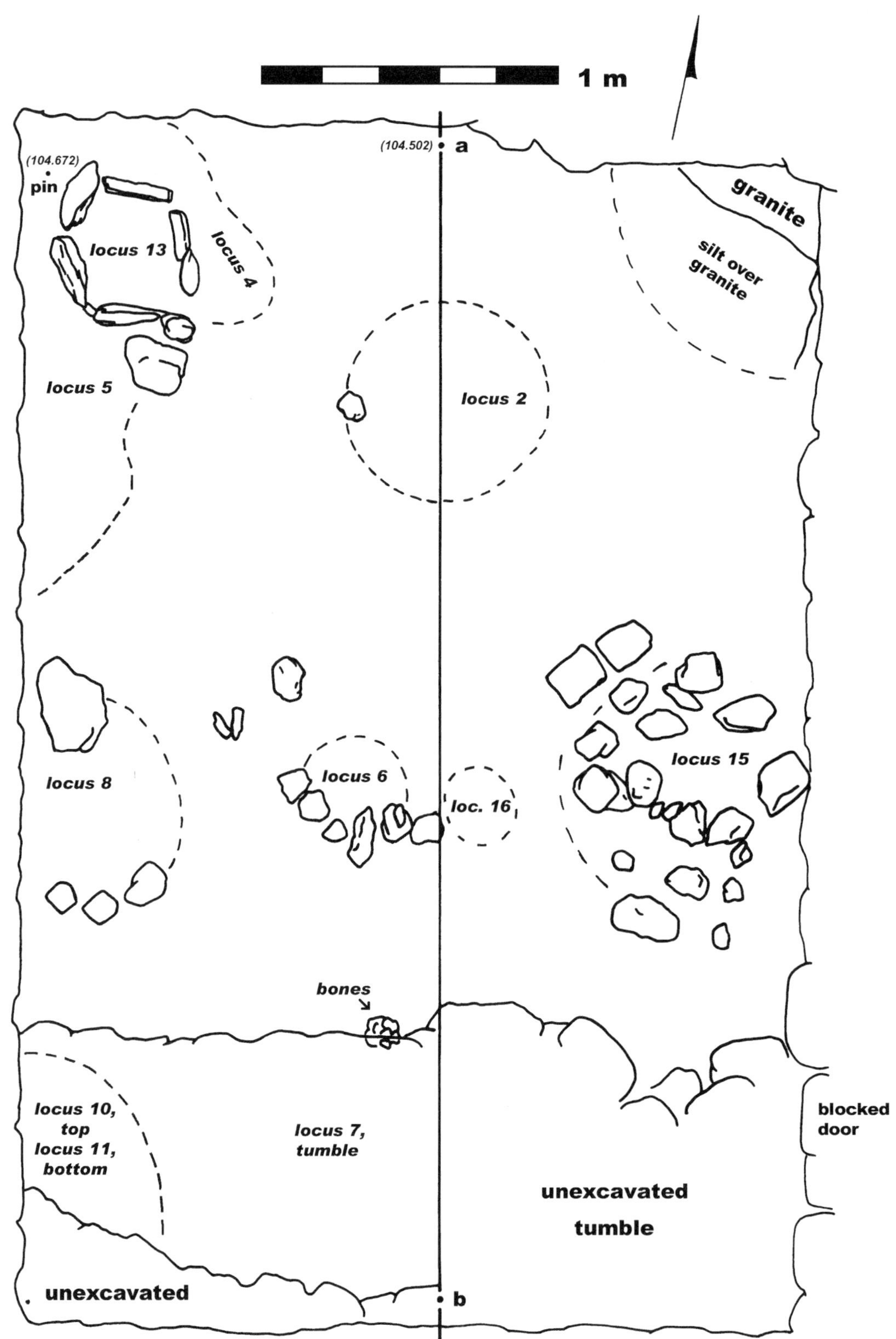

Figure 15. Top plan of Building 177, Room A

covers the whole room, or at least so far as it could be excavated. It is a brownish layer, probably because of the organic matter in it, including dung, fibers, hair, and twine. Especially important finds include the copper/bronze weight (RN 99/239; fig. 40c, pl. 35b), a coin (RN 99/239; fig. 41c), decorated glass, glass beads, a mud(?) plug (RN 99/202), and a "game piece" (RN 99/200; fig. 42s).

Over this, a fine, packed silt (locus 1) was laid down over almost the whole room. It might have been windblown silt somewhat consolidated by one of the rare rains. Into this surface several shallow pits or depressions were sunk (fig. 15, loci 2, 6, 15, and 10/11). Locus 2, clearly visible in section a–b (pl. 30a), was round and neatly defined, but contained nothing but finely laminated silts and a few rocks and white specks. Locus 6 was a smaller, silt-filled depression partly rimmed with stones; it looks more like a potstand than the other installations at this level. Loci 10 and 11 are the top and bottom layers of another shallow depression; the upper locus is ashy, and the lower, mostly fine sand. A burnt nozzle (RN 99/213; pl. 35d) was recovered from locus 10 and one dipinto (RN 99/225; not illustrated) from locus 11. The nozzle was first thought to be the tip of a *tuyere* (though the top of the Hillock is a most unsuitable location for metalworking) but was later relabeled as a lamp fragment. Locus 15 was a fairly large, rough circle of stones with some charcoal at the bottom, and also a coin (RN 99/237; fig. 40d). We do not know whether the now-blocked door to Room D was open at this time. Wall fall at the southeastern corner of Room A obscured the bottom of the door, and fill layers in Room D on the other side were too thin to demonstrate anything one way or the other.

Sometime afterward, the south wall collapsed (locus 7). The dimpled crushing stone in the tumble was probably a used-up crusher employed with other cobbles in the construction of the wall. The topmost infilling of the tumbled stones included modern trash, but also two bricks, one of which (RN 99/204; pl. 16b) had a depression like a door socket, though it is too soft for such a purpose; it is another of the odd "incense burners" discussed in *Chapter 4*. By this time the room — with a collapsed wall — was obviously uncovered. The final layer is a very fine, light, loose layer of windblown silt (locus 0).

Room A, then, seems to have had at least two stages of occupation. One, and perhaps two, stages seem to have been habitation, as marked by the hearth, beads, coins, abundant sherds, and dipinti (and hence presumably wine). Unlike Rooms B and C of Building 93, however, Room A yielded items such as the copper/bronze weight and the fancy "incense burners." The final use of Room A is marked by a surface with a series of shallow depressions, two of which show signs of burning, and the others may have served as potstands. The burnt nozzle remains a puzzle. The door to Room D must have been open while Room A was habitation space, but whether it was open in the last stage is not known. If Room A was an uncovered working space and the door was blocked, then people would have had to climb over the wall, as they do now.

Room B

Room B (fig. 14, pl. 10b), in the middle of Building 177, measured roughly 2.5 × 2.0 m. It had no south wall but opened directly onto Room D. Note the niches in the north walls of Rooms B and C that utilize natural clefts in the granite (pl. 10b). The stratigraphy in the room consisted of shallow layers over granite bedrock. Locus 1 was a thin, fine, surface silt with a little pottery and bone. It overlay locus 2, a more densely packed silt with two ashy patches and a little charcoal, which in turn overlay locus 3, a thin ashy layer over bedrock. Locus 4 was a crevice in the granite filled with an ashy, silty sand and rotten granite. It yielded a grinding stone and a little pottery and bone and may have been fill to level the working floor marked by locus 3.

Room C

Room C (fig. 14, pls. 11a, 30b) (ca. 2.0 × 2.5 m) in the northeast corner of Building 177 had a thin stratigraphic sequence but many small finds. Since it was excavated in two halves, it has more numbered loci, though several of them can be lumped. Loci 1 (east) and 5 (west) are a fine, soft, silty surface sand. Pieces of three dimpled crushing stones (two described as "smallish, flat" and the third as basalt), two beads, a raw emerald/green beryl, some pottery, glass, bone, teeth, and charcoal were recovered. It overlay loci 2 and 6, a brown, silty sand fill with more organic matter such as seeds, wood, charcoal, bone, wool or hair (some colored red and green), and matting as well as bits of pottery, glass, and another raw emerald, a coin corroded to a blank (fig. 40e), and a glass bead. Locus 7 in the western half of the room was another ashy, silty layer with much charcoal, some bone, wood, pottery, a bit of eggshell, glass fragments, a coin (fig. 40f), an emerald, and a glass bead. Loci 3 and 4 in the east half of the room were fill in pockets in the granite bedrock. Locus 3 was a small patch of light-colored fill, and the locus 4 fill yielded some sherds, bone, charcoal, and another bead. Locus 8 in the northwest corner was a pocket of brown fill with burnt bone, and locus 9, along the west wall of Room C, was the silty sand over bedrock.

The bottom of locus 2/5 seems to have been a floor, immediately over bedrock on the north and over fill in granite pockets in the south end of the room. Judging from the small finds, this room might have had more storage functions than Room B, which had only three walls. The five dimpled crushing stones (three from locus 1) from this room could have been worn-out stones used in wall construction, but it is also true that a number of crushing and grinding stones were noted in Room A and many more just outside Building 177.

Room D

In order to permit access to the excavations in Rooms A, B, and C, Room D (fig. 14, pl. 11b) was only excavated along its south wall. The stratigraphy is similar to that in Rooms B and C: a fine surface silt over a compact silty surface, over bedrock or fill in pockets in the bedrock. Loci 1 (east) and 6 (west) are the surface silt. At least one grinding stone, some pottery, glass fragments, bone, charcoal, and four beads were retrieved. Locus 2 was a compact silty layer with ash, burnt bone, and two more glass beads. It overlay granite bedrock on the east and loci 3 and 4 on the west. The former was an ashy, brown, sandy patch with much bone, some sherds and charcoal, and a few seeds, over bedrock. Locus 4 was a depression in the granite bedrock, as were loci 5, 7, and 8 at the western end of the trench. Locus 5 yielded a little pottery, bone, and charcoal, but the other fill pockets were nearly sterile gritty sand and decayed granite.

Building 181

Building 181 (fig. 16, pl. 12) was excavated as a sample of the numerous one-room outbuildings at Bir Umm Fawakhir. “Outbuildings” are simply one-room, detached structures with little or no evidence of domestic use, and they range from neatly built, quadrilateral single rooms to rough stone structures on the hillsides, to crude walls partly enclosing the space under an overhanging boulder. A few seem to be guardposts (e.g., Buildings 75 and 236), but the use of the others is uncertain. Judging from the kitchen areas in Dumps 1 and 2, cooking was done in the open air. Some of the smallest outbuildings discreetely tucked behind boulders (e.g., Buildings 132 and 171) look like latrines, but Building 181 showed no hint of such usage, or for animal shelter. It may have been a temporary storage facility for items that did not need special protection from the elements or thieves.

Building 181 was surveyed during the 1997 season (Meyer 2011, p. 66, figs. 21b, 41a). It is actually a utilized space under some large boulders. Two huge boulders with a gap between them and smaller boulders on top open eastward. The mouth of the space is almost closed by another boulder, so it needed only the construction of a short, rough wall on the north to close off a small space. Two grinding stone fragments were built into the wall, and three concave grinding stones, pieces of both upper and lower rotary grinding stones, and a shallow looters’ hole were noted outside the “door.” A dipinto, surely placed there recently, rested on one of the boulders.

The stratigraphy in Building 181 was straightforward. Locus 1 was a fine, silty sand about 3 to 5 cm thick with some sherds, glass, bone, and a little charcoal. Layer 2, below, consisted of a more compact fill alternating between fine, silty sand and coarser sand, probably wind-laid and about 40 cm thick. Small bits of pottery, bone, some charcoal, shell, three beads, and one “mano” type of grinding stone were recovered. Locus 3 below that was a still more compact sandy, gritty layer with very few sherds, down to bedrock.

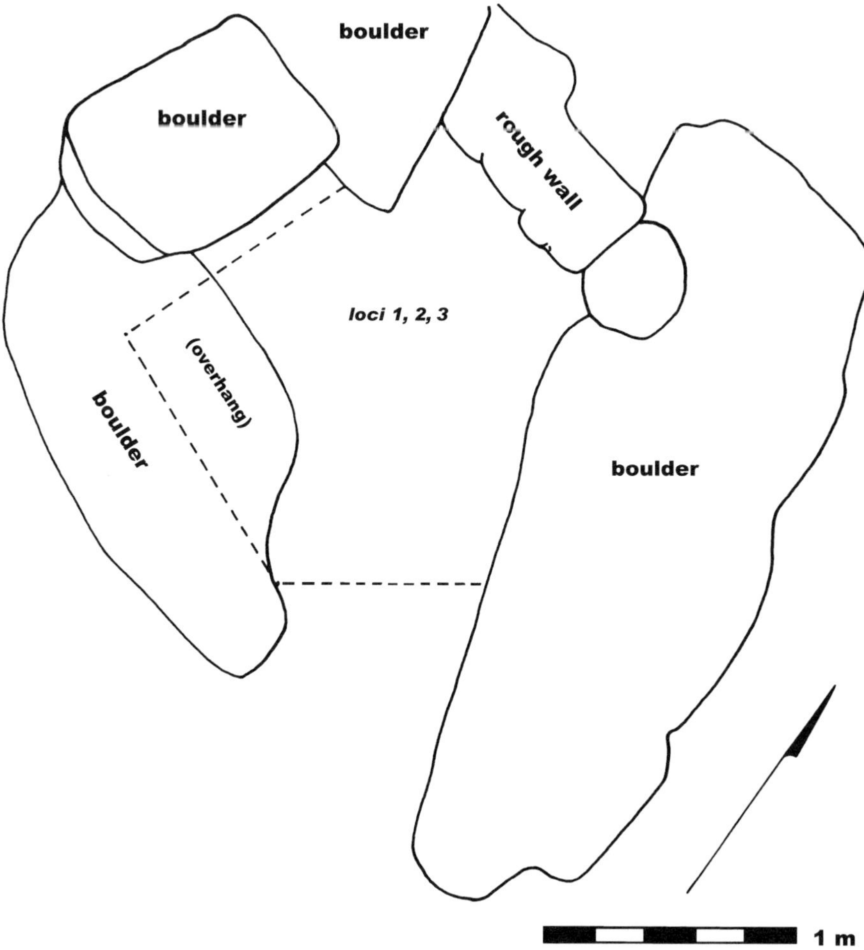

Figure 16. Top plan of Building 181

Conclusions

First and foremost, the evidence for multiple floor layers in some of the rooms indicates at least three occasions of occupation, interspersed by abandonment long enough for windblown sand to cover, say, the intact pots at the bottom of Dump 1 and Building 93, Room C, or rubbish to tumble downslope and cover floors or features. This suggests that ancient Bir Umm Fawakhir, like the granodiorite quarries at Mons Claudianus, was occupied only when the powers that be sent workmen into the desert to mine and reduce the gold ores, and supported them for the duration of the work. When the operations became unnecessary or untenable, the workmen moved on, to return when and if the mines were reopened.

The discovery of kitchen areas under both Dumps 1 and 2 strongly suggests that cooking was an outdoor activity. This makes sense. The desert is hot in the daytime, extremely so in the summers, so cooking indoors would have been even more insufferable. Rain is highly unlikely, and if one of the rare flash floods hit, dinner would have been moot. On the other hand, the desert does grow cold when the sun sets in the winter, so little hearths like the one in Building 177, Room A, or the potstand with evidence of burning around it in Room B of Building 93, would have been welcome now and again. Whether people ate indoors, as suggested by the iron ladle and potstand in Room B of Building 93, or outdoors is unknown, though this may well have varied from season to season as protection from the sun or wind, or warmth or shade was desired.

The use of the many one-room outbuildings at Bir Umm Fawakhir is still unclear, though cooking seems more unlikely than before. Building 181 showed no signs of being a latrine or animal shelter, but that does not exclude such usage for other buildings. We can only reiterate our earlier conclusion that the small, somewhat removed outbuildings with narrow entrances could have been used for latrines, the larger ones with wider doors for animals, and quite a few for storage or perhaps crafts like rope making. It is entirely possible that an outbuilding could be used for different activities in the course of its use-life.

Buildings 93 and 177 also show some signs of shifting usage. Rooms C and D look like the core of Building 93, and Room C at least has three floor levels; Room E was attached at some point, but excavations did not go far enough to indicate at what stage this took place. Rooms A and B look like an expansion of Building 93, a conclusion tentatively supported by the presence of only one or two floor levels. Room F may have been a one-room independent structure originally; A and B look squeezed in between it and Room C. Room A in Building 177 likewise seems to have had two or three occupation levels, of which the first one or two seem to be more domestic and the topmost one dominated by shallow hearths and pot emplacements. The layout of Bir Umm Fawakhir always did look rambling and unplanned, but now we can say with more confidence that it was built up house by house, by room, by addition, by renovation, by "capture" of nearby structures, as needed.

The miners were men. It has never been suggested, much less proven, that women or children hacked quartz ore out of the granite. They may, however, have carried baskets of lumps of ore from the mines to the crushing stations, and women may have milled the crushed ore fine enough for washing. At Bir Umm Fawakhir we have only the most meager suggestions that women were present, mostly in the form of personal ornaments such as beads and the copper/gold bracelet, and even this assumes men did not wear jewelry. There is no direct proof of children. One baby bone or even an incompletely fused epiphysis from one of the cemetery areas would speak volumes, but unfortunately, only the scrappiest shreds of bone were noted and the cemeteries were never systematically investigated. That said, we do think women and families were present. As any sailor can attest, men can cook, wash, and haul water, but in the ancient Egyptian world, these tasks generally fell to women and children, and again as any sailor can attest, "there is nothing like a dame." Women and prostitutes are certainly attested in the ostraca from the earlier, Roman period *praesidia* at Maximianon (Wekalat Zarka) and Krokodilô (Wadi Mweh) on the Hammamat road. There are even a few mentions of female water drawers and spinners (Cuvigny 2003, pp. 374–97). On the other hand, it is somewhere between possible and probable that the male to female ratio was skewed. Cross-culturally speaking, mining towns are usually short of females, and the newer and shorter-lived they are, the fewer the women (Lawrence 1998).

Finally, two houses and one outbuilding represent 1.3 percent of the 237 structures mapped in the main settlement, not counting the hundreds of others in the outliers. So, as is usual in archaeological reports, we have to temper all conclusions with the acknowledgment that excavation of more houses not merely could but certainly would change our present understanding of the site.

Chapter 3

Pottery

Carol Meyer and Lisa A. Heidorn

The quantity of potsherds from Bir Umm Fawakhir is daunting; that, after all, is the name of the site, "Well of the Mother of Pots." We collected all sherds from the excavation areas, but lacked time and personnel to sort, type, describe in detail, and draw any but the most important diagnostic sherds. Surface layers and ones determined to be very mixed, such as the top layers of Dump 2, could only be poured out on the table, scanned, and roughly tabulated. Sherds from more reliable excavated loci were sorted and tabulated by ware and shape, if determinable. Selected sherds were drawn in the field, and most were returned to the site; a few were registered and stored in the Antiquities magazine in Quft.

Since the first season at Bir Umm Fawakhir, in 1992, our understanding and treatment of the pottery have evolved significantly, and important corpora from other sites have been published. Originally we grouped the pottery by findspot (e.g., around the wells) and shape (Heidorn 1995, 2000), but for the 1996 and 1997 survey seasons, we emphasized the wares. We still sorted by site (Wadi el-Sid, main settlement, or outlier) and, if possible, part of the site (e.g., sample from vicinity of Building 177) and then by ware (imported, pink, marl, silt, and less common wares). Within these groups we displayed the pottery starting with most open forms, such as shallow dishes, to most closed, such as jugs. For this report, all sherds are sorted first by ware and then by shape. Almost all come from the two excavation zones, Building 93 and the Hillock.

We grouped most of the 1999 potsherds into several fabric or ware groups:[14]

- "African Red Slip" pertains to fine, imported vessels. We are following Hayes' terms, typology, and dating. He describes African Red Slip (ARS) as shiny but not glossy like terra sigillata. The fabric has a "fairly coarse, rather granular appearance." It ranges from orange-red to brick-red and often has lime impurities, generally small but occasionally larger. Fine quartz is often present, and sometimes black particles. African Red Slip is characteristically slipped (Hayes 1972, pp. 13–14). It was produced in a region of what is now Tunisia in the fourth to seventh centuries and was widely exported (Hayes 1972, p. 472), though both production and export were affected by the Vandal incursions (Hayes 1980, p. 516) in the early fifth century.
- "Eastern Desert Ware" is handmade pottery special to the Eastern Desert of Egypt and northeast Sudan. It is usually dark, unevenly fired, burnished, and decorated with incised designs. Most of the forms are open bowls or cups, but closed forms do occur.
- "Pink ware" is made from the pink kaolinite clays mined at Aswan, usually finely tempered, ranging from pink to orange in breaks. The finer red-slipped or washed vessels can also be termed Egyptian Red Slip A.
- "Marl ware" is a term that covers a wide range of calcareous rich fabrics made from desert clays, normally pale buffs or tans with light cream or white surfaces.
- "Nile silt ware," the largest part of the Bir Umm Fawakhir corpus, is made from Nilt silt clays, tempered with calcareous, quartz, or organic matter. They are often red-brown in color, ranging to orangey at times, and may be slipped, in which case they may be termed Egyptian Red Slip B.

---

[14] Definitions of terms are based in part on the pottery study from Mons Porphyrites (Tomber 2001, pp. 243–44).

- "Uncertain fabric" indicates wares that we could not readily identify. Ware descriptions can be very time consuming, and exotic wares such as that from the Western Desert or mixed clays or misfired pieces can be difficult to categorize.
- "Amphoras" refers to a variety of large storage or shipping vessels; here, we follow the standard labels such as Late Roman Amphora 1.

The intention was to draw a sherd outline on a reconstructed vessel form if the sherd represented less than a fourth of the vessel, but this could not always be done. Thus, if the sherd outline is shown on the drawing, it is a small piece of the vessel, but if there is no sherd outline, then it could be anything from a small fragment to a nearly complete vessel. Most of the complete or nearly complete vessels were registered.

We include a fair number of comparanda because the ceramics remain our most important dating evidence for the site. Comparanda for sherds are generally given in order of geographical proximity: first examples recovered in previous seasons at Bir Umm Fawakhir, then ones from the Eastern Desert, then from closer parts of the Nile valley, and then more from distant sites. Very few Coptic/Byzantine-period kiln sites in Egypt have yet been discovered, but we can at least say that some types are more likely to have come from the south, for example, the Aswan area, or the eastern Mediterranean, such as the Late Roman 1 amphoras. Unhappily, there is as yet very little Coptic/Byzantine-period pottery published from Coptos, which is assumed to have been a major if not the major starting point for caravans serving ancient Bir Umm Fawakhir (but see Herbert and Berlin 2003). Very ruined Christian churches have been reported west of the central Min Temple area (Petrie 1896, p. 25; Weill 1911, pp. 131–33), and S. Herbert (1999, p. 656) suggests that the size of the complex indicates a Coptic metropolis.

Most Coptic/Byzantine-period pottery forms are broadly dated, and so far the results from the upper and lower levels of the Bir Umm Fawakhir excavations do not help us much in defining earlier versus later forms. We only have three relatively deep trenches: Building 93 Room C, Dump 1, and Building 177 Room A. What we can say, however, is that the Bir Umm Fawakhir corpus is an unusually unified one. Whatever the exact time range of the habitation of the village and the exploitation of the mines, there is only a little pre-Coptic/Byzantine pottery and virtually none later than roughly the end of the sixth century A.D. These kinds of pots were used together, whether that means precisely this decade or that.

Pottery Descriptions

Figure 17. Imported, Eastern Desert, and Pink Wares

African Red Slip

1. Large bowl, fire blackened. Interior and exterior 2.5YR 5/8; fabric 2.5YR 5/6. African Red Slip, green and white bits. Dump 2, locus 11. The diameter might be smaller, but we have no means of rechecking the sherd. The ware is described as African Red Slip and not the somewhat softer Egyptian Red Slip A (Hayes 1972, pp. 387–88). Bowl 1 may be compared to Hayes form 91D, dating to about A.D. 600–650 (Hayes 1972, pp. 140–44).[15] A red-slipped bowl with a "short stubby flange" from Carthage, ca. 533–550 in date, may also be comparable (Fulford 1984, p. 75, fig. 22:74-3).
2. Feather-rouletted sherd (RN 99/226). 10R 6/6 to 6/8 surface; 10R 6/6 fabric. African Red Slip, hard fired; small black bits, some large white and red bits. Surface, dump south of Building 177. The rouletting on sherd 2 is probably most like that on Hayes' form 91A, a flanged bowl with interior feather rouletting datable to the mid- to late fifth century (Hayes 1972, pp. 140, 142).
3. Stamped sherd (RN 99/226). Reddish color. African Red Slip. Building 13, surface. Stamped rosettes, like the one on sherd 3, are a fairly common motif, and the larger rosettes are especially common on forms 59A and B, 61A, and 67 (Hayes 1972, pp. 238–39). Form 59 is a plate with stamped decoration datable to the mid-fourth century to 400, and not later than 420 (Hayes 1972, pp. 96–100); some form 59A dishes have been found with coins datable to 330–335 to 341–346 (Hayes 1980, p. 500). Form 61 in general is a broad, shallow bowl or "flat-based dish" with a long history (Hayes 1972, pp. 100–07), but form 61A in specific seems to have ended about 380 or a little after (Hayes 1980, p. 516). Finally, form 67 is a "large bowl" with stamped decora-

[15] Form 91 in general may go back to the end of the fourth century (Hayes 1977, p. 282), though forms 91A and 91D in specific are not mentioned.

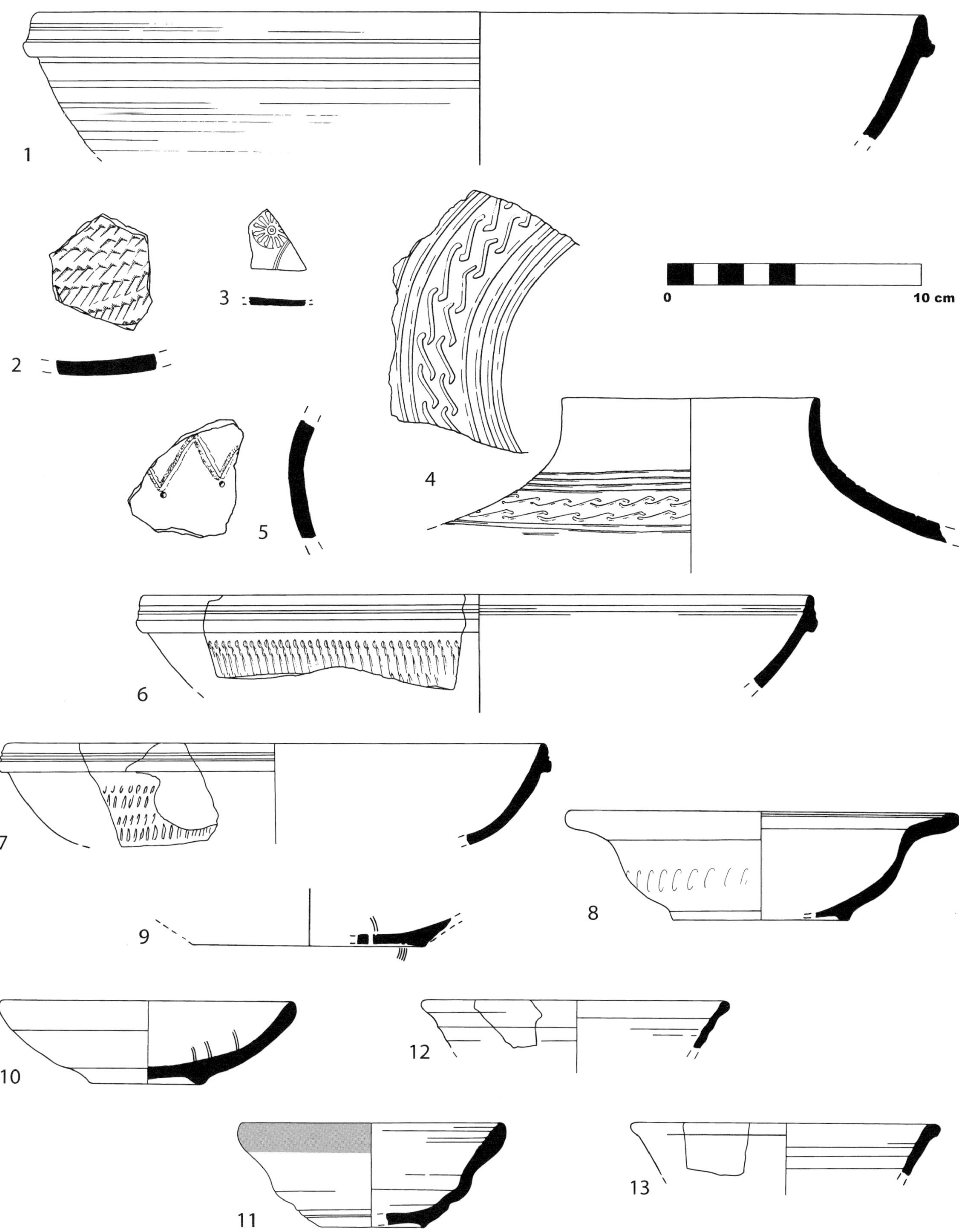

Figure 17. Imported, Eastern Desert, and pink wares

Figure 17. Imported, Eastern Desert, and Pink Wares (cont.)

tion, if not usually rosettes. It is said to be quite common from the late fourth to early fifth century (Hayes 1972, pp. 112–16; Hayes 1977, p. 283), but the Bir Umm Fawakhir sherd is too small to determine whether it came from a plate or a bowl.

Forms 59 and 61 are similar to some silver dishes from Niš (Hayes 1980, p. 520), though no dates are given. Form 67, too, seems to be based on silver prototypes, some of which can be dated as early as ca. 325, though ceramic form 67 seems to be later (Hayes 1980, p. 519).

Handmade

Eastern Desert Ware, handmade pottery like sherds 4 and 5, has been thoroughly studied by Hans Barnard. He says that the peak of production occurred in the fourth–sixth centuries, though examples may occur as early as the third and as late as the eighth century A.D. (Barnard 2008a, p. 132; Barnard 2008b, p. 1). Eastern Desert Ware is widely distributed in the Eastern Desert of Egypt, from Bir Umm Fawakhir and Quseir al-Qadim in the north to Tabot (about the latitude of Suakin in Sudan) in the south. It has also been found at Nile valley sites south of Aswan from Beit al-Wali (immediately north of Kalabsha) to Qasr Ibrim, and even a few pieces as far as the Fifth Cataract (Barnard 2008b, p. 2). Not surprisingly, a large number were recovered from Berenice and nearby sites (Barnard and Rose 2007). This kind of pottery seems to have been made in the desert by desert dwellers (Barnard 2008b, pp. 40, 63), and all tested sherds indicate the use of Eastern Desert Ware vessels for food rather than, say, water (Barnard 2008b, p. 82). The remote site of Biʾr Minayh, roughly 45 kilometers south of Bir Umm Fawakhir as the crow flies, appears to have a far higher proportion of Eastern Desert Ware than Bir Umm Fawakhir, some 30 out of 107 published sherds (Lassányi 2010b, pp. 285–88). The function of Biʾr Minayh remains enigmatic, though the water well was clearly an important resource for travelers and nomads for millennia. The site can, however, be reached only by a detour from the Coptos-to-Berenice road. The drystone huts are quite similar to the smaller of the Bir Umm Fawakhir houses, and there are mineralized quartz veins in the surrounding granites, but no evidence for serious, prolonged mining (Vasáros 2010, pp. 205–06). Several dozen Eastern Desert Ware vessels, mostly cups, deep bowls, or beakers, are published from the cemeteries at Kalabsha South and Wadi Qitna (immediately south of Kalabsha; Strouhal 1984, pp. 157–77; Barnard 2008b, pp. 158–63, 179–82, nos. 161–224). Other examples, some decorated deep bowls, come from "round graves" or tumuli in the Wadi Allaqi, which stretches from the east bank of the Nile in the far south of Egypt into north Sudan, but no precise location or ware was noted (Castiglioni, Castiglioni, and Vercoutter 1995, p. 159). A few pieces of Eastern Desert Ware were picked up on the surface of Bir Umm Fawakhir in previous seasons, but we now have two fragments from excavated contexts.

4. Jar. Large black (firing?) spot on red brown. Surface 2.5YR 5/6; core and firing spot 7.5YR 4/1. Handmade; worn down but perhaps once burnished. Much sand and small white (limestone?) bits. Dump 2, locus 2. Although this jar finds few parallels, its fabric and method of decoration are clearly in the Eastern Desert Ware tradition. The "running dog" motif between the parallel lines is common on other Eastern Desert Ware forms (e.g., Barnard 2008a, p. 144, fig. 5:232, 239, 244). The lower part of a handmade bowl with similar repetitive decoration and a small jar with incised decoration were published with the Bir Umm Fawakhir 1992 pottery (Heidorn 1995, pp. 84–85, figs. 29:j, 30:f). The "lazy S" or running dog motif is well represented in the Biʾr Minayh corpus, which includes at least one necked jar (Lassányi 2010b, pp. 285–86, jar is no. 82).
5. Body sherd, burnished surface, gouged decoration of zigzags. Black interior 10R 5/4 to 4/2; fabric 10R 4/1. Handmade; abundant medium-size and large white bits and chunks. Dump 2, locus 2. From the 1992 season, see a handmade jar with incised zigzag decoration (Heidorn 1995, p. 85, fig. 30:f).

Pink

All or most of the pink wares at Bir Umm Fawakhir are assumed to originate from the Aswan region, where the kaolinite desert clays are found. The kaolinite clay is mixed with varying amounts of silt. The fabric is sometimes called Egyptian Red Slip A, but since not all the Bir Umm Fawakhir pink fabric sherds are slipped, we simply describe them as "pink."

6. Large polished bowl with chattered decoration. 10R 5/8. Pink, fine fabric, abundant red and white (quartz) bits. Dump 2, locus 11 (tabun exterior). Bowl 6 is very like Hayes forms 83 and 84, which are generally assumed to be among the earliest imitations of African Red Slip in Egyptian Red Slip wares, dating from the fifth to the beginning of the sixth century A.D. (Hayes 1972, p. 388). There is a similar but shallower bowl from the 1993 season (Heidorn 2000, p. 84, fig. 55:26). See also a bowl from Shenshef, pink with matte orange-brown slip, different rouletting, fifth century and probably into sixth; similar to African

Red Slip form 82 (Tomber 1998, p. 171, fig. 6-4:32). At the Seti Gurna temple, see another shallow dish, similar decoration, Egyptian Red Slip Ware A, dated to the fifth to early seventh century on parallels (Myśliwiec 1987, pp. 104–05, nos. 1044–46).

7. Bowl with grooved rim and chattering. Exterior 2.5YR 6/8, interior and core 10YR 5/8. Pink ware; white and red bits, sand. Dump 2, locus 3. For a bowl with grooved rim but simpler decoration from earlier season, pink fabric, red slip inside and out (10R 5/8), see Meyer and Heidorn 2011, p. 120, fig. 32:108. See also reference to a shallow dish from Seti Gurna, cited above, and no. 1042 (Myśliwiec 1987, pp. 101, 104). A bowl from the Monastery of Epiphanius, late sixth to early seventh century, has a similar form but no chattering (Winlock and Crum 1926, pp. 86–87, fig. 37:L). Similar shallow bowls or cups from Elephantine are sometimes chattered, often have stamped decorations, and are dated to the last quarter of the fifth century to the third quarter of the sixth or a little later (Gempeler 1992, p. 73, fig. 18:314).
8. Small bowl with grooved rim and very shallow ovals or chattering. Interior and exterior 5YR 5/6, core 5YR 6/4. Pink fabric; white, red, and black bits, sand. Dump 2, locus 1 (surface). There are several examples from earlier seasons: a shallow bowl (Heidorn 2000, p. 84, fig. 55:6); a shallower bowl with broader rim and no chattering, pink fabric (Meyer and Heidorn 2011, p. 130, fig. 37:162); and a shallower bowl with flatter rim, pink fabric (2.5YR 6/6), no chattering, slip inside and out (2.5YR 5/8) (Meyer and Heidorn 2011, p. 146, fig. 45:242). At Elephantine, see perhaps type T215a, much shallower, no rouletting, from beginning to middle of fifth century A.D. (Gempeler 1992, p. 68).
9. Grooved plate base with mend hole. Body 5YR 7/4, faint remnants 2.5YR 5/8 slip. Pink ware; fine red, black, and white bits, few medium red, white, black bits. Dump 2, surface.
10. Small cup. Interior 5YR 6/8, exterior 5YR 5/6 with 2.5YR 5/6 rim. Pink fabric; black, red, white bits, mica, sand. Dump 1, locus 2. A possible parallel from Elephantine is type T328, a "small deep cup," fabric IA with red slip, dated to second quarter of fifth century to end of fifth or early sixth century (Gempeler 1992, p. 97, fig. 40:18).
11. Cup with red-slipped rim. Core 7.5YR 7/4, interior 7.5YR 6/6, exterior 7.5YR 7/6, exterior rim 2.5YR 5/6. Pale fabric, Aswan fine ware; numerous red, black, white bits, sand, fine chaff. Surface find. For similar cups from previous seasons, see Heidorn 2000, p. 86, fig. 56:43; and Meyer and Heidorn 2011, p. 130, fig. 37:164. A pink bowl, slipped, with a brighter red slip at the rim, is reported from Biʾr Minayh (Lassányi 2010b, pp. 275, 277, no. 31). At the Seti Gurna temple, see perhaps vessel no. 1142 (Myśliwiec 1987, pp. 107–08). From Elephantine, see a small, deep cup, form 326, some examples with red rim, fabric IA, late fifth perhaps as late as early seventh century (Gempeler 1992, p. 97, fig. 40:12), and also some small red-rimmed bowls of slightly different form, second half of fifth century (Kaiser et al. 1975, p. 74, fig. 11b–d). There is a somewhat larger cup from Ashmunein made of pink clay with a dull orange slip and a dark brown exterior rim, datable about mid-fifth to early eighth century (Spencer and Bailey 1986, pp. 32, 97 no. H52). Small cups or bowls of Aswani fabric, many with brown or reddish rims are said to be relatively abundant; the cup illustrated (H.1.6) is datable to the latter half of the sixth century (Spencer, Bailey, and Burnett 1983, pp. 26, 38, 118). J. Faiers (2005, p. 67) describes some Egyptian Red Slip A cups with cream or yellow slip, possibly from the Luxor area, but most often considered Aswani.
12. Small cup or bowl. Fabric 7.5YR 6/6, white-slipped surface ca. 2.5YR 8/2 but hard to see. Aswan fine ware; small to medium-size black and white bits. Dump 2, locus 11 (tabun exterior). From Shenshef there are some shallow bowls with similar profiles, white slipped, Aswani fabric but granular and somewhat coarse, datable to the fifth and early sixth century (Tomber 1998, pp. 172–73, fig. 6-4:41–43).
13. Small cup or bowl. White slipped surfaces 2.5YR 8/2, fabric 2.5YR 6/3. Aswan fine ware; medium amount of small red, black, white bits. Dump 2, locus 2. Among the Seti Gurna temple corpus there are some deep cups with simple walls, generally datable to the fifth to early seventh century (Myśliwiec 1987, pp. 116–17, nos. 1318–19).

Figure 18. Stamped Plates and Dishes

Figure 18 shows a range of dishes with stamped decoration. Judging from the ones whose shape can be at least partly determined, they are shallow bowls or plates with low ring or pedestal bases. All the sherds are surface finds except for number 15, excavated from Building 177, and it is too shattered to see any foot or base. Almost all the stamped dishes are relatively fine, polished, and orange or red slipped; they are among the best-made pottery on site. The stamps include both Christian symbols such as crosses or palm branches, and perhaps the bird on number 16, but others are simpler flowers, rosettes, circles, or sunbursts. There is an extensive corpus of stamped plates, bowls, and dishes from Elephantine, and even the stamps themselves for producing the decoration (Gempeler 1992, figs. 2, 9, 11–18, 20–22, 39, 43, 45, 50–53, pls. 2–24).

14. Stamped plate, rosette design (RN 99/233; pl. 31a). Fabric 5YR 7/6, 2.5YR 6/8 surface. Pink; fine black and white bits, a few medium black bits. Dump behind Building 181, surface; sherds do not join. Some Elephantine type 204 plates are similar; they date from the third quarter of the third to around the middle of the fifth century A.D., perhaps later still. The shape is an imitation of Hayes North African 31 (Gempeler 1992, p. 65, fig. 9:4–5). See also the somewhat earlier, unstamped type T203a, imitation of Hayes 50, datable to the last quarter of the third to the second half of the fourth century (Gempeler 1992, p. 65, fig. 8:11).
15. Stamped plate, splintered; concentric circles in center with radiating palm leaves (RN 99/236). Color not noted. Building 177, Room A, locus 12. There were some sherds with a palm-leaf stamp from previous season: a flat sherd (Heidorn 2000, p. 88, fig. 57:57); a stamped plate or dish with a low ring base, pink fabric; and a flat sherd with palm fronds and circle-and-dot stamps (Meyer and Heidorn 2011, pp. 126, 128, figs. 35:136, 36:160). The shape of the plate is closest to Hayes types 75 and 76, both datable to the middle of the fifth century (Hayes 1972, pp. 122, 124–25). There is a good parallel from Antinoopolis (Antinoë) both for shape and stamped decoration (Guerrini 1974, p. 78, fig. 17:1, pl. 33:4). See also a stamp decoration from Ashmunein, Egyptian Red Slip A, second half of fifth to sixth century (Bailey 1996, p. 57, fig. 5:18, pl. 4). The design is very similar to Elephantine stamp type 12, a palm branch with triple midrib (Gempeler 1992, p. 34, pl. 6:4), and palm leaves and circles may be seen on two shallow dishes of a common type, pink ware, second half of fifth to perhaps middle of sixth century (Gempeler 1992, p. 67, fig. 11:3–4).
16. Stamped sherd, "duck" in center (st-3), leaves and sunbursts stamped around it (RN 99/226). Color not noted. Surface find. A shallow dish and a flat sherd from the Seti Gurna temple have similar leaf or leaf-and-sunburst stamps but do not preserve any central stamp. Both are Egyptian Red Slip Ware A and are datable to the "Late Roman" period (Myśliwiec 1987, pp. 99–102, nos. 1000–01). There are many bird stamps at Kellia. Most are used in a circle around the bottom of a plate or dish, but at least one is stamped in the center (Egloff 1977, pls. 13, 37:5). Kellia was founded ca. A.D. 338, but the excavated remains are mostly sixth–seventh century (Cannuyer 2001, pp. 34–35). For a painted bird in the center of a dish with a high ring base from Elephantine, see Gempeler 1992 (p. 104, fig. 46:8).
17. Stamped dish (or plate), design of circle and dots ("faint flowers") (RN 99/226). Pink with red slip. Dump 1, surface. There is an almost identical stamp decoration on a footed plate or bowl sherd from the 1993 season (Heidorn 2000, p. 90, fig. 58:118). The rosette design is the Elephantine stamp type 28a (Gempeler 1992, p. 69, fig. 12:14). See also types T226a and T227, imitating Hayes form 104; T226a dates to mid-fifth to the first quarter(?) of the sixth century A.D. (Gempeler 1992, pp. 72–73, figs. 16:16, 17:1).
18. Stamped sherd with XP cross, red slip (RN 99/226). Silt, very coarse. Dump 1, locus 1. A shallow dish from the Seti Gurna temple, Egyptian Red Slip Ware "C" with a similar cross stamp facing the other way suggests a late fifth or early sixth century date (Myśliwiec 1987, pp. 101–02, no. 1003). A quite similar cross was stamped on a "Samian" dish from the Monastery of Epiphanius, late sixth to early seventh century (Winlock and Crum 1926, pl. 32:B, center bottom). The stamp design is similar to Elephantine stamp type 58; see also similar stamps on dishes of type T219, shallow bowls or cups, pink fabric, second quarter of the fifth to last quarter of the sixth century (Gempeler 1992, pp. 69–70, fig. 13:7–8).
19. Stamped sherd, elaborate cross design (RN 99/226). Red slip, peeling. Dump behind B13. There is a shallow dish or plate with a very similar cross, pink ware, from the 1996–1997 corpus (Meyer and Heidorn 2011, p. 128, fig. 36:158). A similar "jewelled cross" is stamped on the base of a dish from Amarna, dated to the first half of the sixth century (Faiers 2005, p. 80, fig. 2.8:77). At Elephantine another very similar cross stamp may be seen on a flat pink ware dish of a type datable to the second quarter of the fifth to the early seventh century (Gempeler 1992, p. 69, fig. 12:11). The design itself is the Elephantine stamp type 58 (Gempeler 1992, p. 37, pl. 19:3), though sherd 19 is not well enough preserved to show the loop of the Christogram.
20. Stamped sherd, arm of cross (RN 99/226). Orangish body 2.5YR 7/4, darker red-orange slip 2.5YR 6/6. Abundant red and black bits, some medium-size red bits. Dump 2, surface.
21. Stamped sherd, concentric circles (RN 99/226). Tough orange fabric 2.5YR 6/8, slip 10R 6/8. Abundant small black bits, some medium black bits. South of Building 177, surface. Circle stamp decorations may be seen on flat- or virtually flat-based plates from the Seti Gurna temple, Egyptian Red Slip Ware A, called "Late Roman" in date (Myśliwiec 1987, pp. 99–100, nos. 989–90).
22. Stamped plate, rosette design (RN 99/226). Surface 2.5YR 5/8. Fabric not visible. South of Building 177, surface. A good parallel for the stamp design may be seen on a plate from the Seti Gurna temple, "Late Roman" in date (Myśliwiec 1987, pp. 99–100, no. 991). The design is Elephantine stamp type 27, a dotted rosette (Gempeler 1992, p. 35, pls. 6:2, 6; 11:6; 12:2, 4; 14:1–2).

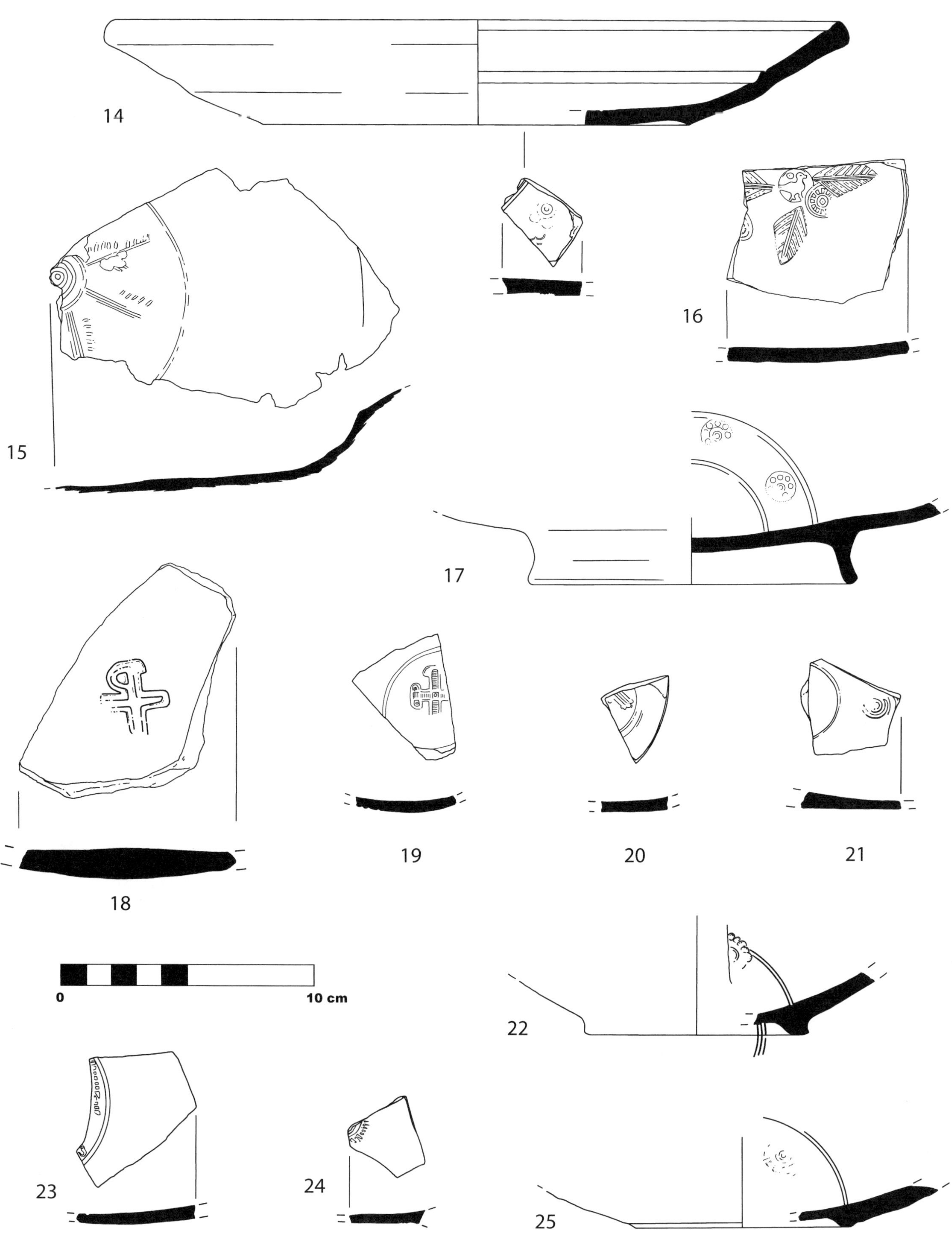

Figure 18. Stamped plates and dishes

Figure 18. Stamped Plates and Dishes (cont.)

23. Stamped plate, remnant of palm-leaf design and perhaps bit of the arm of a cross (RN 99/226). Fabric 2.5YR 5/4, slip 10R 5/6. Abundant small black and white bits, some large white bits. Building 177, surface.
24. Stamped sherd, part of a sunburst (RN 99/226). Fabric 10R 5/6, bright orange slip 10R 6/8. Abundant small red, white, black bits, some medium white bits. Building 177, surface. There is a sherd with similar stamped decoration from the 1993 season (Heidorn 2000, p. 86, fig. 56:28).
25. Stamped sherd, faint rosette or sunburst (RN 99/226). Fabric 10R 6/6, remnant orange slip 10R 6/8. Very fine red and black bits. Building 177, surface. For parallels for stamp, see no. 22, above.

Figure 19. Pink and Aswani Fine Wares

26. Bowl with flanged rim. Fabric 2.5YR 6/6, red slip 2.5YR 6/6 to 6/8. Pink ware; very fine temper, little sand. Building 93, Room C, locus 16. From the 1996–1997 corpus there is a bowl of similar shape but in silt ware (Meyer and Heidorn 2011, p. 116, fig. 30:85). See also a sixth- to seventh-century parallel at the Esna hermitages (Jacquet-Gordon 1972, pl. 222:34). At the Seti Gurna temple there are some small deep cups with fat rims, Egyptian Red Slip Ware C, generally datable to the fifth to early seventh century (Myśliwiec 1987, pp. 109–11, nos. 1200, 1212). An Egyptian Red Slip B bowl from Amarna with a more emphatic flange but similar carination is datable to ca. mid-fifth to mid-sixth century (Faiers 2005, p. 81, fig. 2.9:83). For a parallel from Elephantine, see type T318a, "deep cup," fabric IA with red slip, common, dated to last quarter of the fourth to second quarter of the sixth century (Gempeler 1992, p. 94, fig. 36:5–6).
27. Bowl. Fabric 5YR 7/4, slip 2.5Y 8/2. Pink ware; fine red and black bits, few large white bits. Dump 2, locus 5. At Elephantine similar bowls of type T203b, fabric IA with red slip, are said to be common and datable to the second half of the fourth century to the fifth or sixth century (Gempeler 1992, p. 65, fig. 8:9).
28. Bowl. Fabric 5YR 7/4, yellow-cream slip 10YR 8/3. Pink ware; fine black specks, few large white bits (sand), few large red-brown bits. Building 177, Room A, locus 7.
29. Deep bowl with tough white post-break concretion. Fabric 7.5YR 7/3 to 6/2 (grayish), surface 2.5YR 6/6 where not covered by concretion. Pink ware; many fine black bits, a few larger. Dump 2, locus 4 middle strip. There is a deep conical cup with simple walls and rim from the Seti Gurna temple corpus, generally datable to the fifth to early seventh century (Myśliwiec 1987, pp. 116–17, no. 1319). For a parallel from Elephantine, see a simple cup, type T316b, fabric IA, not very common, dated to middle of fourth to sixth century (Gempeler 1992, p. 93, fig. 35:13).
30. Low ring base. Core 5YR 7/6, interior and exterior surfaces 5YR 7/8. Pink ware; red, white, and black bits, sand. Dump 2, surface. Note a ring base of a hard, pink fabric in the 1996–1997 corpus (Meyer and Heidorn 2011, p. 120, fig. 32:114).
31. Grooved ledge rim of small bowl; diameter might be much greater. Fabric 2.5YR 7/6, worn slip 10R 5/8. Pink ware; abundant black bits, few medium-size white and red bits. Building 181, surface. The shape may be an imitation of Hayes form 67,[16] an earlier form of African Red Slip imitated in Egyptian Red Slip. For an example from the 1993 season at Bir Umm Fawkhir, see a bowl with this type of rim but of greater diameter and more of the side preserved, with a smoothed, slipped exterior, and a "dense fabric, no visible temper" (Heidorn 2000, p. 90, fig. 58:102). A wider, shallow bowl of Egyptian Red Slip Ware A from the Seti Gurna temple has a similar grooved rim and is generally datable to the fifth to early seventh century (Myśliwiec 1987, pp. 101, 103, no. 1032). An Egyptian Red Slip A platter from the Amarna area has a similar rim shape, greater diameter (48 cm), traces of rouletting under the rim, and dates to perhaps the late sixth to second half of the seventh century (Faiers 2005, p. 183, fig. 3.2:8). See perhaps a "sigillata" vessel from Kellia, sixth–seventh century (Egloff 1977, pl. 43:12). From Elephantine there is a shallow dish, almost the shape of a squashed patella cup, type T211a, said to be a common form, fabric IA with red slip, datable to second half of the fourth to second half of the fifth century (Gempeler 1992, p. 67, fig. 10:10).
32. Cup with painted lines at interior rim. Fabric 2.5YR 7/8, white slip 2.5Y 8/2, paint now faded to red-brown. Pink ware. Building 93, Room C, locus 5. This is one of the most common "type fossils" among Coptic/Byzantine-period pottery. For examples from previous seasons, see Heidorn 2000, p. 84, fig. 55:11; and Meyer and Heidorn 2011, p. 130, fig. 37:166. Hayes (1995, pp. 34–35) states that at Berenice an "Aswan type" of small, simple, shallow bowl with inset base and brown to black lines inside the rim tends to confirm the fifth-century dating. A nice parallel was retrieved from Shenshef as well: a shallow cup, red-brown with yellow-cream slip inside and out, two horizontal brown lines painted inside just below the rim (Tomber 1998, p. 172, fig. 6-4:46). A smaller, simple cup, pink fabric, white slip inside and out, painted ochre line, was recovered from a grave (tumulus no. 3) at Biʾr Minayh (Lassányi 2010b, p. 278, no. 34). Two bowls are illustrated from Mons Porphyrites Lycabettus Ramp, both Aswani fabric, white slip, black bands painted inside, Late Roman in date (Tomber 2001, p. 282, fig. 6.19:9–10), and another from the animal lines at Badia (Tomber 2001, p. 300, fig. 6.34:15). From the Seti Gurna temple corpus, see cup no. 1301, Egyptian Red Slip Ware A with painting, datable to the fifth to eighth century (Myśliwiec 1987, pp. 114–15). Good examples may be seen at Ashmunein, Aswan fine ware with thick white slip, one or two dark brown bands painted inside, before A.D. 500 (Bailey 1966, p. 58, pl. 4 fig. 5:35–36). Similar painted cups were found at Esna, red or white slip, sixth century or later (Jacquet-Gordon 1972, pl. 219:3). As might be expected, similar painted cups are well attested at Elephantine: types

[16] For the dating of Hayes form 67, see sherd 3, above.

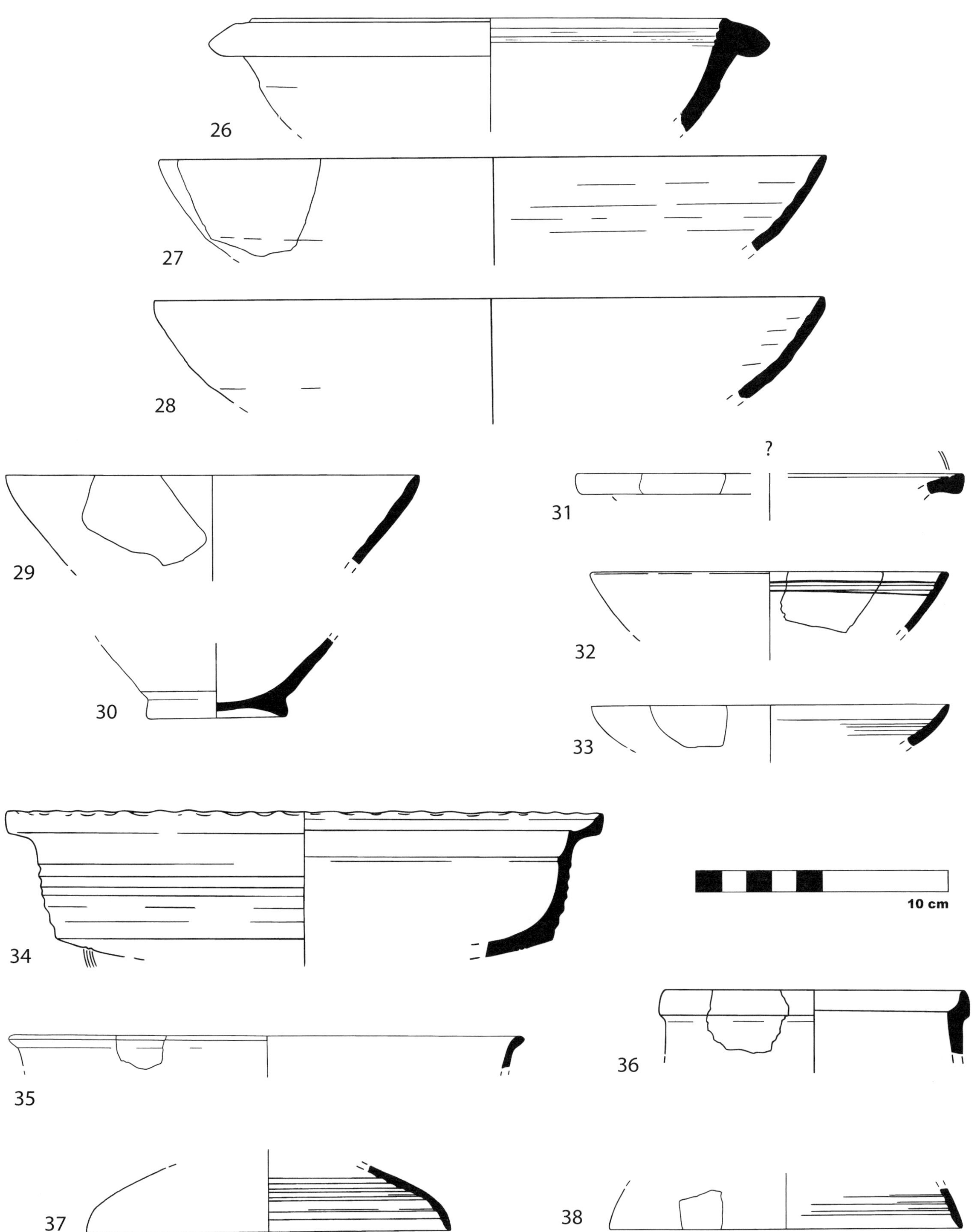

Figure 19. Pink and Aswani fine wares

Figure 19. Pink and Aswani Fine Wares (cont.)

T316a and T316b, fabric IA, white slip and paint, ca. middle of fourth to sixth century, and a shallower form T232, same fabric, late fifth to seventh century (Gempeler 1992, pp. 74–75, 93, figs. 20:1, 35:12 and 14). Note a small cup from Antinoopolis, 11.3 cm in diameter, pink clay, white slip, black paint on rim, fifth–seventh century (Guidotti 2008, pp. 327, 380, no. 193). From the Kalabsha area south of Aswan, see some cups of white-yellow clay with dark brown bands painted inside (Ricke 1967, pp. 52, 62, fig. 69:T/24.3, fig. 72:B7/10 and B7/8), and eight more from the Wadi Qitna cemetery (immediately south of Kalabsha), generally dated to the second half of the third through the fifth century (Strouhal 1984, pp. 146–47, nos. P676, P677, table 29). There are even a few from Sayala (dated to late third century), made of a pale fabric with brown interior painted lines, though this kind of shallow cup is less common than deeper beakers and cups (Kromer 1967, p. 103, fig. 33:10).

33. Shallow cup (or lid?), finely ridged but blackened interior, rough surface. Surface 2.5Y 7/3; fabric 7.5YR 6/4. Aswan fine ware or perhaps marl fired to white surface; fine black and white sand with some medium-size bits. Building 177, Room A, locus 9. See a nested group of six complete and two chipped bowls from Berenice, Aswan white-slipped, wheelmarks, no decoration, datable to the fifth century (Tomber 1999, p. 144), and also a shallow cup from Shenshef, fifth and probably into sixth century (Tomber 1998, p. 172, fig. 6-4:44). There is a similar cup form at Elephantine, type T223, fabric IA with red slip (not creamy), not common, dating uncertain perhaps fifth century, but compare to Hayes form 53B (Gempeler 1992, p. 71, fig. 15:8–10). If number 33 is a lid rather than a cup, see an example from Amarna, no. 402, M4 fabric (hard, brittle, very fine silt), fifth–eighth century (Faiers 2005, p. 157, fig. 2.53:402). For a silt example, see no. 1394 from Gurna (Myśliwiec 1987, pp. 118–19).

34. Casserole with piecrust rim, sooted exterior, blackened rim. Fabric 2.5YR 6/8. Temper not noted. Dump 1, locus 12 northwest. From Elephantine, type K222a, a common form of casserole, usually fabric IIIA but sometimes IIB, second half of fifth century (Gempeler 1992, p. 152, fig. 86:5–7) is comparable. From farther south, there is a "brown clay" example from Bab Kalabsha "Berg Kapelle," X-Group (Late Roman–Byzantine period) (Ricke 1967, p. 46, fig. 66:BK/35b).

35. Large bowl (? diameter uncertain). Fabric 5YR 7/4, surfaces 10YR 7/4. Abundant black bits; red bits and chunks; some white bits. Building 181, locus 2.

36. Jar rim, smoothed but interior somewhat rough. Orange 2.5YR 6/8 with gray core. Pink ware; very fine sand(?), a few white (limestone?) bits. Dump 2, locus 5 middle strip.

Numbers 33, 37, 38, 59, and 60 are problematic. They could be shallow bowls or lids; the range of colors and fabrics does not help identification except in the case of 59 and 60. Number 33 is tentatively called a bowl on the basis of the half dozen stacked bowls from Berenice. Number 33 is blackened inside, but that is not conclusive as it could have happened after it was discarded. Most but not all identifiable lids from other sites have knobs on top, which neither 37 nor 38 preserve; they are tentatively called lids because they are unusually rough and ridged inside. Numbers 59 and 60 are called lids because in addition to being rough and ridged inside and quite thin, they are porous, which would make them poor choices for a bowl or cup. Sherd 60 is such a small fragment that the diameter of the lid could be less and the angle steeper. As reconstructed, however, it is too thin and shallow to be used for much other than a lid. Lids would certainly have been quite useful at ancient Bir Umm Fawakhir not only for cooking but for reducing evaporation of fluids in a hyperarid desert and for fending off flies and other pests. It is also conceivable that other kinds of cups or bowls were used as lids occasionally. In the case of numbers 37, 38, 59, and 60 we are quite aware that our tentative identifications as lids rather than bowls could be overturned.

37. Lid. Surfaces 10YR 8/2, fabric 7.5YR 7/2. Aswan fine ware; some medium-size and fine red bits. Dump 2, locus 2.

38. Lid. Cream or very pale pink 2.5YR 8/2. Aswan fine ware(?); fine temper, some red bits, medium black bits. Building 93, Room E, locus 3 (screen). For a marl lid from Tôd with a similar simple rim, see Pierrat 1996, p. 191, pl. 2:13.

Figure 20. Pink and Marl

Pink

39. Bottle neck with combed decoration, diameter uncertain; perhaps the upper part of a bulbous-necked jar or flagon. Surfaces 2.5Y 8/2, fabric 7.5YR 7/4. Building 177, Room A, locus 7 surface. Aswani fabric; small white and black bits, a few medium-size white bits. At Amarna, shape no. 192 is similar but is less angular below the rim collar. It is called a cup or bowl, has a cream slip running over the rim, and is made of fabric M1 (hard silt with straw, large white bits, other tempering) and is datable to the middle of the sixth century (Faiers 2005, p. 108, fig. 2.24:192). See also a bulbous-necked flagon with ridges rather than combing, perhaps a mix of Nile silt and marl, probably fifth century (Faiers 2005, p. 142, fig. 2.46:310). A somewhat similar rim may be noted from the South Church context 9108b at Ashmunein, made of local silt, datable by African Red Slip types to ca. 420 to 450/460 (Bailey 1996, pp. 75, 85, fig. 42:17). Another parallel is not so well dated (Bailey 1996, fig. 57:2).

40. Funnel? Surfaces 10YR 8/3 cream; fabric 2.5YR 6/6. Pink; fine white bits, a little fine to medium-size red bits, a few medium-size white bits (sandy). Building 93, Room A, locus 3. For shape, see perhaps a "carinated bowl," also lacking a bottom, from the

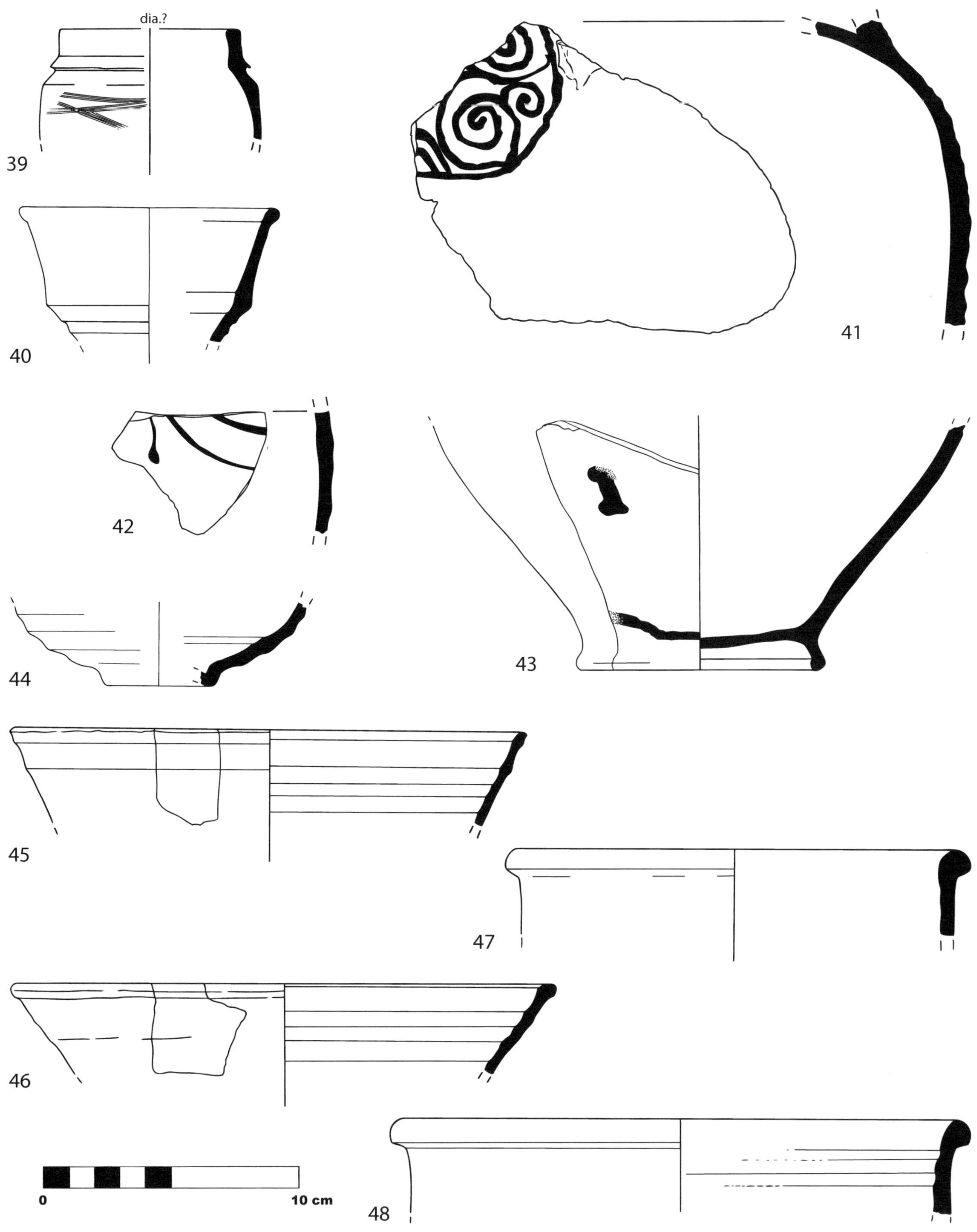

Figure 20. Pink and marl

Figure 20. Pink and Marl (cont.)

1992 season (Heidorn 1995, p. 88, fig. 30:l). A large funnel (dia. 14 cm) is published from the Monastery of Epiphanius, red fabric, white slip (Winlock and Crum 1926, p. 93, fig. 49:E). Another funnel is reported from Esna, fabric II (red-orange, black in break; large particles of all sorts, lots of chaff), sixth century or later (Jacquet-Gordon 1972, pl. 229:6). Two possible funnels from Amarna have a very different shape; one (no. 382) was a *qadus* base with a hole bored through it after firing (Faiers 2005, p. 153, fig. 2.52:382–83). Although funnels are attested in pottery corpora of this period, number 40 lacks a tip or base, so it is hard to determine whether it is a funnel or a cup. For a carinated cup shape, see perhaps a "Roman white marl" deep cup from Coptos, topmost level (Herbert and Berlin 2003, p. 126, fig. 100:R3+.14). Note also a deep cup from Elephantine, type T303b, fabric IA with red (not cream) slip, third quarter of the second to perhaps early third century, harking back to a terra sigillata prototype in Gaul (Gempeler 1992, p. 90, fig. 33:12–14).

41. Large decorated jar. Black paint; slip 10YR 7/2, pinkish interior and fabric 5YR 7/4. Pink; sand, black bits, red chunks. Building 93, Room C. Spiral decoration is not rare at Bir Umm Fawakhir (cf. Meyer and Heidorn 2011, fig. 37:171, fig. 40:196–97), but curlicues are. The diameter of vessel 41 is uncertain, but see perhaps a large closed pot or "Topf" from Elephantine, type K431, diameter 30 cm, ribbed exterior, smooth interior, painted, fabric IV (porous), one example only, probably sixth century (Gempeler 1992, p. 173, fig. 105:2).
42. Body sherd with spiral painted decoration. 2.5YR 5/6 with black paint. Pink ware: fine red and black bits, few medium-size bits. Dump 2, locus 5 middle strip. Spiral painted decoration is quite common, for instance, a sherd from the 1992 season (Heidorn 1995, p. 84, fig. 29:q), and a pink jar(?) sherd from the 1996–1997 corpus (Meyer and Heidorn 2011, p. 130, fig. 37:171). See also a sherd from Shenshef, coarse pink Aswani fabric, dark red-brown to purple paint over yellow to brown slip over white under slip, fifth and probably into sixth century (Tomber 1998, p. 174, fig. 6-5:47). There are many spiral decorated vessels in the Seti Gurna temple corpus (Myśliwiec 1987, pp. 144–45). At Antinoopolis there are a number of spiral painted jars and jugs with one or two handles, dark pink or pink clay with white slip, fifth to seventh century in date (Guidotti 2008, pp. 345–46, 397–99, nos. 320, 324–27, 332).
43. Base of large bowl with black painted "bone" and dribbles of black and white paint. Fabric and interior 5YR 7/6, exterior slip 10R 5/6. Pink; abundant sand; white, red, and black bits. Building 93, Room C, locus 20. From Elephantine, see ring base on a painted vessel (different decoration), fabric IA with 10R 6/5 red slip, end of fourth to first half of seventh century (Gempeler 1992, p. 162, fig. 94:7).
44. Small kick-up base. Core 7.5YR 8/6 to 7/6; exterior 5YR 7/4 to 7/6; interior medium brown-yellowish cast 7.5YR 5/6. Pink, thin. Dump 2, locus 2. There may be a similar jug base from Elephantine, type T840, fabric IB, one example only, date uncertain (Gempeler 1992, p. 144, fig. 80:11).

Marl

45. Bowl. Surfaces 10YR 7/2, fabric 5YR 7/4. Marl; small red and black bits. Dump 2, locus 5 north strip. A series of marl bowls with splayed, ribbed walls and push-up button bases are said to be common at Mons Porphyrites, Late Roman in date (Tomber 2007, p. 195, fig. 6.9:99–101).
46. Bowl, some soot interior and exterior. 10YR 6/2. Marl; fine white bits. Dump 2, locus 4 middle strip. For a conical marl bowl with smoother walls from a previous season, see Meyer and Heidorn 2011, p. 142, fig. 43:218. A cooking pot of a hard silt fabric from Amarna has the same sort of rim, sides, and blackening, but in addition preserves a slightly convex base, probably fifth century in date (Faiers 2005, p. 115, fig. 2.28:205). If inverted, note also a lid from Esna, similar shape (plus a knob) but different fabric (Jacquet-Gordon 1972, pl. 229:4).
47. Jar or deep bowl. Fabric and surface 2.5Y 7/3. Marl probably; many small white bits, some medium-size white bits (quartz). Dump 2, locus 5 middle strip. See comparanda for number 49, below.
48. Jar or deep bowl. Surfaces and core 2.5Y 8/2. Marl; red and white bits, sand. Building 93, Room C northeast, locus 5. There is a series of deep cooking pots from Kellia, silt fabric, painted, but with similar rim form and ridged interior, from a locus datable to A.D. 650–730 (Egloff 1977, p. 97, pl. 45:9). See also comparanda for number 49, below.

Figure 21. Marl

49. Large, deep bowl. Surfaces 2.5Y 7/2 to 7/4, fabric 10YR 7/2. Marl probably; medium amount black and white bits, a little chaff, fine sand. Dump 1, locus 2 (ashy). Wide-mouthed marl jars are known from Late Roman contexts at the Qurna Seti temple (see Myśliwiec 1987, pp. 153–54, nos. 1934, 1938), although the rim forms are not a precise parallel.
50. Large handled pot. Surfaces 2.5Y 7/2 to 8/2, fabric 2.5Y 7/2. Marl; abundant sand, medium amount black bits, a few red bits. Dump 1, locus 2 (ashy). There are some examples from previous seasons: a similar jar sherd without a handle (Heidorn 1995, p. 85, fig. 30:e) and a jar with a handle (Heidorn 2000, p. 86, fig. 56:41). There is a parallel at Shenshef in a marl jar, fifth–early sixth century (Tomber 1998, pp. 174–75, no. 57). At Tôd, see a "rare type of marl" jar, but the dates are early, perhaps as far back as the second century to early fourth (Pierrat 1996, p. 192, pl. 2:15). From Esna, see a very large, tall storage jar with four handles at rim, fine incised line decoration, fabric IV (white, gray, or beige with greenish cast, often pink in break; temper large black particles, grog; porous), sixth century or later (Jacquet-Gordon 1972, pl. 224:3).

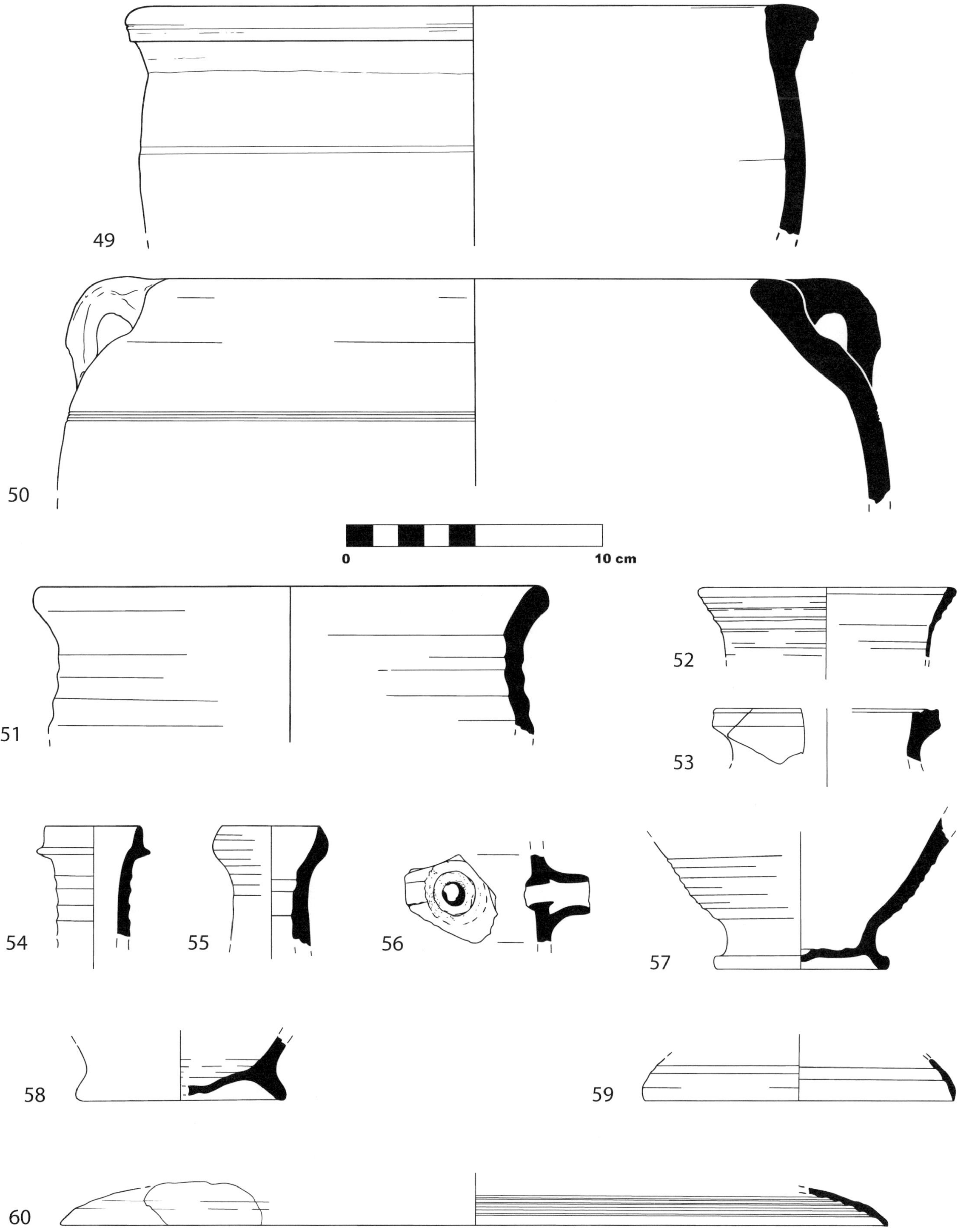

Figure 21. Marl

Figure 21. Marl (cont.)

51. Jar or *qadus*. Exterior 10YR 7/2, interior 2.5Y 7/2, fabric 10YR 8/4. Marl; red chunks, sand, black bits, maybe a little chaff. Dump 2, locus 5 (middle strip). Some examples from previous seasons include: a jar with a more sharply profiled rim (Heidorn 1995, pp. 82–84, fig. 29:f), and two marl jars (Meyer and Heidorn 2011, pp. 142, 150, figs. 43:222, 47:253). There is a parallel at al-Heita in the Eastern Desert, "blue-gray fabric with lime, cream wash exterior and over onto rim interior," datable to fifth–seventh centuries (Sidebotham, Zitterkopf, and Riley 1991, p. 616, fig. 38:125). Marl "storage jars" or *qawadis* were also found at Qurna (e.g., Myśliwiec 1987, pp. 163, 166–67, no. 2044). The shape but not the fabric has a parallel at Esna, sixth century or later (Jacquet 1972, pl. 228:2). If this jar and its kin are in fact *qawadis*, then the question arises as to what such water jars were doing in the desert. See Brun and Reddé 2011, p. 20, for a discussion of water-lifting devices in the Eastern Desert in the Roman period.
52. Jar neck. 5Y 8/3. Marl. Dump 2, locus 5 (ashy). There is a more conical example from the 1993 season (Heidorn 2000, p. 90, fig. 58:110). From Shenshef, there is a more conical everted neck jar with a much thicker rim, perhaps marl (very sandy with a few limestone bits), pink-brown fabric (10R 6/6) with buff surfaces (5YR 8/4 to 7/4), fifth and into sixth century (Tomber 1998, pp. 174–75, fig. 6-5:55).
53. Casserole(?), diameter uncertain. 7.5YR 6/3. Marl. Building 93, Room E, locus 3 (screen). For a silt "casserole" with similar profile from previous season, see Meyer and Heidorn 2011, p. 122, fig. 33:123.
54. Bottle neck. Light pinkish beige fabric 5YR 7/4; surface 10YR 8/2. Marl; red and black bits, large white bits. Building 93, Room C northeast, locus 3. At Tôd there is a parallel in a marl bottle neck datable to the fourth–fifth century (Pierrat 1996, p. 197, pl. 5:67). For a bottle neck from Antinoopolis, fifth–seventh century, fine pink Aswan paste, with white slip, see Guidotti 2008, pp. 322, 379, no. 178.
55. Bottle or jug neck; black smudges on exterior rim and streak down neck may be remnant paint or ink. Exterior and interior 2.5Y 8/2, core 2.5Y 7/2. Marl(?); white, black, and red bits, sand, chaff. Building 177, Room C east, locus 2. There is a good parallel at Tôd, marl fabric datable to the end of the fifth to middle of the seventh century (Pierrat 1996, p. 202, pl. 7:107). A series of filter jars with tall necks, some without handles (types 207 and 208), from Kellia are generally pink, gray, or light brown, many with a porous fabric, datable to the fifth century (Egloff 1977, pp. 121, 126, pl. 66:5, 7).
56. Spout. Fabric 10YR 7/3, surface 5Y 8/2. Marl; abundant fine sand; many small red and black bits. Dump 2, locus 9. Note a flask with spout and neck strainer from the 1993 season (Heidorn 2000, p. 90, fig. 58:113). There is a marl spout from Biʾr Minayh (Lassányi 2010b, p. 280, no. 50). A small two-handled silt water jar was excavated from the cellar of a house in the Seti Gurna temple area, datable to the fifth to early seventh century (Myśliwiec 1987, pp. 172–73, no. 2122).
57. Base of large bowl or jar. Surface and fabric 10YR 8/3. Marl; much sand, abundant black, gray, red bits; red and gray chunks (granite?). Dump 1, top 5 cm.
58. Base of bowl or jar. Interior and base 5Y 7/4, exterior 5Y 6/1. Marl; red and white bits, sand. Building 93, Dump 2, locus 5 (middle strip).
59. Lid. Surfaces 10YR 8/4. Marl; medium amount small to medium-size sand; few medium-size black bits; porous. Dump 2, locus 3. See discussion of lids at number 37, above.
60. Shallow lid, sharply ribbed interior; diameter perhaps smaller. Fabric 5YR 7/4. Marl; fine red, white, black bits; some large red grits. Building 181, locus 2.

Figure 22. Silt Plates and Bowls

61. Large plate. 5YR 5/3 with thick, dark gray core. Silt; fine sandy temper, a few black bits. Building 93, Room C northeast, locus 14. The shape may have a parallel in some very large plates from Elephantine, fabric IA (pink), with a ring base (where preserved), late sixth to the beginning of the seventh century (Gempeler 1992, p. 87, fig. 31:1–3).
62. Shallow dish with grooved rim, fire blackened. Exterior 5YR 5/2 to 5/4, interior 5YR 4/1 to 4/3, core 5YR 5/6. Silt; white and black bits, mica. Building 93, Room A, locus 4. There is a shallow silt bowl of smaller diameter but very similar rim in the 1996–1997 corpus (Meyer and Heidorn 2011, p. 118, fig. 31:99). For a bowl with triangular lip, Egyptian Red Slip B ware (red-brown to orange-brown with red-brown slip) from Shenshef, fifth and probably into sixth century, see Tomber 1998, p. 174, fig. 6-5:52; note also that nos. 51 and 53 have reeded or grooved rims. There is a very similar shallow dish in the Seti Gurna temple corpus, Egyptian Red Slip Ware C, generally datable to the fifth to early seventh century (Myśliwiec 1987, pp. 111–12, no. 1250). Not much pottery was published from Jême at Medinet Habu, but a group (U') of shallow dishes includes one (vessel e) with a profile similar to our number 62. The Jême dishes are described only as Late Roman "imitation terra sigillata," but they were found in a "large mud storage vessel" together with a bell-shaped large bowl (Hölscher 1954, p. 76, pl. 48) similar to number 109, below. Two Egyptian Red Slip B dishes with similar rims from Amarna are probably sixth century in date (Faiers 2005, p. 84, 184, figs. 2.10:92, 3.3:13). At Kellia, a shallow plate (type 31) has a less squatty profile but a similar rim and fabric, including mica bits, probably fifth century (Egloff 1977, pp. 79–80, pl. 39:11).
63. Base of plate or shallow dish. 2.5YR 5/6 with gray core. Silt; fine white and black bits, a few medium-size black bits. Building 93, Room D, locus 3.

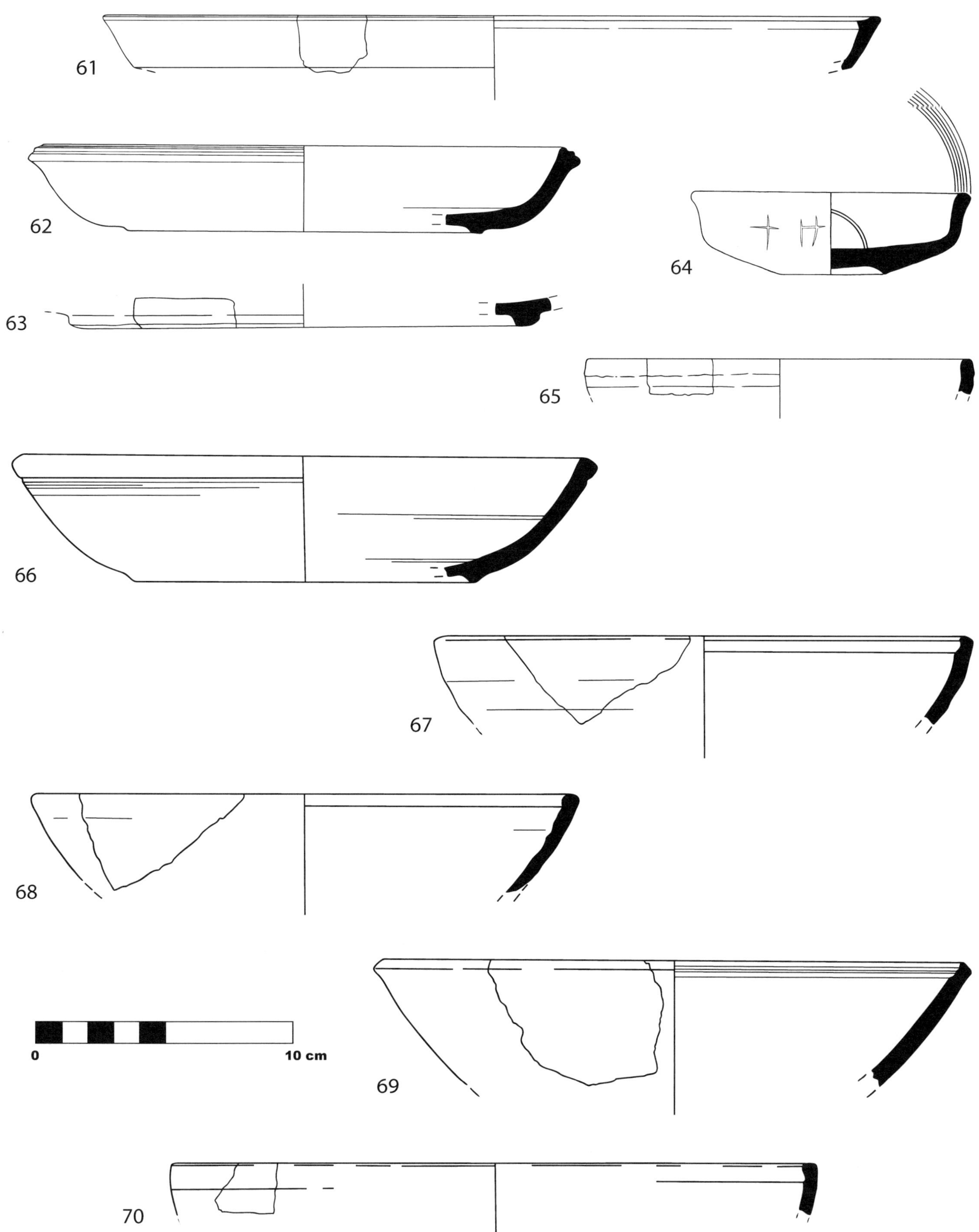

Figure 22. Silt plates and bowls

Figure 22. Silt Plates and Bowls (cont.)

64. Small cup or bowl with inscribed marks on side, shallow grooves on rim (RN 99/215; pl. 31b). Interior 2.5YR 5/8, core and exterior 2.5YR 6/8. Silt fabric, temper not visible. Dump 2, locus 3. There is a parallel at Kellia, a cup with sharper carination (type 45), surface find (Egloff 1977, p. 83, pl. 40:15). For a possible parallel at Elephantine, see type T307, "small deep cup" with no grooves or ridges, fabric IA, red slip, third century (Gempeler 1992, p. 91, fig. 34:1). Another possible parallel may be seen at Buto, silt cup, no base, sixth and into seventh century (Ballet and von der Way 1993, p. 7, fig. 3:14).
65. Bowl with rough surface. Slip 2.5YR 5/6, fabric 5YR 6/6. Silt; abundant black and white sand, some medium-size white bits. Building 177, Room C east, locus 2.
66. Large bowl, rim and base fire-blackened. Interior 5YR 5/4 to 7.5YR 3/1, exterior 2.5YR 5/4, core 5YR 4/4 to 7.5YR 2/1. Silt; red bits, sand, mica. Building 93, Room B west, locus 6. See also a large, shallow bowl from the 1993 season (Heidorn 2000, p. 88, fig. 57:79).
67. Large bowl. Surfaces and slip 10R 5/6, fabric 2.5YR 5/6. Silt. Dump 2, locus 2. Without bases it is hard to find good parallels for these simple bowls, but see perhaps type T327b from Elephantine, pink fabric, second half of fifth to early sixth century (Gempeler 1992, p. 97, fig. 40:15–16).
68. Large bowl. Fabric 2.5YR 5/6, slip 2.5YR 4/6. Silt; very scaly red-brown fabric; chaff; fine white bits (sand?); a little medium-size white and fine black bits. Building 177, Room A, locus 12. There is a similar large silt bowl from the Seti Gurna temple, datable in general to the fifth to early seventh century (Myśliwiec 1987, p. 118–19, no. 1408). A similar large red-slipped bowl from Amarna, said to be "badly abraded inside," is probably datable to the fifth–sixth centuries (Faiers 2005, p. 89, fig. 2.13:114).
69. Large, conical bowl, sooted interior and exterior, splintery. Fabric 5YR 6/4. Silt; small black and white bits. Dump 1, locus 2 (ashy).
70. Large bowl. Slip 2.5YR 4/6, fabric 5YR 5/4. Silt; perhaps lightly fired; medium amount white sand with some larger grains. Dump 2, locus 8.

Figure 23. Large Silt Bowls and Beakers

71. Large bowl. Red-brown slip 2.5YR 4/6; red-brown fabric 2.5YR 5/6. Silt; abundant fine black bits, a few fine or large white bits, a few medium-size black bits, a little chaff. Dump 1, locus 4. See a similar large, simple, silt bowl from the Seti Gurna temple, fifth to early seventh century (Myśliwiec 1987, pp. 118–19, no. 1377).
72. Large bowl with incurved rim. Exterior slip; fabric 5YR 5/4. Silt; sand, some medium size quartz grains. Dump 2, locus 11. There is also a large bowl with an incurved rim from the 1992 season (Heidorn 1995, p. 81, fig. 28:j). Note some large, footed beakers from Elephantine, type T608a, often but not always painted, pink ware, datable to the beginning of the fourth to the sixth century (Gempeler 1992, p. 125, fig. 71:11–13). For a similar vessel, see Bab Kalabsha, X-Group (Late Roman–Byzantine period), large bowl on ring base, yellowish clay (Ricke 1967, p. 63, fig. 72:B8/10), or a smaller example of red clay with vertical slashes of paint (Ricke 1967, p. 68, fig. 80:E/w.2). Another, smaller cup with a similar profile comes from Sayala, a site dated to the late third century (Kromer 1967, pp. 99–100, pl. 32:1).
73. Large, painted bowl. Orange paint on red-brown, rough surface. Surfaces and fabric 2.5YR 5/6; orange paint 5YR 7/8 on red-brown slip. Silt; sand, gray chunks. Building 177, Room A, surface. There are some similar beakers from previous seasons: one with black over white splotches on a red rim band, and another smaller goblet with two rows of black splotches (Heidorn 2000, pp. 84, 88, figs. 55:17, 57:71); two large goblets, pink fabric, red slip, black and yellowish white painted blobs (Meyer and Heidorn 2011, p. 130, fig. 37:167–68). See similar vessels at Berenice: some red-slipped beakers of "Aswan type" often with black and cream vertical stripes or blobs (Hayes 1995, pp. 34–45, citing Adams 1986 and Strouhal 1984); a large beaker with similar decoration, "large variant of Aswan Red Slip ware," said to be standard fourth–fifth-century type (Hayes 1996, p. 178); and a somewhat smaller goblet with splashed decoration, Aswan pink ware (2.5YR 6/6 with darker slip), fifth and probably into sixth century (Tomber 1998, p. 172, fig. 6-4:40). The Seti Gurna temple corpus includes a series of large silt beakers or bowls with splashed-on black-and-white decoration, and Myśliwiec (1987, pp. 94–95, 97, nos. 976–979) notes parallels with Nubian X-Group ceramics of the fourth to early sixth centuries.17
74. Large bowl. 5YR 5/6. Silt; temper not noted. Dump 1, locus 4. The ridge or residual flange on the outside seems to have no parallels so far.
75. Bowl with thick triangular rim, polished surface. 7.5YR 5/6. Silt; fine black bits, a few larger black bits. Building 181, locus 1. From the Seti Gurna temple there is a bowl with very similar rim, dated in general to the fifth to early seventh century (Myśliwiec 1987, pp. 107–08, no. 1156). See an example from Bab Kalabsha, yellow-white clay, flat base, X-Group (Late Roman–Byzantine period) (Ricke 1967, p. 49, fig. 68:T/19).
76. Large bowl. Brown fabric and surfaces. Silt; fine sand, small black bits. Building 93, Room E, surface silt. There is a flat-bottomed silt bowl from the 1996–1997 seasons (Meyer and Heidorn 2011, p. 132, fig. 38:175). Note a bowl with a similar rim, Egyptian

---

[17] What the apparent absence of "degenerate vine leaf" or "splashed decoration" painting at Kellia (Egloff 1977) may mean in terms of distribution or chronology of decorative styles is unclear, but, given the size of the corpus of painted pottery at Kellia, its absence is noteworthy.

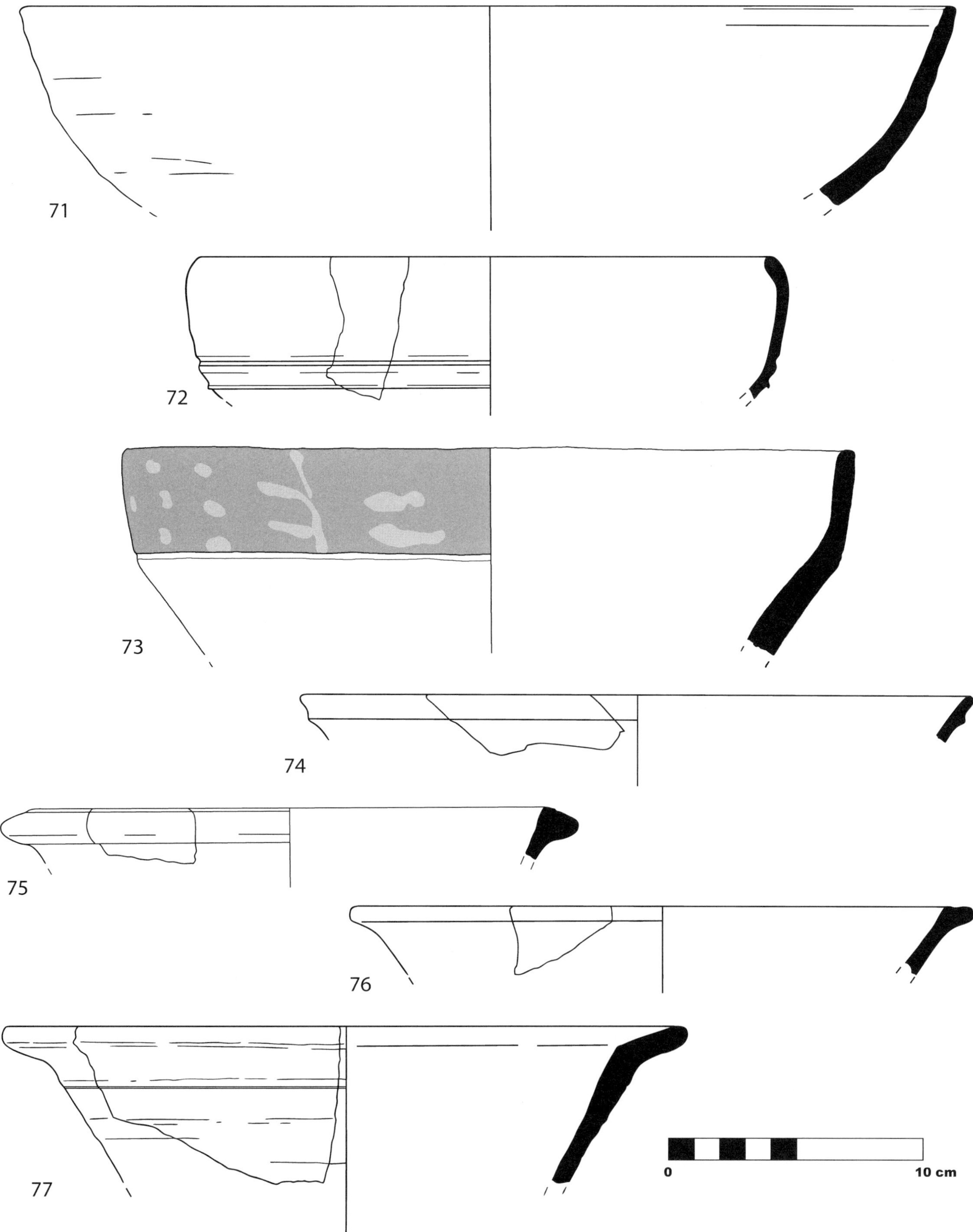

Figure 23. Large silt bowls and beakers

Figure 23. Large Silt Bowls and Beakers (cont.)

Red Slip Ware C, from the Seti Gurna temple, perhaps sixth–seventh century in date (Myśliwiec 1987, pp. 112–14, no. 1272). A somewhat thicker Egyptian Red Slip H bowl from Amarna seems otherwise quite similar (Faiers 2005, p. 98, fig. 2.18:147). From Elephantine, there is a type of bowl T302 with a similar rim, a simple, low ring base, pink fabric, first to fourth century (Gempeler 1992, pp. 89–90, fig. 33:8).

77. Large bowl with flaring rim. Surfaces 5YR 5/6, dark gray core 2.5YR 3/1. Silt; abundant sand in fine to medium-size grains, a little chaff. Dump 1, top 5 cm.

Figure 24. Silt Bowls and Casseroles

For a range of similar silt bowls or casseroles, see examples from the Seti Gurna temple, generally fifth to early seventh century in date (Myśliwiec 1987, pp. 119–21, esp. nos. 1419, 1435–1437, 1440, 1442–1443).

78. Bowl with jutting or everted rim. 5YR 5/6. Silt; fine white bits, a few large red bits. Building 93, Room A, locus 4. See perhaps a small casserole from Elephantine, type K201a, pink fabric, datable as early as the second half of the first to fourth century (Gempeler 1992, pp. 149–50, fig. 84:5).

79. Carinated bowl. Fabric and surfaces 2.5YR 5/6. Silt; sand, medium amount white and black bits. Building 181, surface. A silt casserole at Biʾr Minayh has a similar rim (Lassányi 2010b, pp. 282–83, no. 62). A silt cooking dish from Amarna with a flattened, grooved rim, red slip inside and out (Faiers 2005, p. 115, fig. 2.28:204) seems to be the sole close parallel in the sizeable Amarna corpus of cooking pots. A fifth-century cooking pot from Kellia (type 88) has a similar rim, sides, and fabric but also two horizontal handles (Egloff 1977, p. 95, pl. 44:6).

80. Carinated bowl. 2.5YR 5/6. Silt; some very fine white and black bits, abundant small white and black bits, a little mica, a few large red bits. Dump 2, locus 5 (middle strip).

81. Carinated bowl, rim painted white with black spots. 2.5YR 5/6. Silt. Dump 2, locus 4 (middle strip). A silt casserole from the 1993 season has a larger diameter but a very similar rim with painted spots (Heidorn 2000, p. 88, fig. 57:82). There is a similar bowl from the Ashmunein Church site, slipped overall, white band with black blobs atop, middle of fifth century (Bailey 1996, p. 62, pl. 7:54–55).

82. Carinated bowl or casserole. Core 2.5YR 5/6, exterior surface 10R 5/6. Silt; white chunks and bits. Dump 1, locus 4.

83. Carinated bowl or casserole, misshapen rim. Fabric and surface 10R 5/8. Silt; fine sand, some medium-size white bits (limestone?). Building 181, locus 1. There is a parallel from Shenshef, red-brown Nile silt casserole with beaded rim, fifth and probably into sixth century (Tomber 1998, p. 176, fig. 6-6:67). At Elephantine note a type of "saucepan," K110, with a shallower, rounded body, red-brown fabric with white spots painted on rim, probably fourth–fifth century in date (Gempeler 1992, p. 147, fig. 82:18).

84. Carinated bowl or casserole. Surfaces 2.5YR 5/6, core 2.5YR 4/6 to 4/8. Silt; black bits, sand, mica. Dump 2, locus 2. Several "wide, shallow bowls" are noted from the Wadi Qitna cemetery (immediately south of Kalabsha), generally dated to the second half of the third through the fifth century, and one of the published ones resembles number 84 (Strouhal 1984, pp. 114–15, no. P762).

85. Deep bowl, surface sooted. Fabric 7.5YR 6/4. Silt. Building 93, Room A, locus 6. For an example from a previous season, see the silt casserole in Heidorn 2000, p. 88, fig. 57:82.

86. Casserole or basin. Remnant reddish slip 10R 5/4, fabric 5YR 5/6. Silt; abundant small black and white bits, some medium-size white bits. Dump 2, locus 2.

87. Basin or casserole, surface smoothed, perhaps slipped. Gray surface gley1 4/1, core 2.5YR 4/3. Silt. Building 177, Room A, locus 1 southwest (surface).

88. Carinated bowl, white painted arches. Core 10R 5/8, surfaces 10R 5/6. Silt; white and red bits, sand. Dump 1, top 5 cm. The type is well attested in finds from previous seasons: a casserole very similar in shape but undecorated, and a deep, footed bowl with painted arch decoration (Heidorn 2000, p. 88, fig. 57:83, 81); a casserole with white spots, another with much thicker walls and black painted arches, and two more with white spots and arches or a wavy stripe (Meyer and Heidorn 2011, pp. 132, 134, figs. 38:179–80, 39:181–82). At the Seti Gurna temple there is a similar silt casserole with white zigzags, datable in general to the fifth to early seventh century (Myśliwiec 1987, pp. 120, 122, no. 1469). At Esna, see some "bowls without feet," fabric I (chocolate brown, tempered with small black or white grains, quartz, mica, usually red slipped), sixth century or later (Jacquet 1972, pl. 220:7). There are also some examples from Antinoopolis, carinated bowls with simpler rims, painted arches on the sides, pink to dark pink to chocolate clay (Guidotti 2008, pp. 335–37, 388–91, nos. 258–78). Among the many types of carinated cooking pots from Kellia, see especially type 98, a shallow variety with painted arches, locus date of A.D. 650–730 (Egloff 1977, p. 97, pl. 45:8).

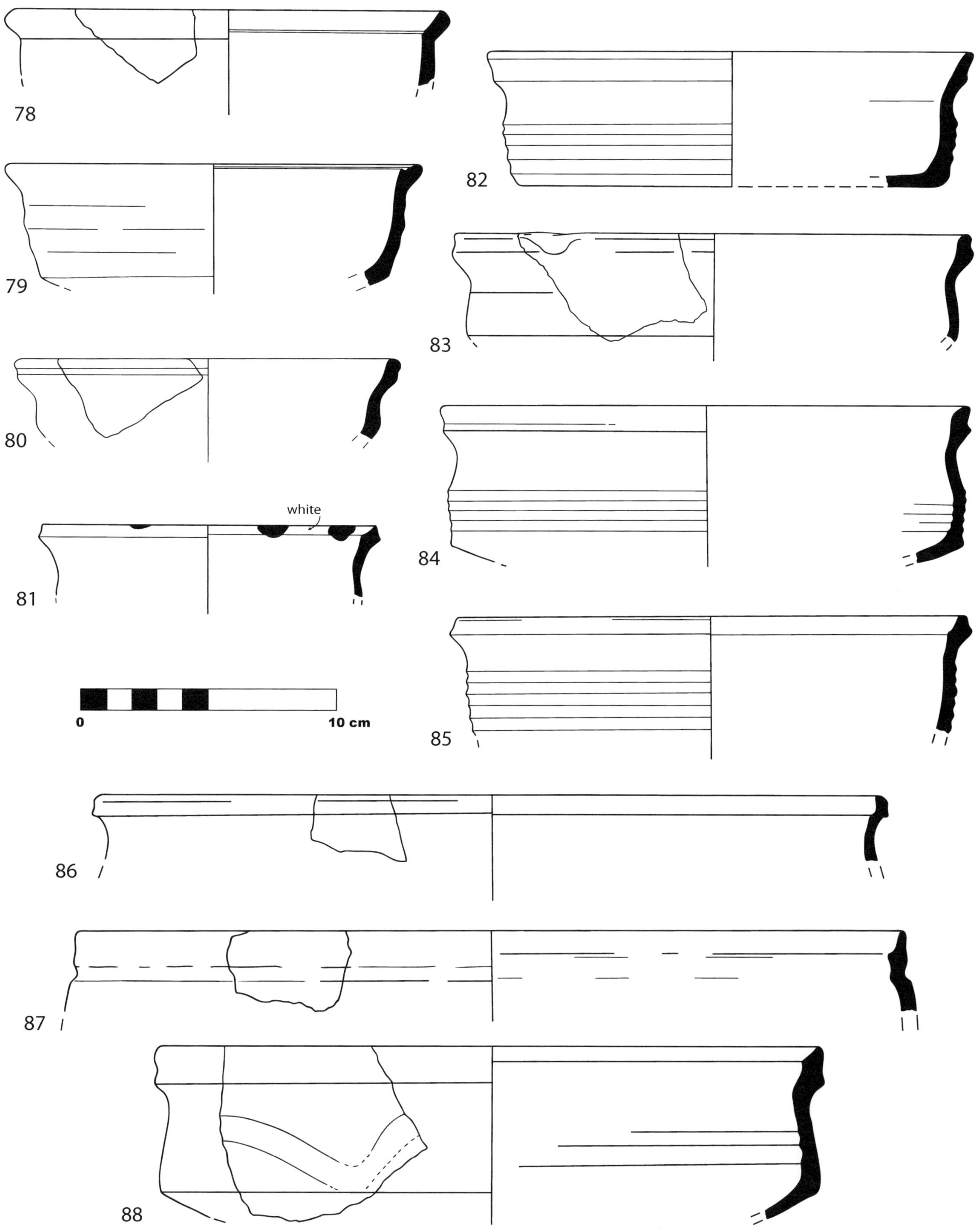

Figure 24. Silt bowls and casseroles

Figure 25. Silt Casseroles and Carinated Bowls

89. Casserole with piecrust rim, finely ribbed, exterior sooted. 2.5YR 5/6 with thin gray core. Silt; sand; many black bits, some medium-size quartz grains. Building 177, Room A, locus 14 (screen). There is a similar cooking pot from Shenshef, piecrust rim, red-brown with purple-black painted spots, fifth into sixth century (Tomber 1998, p. 176, fig. 6-6:63). At Badia, a road station on the other side of the mountain from Mons Porphyrites, there is a cooking pot of very hard silt fabric, piecrust rim, Late Roman in date (Tomber 2001, p. 301, fig. 6.35:37). From the Seti Gurna temple, see some dark red-brown examples, fifth to early seventh century (Myśliwiec 1987, pp. 149, 151, nos. 1902–03). A bowl with a piecrust rim, silt fabric, Amarna, A.D. 350–525 in date, has a more angular body but is otherwise quite similar (Faiers 2005, p. 117, fig. 2.29:214). From Ashmunein, a brown clay "cooking pot" with a piecrust rim is similar (Bailey 1996, p. 66, pl. 10:35), but a brown clay "casserole" with a piecrust rim and a burnt bottom, probably fifth century in date, is an even closer parallel (Bailey 1996, p. 69, pl. 13:32). At Kellia, type 108, datable to ca. 450–500 (or later), has a slightly different ledge rim inside but is otherwise a good parallel (Egloff 1977, p. 98, pl. 46:10). From Elephantine, note types K343a and K343b, open pot forms with a ledge on the rim to support a lid, red-brown fabric, fifth century in date (Gempeler 1992, p. 160, fig. 93:1–5), or better still, type K223a, red-brown fabric, not common, probably second half of fifth century (Gempeler 1992, pp. 152–53, fig. 86:11).

90. Casserole with piecrust rim. 2.5YR 5/6 throughout. Silt; very crumbly and flaky; if slipped, can no longer tell; abundant sand, a few white bits. Dump 1, locus 13 (interior of tabun 1). There is a very similar silt casserole rim from the 1996–1997 seasons (Meyer and Heidorn 2011, p. 134, fig. 39:184). For a similar casserole from Antinoopolis, pink clay, exterior blackened, fifth–seventh-century date, see Guidotti 2008, pp. 309, 369 no. 99, and comparanda to number 89, above.

91. Cooking pot or casserole. Surfaces 10R 5/6, fabric 2/5YR 5/4 to 5/6. Silt; friable; abundant white bits and chunks; a little sand and black bits; perhaps a little chaff. Building 177, Room A, locus 7. There is a similar "collared pot" from Esna, fabric Ia (fine, red-brown with temper of small black or white grains, quartz, some mica, sometimes chaff), sixth century or later (Jacquet 1972, pl. 225:21). See also perhaps a collared cooking pot from the Seti Gurna temple, fifth to early seventh century (Myśliwiec 1987, pp. 149–50, no. 1867).

92. Deep bowl with thick, rounded rim, rough red slip, diameter possibly greater. Fabric 5YR 6/6, slip 2.5YR 5/6. Silt; sand, black bits. Building 93, Room A, locus 4. A large marl bowl with a similar shape was recovered from the surface of Bir Handosi (Sidebotham, Barnard, and Pyke 2002, p. 204, fig. 13:23), an isolated, Late Roman site roughly 50 km southeast of Bir Umm Fawakhir.

93. Large, deep(?) bowl, red slip, traces of white paint. Fabric 2.5YR 6/6, slip 7.5R 5/6. Silt; sand; abundant small and medium-size red bits, some medium-size quartz grains, medium black bits. Building 177, Room C east, locus 2.

94. Large, deep bowl with thick, rounded rim. Surface 10YR 8/2 (cream), interior 5YR 6/6. Silt(?); many fine black and white bits, some medium-size black and white (quartz) bits. Building 93, Room A, locus 4. The type is well attested from previous seasons: perhaps a bowl with painted blobs on rim (Heidorn 1995, pp. 81–82, fig. 28:c); a large silt bowl with a similar rim but also small lug handles (Heidorn 2000, p. 84, fig. 55:7); a large, deep, red-brown silt bowl with two lug handles, and a large bowl rim, no handles preserved (Meyer and Heidorn 2011, pp. 116, 122, figs. 30:87, 33:118). For a possible parallel from Shenshef, see a bowl with an enlarged beaded rim, dull orange-pink marl (2.5YR 6/6) with matte brown slip (10R 3/1) inside and out, datable to fifth and probably early sixth century (Tomber 1998, p. 174, fig. 6-5:56). Another possible parallel may be seen at Elephantine, type K105, a "saucepan" with a thick rim, fabric IB, fourth century (Gempeler 1992, p. 147, fig. 82:13).

95. Large, deep bowl with thick, rounded rim. Fabric 2.5YR 6/6, surface obscured by concretions but probably same. Silt(?); abundant small white bits, some small black bits. Building 93, Room A, locus 4. There are several examples from previous seasons: a large, carinated bowl with a club rim and black painted spots on the rim; another large, unpainted, carinated bowl with a knob rim; and a large, deep, ribbed bowl with an emphatic club rim (Heidorn 1995, pp. 81–82, 89, figs. 29:c and 30:n; Heidorn 2000, p. 90, fig. 58:104). A marl bowl from the surface of Umm Howeitat Bahri, a small Late Roman site north of Bir Umm Fawakhir, has a very similar rim shape (Sidebotham, Barnard, and Pyke 2002, p. 197, fig. 6:7). From the Seti Gurna temple there is a large silt vat with a club rim, generally datable to the fifth to early seventh century (Myśliwiec 1987, pp. 154, 156, no. 1954).

96. Large, deep, handled bowl with thick, rounded rim and red slip. Fabric 10R 6/6, slip 10R 5/6. Silt(?); small to medium-size black and white bits. Dump 2, locus 5 (middle strip). Another handled sherd, probably from the same vessel, was also recovered. The form has been reported from previous seasons: a large, deep, ribbed bowl with a rounded rim and handles (Heidorn 2000, p. 84, fig. 55:7) and another example nearly complete from rim to base (Meyer and Heidorn 2011, p. 116, fig. 30:87).

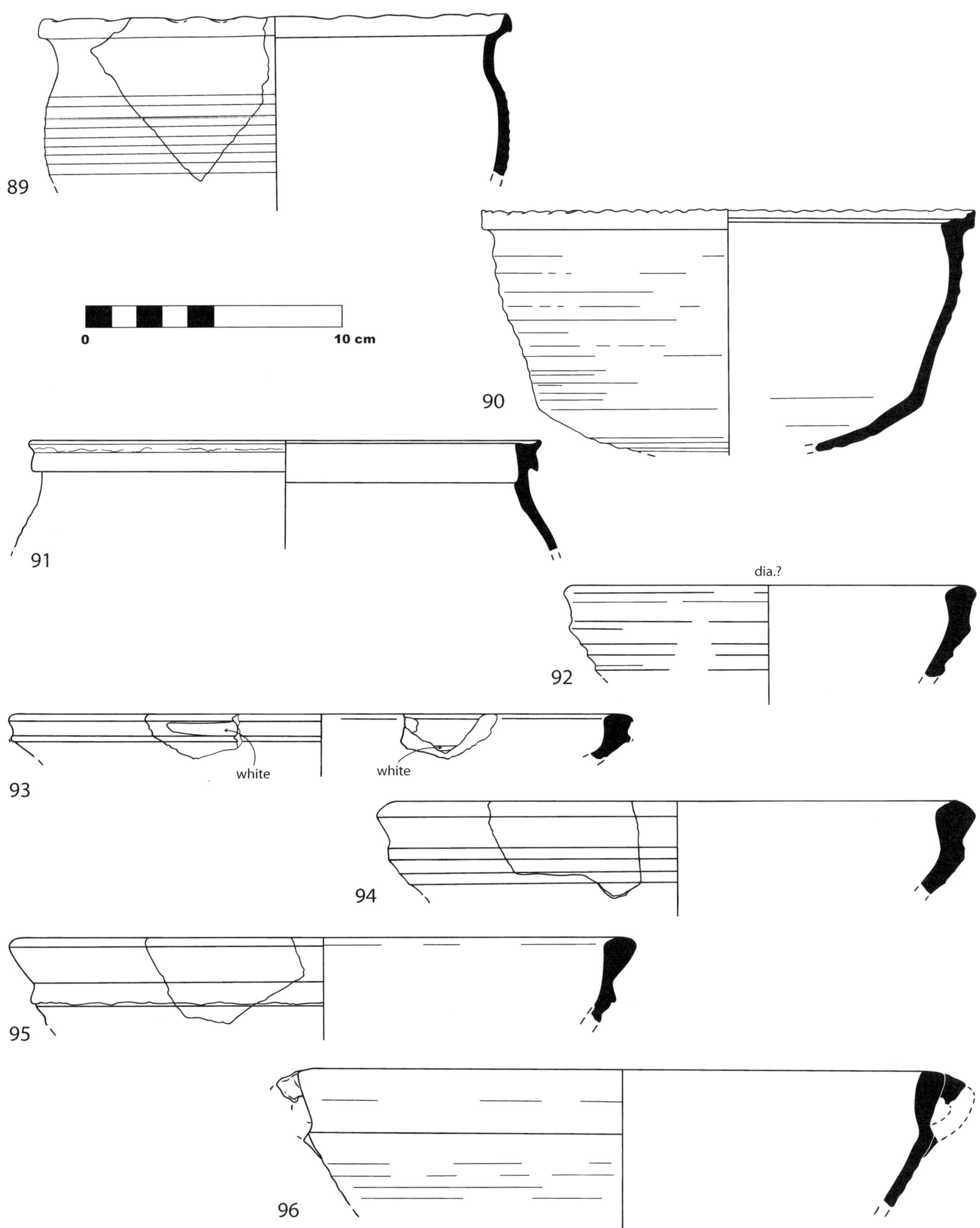

Figure 25. Silt casseroles and carinated bowls

Figure 26. Silt Large, Deep Bowls

97. Large, deep bowl. Pale buff surface 7.5YR 8/2, dark brown core 2.5YR 5/4 to 3/4. Silt; sand, white bits, burnt-out chaff. Building 177, Room A, locus 12. From the 1993 season, see perhaps a large, deep, ribbed casserole with an elaborate rim and basket handles (Heidorn 2000, p. 84, fig. 55:19).
98. Large, deep bowl with corrugated rim. Pale surface 5Y 8/2, orangish fabric 5YR 6/8. Silt; sand; red and white (limestone?) bits. Building 93, Room A, locus 4. Similar bowls are known from previous seasons: a carinated "cooking pot" with horizontal handles, ribbed body, and a corrugated rim (Heidorn 1995, p. 88, fig. 30:k), and another good example with a similarly corrugated rim (Meyer and Heidorn 2011, p. 136, fig. 40:192). There is a parallel at Tôd, marl fabric, end of fourth and fifth centuries (Pierrat 1996, p. 196, pl. 5:57). At Kellia, a large carinated bowl with a double piecrust rim (pinched in from both sides), made of a soft, porous, red-brown fabric, is datable to the early fifth century (Egloff 1977, p. 152, pl. 81:3).
99. Large, deep bowl. Red-brown fabric 2.5YR 4/6 and surface, perhaps slipped. Silt; fine sand, abundant small black and white bits. Dump 2, locus 8. If, and only if, the base turns in abruptly to make a shallow pan rather than a deep bowl, there is a possible parallel in a "shallow casserole" from Mons Porphyrites, early second century A.D. (Tomber 2007, p. 197, fig. 6.10:16).
100. Large, deep bowl. 5YR 5/4. Silt, soft; fine white bits. Building 93, Room A, locus 4. Note two large, deep bowls with the same kind of rim from the Seti temple at Gurna, but with white painted arches on the body (Myśliwiec 1987, pp. 130–31, nos. 1558–59).
101. Large, deep, handled pot, gouge near one handle. Fabric and interior 2.5YR 6/4, red slip exterior 2.5YR 4/6. Silt; small red bits, white bits, sand. Building 177, Room A, locus 7. Similar vessels are reported from previous seasons: a "cooking vessel" with handles, a smaller, handled "cooking pot" (Heidorn 1995, p. 85, fig. 30:b; Heidorn 2000, p. 88, fig. 57:84), and perhaps a marl "cooking pot" with a similar rim and handles but combed decoration (Meyer and Heidorn 2011, p. 150, fig. 47:252). At Elephantine, note type K318, an open jar form with handles, pink fabric, date uncertain (Gempeler 1992, p. 157, fig. 90:9–13).

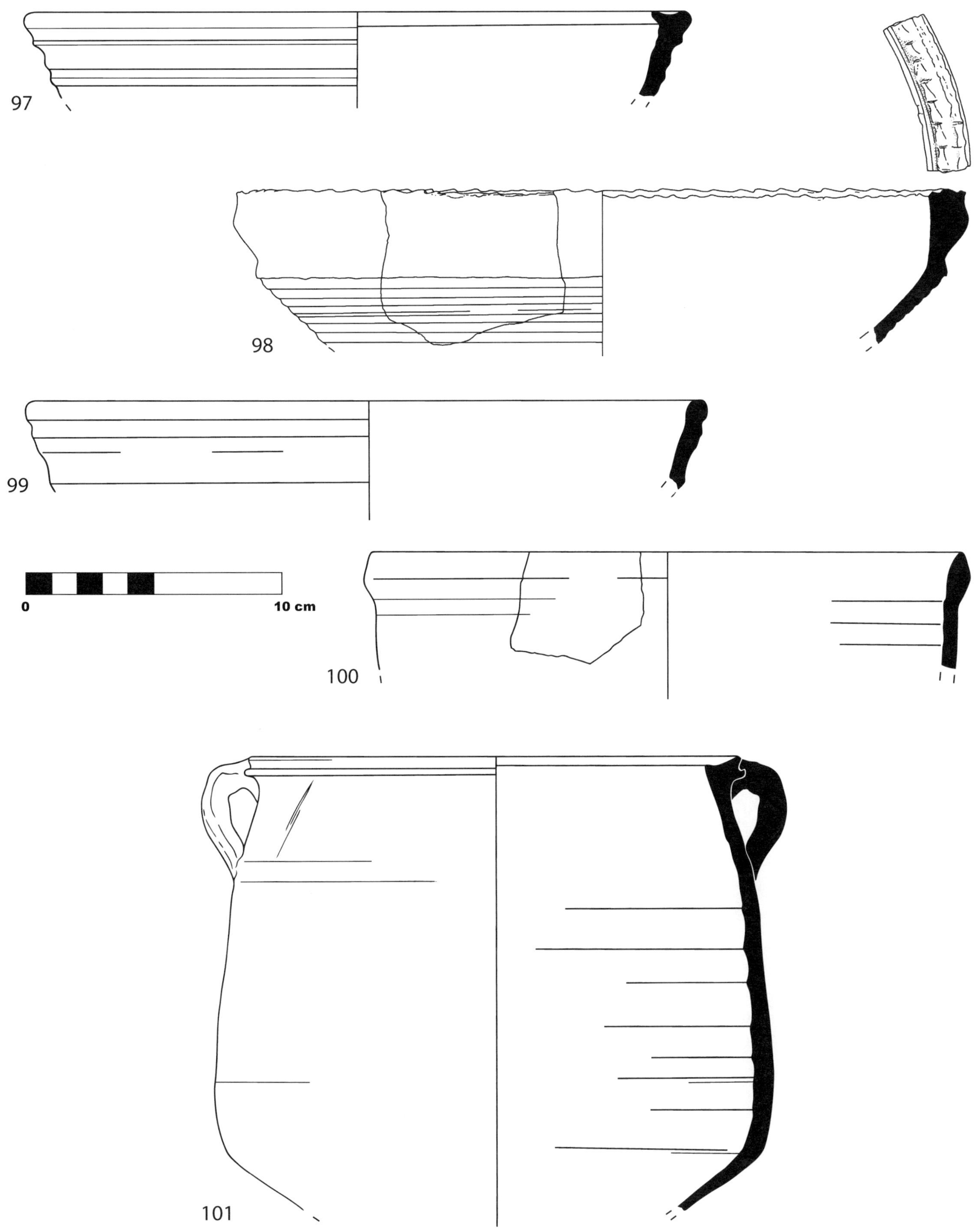

Figure 26. Silt large, deep bowls

Figure 27. Silt Large, Deep Bowls, or "Kraters"

A series of large, deep bowls may have served as "kraters" or wine-mixing bowls at ancient Bir Umm Fawakhir. Judging from the number of amphoras, wine was available, and we assume that, in accordance with ancient etiquette, it was mixed with water before consumption.[18] Most of the kraters are neatly finished, and some are elaborately decorated. Curiously, there are relatively few parallels for the rim treatment or shape of the kraters, especially the bell-shaped ones like 104, 109, 112, and probably 105 and 113. The large, deep bowls from Elephantine, for instance, generally have a distinct ridge or slight shoulder (cf. Gempeler 1992, fig. 113). As of writing, then, the probable area of manufacture of this group of Bir Umm Fawakhir vessels remains unknown.

102. Small krater with trace of black paint. 10R 5/4 fabric with grayish core, worn 10R 5/8 slip inside and out. Silt; sand, some medium-size black and quartz grains. Dump 2, locus 8. It seems to be similar to a more complete example from Amarna, Egyptian Red Slip B, probably fifth century (Faiers 2005, pp. 206, 208, fig. 3.14:105).

103. Krater or basin with club rim. Surface 2.5YR 5/6, orange fabric 2.5YR 6/8 with grayish core. Building 93, Room A, locus 3. The shape of the rim has a parallel in a decorated marl (perhaps Egyptian Red Slip A) basin from the surface of Bir Handosi, a small, remote site southeast of Bir Umm Fawakhir (Sidebotham, Barnard, and Pyke 2002, p. 204, fig. 13:20).

104. Krater, black blobs on white paint on rim (RN 99/218; pl. 32a). 10R 5/4 interior and exterior. Silt; breaks not visible but perhaps some chaff on surface. Surface find, about half of pot extant, restored in field laboratory.

105. Krater with thick, grooved rim. 5YR 6/6 with grayish core. Silt. Building 177, Room A, locus 3 southeast. For a parallel from Shenshef, see a basin with a sharply everted, grooved rim and double lip, slightly sandy Nile silt ware, datable to the fifth and probably early sixth century (Tomber 1998, p. 174, fig. 6-5:58). A silt bowl from the Amarna area, probably fifth century, with a square, reeded rim, orange slip inside and out, is similar in form but also bears remnants of painted crosshatch decoration (Faiers 2005, p. 208, fig. 3.15:113).

106. Krater with everted, grooved rim, reddish slip, black frond-like decoration painted on white band below rim. Core 2.5YR 6/2 to 6/4, exterior slip 2.5YR 5/6. Silt; sand, some small black bits, burnt-out chunks or "bursters" on interior surface. Dump 1, locus 4.

[18] Since all sherds and other materials must remain in Egypt, it was not possible to test any sherds for residues.

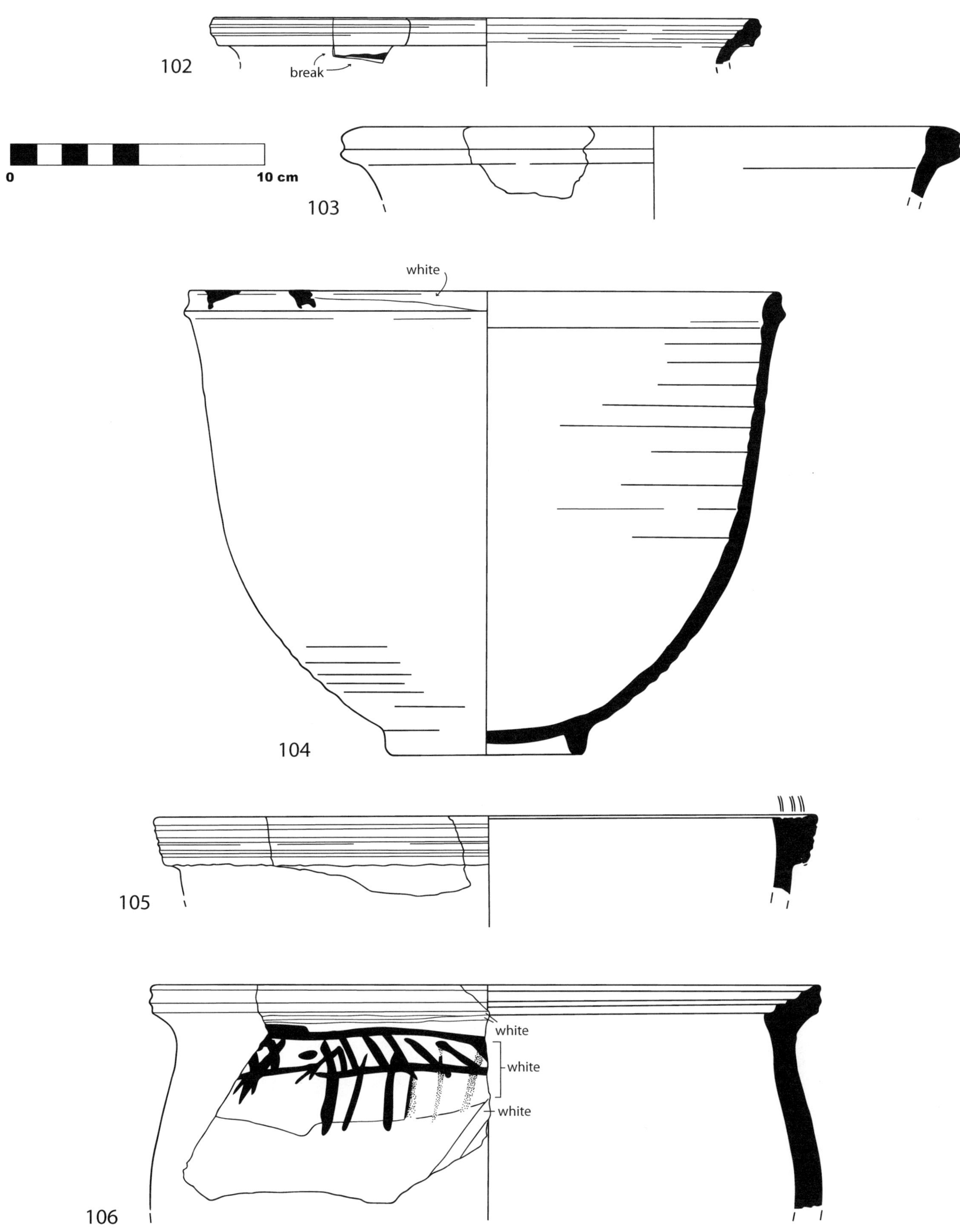

Figure 27. Silt large deep bowls, or "kraters"

Figure 28. Silt Large, Deep Bowls, or "Kraters"

107. Krater with red slip, black painted designs on white painted bands, now flaking off. Fabric and surfaces 2.5YR 6/6, slip 10R 5/6. Silt; a few white bits. Dump 2, locus 6. There are some parallels from previous seasons: a somewhat smaller krater with the same sort of crosshatch decoration below the rim and a similar but painted rim; and a very similar vessel with the same sort of painted decoration (Heidorn 1995, p. 85, fig. 30:a; Heidorn 2000, p. 86, fig. 56:29). A large (dia. 30 cm) silt bowl with a much flatter but similarly grooved rim and crosshatch paint on the body is reported from the Late Roman site of Bir Handosi (Sidebotham, Barnard, and Pyke 2002, p. 204, fig. 14:25).

108. Krater with black painted rim, red-brown stripes on white band below rim. Core 2.5YR 5/4 to 10R 6/6 to 4/1; interior surface 2.5YR 4/1; exterior surface 2.5YR 5/4. Silt; sand, white bits, burnt-out chaff. Dump 2, locus 2. From the Seti temple at Gurna, see a large vessel with a flat, overhung, painted rim and painted upper body (Myśliwiec 1987, pp. 134–35, no. 1600). There is a good parallel at Tôd, end of fourth and fifth century, in a large jar with painted bands (Pierrat 1996, p. 196, pl. 4:54). A smaller bowl from the Amarna area has a similar shape, painted black stripes on the exterior and dots atop the rim (Faiers 2005, p. 203, fig. 3.12:94). For a parallel from the Bab Kalabsha cemeteries, see a bell jar with a thick, flat rim, undecorated, yellowish clay, X-Group (Late Roman–Byzantine period) (Ricke 1967, p. 65, fig. 79:E/a). There is another possible parallel from Elephantine, a somewhat smaller open pot, pink fabric but with a similar square rim and stripes of black over white paint, datable to the third–fourth centuries (Gempeler 1992, p. 155, fig. 89:5).

109. Krater, red slip, incised mark, slightly elliptical at rim (27.9–29.7 cm across) (RN 99/222; pl. 13a). Slip 10R 6/6 to 5/6 to blackish streaks; no break to show fabric. Silt. Building 93, Room C northwest, in locus 18 fill, resting on locus 19 floor. Found upside-down on lowest floor excavated in Room C (pl. 24c). Among the relatively few published pottery finds from Jême at Medinet Habu there is a large, deep bowl like the bell-shaped number 109 but with a simpler rim. The Jême vessel is described as "coarse red clay, smoke blackened outside," and it was found in a "mud storage vessel" with six shallow dishes (Hölscher 1954, p. 76, pl. 48), one of which resembles our number 62. For similar vessels from Esna, see some more large, bulging jars, some slipped, in fabric III (red-orange, black in break, tempered with large particles of all sorts), datable to the sixth century or later (Jacquet 1972, pl. 223:15). A "jar with a double-lip rim" from Shenshef, slipped, of Nile silt, datable to the fifth and probably early sixth century, is described as "possibly a *saqiya* pot" (Tomber 1998, p. 176, fig. 6-6:61). At Elephantine, types K502 and K505 of the third–fourth centuries, and K509 of uncertain date, may have had similar functions though the finishing and rims are different and they are not bell-shaped (Gempeler 1992, pp. 181–82, figs. 113:1, 7, 114:3).

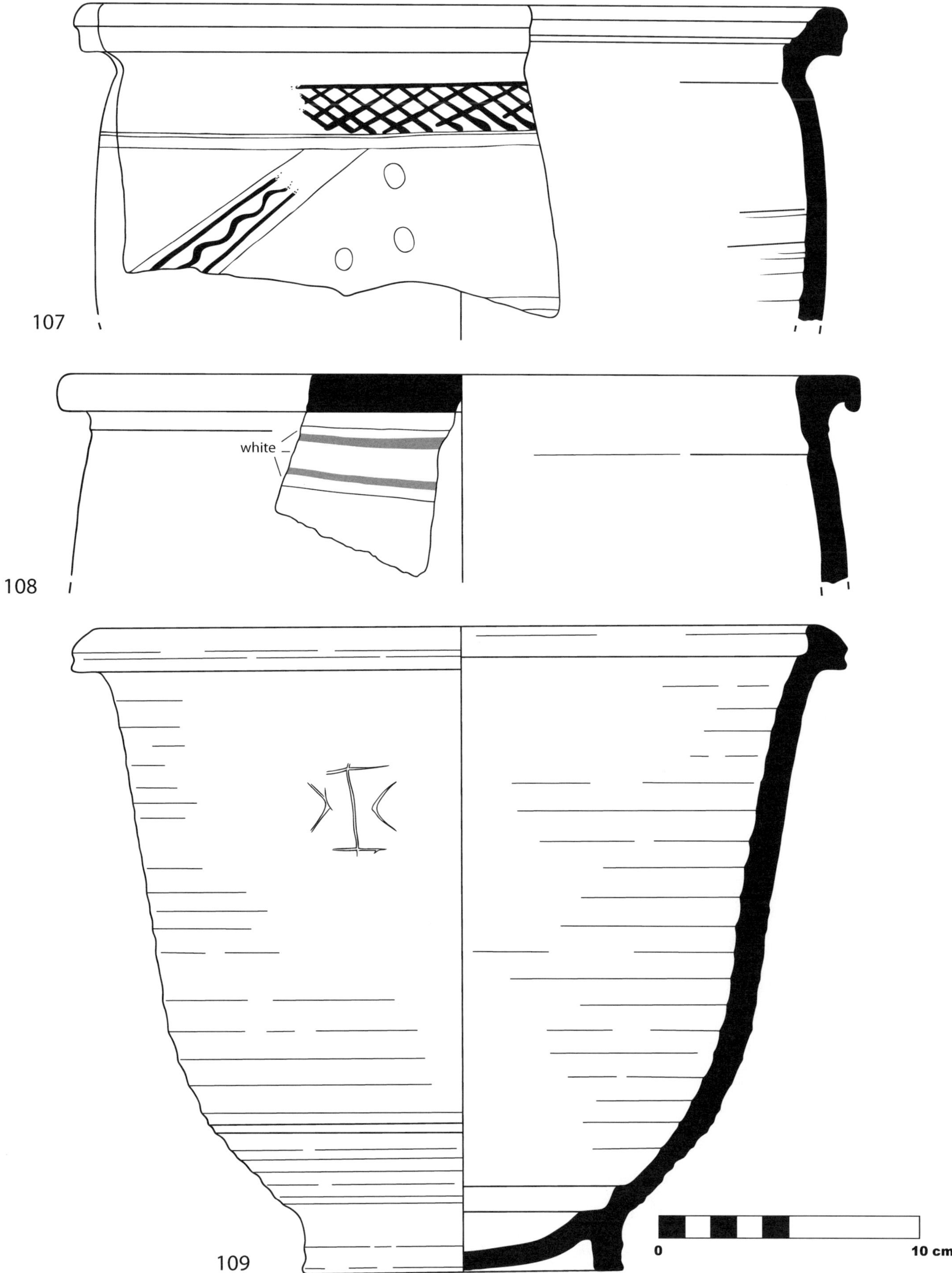

Figure 28. Silt large deep bowls, or "kraters"

Figure 29. Silt Large Deep Bowls, or "Kraters," and Vats

110. Krater, surfaces blackened. Fabric 5YR 6/4. Silt; abundant small red and sand bits, some medium-size sand. Dump 2, locus 10 (ash around "SW tabun").

111. Krater(?), very rough, combed surface. Exterior 7.5YR 4/2, interior fired to 7.5YR 5/4, gray core. Silt; much chaff; a few white bits. Building 177, Room A, surface.

112. Krater with grooved rim, red slip. Fabric 2.5YR 6/6, slip 10R 5/6. Silt; sand, a few small white and black bits, chaff. Dump 1, locus 2 (ash).

113. Large krater, grooved rim, red slip, black painted decoration below rim, rim blackened. Fabric 10R 6/8 to 6/6, slip 10R 4/8 to 5/6. Silt; black bits and chunks; red and white chunks; perhaps chaff. Building 177, Room A, locus 5. From the 1992 season, see a smaller krater with a similar squarish rim and some paint traces (Heidorn 1995, p. 78, fig. 28:a). There are several "kraters" from Biʾr Minayh, but number 46, of red-brown Nile silt fabric with a reddish slip and black and white painted decoration, from tumulus no. 1, is the closest match for any of the Bir Umm Fawakhir vessels (Lassányi 2010b, pp. 278, 280, no. 46). Note a somewhat smaller (dia. 32 cm) large bowl, brown fabric with some mica, orange exterior and painted brown-purple lines from the Amarna area (Faiers 2005, p. 192, fig. 3.7:46).

114. Decorated sherd, perhaps from a krater or a globular jar, very smooth, black paint on dirty white paint and red slip or paint. Red surface 10R 5/6, gray core 10R 3/1. Silt. Dump 1, locus 7. This is a very common kind of decoration. For dating, see Pierrat 1996 for examples from the end of the fourth to the end of the fifth century, and Gempeler 1992 for examples datable to the second to third quarters of the fifth century. A good parallel for the design may be seen on a very large pot from Kellia, indirectly dated to the seventh century (Egloff 1977, p. 140, pl. 74:5).

115. Very large vat, diameter > 50 cm. Surfaces 10R 5/6 with 10R 4/1 gray core. Silt; sand, many black bits; chaff. Dump 1, top 5 cm. See a very large silt vessel with the same "unusual" rim from the Seti temple at Gurna (Myśliwiec 1987, pp. 154, 156–57, no. 1955). A group of "large, thick-walled storage jars of varying shape" is noted from the Wadi Qitna cemetery (immediately south of Kalabsha), generally dated to the second half of the third through the fifth century, and one of them, P775, red-brown fabric, is similar to our 115 (Strouhal 1984, pp. 118–19).

116. Basin or vat. Interior dark brown 10R 4/3, exterior 2.5YR 6/2 to dark gray 10R 5/1. Silt; some white bits; chaff; chunks (unmixed clay?). Dump 1, locus 4. A possible parallel is Elephantine type K512, a very deep, heavy basin of pink fabric with a red slip, second quarter of the fifth and probably into the seventh century (Gempeler 1992, p. 182, fig. 114:1).

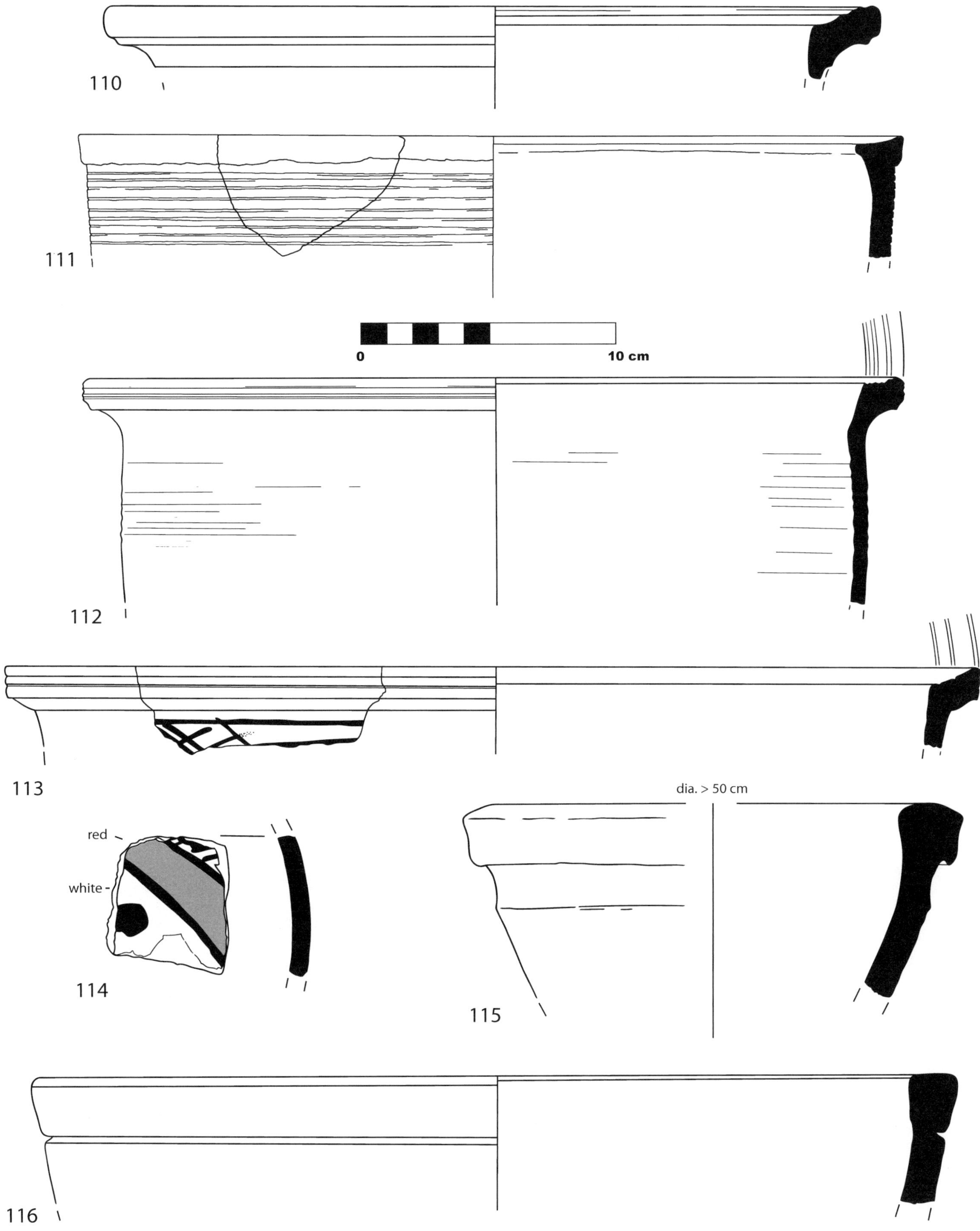

Figure 29. Silt large deep bowls, or "kraters," and vats

Figure 30. Silt Vats and Basins

117. Vat. Gray 2.5YR 4/1. Silt; chaff, medium amount small to medium-size sandy bits, no black bits visible. Building 93, Room B west, locus 3.

118. Basin with club rim, sooted interior. Exterior surface 10R 4/8, fabric 10R 6/8 to 6/2. Silt; abundant fine white and black bits. Dump 2, locus 4 (middle strip). There is a similar large, open, silt vessel from the Seti temple at Gurna (Myśliwiec 1987, pp. 154, 156, no. 1954).

119. Basin with club rim, red-brown slip, blackened. Fabric 2.5YR 5/4 to 5/2 at core. Silt; abundant medium-size to large white bits; some medium-size red bits, a few medium-size black bits. Dump 2, locus 9 ("pot 1"). A silt bowl with a "short, everted, squared rim" from the Amarna area is quite similar and may be datable to the fifth century by comparison to examples from Ashmunein (Faiers 2005, p. 102, fig. 2.20:170). If the sides were more slanted it would resemble a basin from Elephantine, type K516, rare, probably fifth–sixth century (Gempeler 1992, p. 183, fig. 115:8).

120. Basin with club rim, red slip. Core and surface 2.5YR 5/6. Silt; white bits, a few black bits. Building 93, Room C northeast, locus 2. For a similar shape, see a large marl basin from the 1996–1997 corpus (Meyer and Heidorn 2011, p. 118, fig. 31:95). See also the parallel from the Seti Gurna temple for 118.

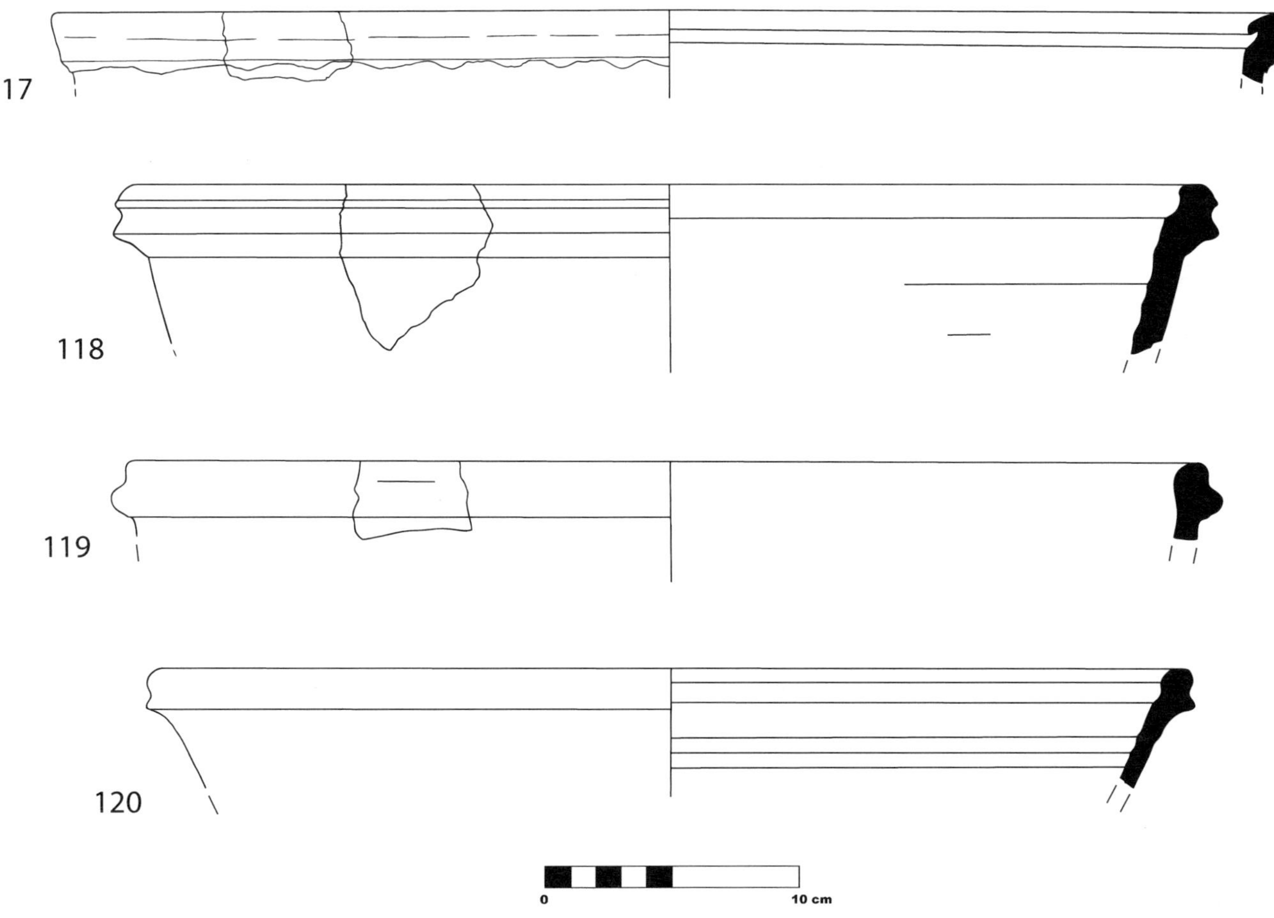

Figure 30. Silt vats and basins

Figure 31. Silt Basin and Jars

121. Basin with club rim, red slip, diagonal gouge on outside. Slip 2.5YR 5/6 exterior and interior, fabric 5YR 6/4. Silt; sand, small black and white bits, a few white chunks. Building 93, Room C northwest, locus 18. There are similar vessels from previous seasons: a plain krater with similar rim; and a "wide-mouth jar" with a channeled rim, reddish fabric (Heidorn 1995, p. 84, fig. 29:h; Heidorn 2000, p. 88, fig. 57:87).

122. Jar rim and part of neck. Fabric 2.5YR 6/8, gray core 2.5YR 5/1. Silt; fine black and white sand, some medium-size black and white bits. Building 93, Room E, locus 2. A silt jar with an "everted pulley rim" from Amarna is quite similar in form but a little thicker (Faiers 2005, p. 125, fig. 2.34:259).

123. Jar(?) 2.5YR 5/8. Silt; medium black and white bits. Building 93, locus uncertain.

124. Jar rim and neck. 7.5R 5/6. Silt, well fired and fine tempered; few small black bits. Building 177, Room A, locus 7 (screen). See the top half of a small jar with black and white painted decoration, fine "metallic" silt fabric, from the 1996–1997 seasons (Meyer and Heidorn 2011, p. 146, fig. 45:244). A possible parallel from Shenshef preserves more of the vessel. It has a globular, ridged body, silt fabric, mouth diameter greater than the Bir Umm Fawakhir example, thin wash running to base of neck on inside and out, fifth to early sixth century (Tomber 1998, p. 176, fig. 6-6:65).

125. Jar(?) with ridged neck. 2.5YR 5/6. Silt(?); small to medium-size white bits, a few medium-size red and black bits. Dump 1, locus 12. The closest example from a previous seasons is probably a silt jar with a similar rim but a thicker body (Meyer and Heidorn 2011, p. 148, fig. 46:246). The ridged neck and profiled rim resemble some of the *qawadis* from Amarna, but the fabric of number 125 differs from the "corky" silt Amarna fabric (Faiers 2005, p. 151, fig. 2.50:355, 358–60).

126. Large jar. Surfaces 2.5YR 4/4, core 2.5YR 4/6 to 10R 4/6 to 7.5YR 5/1 at rim. Silt; white and black bits, mica. Dump 1, locus 2. See perhaps some short-necked silt jars from the Seti temple at Gurna, all published examples painted, no. 1681 for rim shape and no. 1715 and similar for the vessel shape (Myśliwiec 1987, pp. 140–43). A good parallel may be seen in a Nile silt cooking pot from Ashmunein (Bailey 1996, p. 65, pl. 9:8). D. Bailey says that "despite the clay source being Nile silt and the utilitarian nature of the product these vessels are beautifully made, lightweight, and presumably strong" (Bailey 1996, pp. 64–65). There are some much smaller two-handled pots with similar rims and upper bodies, red-brown fabric, type K409, late first to third century (Gempeler 1992, p. 169, fig. 101:12–13).

127. Jar. 2.5YR 5/6. Silt; fine black bits, a few large black bits. Building 177, Room C west, locus 1. See perhaps a silt cooking pot with a lid-seated rim inside and a ribbed body (not preserved on 127) from Amarna (Faiers 2005, p. 119, fig. 2.30:226).

128. Globular jar with grooved rim, gritty surfaces. 7.5YR 5/6. Silt; abundant black and white bits, some medium-size white bits (quartz). Building 177, Room D west, locus 2. From the 1996–1997 corpus, see a silt "casserole" with a short neck and thin walls (Meyer and Heidorn 2011, p. 122, fig. 33:123). A Late Roman silt "globular cooking pot with upright, double-lip, lid-seat rim" is published from Mons Porphyrites (Tomber 2001, p. 291, fig. 6.23:51). See perhaps some globular silt jars with short, vertical necks from the Seti Gurna temple, dated to the fifth–seventh century (Myśliwiec 1987, pp. 146, 148, nos. 1817, 1820). For a parallel from Esna, see a jar with similar shape and rim but painted, fabric Ib, sixth century or later (Jacquet 1972, pl. 225:25). There is a similar orange-brown silt cooking pot from the Ashmunein South Church site, dated later than A.D. 450 (Bailey 1996, pp. 65, 67, pl. 11:41).

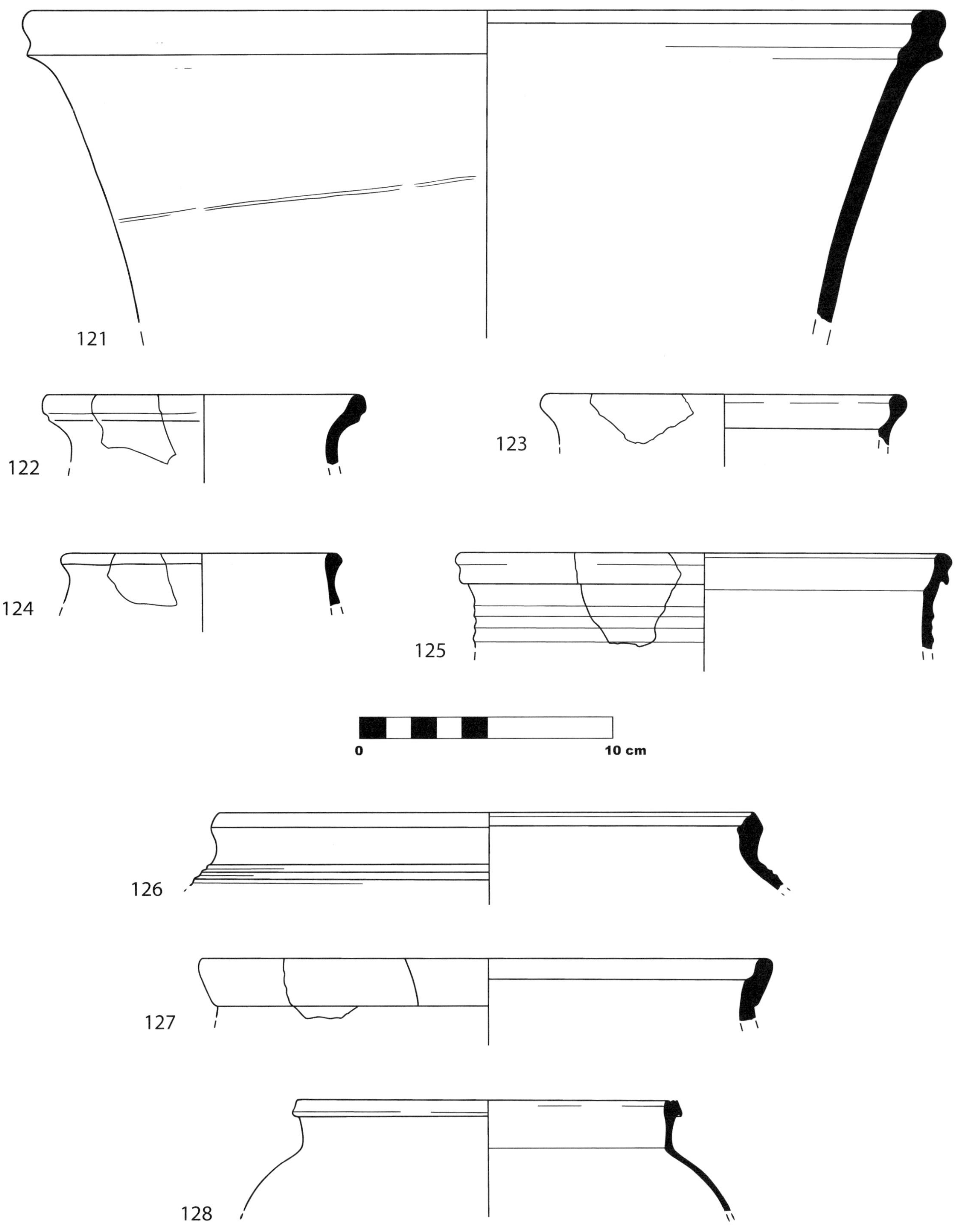

Figure 31. Silt basin and jars

Figure 32. Silt Jars

129. Globular jar, thickness approximate (RN 99/219; pl. 13b). Interior and exterior surfaces 10R 5/6. Silt; cannot see temper. Dump 1, locus 17, found with no. 135 (pl. 7). From the 1996–1997 corpus, see a globular silt cooking pot and a similar though ribbed pot (Meyer and Heidorn 2011, pp. 118, 142, figs. 31:101, 43:223). The latter may be compared to a cooking pot from Shenshef, very fine Nile silt, exterior ribbed, fifth and probably into sixth century (Tomber 1998, p. 176, fig. 6-6:66). Pot 1822 from the Seti Gurna temple corpus (Myśliwiec 1987, p. 146) is similar but has no good dating. Another possible parallel is a closed pot from Elephantine, type K476, red-brown fabric, uncommon, date uncertain (Gempeler 1992, p.179, fig. 112:1). A "cook pot" from Akoris, early sixth century, seems to have a rim that is curled or lipped inward but the shape is otherwise quite similar, even to the rounded base. No drawing is provided with the photograph, however (Kawanishi and Tsujimura 1988, pp. 27, 31, pl. 17:2). The form of jar number 129, which is quite simple, has even earlier parallels, such as a Ptolemaic (second century B.C.) pot from Tôd, *remblai* no. 2, made of silt with vegetal and mineral temper, ranging in color from red-pink to orange-red, thicker shoulder, no base preserved (Pierrat-Bonnefois 2000, p. 324, fig. 277).

130. Jar, exterior smoothed but still somewhat rough, sooted. 2.5YR 5/6. Silt; chaff, abundant black and white bits, some medium-size white bits. Dump 2, locus 10. See discussion of number 129, above.

131. Jar with ridged neck. Core and surfaces 2.5YR 5/6. Silt; fine sand, white bits, a few black bits. Dump 2, locus 2.

132. Large jar. Fabric and surface 2.5YR 5/6. Silt: fine red and white bits. Building 177, Room D west, surface. A wide-mouthed silt jar with two grooves on the outside of the rim, from Amarna, undated surface find, is very similar (Faiers 2005, p. 127, fig. 2.34:267).

133. Large jar, slipped exterior and into interior of rim. Fabric 2.5YR 4/6 with same color slip; unslipped interior surface 7.5YR 7/3. Silt, coarse; chaff, large white (limestone?) bits and quartz. Building 93, Room D, locus 3. There is a cooking pot from Biʾr Minayh with a similar, gently everted rim, silt fabric, reddish pink wash inside and out, excavated from trench 01/5 locus 1 (Lassányi 2010b, pp. 282–83, no. 60)

134. Large jar, slipped exterior and into interior rim. Fabric 2.5YR 5/6, slip 7.5YR (worn). Silt; sandy, abundant medium-size and large white bits (limestone and sand), a few medium-size red bits. Building 93, Room D, locus 3.

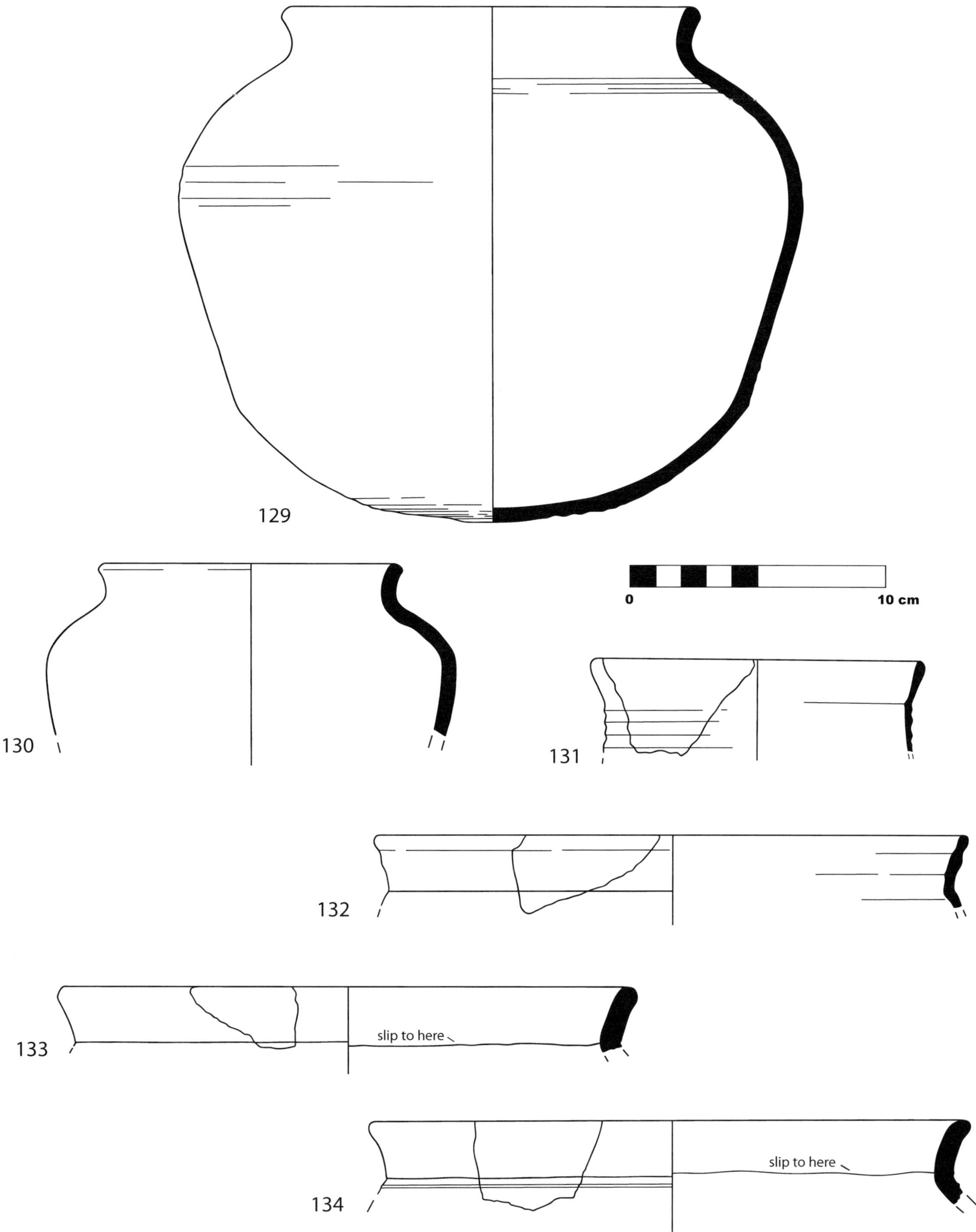

Figure 32. Silt jars

Figure 33. Silt Jars (cont.)

135. Jar with five holes in bottom, possibly for making cheese; thickness approximate (RN 99/220; pl. 14). Exterior 5YR 6/2. Silt, cannot see temper. Dump 1, locus 17, found with jar number 129 (pl. 7). There are some similar baggy storage jars or *qawadis* from from the Seti temple at Gurna, for example, no. 2044, but the bases are missing (Myśliwiec 1987, pp. 166–67). Likewise from Elephantine, type K438 is a large, baggy pot, red-brown fabric, one example and that lacking a base, date uncertain (Gempeler 1992, p. 174, fig. 106:7). Some vessels from Amarna have holes pierced in the bottoms, but the shapes are quite different (Faiers 2005, pp. 162–63, 206–07, figs. 2.58:424–25, 3.14:103); some are more like colanders (Faiers 2005, pp. 147–48, fig. 2.48:350–52).

It is tentatively suggested that the pair of vessels, numbers 129 and 135, were used for making cheese. The wide-mouth pot 129 could have held milk, and jar 135 could have drained the whey. Making cheese would have been a good solution to the problem of keeping milk in a hot desert. There is also some evidence for consumption of cheese at a desert site. A corpus of ostraca and other texts from the monastery at Wadi Sarga, on the edge of the desert 24 kilometers south of Asyut (Thompson 1922, p. 1), is most interesting in respect to food supplies. Wine is by far the most important commodity, accounting for about fifty-two references, followed by grain with about eighteen. Cheese is mentioned five times (Crum and Bell 1922, pp. 137, 153, 155, 180), roughly as often as dates, oil, bread or loaves, and "pickle." The biggest single receipt of cheese seems to have been "16 *orgon* of cheese, 6 *askalone*[19] of cheese" (Crum and Bell 1922, pp. 152–53). Vinegar, beans, vegetables, lentils, meat, salt fish, salt, and honey have only one or two mentions each (Crum and Bell 1922). The texts are slightly later than Bir Umm Fawakhir, which is to say early seventh into the early eighth century (Crum and Bell 1922, p. 9), but they do present an interesting picture of food and other supplies carried to a site on the desert edge, mostly by camel loads.

136. Large jar with lightly ridged shoulder. Exterior 10R 5/6, interior 10R 4/3 (grayish). Silt, very coarse; sand, white and black chunks, chaff. Building 93, Room D, locus 3. For the shape, see perhaps two large marl jars from the 1996–1997 corpus (Meyer and Heidorn 2011, pp. 142, 150, figs. 43:222 and 47:253). This could conceivably be the top of a *qadus*; cf. Tôd (Pierrat 1996, p. 200, pl. 7:97), but without the base it is impossible to know.

137. Jar with slightly ridged shoulder and incised Vs or Xs, slipped. Fabric 10R 5/6 to grayish 10R 4/2, slip blackened or smudged 10R 5/6. Silt, coarse; chaff, very large red chunks, many medium-size red and white bits. Building 93, Room D, locus 3. There are some silt jars with short, flaring rims from the Seti temple at Gurna with painted (not incised) decoration, dated approximately to the fifth to early seventh century (Myśliwiec 1987, pp. 140–41, nos. 1699–1700). For a possible parallel from Esna, see a large storage jar with a different rim but incised lines, fabric III, sixth century or later (Jacquet 1972, pl. 224:6).

[19] The *askalonion* was a measure used for wine or cheese, but what that amount may have been is not known (Crum and Bell 1922, p. 20).

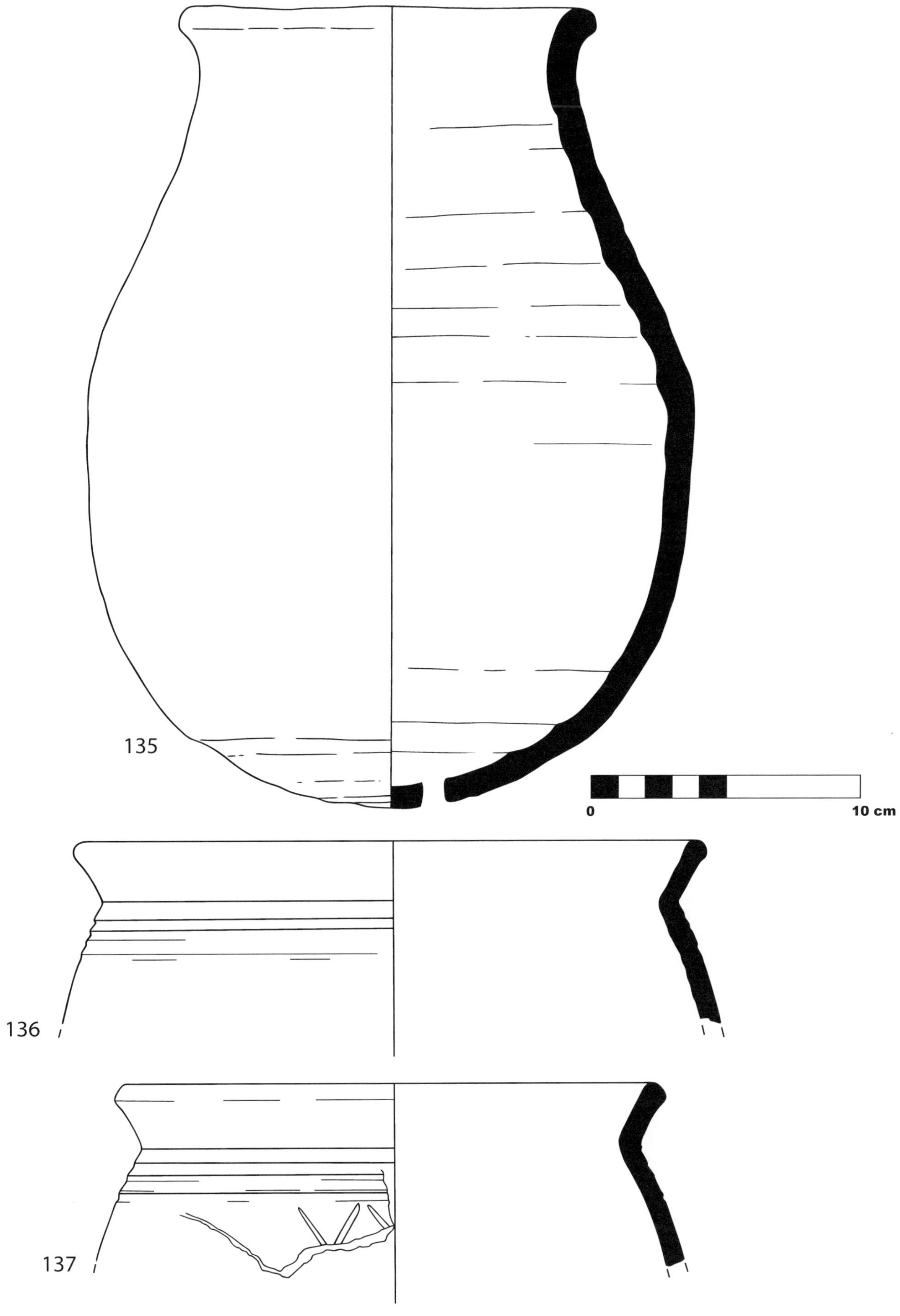

Figure 33. Silt jars

Figure 34. Silt and Uncertain Fabrics

138. Large, red-slipped jar with remnant black paint (RN 99/234; pl. 32b). More sherds from same vessel found but not drawn. Fabric 2.5YR 6/6, slip 7.5YR 6/6. Silt, somewhat porous; small black and white bits, chaff. Surface find in dump behind Building 61. From Mons Porphyrites, Lycabettos Ramp, Late Roman, see perhaps a silt "wide mouth bowl or jar" with similar form but different decoration (Tomber 2001, p. 282, fig. 6.19:8). There is a similar silt jar, no. 1571, from the Seti temple at Gurna with worn dark brown-violet decoration; see perhaps jar no. 1662 as well (Myśliwiec 1987, pp. 132–33, 139–40). There are some very similar shapes from Amarna, fifth–sixth century in date, M2 fabric (hard to fine silt, red-brown with thin red/black core), sloppily decorated in different red and black patterns (Faiers 2005, pp. 134, 138, fig. 2.42:283–86). The decorations differ from the Bir Umm Fawakhir jar though similar looped painting may be seen on other sherds (Faiers 2005, pp. 143, 145, 194, figs. 2.47:327, 329 and 3.8:62, 64). See also a coarser variant from the Ashmunein Church site, perhaps early seventh century (Bailey 1996, pp. 83–84, pl. 25:1). A jar from Esna has a neck that slopes in rather than standing vertical like the Bir Umm Fawakhir example, and different decoration, fabric III, probably later than A.D. 500 (Jacquet-Gordon 1972, pl. 223:G10).

139. Bottle with very narrow opening, thick red slip, black paint on interior of mouth flange. Fabric 5YR 6/8. Silt. Dump 1, locus 1. This sort of sherd remains something of a puzzle. From the 1993 season, see the "base of a small jar" with a thick, red, burnished slip; the center is broken away, but if flipped it might be a bottle neck with extremely small opening (Heidorn 1995, p. 87; fig. 30:g). On the other hand, the "small, high base" with a "waxy red slip inside and out" from the 1996–1997 corpus is complete enough to show that it was a closed base (Meyer and Heidorn 2011, p. 132, fig. 37:174). There is also a marl bottle neck and mouth with a different rim shape but a similarly very narrow opening (Meyer and Heidorn 2011, p. 136, fig. 40:194), so bottles with extremely restricted openings are reasonably well attested at Bir Umm Fawakhir. There is a single parallel at Elephantine, a silt flask rim and neck, pink fabric, type T709, third–fourth century (Gempeler 1992, p. 134, fig. 76:13).

Bases

In the vessels where bases are preserved, many are rounded or convex rather than footed. Thus a rounded base broken into small sherds would be nearly unidentifiable. The ring bases illustrated here could have come from a range of deep cups, bowls, or jugs.

140. Ring base, blackened. Surfaces 7.5YR 7/6 to 10YR 3/1, core dark gray 10YR 3/2. Silt; sand, red and black bits. Dump 1, locus 7.

141. Ring base. Exterior 7.5YR 6/4, interior 7.5YR 5/4, core 7.5YR 6/6 to 10YR 4/1 (gray). Silt; sand, mica, white bits. Building 177, Room A, locus 12.

142. Ring base. Exterior 5YR 7/8, interior 5YR 5/6, core 2.5YR 5/6. Silt; black and white bits. Building 177, Room A, locus 12.

143. Ring base. Interior 2.5YR 5/4, exterior 2.5YR 5/6, core 2.5YR 4/8. Silt; white and black bits, much mica on surface, some red bits. Dump 2, locus 2.

144. Ring base, jar(?). Exterior 7.5YR 6/4 to 10R 5/4, interior 10R 5/4, core 2.5YR 5/6. Silt. Building 177, Room A, locus 7.

145. Large, high ring base. Core 2.5YR 5/4, surface 2.5YR 6/4 (whitish coating or concretion, hard to see surface). Silt, hard fired; sand, white, black, and red bits. Dump 1, locus 4.

Uncertain Fabric

146. Bowl, surface smoothed but still somewhat rough. 2.5YR 6/8. Mixed clay(?); chaff, abundant medium-size black and white (limestone?) bits. Building 177, Room A, locus 12 to gebel. There is a parallel in a deep cup from the Deir al-Barsha survey, silt B2 fabric with red-slipped interior and exterior, burnished, dated to sixth century by reference to Ashmunein (Op de Beeck and Hendrickx 2011, p. 344, no. 43). Lecuyot and Pierrat (1992, pp. 174–75, fig. 2, middle left) published a similar deep bowl of mixed clay (perhaps silt and Aswan kaolinite) but gave it a late date, mid-seventh to mid-ninth century.

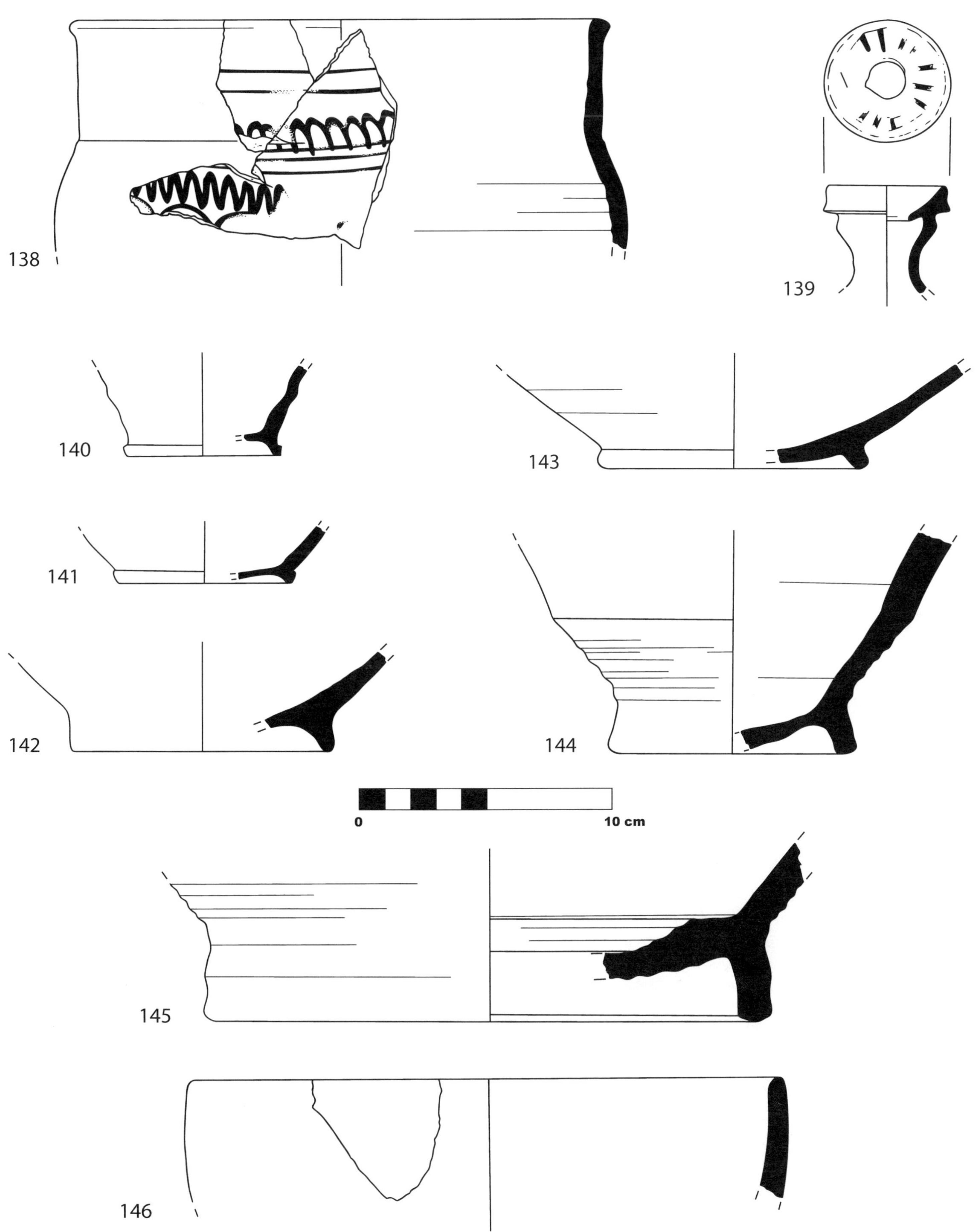

Figure 34. Silt and uncertain fabrics

Figure 35. Uncertain Fabrics and Amphoras

Uncertain Fabrics

147. Rim of small bowl or jar(?), slight groove under rim filled with black paint. 2.5YR 5/8. Uncertain ware; black and white (quartz) bits. Dump 2, locus 11 (exterior of pot 2).

148. Rim of jar. Gray-brown fabric 5YR 6/4, creamy surface 2.5Y 8/2. Uncertain ware; small black bits. Building 93, Room C, locus 18 northwest.

Amphoras

Amphoras were very common at Bir Umm Fawakhir, but there were many examples of a few types. The most common was the Late Roman Amphora 1 (LRA1) type, many sherds of which are included in the section on dipinti in *Chapter 4*. For reference, two complete examples of Late Roman 1 amphoras with dipinti from earlier seasons (Heidorn 2000, p. 39, fig. 59:111; Meyer 2011, p. 155, fig. 49) are reproduced in figure 36. In addition to the parallels cited in previous publications, there are several Late Roman 1 amphoras from Biʾr Minayh, including two amphoras from a grave or the vicinity of a grave at Biʾr Minayh (Lassányi 2010b, pp. 284–85, nos. 71–79). This supports our earlier observation of large quantities of big amphora sherds in the vicinity of graves at Bir Umm Fawakhir.

Cheese and other foodstuffs were briefly noted with the "cheese pot" number 135, above, but the Wadi Sarga texts are especially interesting in regard to the wine supply to a monastery on the desert fringe. Wadi Sarga is about 24 kilometers south of Asyut and dates to the early seventh to early eighth century (Crum and Bell 1922, p. 9), a little later than Bir Umm Fawakhir. At Wadi Sarga, however, not only is wine by far the most abundantly attested commodity with at least fifty-two references, but the amounts are impressive. The wine jars are not carried in by the camel load but by the camel caravan, "sixty-eight large measures" of wine on one occasion (Crum and Bell 1922, p. 159) or 115 *cnidia*[20] on another (Crum and Bell 1922, p. 160).

Late Roman 1 amphoras were produced on Rhodes, Cyprus, and in southeastern Turkey (Cilicia), and perhaps northwest Syria, and some copies even in Egypt (Pieri 2005, p. 80). In the fifth through seventh centuries, a variant with a vertical neck (LRA1B) was by far the most common type of amphora in the eastern Mediterranean (Pieri 2005, p. 76). Aston (2007, pp. 434–38) refines this somewhat and says that vessels of this form (LRA1) originated in Cyprus, the Cilician coast of Turkey, and Syria, and they are generally datable to the sixth to seventh centuries.

149. Late Roman Amphora 5, neck, shoulder, handles, exterior described as ridged. Exterior slip 10YR 7/2, surfaces 5YR 5/8 with gray core. Tempered with sand, white chunks, a little black. Building 93, Room C northwest, locus 11. This type of amphora is reported from a wide range of sites in Egypt. At Esna there is a baggy amphora, fabric VI (pink to salmon red with white or beige surface), sixth century or later (Jacquet 1972, pl. 227:11). From Elephantine, Gempeler (1992, pp. 199–200, fig. 124:3) describes a baggy, round amphora type K766, clay type VI or VII, not common at Elephantine but datable to the late sixth to seventh century, perhaps comparable to Abu Mena amphoras. See perhaps some amphoras from Antinoopolis with shorter necks and square rims, yellowish white clay, fine and compact fabric, broadly dated to the fifth–seventh centuries (Guidotti 2008, pp. 353, 404, no. 371). At Kellia, examples dated to the seventh century are said to have come from Abu Mena, about 50 km away (Egloff 1977, pp. 117–18, pl. 60:4).

    In general, bag-shaped Late Roman 5 amphoras were manufactured over such a long time span, from the fourth to the tenth centuries (with earlier prototypes), in such a variety of more or less squat or slender forms, that it is hard to devise a solid typology and dating (Pieri 2005, pp. 114–15). The Late Roman 5 amphora type is of Palestinian origin, but amphoras of this shape were produced in Egypt (Alexandria) from the late sixth century A.D. through the seventh century (Mareotis region and Abu Mina) and even as late as the second half of the twelfth century (central Sinai) (Dixneuf 2011b, p. 143).

    The most distinctive surviving feature of number 149 is the handles high on the shoulder, almost touching the base of the neck. It may therefore be Pieri's variant "Type 3" of Late Roman 5, which has a bright orange to light beige fabric and sandy temper with quartz and calcite [*sic*]. The form was widely distributed from Albania to Istanbul, throughout Palestine, Jordan, and Egypt, and may be datable to the early sixth to the end of the seventh centuries (Pieri 2005, pp. 117, 119–21).

150. Late Roman Amphora 7, Egyptian amphora body segment (pl. 40a). Reconstructed in field lab (lab-7; see *Chapter 7*), color and temper not noted. Silt. Surface find. This common type of amphora is generally dated to the sixth and seventh centuries (Elephantine: Gempeler 1992, pp. 195–96, fig. 126:7; Seti temple at Gurna: Myśliwiec 1987, pp. 163–64, no. 2024; Epiphanius:

[20] The κνίδιον was a measure used apparently only for wine, at least at Wadi Sarga (Crum and Bell 1922, p. 22)

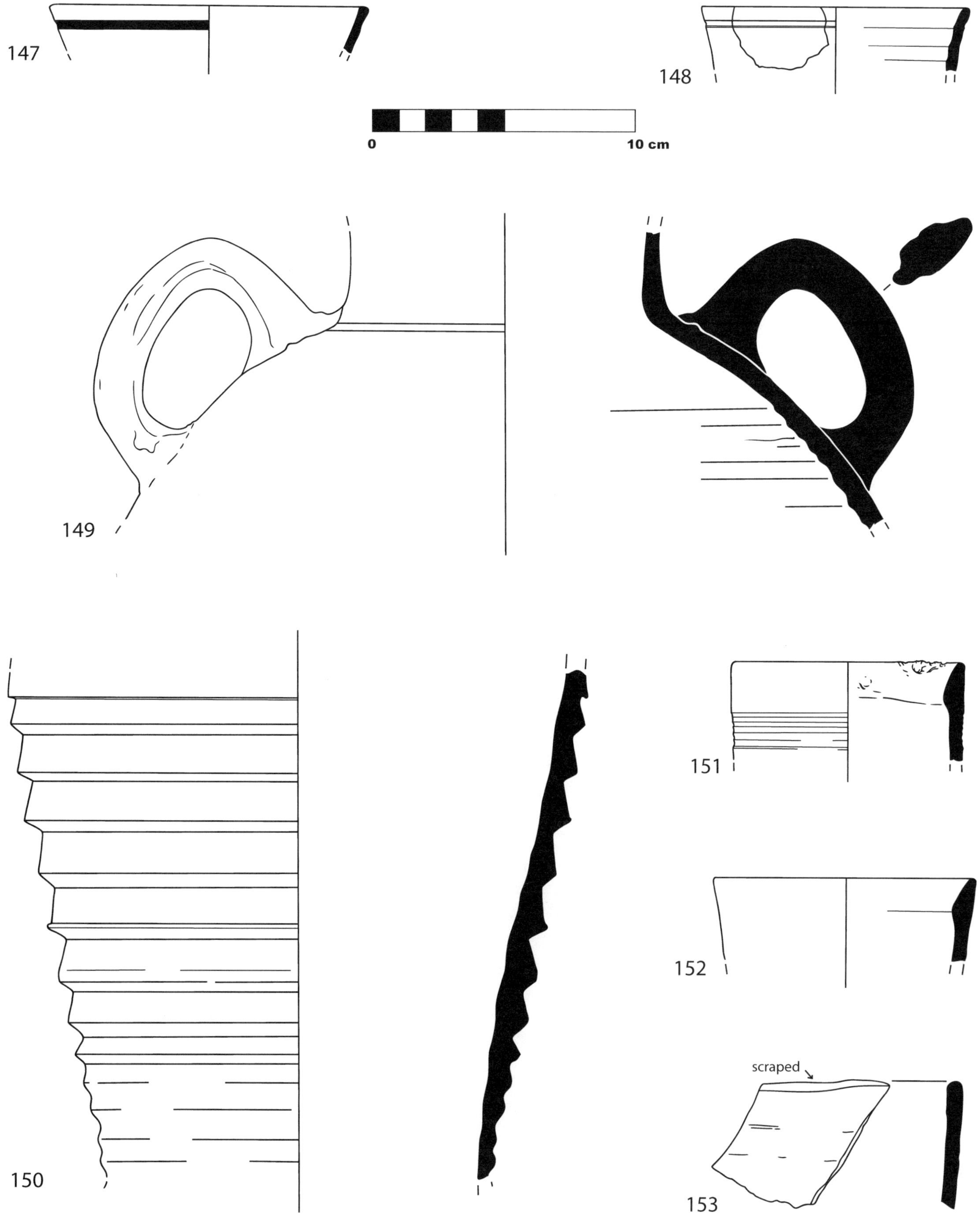

Figure 35. Uncertain fabrics and amphoras

Figure 35. Uncertain Fabrics and Amphoras (cont.)

Winlock and Crum 1926, pp. 78–79; Esna: Jacquet 1972, pl. 227:4, 7; masses at Antinoopolis: Guerrini 1974, pl. 37:3; Kellia, said to be seventh century: Egloff 1977, pp. 114–15, pl. 58:6; general discussion of Late Roman Amphora 7 type, Ballet and Dixneuf 2004). Aston (2007, p. 424), however, gives a somewhat earlier date, fifth to sixth century. The Late Roman 7 amphoras at Amarna are especially well studied. They were probably used primarily to transport wine and olive oil, but some have been shown to have remains of fish bones, acacia pods, and olives. Once emptied of their original contents, amphoras were often reused for a wide variety of purposes (Pyke 2005). The type is said to be very common in Middle Egypt, though at Elephantine at least half of the tested sherds were made of local clays (Aston 2007, p. 424). Pieri (2005, p. 132) would extend the dating to the fifth through seventh centuries and notes how uncommon the form is outside Egypt. At Wadi Qitna (immediately south of Kalabsha) red-brown amphoras (type B1) were very common, and at least one variant was tall and slender with shingled sides like 150. Strouhal says that "Amphora of the B1 type occurred in practically all graves containing pottery" and many sherds preserved "the original layer of resin which pre[v]ented the liquid contents from leaking through the badly-fired walls and could simultaneously have served to preserve the contents (for example, wine)" (Strouhal 1984, pp. 140–41).

151. Keay's type 55 Tunisian amphora, fine ribs on neck, sloppy finish on interior and rim. Marl type import[?]. Fabric 10R 6/6, grayish core 10R 6/3. Tempered with abundant black bits, some white bits. Building 93, Room C northwest, locus 15. Keay's type 55 is dated from the end of the fifth through the first half of the sixth century, ca. 500–650 A.D. (Keay 1984, pp. 91, 289–93). There is a good parallel for the shape of 151 at a small site near Deir al-Atrash in the Eastern Desert, fabric 10YR 5/3 fired to pale orange at edges, cream colored (10YR 7/4) exterior (Sidebotham, Zitterkopf, and Riley 1991, pp. 614–15, fig. 35:103). The best parallel from Carthage has a straight neck with fine exterior ribs and a thickened interior rim, though the thickened part is more of a ridge than a triangle. It is called a *spatheion* and dates later than ca. A.D. 475–500 (Peacock 1984, p. 135, fig. 40:66).

152. Keay's type 55 Tunisian amphora, well smoothed, tough fabric. Surfaces 7.5YR 7/2, fabric 2.5YR 6/6 to 6/4. Very fine, sandy temper. Building 93, Room C northwest, locus 3. See parallels for 151, above.

153. Amphora sherd used as scraper. Building 93, Room C northwest, locus 16.

Amphoras and amphora pieces were used in many secondary contexts. There are several large sherds like 153 that have clearly been worn down on one side, though what they were used for is not known.[21] In Building 93, Rooms B and C, segments of ridged Late Roman 7 amphoras were set in the floor, apparently as potstands, and the kitchen in Dump 2 included the top part of a Late Roman 1 amphora set upside-down next to the tabun. At other sites amphoras were used in wall construction, as at Mons Claudianus, or oven lining or even part of a harbor's "hard," as at Quseir al-Qadim (Peacock and Blue 2006, pp. 70–73).

In conclusion, the sherds presented here confirm the general fifth–sixth century date of Bir Umm Fawakhir. That some forms or styles seem to have begun earlier, in, say, the fourth century, and ended later, in, say, the seventh century is only to be expected. Three complete vessels (numbers 109, 129, and 135) were recovered from some of the lowest levels excavated, but none of them is tightly tied to closely dated vessels elsewhere. Readily datable material such as legible coins or texts has not yet been recovered from Bir Umm Fawakhir, much less from a closed context. We would, however, like to suggest a possible use for some of the vessels. The ribbed pots and casseroles with ledges to support lids have long been identified as cooking pots, but if vessels 129 and 135 were in fact used for making cheese, then we have another identification of at least ad hoc use of two kinds of jars. Given the large number of Late Roman 1 amphoras on site, and hence wine, there should be something to drink it with. In fact, small cups in a variety of wares and finishes, including the distinctive shallow cups with a white slip (e.g., no. 32), form a large part of the corpus, as do some large, deep, often decorated bowls that could have served as "kraters" for mixing wine and water. Testing for residues seems a reasonable next step.

[21] Reused and recycled amphoras or sherds are treated extensively in Peña 2007, including disks and tools or scrapers (pp. 152–59) and hearths or supports (pp. 149–52).

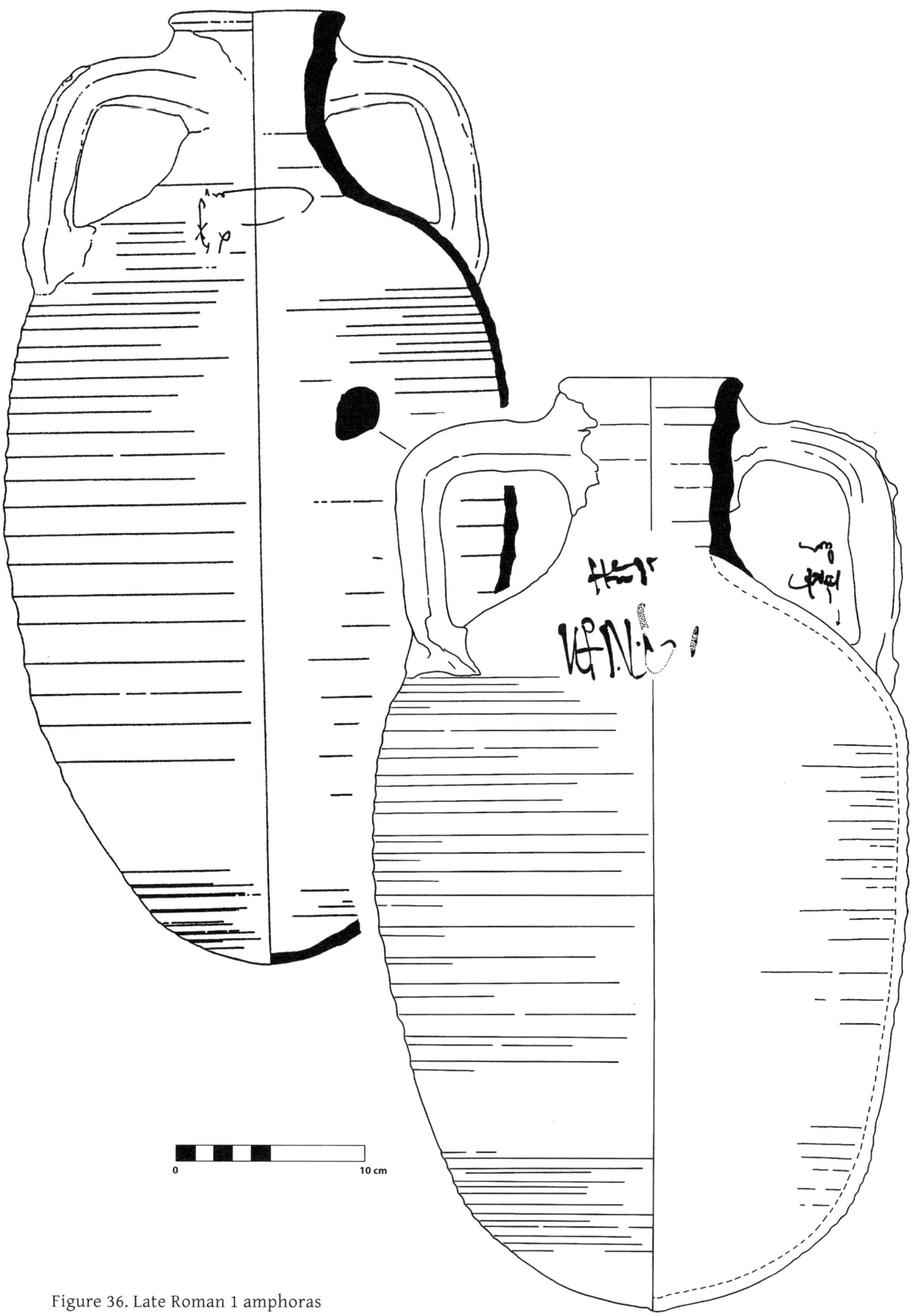

Figure 36. Late Roman 1 amphoras

Chapter 4

Dipinti, Coins, and Small Finds

Carol Meyer

Dipinti

As in the previous survey seasons (Wilfong 2000; Meyer 2011, p. 155, figs. 50–52), many dipinti were recovered, both from the excavations and from the surface (figs. 37–39). Sixty-six in all were tallied, including the Late Roman 1 amphora reused in the Dump 2 kitchen; all are tabulated in *Appendix B*, numbers RN 99/223 through RN 99/225. The dipinti are notations scribbled in red ink on the shoulder, body, and sometimes the neck of Late Roman 1 amphoras. Since the ink is fugitive, the writing highly cursive, and the sherds often small, the dipinti are not very legible.

Fournet and Pieri's 2008 study of the Late Roman 1 amphoras at Antinoopolis indicates that they were used for wine (and not, say, oil or garum) and were scribbled all over in the course of being traded. The inscriptions may be grouped into four types: (a) a large scrawly one on the shoulder in front, (b) another one scribbled above it, (c) names and numbers in small letters under a handle, and sometimes (d) a large-letter inscription on the neck. Type a usually starts with a large Christogram, two or three illegible letters, a vertical slash or cross, and numbers indicating the quantity in the container, so many ξέστησ or *sextarii*. There may also be abbreviations of sacred names such as Θε(όσ) or κύρ(ιοσ) (Fournet and Pieri 2008, pp. 184–202). At Bir Umm Fawakhir, note the Christogram in figure 37d, figure 38g, and the XM that stands for XMΓ (Χριστὸσ Μαρίασ γέννα) in figure 37c (the sherd in figure 39k [RN 99/197] is not strictly a dipinto, but it is shown with them because it has a couple of letters, "XM..."). Fournet and Pieri suggest that "notre mystérieuse séquence [the Christograms, etc.] était superflue" and that the elements, stylized to the point of illegibility, "ne devaient pas cacher des données capitals sur le plan commercial" (Fournet and Pieri 2008, p. 187). The occurrence of such dipinti from Gaul to Egypt does, however, attest to standardization and commercialization on a grand scale. The little inscriptions (type c) generally contain two names (though seldom the same two at Antinoopolis) and some numbers. Gascou, treating the dipinti from Saqqara, reads the first line as a personal name, the second line (at least in the two cases cited) as "potter," and the third line as a number. In this case the small type c inscriptions would relate to the production of amphoras in a given workshop (Gascou 1978, pp. 26–27). Fournet suggests that the name in the second line could be a patronymic. Or, given the generally Greek names such as "Paulos" or "Kyrillos" in the first line versus the more local names such as "Angilas" in the second line, the two names might refer to a major trader or merchant and a local producer. The numbers in the last lines are so high that they could be lot numbers, such as a batch of amphoras or the wine in them. Thus, very tentatively, the little type c inscriptions could pertain to the collection of various local wine sources by a major trader at an emporium on the coast, but the question needs further analysis (Fournet and Pieri 2008, pp. 195–99).

Sites such as Berenice and Bir Umm Fawakhir are large, well supplied, and more or less long-lived, but the presence of Late Roman Amphora 1 sherds and dipinti at Biʾr Minayh attests to the importance of hauling wine amphoras to even the most remote, short-lived sites in the Eastern Desert (Almásy 2010, pp. 194–96; Lassányi 2010, pp. 284–85), or even as far south as Kalabsha South and nearby Wadi Qitna (Strouhal 1984, pp. 154–56; Vidman 1984, pp. 219–22).

A number of type c small inscriptions are shown in figures 37a, 38c, 39c–j. If dipinto 39f (pl. 33a) is indeed to be read "τετρα" and the small inscription in Meyer 2011, figure 49 as "γλ . κ ...," perhaps "four" and "sweet," respectively, then perhaps the little type c inscriptions may at times carry information about the

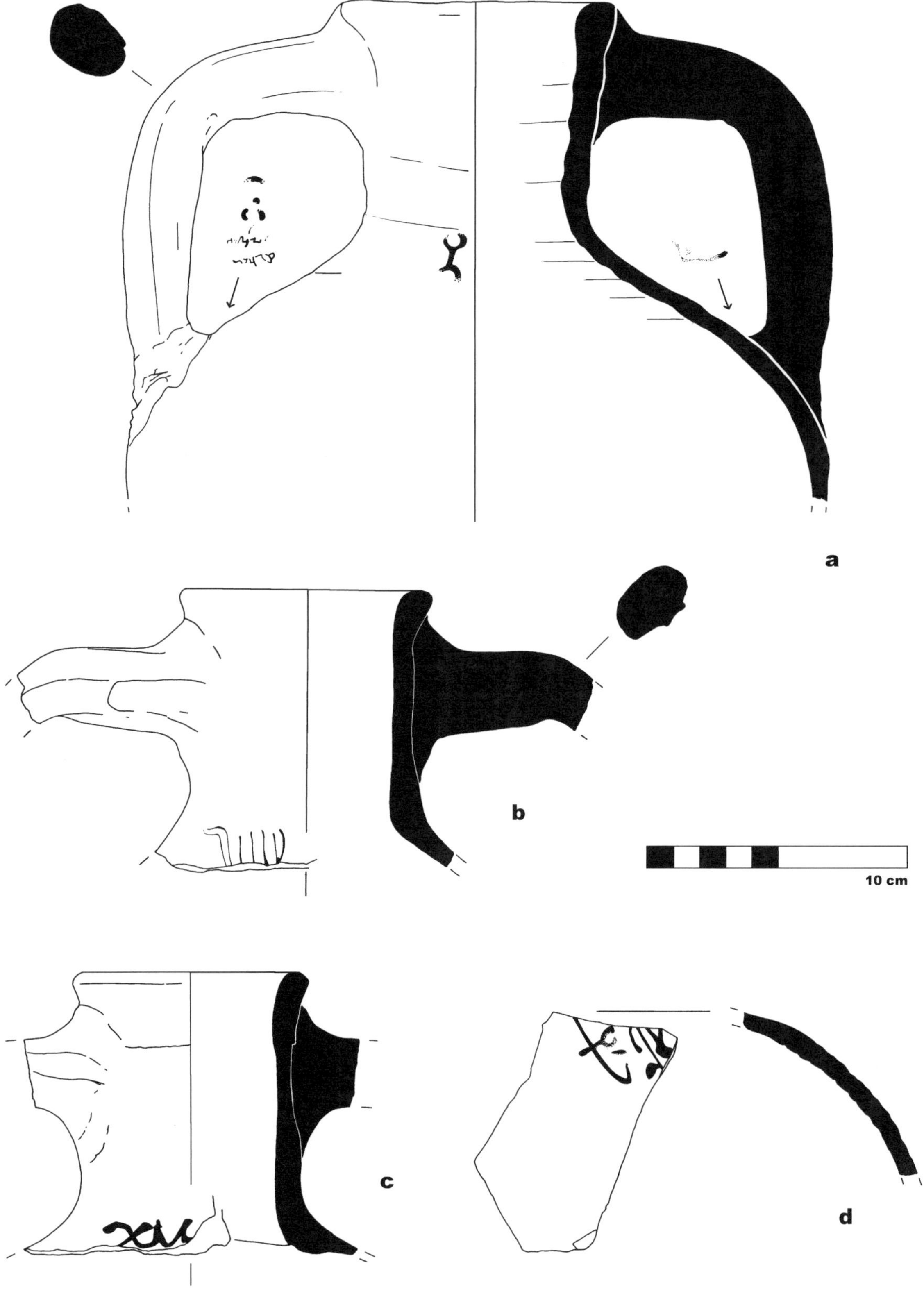

Figure 37. Dipinti

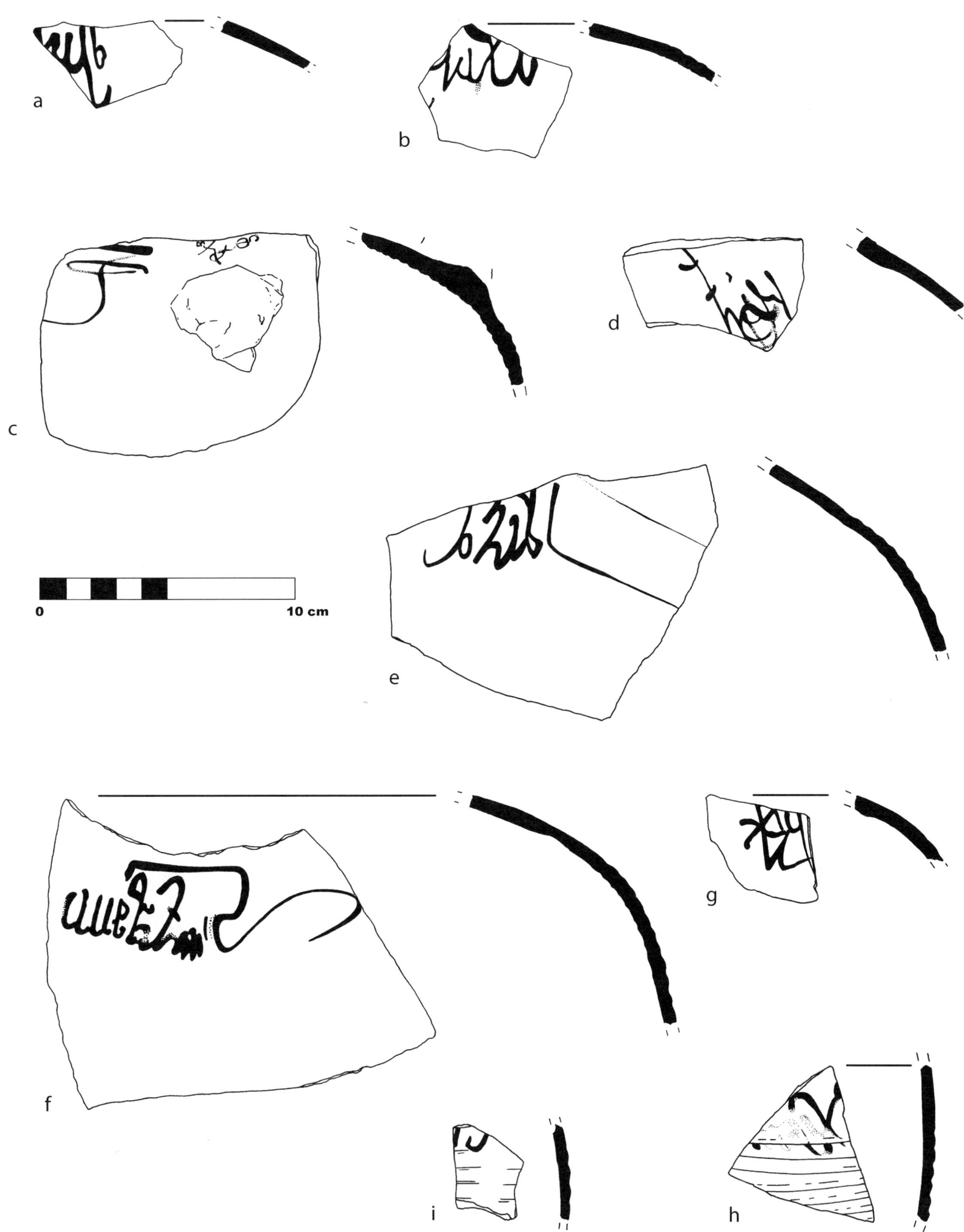

Figure 38. Dipinti (*cont.*)

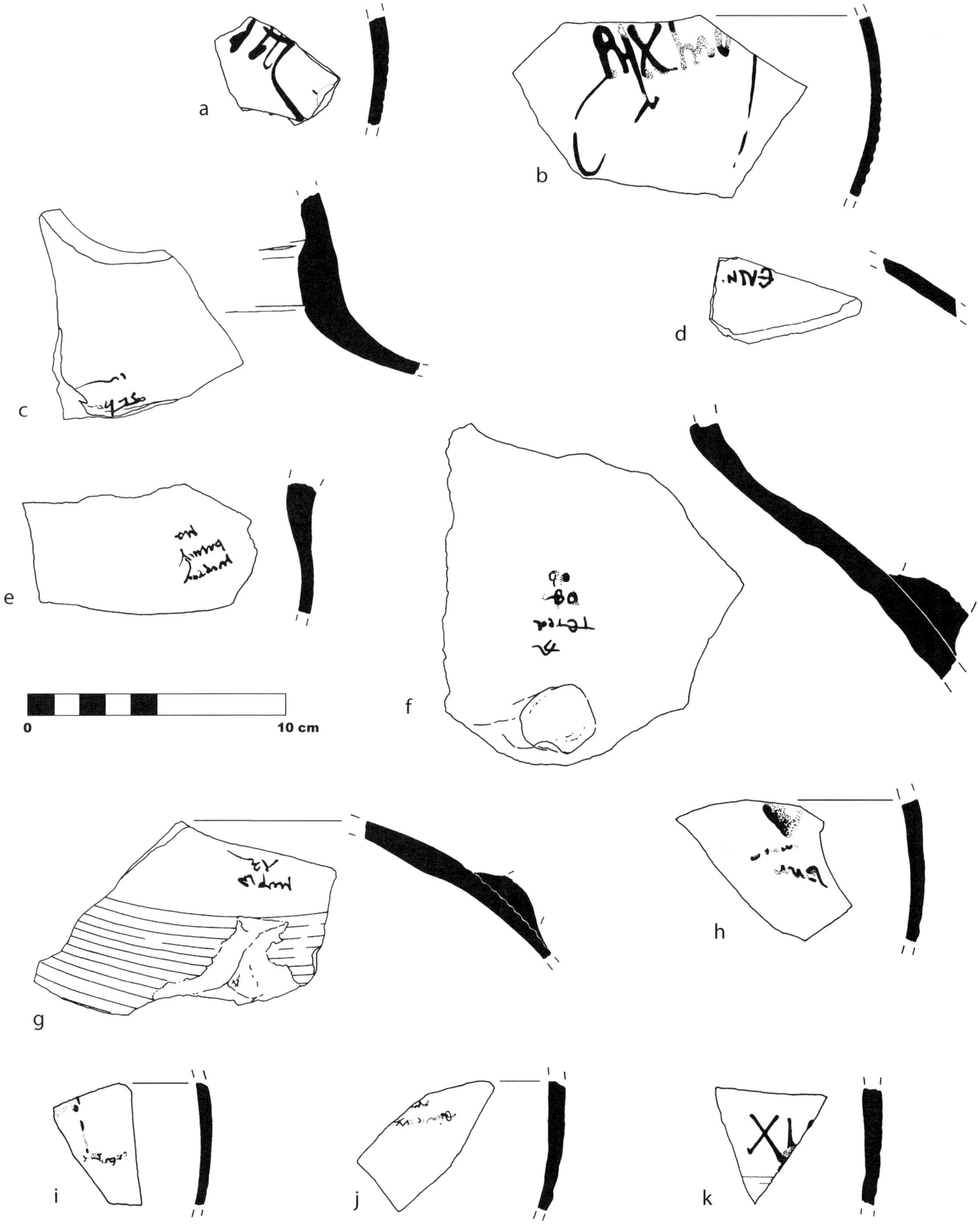

Figure 39. Dipinti (*cont.*)

contents. Apart from the type a Christograms in figures 37d and 38g, the other large, scrawly inscriptions could be type a or b; they are too broken to be certain.

Coins

The few coins recovered from the Bir Umm Fawakhir 1999 excavations are small, bronze, and poorly preserved (RN 99/237; fig. 40a–f). (For the conservator's report, see *Chapter 7*.) The paucity of coins is not surprising, given that there was and is little to spend money on in the desert. Most Byzantine coin catalogs deal with gold, silver, and large bronze coins; very few include minuscule bronze ones. The most likely mint for the Bir Umm Fawakhir coins is Alexandria, but coins from there are far less extensively published than those from, say, Constantinople or even Carthage. The geographically closest, large, well-published coin corpus is that from Antinoopolis (Castrizio 2010). One of the few things that can be stated about the Bir Umm Fawakhir coins is that none has a distinctive stamp such as a cross, chi-rho monogram, or a large character such as "I" for a denomination. Despite their poor condition and the shortage of comparanda, the coins, so far as can be determined, do seem to date to the late fourth to sixth century A.D. All coins are presented at a scale of 2:1 in order to show the details.

a. Bronze coin, dia. 11.57 mm (fig. 40a). Building 93, Room C northwest, locus 18. The reverse appears to have had a wreath; the obverse is completely worn away.

b. Bronze coin, dia. 11.59 mm (fig. 40b). Building 93, Room C northwest, locus 18. The reverse may have had a wreath; the three circles inside it are fairly clear. The most striking feature of the obverse is that the emperor is facing left rather than right or full face. There is no trace of an inscription around the head and little room for one. For a left-facing emperor, see a gold solidus of Leo I (A.D. 457–474) (Goodacre 1957, p. 41; Tolstoï 1968, pl. 8:15–16), a silver coin of Anastasius (A.D. 491–518) (Tolstoï 1968, pl. 12:14), and a coin of Constantius II from Berenice, discussed below.

c. Bronze coin, dia. 9.56 mm (fig. 40c). Building 177, Room A, locus 3. What looks like the Angel of the Annunciation on the reverse may be a winged victory or an armed figure. The right arm is raised and does not seem to be holding a cross on a pole, as is often depicted. What may be either a wing or an arm holding a shield may be seen on the viewer's right. For a similar figure on the reverse of tiny bronze coins, see four coins from Antinoopolis: one is datable to Valentinian II (ruled the Western empire A.D. 383–392; Castrizio 2010, p. 198, no. 8) and the rest to Theodosius (ruled A.D. 379–395; Castrizio 2010, p. 182, no. 19; p. 198, no. 7; p. 247, no. 4). A somewhat larger coin (ca. 2 cm dia.) from Berenice shows an armed figure striding to the left toward two kneeling figures. The obverse depicts the emperor Constantius II (ruled A.D. 337–361) with a beaded crown, facing left (Sidebotham and Wendrich 1999, p. 190). Much more generally, the victory motif also appears on a coin of the time of Arcadius (ruled A.D. 395–408; Goodacre 1957, p. 24; Tolstoï 1968, pl. 3:107) and perhaps a tiny bronze coin of Marcian (ruled A.D. 450–457; Castrizio 2010, p. 186, no. 44). See also a small gold coin of Anastasius (A.D. 491–518) that shows a victory with upraised arms moving to the viewer's left (Tolstoï 1968, pl. 15:127) and another gold coin of Justinian (A.D. 527–565) with a winged victory holding an orb with what appears to be a star below (Goodacre 1957, p. 70).

d. Bronze coin, max. dia. 9.56 mm (fig. 40d). Building 177, Room A, locus 15 (stone circle). The unusual headdress, sunken eye, large nose, defined lips, folds of the cloak, and lack of inscription are fairly well preserved on the obverse, but no convincing parallels have yet been found. The reverse probably had a spiky wreath or perhaps a crude inscription, but that side is now worn to a barely raised "C" shape.

e. Badly corroded bronze coin, max. dia. 9.51 mm (fig. 40e). Building 177, Room C west, locus 2. No design is preserved on either side.

f. Very small bronze coin, dia. 8.47 mm (fig. 40f). Building 177, Room C west, locus 7. The reverse preserves much of a wreath and a few scraps of letters, apparently the common "VOT MVLT" inscription with some numerals (perhaps XX). The obverse shows a few remnant letters of an encircling inscription and a fairly clear bust. The straight headbands ending in dots, prominent eyebrow, dot eye, triangular

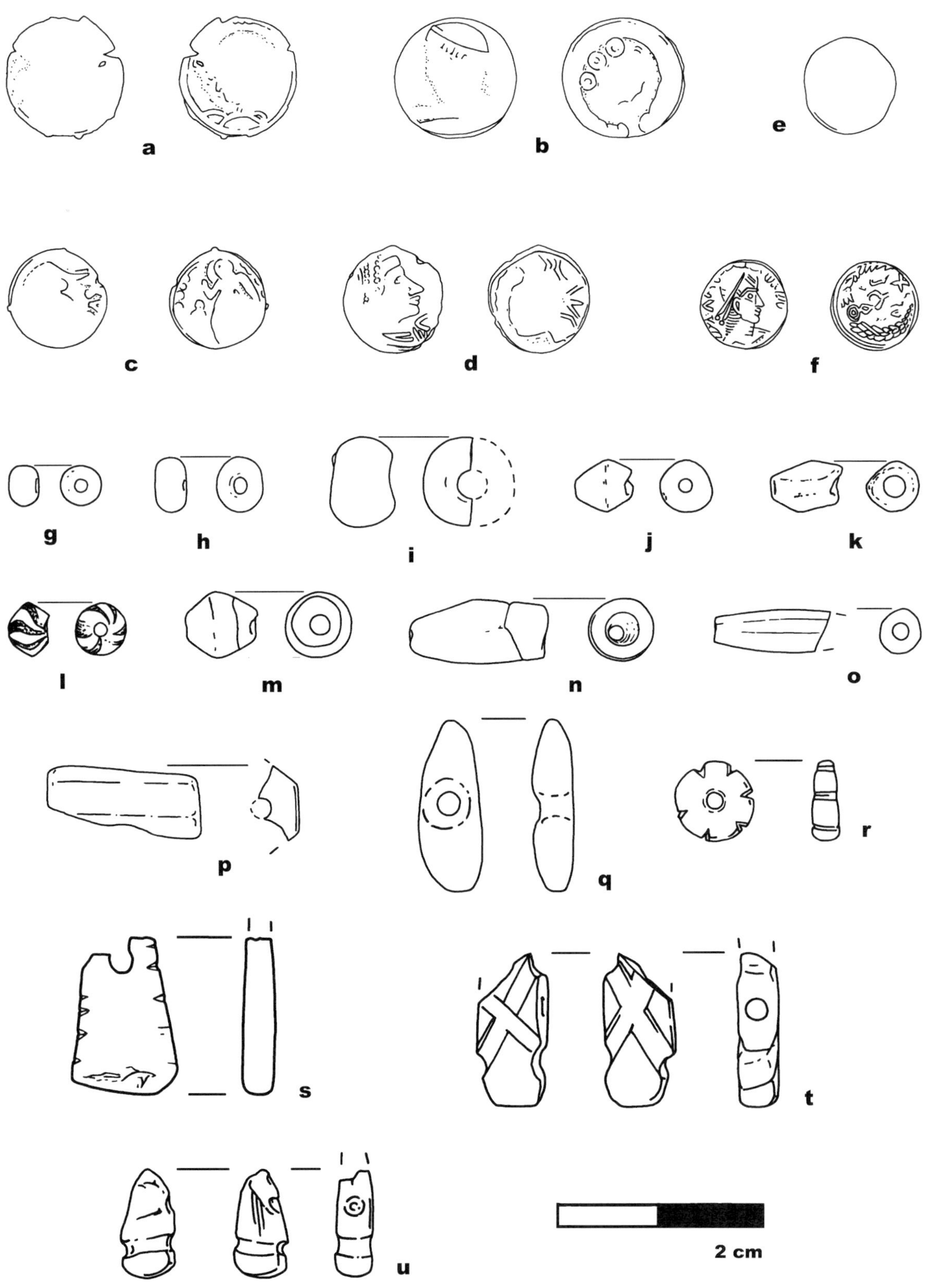

Figure 40. Coins, beads, and pendants

nose, defined lips, and hair rendered as horizontal lines on the neck are visible. There is a tiny *aes* of late fourth to early fifth-century date from Berenice. It has a round-eyed emperor on the obverse and a wreath on the reverse (Sidebotham and Wendrich 1995, p. 48). In general, the best parallels come from the reign of Justinian (A.D. 527–565); see especially a silver siliqua minted in Carthage (Sear 1987, p. 76, no. 253), a very similar silver coin in Tolstoï (1968, pl. 20:57), and perhaps a very small bronze coin also minted in Carthage (Bellinger 1966, p. 168, pl. 44:303.2).

Jewelry

A surprising amount of jewelry was recovered from Buildings 93 and 177. The former yielded twelve beads, a polished agate gemstone, a Bes amulet, and a copper/gold-alloy bracelet. The bracelet (RN 99/230; fig. 41a, pl. 33b) was so green when found that it was assumed to be copper or bronze, but with cleaning and conservation it proved to be a copper/gold alloy. It was found in the fill under a floor of Room A (locus 6), and it looks as if it had been torn in half. The agate gemstone (RN 99/203; pl. 33c) was carved to an oval and highly polished; it could have been set as a ring bezel or part of some other item of jewelry. The copper-alloy Bes amulet (RN 99/240; fig. 41b, pl. 34a) is so small that little can be identified but the three feathers in his headdress. Petrie illustrated a wide variety Bes and Bes-head amulets, many of which are datable to the Roman period. Almost all are made of a glazed material or glass (Petrie 1914, pp. 40–41, pls. 33–34), but one small amulet is bronze (ibid., p. 40, pl. 33:q). By the fifth and sixth centuries A.D., much or most of Egypt should have been at least nominally Christian; Bes was one of the last of the old gods to be worshipped. In fact, we cannot say what cult the ancient Bir Umm Fawakhir miners acknowledged. The Christograms on the wine jars were written where the amphoras were produced or filled, not where it was drunk. The XP stamps on some of the plates were added at the point of manufacture, and whether the miners had much choice in respect to decorative plates is unknown. To date we have found nothing resembling a church, or for that matter any other large administrative or public building. On the other hand, the little Ptolemy III Euergetes chapel dedicated to Min still existed; it survived into the twentieth century.

The beads are mostly glass, small, and not very fancy. Their colors range from black or very dark brown to a range of blues and blue-greens and turquoise, green, bright yellow, or red-orange on black. Many are tiny seed beads (fig. 40g) or rounded (fig. 40h–i). A few were rolled on a slab while still hot to make a bicone (fig. 40j–m) or pressed to make them polygonal (fig. 40o–p). Some are described as "wound," which simply means that a thread of hot glass was wound on a rod, which was then tapped to knock the new bead off the tip. A few beads (fig. 40m–n, pl. 34b) had two different colors wound rather clumsily together; they have exact parallels at Berenice. Such beads are said to be very common in Egypt and date mainly to the second to fifth century A.D. (Then-Obluska, in press). The fanciest beads were striped (fig. 40l, pl. 34c). They were formed from long, thin canes of different colors of glass bundled together and fused to one striped cane. This could be reheated, twisted like a peppermint stick, bits nipped off for beads, punched to make a hole, or further shaped on a slab to make a bicone bead. The bead shown in figure 40l has an exact parallel at Berenice, in a late context (Then-Obluska, in press). One bead (not illustrated) is described as millefiore. More details concerning beads are listed in *Appendix C*. Two beads were made of stone (RN 99/199; fig. 40q–r, pl. 15a–b). The date pit-shaped one is yellowish and black soapstone, and the flower is grayish steatite.

Building 177 yielded twenty-six beads and all three soapstone pendants (RN 99/199; fig. 40s–u). The stone is locally available and so soft that the pendants could have been carved by the ancient Fawakhiris in free time. A small soapstone disk (RN 99/209) could have been a blank for an unfinished ornament. Six more beads were recovered from Building 181, about the only cultural artifacts apart from sherds. The two dumps had almost no jewelry items, only three beads from Dump 2.

The jewelry from the houses, especially Building 93, suggests but does not prove the presence of women at the site. The Bes amulet suggests a desire for divine protection in a hostile landscape and a dangerous profession. More importantly, the jewelry, particularly the copper/gold bracelet and the agate gemstone, support the contention that the miners were paid workers, perhaps even career miners, rather than prisoners or captives. Also, the bits and pieces the excavations recovered from two houses are only what was broken, lost, or discarded, not what was carried away when the workers left or what scavengers picked up later.

Emeralds (Green Beryl)

Much to our surprise, we found ten raw emeralds (green beryls)[22] and a chunk of matrix with more emeralds (RN 99/232; pl. 34d). They came from Buildings 93 and 177, plus one from Dump 2 locus 10. The emeralds/green beryls originated from the mines in the Mons Smaragdus/Sikait region ca. 190 kilometers southeast of Bir Umm Fawakhir as the vulture flies, or ca. 120 kilometers northwest of Berenice on the Red Sea coast. There were no other sources of emeralds within the bounds of the Byzantine empire. The best connection between ancient Bir Umm Fawakhir and Mons Smaragdus would have been the long but well-established desert road from Laqeita (ancient Phoinicon), and then southeast to Berenice; Laqeita is roughly a day-and-a-half march west of Bir Umm Fawakhir. This suggested route is supported to a degree by a small bit of unworked beryl recovered from trench 01/3 at Biʾr Minayh, a remote site reached by a side track from the main Coptos-to-Berenice road (Lassányi 2010a, p. 255). Though emeralds may have been mined earlier, they were not regularly used in jewelry until the Roman period (Shaw 1999). Exploitation of the mines continued through the sixth century and even later (Sidebotham and Wendrich 2000, p. 356; Sidebotham et al. 2004; Sidebotham and Wendrich 2007, p. 297). Emeralds or green beryl occur as six-sided crystals that can be polished and/or drilled to make beads or pendants, though none of the stones from Bir Umm Fawakhir is worked in any way. What they do indicate is a connection between the miners of Bir Umm Fawakhir and the mines in the Sikait area. Raw emeralds were items of value, but we have no way of knowing whether the miners at Bir Umm Fawakhir worked at Mons Smaragdus at one point, knew people who did, or acquired the emeralds via the desert nomads.

Metal Objects

Even including coins and jewelry, metal finds are relatively few. Presumably such valuable items would have been taken away when the site was abandoned or were quickly scavenged thereafter.

The iron ladle (RN 99/228; pl. 34e) was found upside-down on a floor of Room B in Building 93 (pl. 36). It appears to have been hammered out of a long bar of iron. The cross-section of the handle is rectangular, so far as can be determined under the rust. A shallow, round spoon was beaten out of one end and perhaps a hook at the other. The findspot is discussed in *Chapter 2*, and the conservator's report is in *Chapter 7*.

The iron wedge or spike (RN 99/241; pl. 35a) from an upper level of Room B in Building 93 is a rare example of a working tool. At the major granodiorite quarry at Mons Claudianus, tools are quite rare, even though a blacksmith's workshop was excavated (Peacock 1997, p. 190, fig. 6.9). The iron wedge found at Bir Umm Fawakhir could have been used to pound out chunks of ore from the gold-bearing quartz veins. Our 1997 investigation of the mines (Meyer et al. 2005) did not detect any particular pattern of hacking out ore, but the granite around the opencast trenches is rotten enough not to show chisel marks, and the underground mines are at least partly filled with debris, besides being too dangerous to inspect without special equipment and training.

The well-preserved copper/bronze weight (RN 99/239; fig. 41c, pl. 35b) comes from Room A of Building 177, locus 3. Flat, square coin weights date in general to the late fifth to late sixth century, and most are marked only with their denomination (Entwistle 2002, pp. 612–13). In this case, the "NB" is carefully engraved, and a circle is clear over the "N." These are numbers, but we do not know what measurement they

[22] Emeralds are one variety of the mineral beryl ($Be_3Al_2[Si_6O_{18}]$). Beryl may be white and massive like milky quartz, pale blue or green (aquamarine), yellow or golden (heliodor), pink (morganite), red (bixbite), or deep green (emerald) (Hurlbut 1959, pp. 424–26; Mason and Berry 1968, pp. 474–78). The Field Museum of Natural History in Chicago also displays a clear variety (goshenite). The stones recovered at Bir Umm Fawakhir are the deep green emerald variety of beryl, though not flawless and translucent like the best-quality Columbian gems.

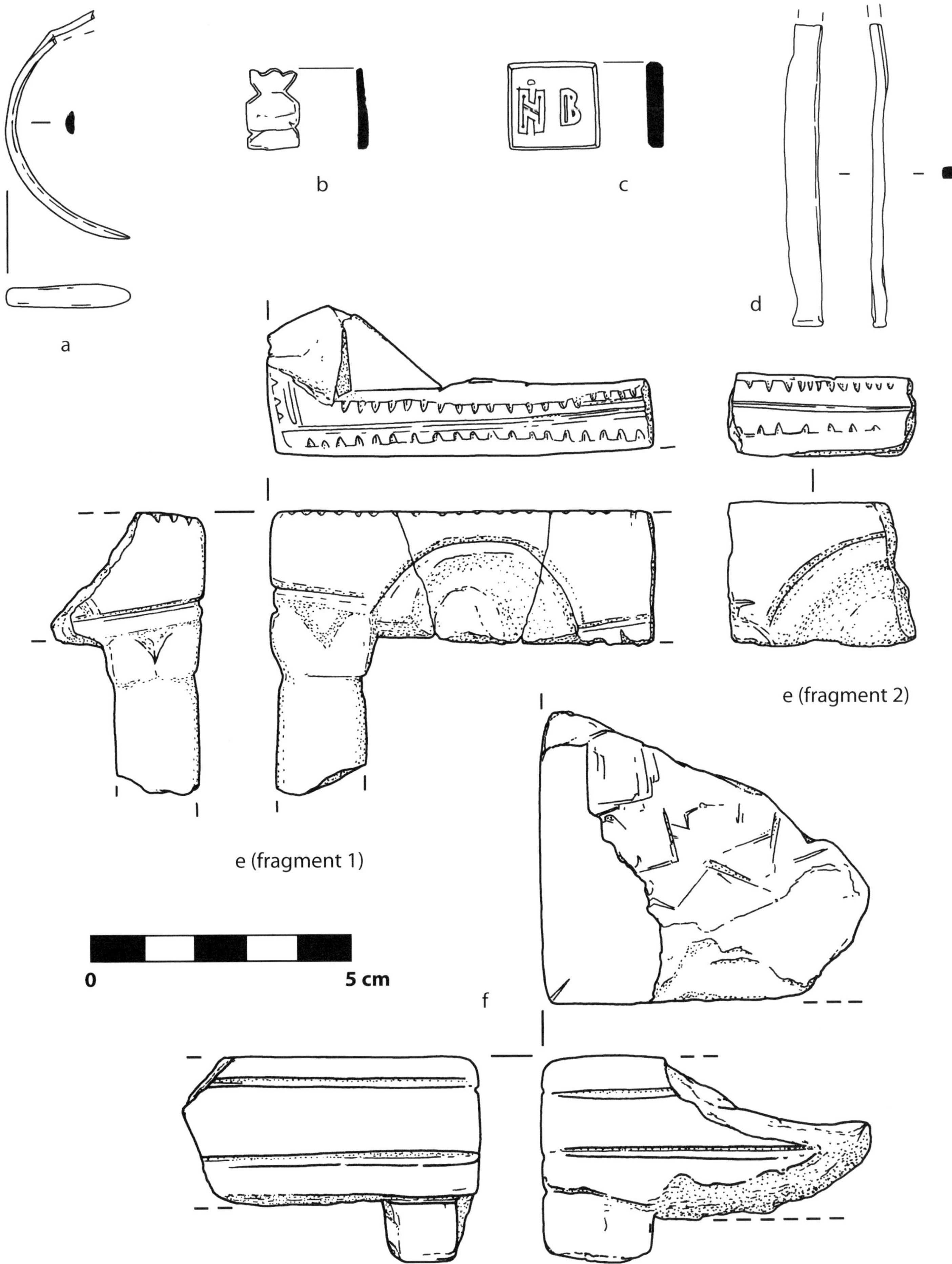

Figure 41. Metal objects and "incense burners"

may represent. Tiny weights and small metal scales are reported from some Late Roman (mid-fourth to mid-sixth century) multi-storied buildings at Berenice. It is suggested that the upper floor was domestic space, the ground floor commercial, and the weights and scales were used for small items of high value (Sidebotham and Wendrich 2007, pp. 97, 105, 216; Sidebotham, Hense, and Nouwens 2008, p. 175; Sidebotham 2011, pp. 268–70).

The copper-alloy strap (RN 99/241; fig. 41d) is in good condition up to the broken-off end, but it is too plain to suggest any particular use. One thin, battered ring (RN 99/241) indicates the existence of lead at the site, but little more.

"Incense Burners"

The previous survey seasons turned up several small, roughly rectangular objects of soft stone with crude, shallow depressions on top and incised decoration on the sides (Meyer 2011, pp. 154–55, fig. 48:i–j). None of the items shows any sign of burning or staining, hence the quote marks around the name.[23] One (Meyer 2011, fig. 48:i) was retrieved near a grave, but the three 1999 "incense burners" were excavated from Building 177, Room A, the crudest from locus 7 (wall fall or "bench") and the others from locus 9 (fill over a floor). The fanciest "incense burner" has a design like a zipper on the rim, arches on the sides, and a foot at the corner carved to resemble a column with a capital (RN 99/227; fig. 41e, pl. 15c). The workmen immediately called it "*kenisah*," or "church," but what if anything it had to do with Coptic religious practice remains unknown. A second carved "incense burner" from the same locus has a short, stubby foot and simpler decoration (RN 99/227; fig. 41f, pl. 16a). The third example (RN 99/204; pl. 16b) came from surface cleaning of the wall fall at the south side of Room A. It is a piece of brick, unbaked but slightly reddened at one side. It was called a "door socket" originally, but mudbrick is a miserable choice for the purpose — especially given the abundance of hard stone at the site — so we think it is actually a crude "incense burner." Parallels are not easy to find, but note two small, roughly rectangular, pink sandstone objects from Biʾr Minayh. They have shallow depressions on top but no signs of burning, so Lassányi suggests they represent miniature altars. Both are decorated with lightly incised lines and triangles, and both were found in tumulus 3 (Lassányi 2010c, pp. 295–96). The funerary connection is supported by two other examples excavated from graves at Bab Kalabsha. Both are small rectangular sandstone basins with shallow rectangular depressions on top. One has diamonds, triangles, and lattices scratched on four sides, the other has four stubby feet and sides carved into an elaborate palm-frond design (Ricke 1967, pp. 69–70, fig. 81:E2/a and E4/b). The largest group of "incense burners," however, comes from the cemeteries at nearby Kalabsha South and Wadi Qitna. Five small rectangular "stone vessels," all made of local Nubian sandstone, were recovered from burial tumuli. One was plain, one had an "H" design scratched on the bottom, and three bore roughly incised lattice or crosshatch designs on the sides (Strouhal 1984, pp. 201–02).

Stone

A few other stone artifacts merit attention. A small, crude, serpentinite bowl (RN 99/205; pl. 17a) or dish was recovered from Building 93, Room B. It has no signs of burning, grinding, or other usage, and it may not even have been finished. A neatly shaped pestle (RN 99/207; pl. 17b) of dark, fine-grained igneous rock came from Building 93, Room A. It has a rounded rectangular cross section and is bashed at the base, as might be expected. Lastly, there is a fragment of the rim of a white, polished calcite bowl (RN 99/198, fig. 42a) from the surface of Dump 2. Calcite is not a local stone but it is found in abundance on the west bank of Luxor.

---

[23] Real incense burners, as indicated by burning or burnt residues, are relatively common elsewhere. Many of the shrines and temples at Berenice yielded incense burners of terra-cotta, stone, wooden bowls filled with sand, and perhaps even reused amphora toes (Sidebotham 2011, pp. 265–66, 268). The small cuboid incense burners studied by Shea (1983) range in date from Isin-Larsa to Islamic times (2000 B.C.–A.D. 800), and in distribution from Mesopotamia to the Levant and Arabia. Their function is indicated by traces of burning and, sometimes, resinous residues.

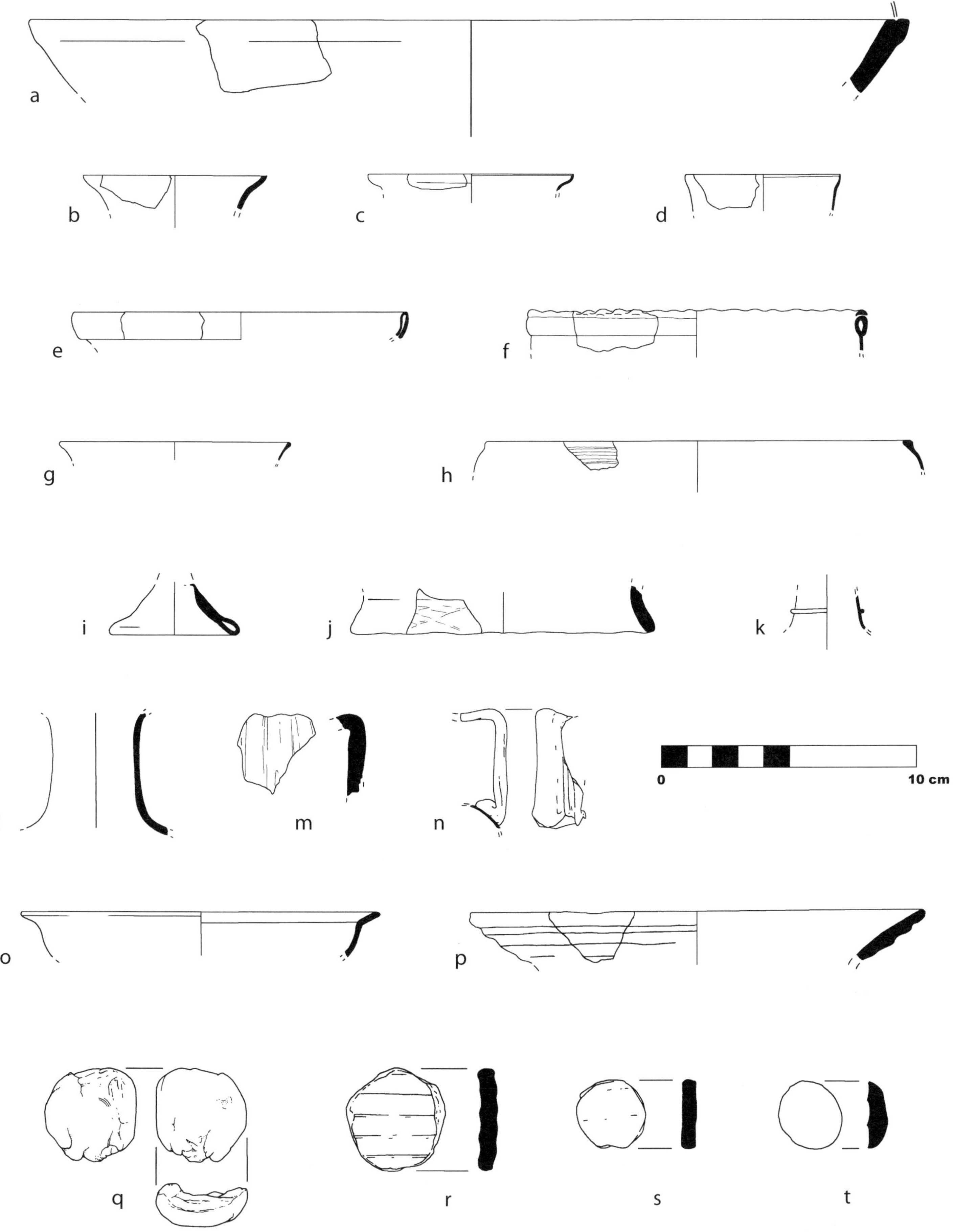

Figure 42. Calcite bowl, glass, faience, mud plug, sherd disks

Glass

All glass recovered from the excavations was inspected in the field house and tabulated, but only beads, diagnostic pieces, and body sherds larger than a thumbnail were kept, registered, and stored in Quft. The beads have been treated above with the rest of the jewelry. Since time was short at the end of the season, all glass was registered as RN 99/195, but the contents of this single register number are broken down in *Appendix C*.[24] That said, even a very small fragment of glass can carry information: cobalt blue is a more costly color than a natural blue-green, opaque reds and oranges are Roman, a very bubbly sherd is probably from poor- to medium-quality glass (though a small bit without bubbles could have come either from a fine vessel or an unbubbly part of a coarser one), an opalescent silvery weathering surface versus a tough black one probably pertain to different glass formulas, and so on. No complete glass vessels were recovered, though the kinds of loci we were excavating — house floors and fill and trash heaps — are not likely to yield anything except splinters. Only a few forms could even be reconstructed (fig. 42), and all but one of those is quite characteristic of the Byzantine/Coptic time range. Where the glass was manufactured is not certain, though Alexandria, or more accurately its vicinity, was long famous as a center of glass production.

Knock-off Rims

Three fragments of beakers or small bowls with knock-off rims were recovered (fig. 42b–d); two are transparent and one, light olive green.[25] One knock-off rim[26] from a bowl with cut decoration was found during the 1996 survey season (Meyer 2011, fig. 48:a), and in general such rims are characteristic of Byzantine/Coptic-period glass vessels.[27] Parallels may be noted, inter alia, at Naqlun, sealed seventh-century locus (Peter Geute, pers. comm.), Jalame (yellowish green bowl; Weinberg 1988, p. 97, no. 481, early fifth century), a very large corpus from Beirut (Jennings 2006, pp. 87–102, mostly fourth–sixth century), a long series from south Syria and Jordan (type BVI. 1112 in Dussart 1998, pp. 80–81, 253, Byzantine through early Islamic periods). Knock-off rims are also characteristic of conical lamps, though none of the thick conical bases was recovered in 1999 (but see Meyer 1994, p. 57, for a sherd recovered in 1992).

Looped-out Rims

For vessels with looped-out, bent rims like figure 42e, see examples from Karanis (Harden 1936, pp. 76–77, pl. 12:117–18); Jalame, early fifth century (Weinberg 1988, pp. 42–43, nos. 25–26); Jerash, early Byzantine (Meyer 1987, p. 189, fig. 6:I); Ain Zara, Jerash, and Amman, fourth century through Umayyad (types BI. 4122 and BI. 413 in Dussart 1998, pp. 64–65, 245); and Beirut, late seventh century (Foy 2000, pp. 256–57, fig. 11:10, 12). The bowl rim with ruffle decoration shown in figure 42f is much less common. Three similar bowls of pale yellow or greenish glass with applied ruffled rims are reported from Armant, second–third century (Harden 1940, p. 121, pl. 85:9–11), though Harden himself seems to have questioned the dating.

Thickened Rims

The slightly thickened rim in figure 42g is not very distinctive, but it could have come from a goblet with a base like figure 42i. See, for instance, some simple, light blue-green, thickened rims at Jerash, early Byzantine context (Meyer 1987, p. 189, fig. 5:S–U). At Carthage such rims are said to be common (Tatton-Brown

---

[24] As used here, "transparent" means the glass is virtually colorless and one can see colors through it. "Translucent" means one can see light through it, and "opaque" means no light comes through except at the very edges.

[25] For further details of findspot and glass quality, see *Appendix C*.

[26] For a reconstruction of a way to make vessels with knock-off or cracked-off rims, see Weinberg 1988, p. 88.

[27] Beveled or knock-off rims may be noted in the first–second-century Roman period as well, though they are not as common as other rim types and some of the vessel forms on which they occur, such as indented beakers (e.g., Quseir al-Qadim, Meyer 1992), are not attested at Bir Umm Fawakhir.

1984, p. 198, fig. 66:29, sixth century, but others range from fifth to seventh century in date). The bowl rim in figure 42h, transparent glass with a greenish tinge and trailed-on white threads, is much more unusual. For an incurved-rim bowl with trailed thread decoration, see a sixth-century example from Carthage (Tatton-Brown 1984, p. 198, fig. 66:27).

Goblet Bases

Looped-up goblet bases such as figure 42i are one of the hallmarks of Byzantine/Coptic-period glass. As Jennings (2006, p. 123) observes, "They are ubiquitous from the fifth century onwards, becoming increasingly common in the sixth century, and carry on [into] the seventh century." For parallels, see Karanis (Harden 1936, p. 172, pl. 16:489); Naqlun from a sealed seventh-century locus (Geute, pers. comm.); Jerash, especially the late Byzantine and early Umayyad pieces (Meyer 1987, p. 199, fig. 8:Y–cc); Beirut (Foy 2000, pp. 253, 257–58; Jennings 2006, pp. 123–27); and Jordan and south Syria (type BIX. 1 in Dussart 1998, pp. 115–21, 267–68).

Straw-marked Base

Bowls and goblets with tooled or cross-hatched "straw-marked" bases like figure 42j are not uncommon in the Coptic/Byzantine period. Note also a tooled base from the 1996–1997 surveys (Meyer 2011, fig. 48:e). Some good parallels may be found at Karanis on some shallow bowls (Harden 1936, p. 54, pl. 11:17, fourth–fifth century; pp. 72, 75, pl. 12:90 and 107, fourth–fifth centuries), and a deep bowl (Harden 1936, pp. 106–07, pl. 14:228). See also a base from Naqlun from a sealed seventh-century locus (Geute, pers. comm.), and a thick, greenish-blue base from Jalame, early fifth century (Weinberg 1988, p. 58, no. 145), and the base of a large, late Byzantine bowl from Amman (type BII. 12, no. 15 in Dussart 1998, pp. 74, 250).

Bottles and Jugs

The bottle neck figure 42k of light blue with a dark cobalt blue trailed decoration is characteristic of Byzantine/Coptic-period glass. See Beirut (Jennings 2006, pp. 163–64, no. 14). The cylindrical bottle neck in figure 42l could have come from a variety of types of bottles, most of which are distinguished by rim treatment. But see bottle neck sherds from Jerash, late Byzantine to early Umayyad contexts (Meyer 1987, p. 202, fig. 9:X and Y), and from Carthage, mostly fifth–sixth century in date (Tatton-Brown 1984, pp. 202–04, fig. 67:65–66).

Handles

The thick strap handles were usually attached just below the rim of a jug and at the shoulder. Thick strap handles like the Bir Umm Fawakhir examples (fig. 42m–n) were applied to vessels from the Roman period through at least the sixth century (cf. Jennings 2006, p. 196), but the very coarse quality of the Bir Umm Fawakhir sherds suggests a date toward the end of this time span. See, for example, a thick handle sherd from Jerash, early Byzantine context, with "stone" (a lump of coarse impurity) in the glass (Meyer 1987, pp. 193–94, fig. 7:P) like the Bir Umm Fawakhir pieces.

Roman Red

The sherd shown in figure 42o and on plate 35c came from a well-made, cast, Roman-period cup or bowl, perhaps a patella cup. Opaque red glass is difficult to manufacture and hence relatively rare. It may be dated roughly to the end of the first century B.C. to the first century A.D. (Jennings 2006, pp. 51–52), though the shape of the Bir Umm Fawakhir fragment looks as if it falls into the later end of this time range. Colorless glass largely supplanted the rich early Roman colors by around A.D. 200 (Harden 1969, p. 62). There is one opaque red glass sherd from Quseir al-Qadim (Meyer 1992, p. 164, pl. 13:303) and a much larger corpus from the royal tombs at Gebel Barkal, mostly first century B.C. (Dunham 1957, pp. 87, 89, 91, 93).

Miscellaneous Small Finds

The very worn rim sherd of a faience bowl (RN 99/211; fig. 42p) from the fill inside the tabun in Dump 2 is also of Roman date. The reconstructed profile is uncertain due to the irregularity of the rim. The sherd is worn to its gritty white core plus a trace of glaze, though no color is left. The faience sherd is another bit of evidence for Roman-period activity at the site (Meyer 2011, p. 28).

The nozzle (RN 99/213) shown on plate 35d probably came from a lamp rather than a *tuyere*. The curve at the bottom means that the nozzle was stubby, like a lamp. On the one hand, lamps, whether ceramic or glass, are poorly attested at the site, but on the other hand, no significant amount of gold smelting is believed to have occurred at or near ancient Bir Umm Fawakhir due to the lack of fuel, though occasional assays might have been undertaken. The findspot, the surface of Room A of Building 177 (locus 10), is no help.

Several mud or plaster plugs from small jars or jugs were retrieved, and one (RN 99/214) from Dump 2 is illustrated in figure 42q. Judging from the small diameter of the rim impressions on the underside, it covered a vessel with a small mouth. Four other plugs from Buildings 93 and 177 were registered as RN 99/202. None of the large amphora stoppers with stamped sealings characteristic of the Roman period was found.

As in previous seasons, several sherd disks were retrieved (RN 99/200; fig. 42r–t), three from Building 177, Room A, and one from Dump 2. All of them appear to have been cut from marl or Late Roman 1 amphora sherds. None is pierced or otherwise worked, so they are labeled "game pieces," though they could have had some other function, such as covering the mouth of a small bottle or jar.

A small cowrie shell (RN 99/201; pl. 18a) had its top ground or sliced off, perhaps to make an ornament of some sort. In addition, thirty-two bags of seashells were registered as RN/194 and are both tabulated in Appendix D. The identifiable shells or fragments include many tiny turritella, at least one ring cowrie, one spotted cowrie and other no longer identifiable cowries, pearly trochus, several pieces of large conches, bleeding-tooth shells, a piece of a tridacna, a small striped univalve like a bonnet shell, and one tiny olive shell; two more cowrie shells and one snail shell are included in *Chapter 5*. Most of the specimens were worn or broken, but more specific identification might be possible for some of the shells. Since the site of Bir Umm Fawakhir is only about 90 kilometers from the Red Sea coast at Quseir, all or most of the shells probably came from there. What is interesting is that so many shells were recovered, some of them tiny, whereas almost no fish bones were found (*Chapter 5*). As for the use, if any, of the shells, note that fifty or so cowrie shells were recovered from the Late Roman Isis temple at Berenice, where they are said to have been used for prognostication (Sidebotham 2011, p. 266).[28]

Most of the wood consisted of fragments, small branches, or twigs probably collected as fuel, but there was one worked wooden peg (RN 99/208; pl. 18b) some 14 cm long. It was recovered from ash-rich locus 3 in Dump 1.

Many bits of rope and twine were recovered (RN 99/181) but all in small bits. Pieces of leather, sheepskin, and unidentified skin were found as well (RN 99/196) but no identifiable worked pieces such as sandals. A number of bits of cloth or fiber were found (RN 99/180, RN 99/186, RN 99/216) including some fragments of colored cloth (RN 99/217) from Dump 2, locus 4; the fragments are discussed in *Chapter 7*.

[28] Raʾis Seif Shared described a folk remedy of ground-up shell like the little turritellas mixed with milk for eye diseases. It is a reminder that all medicine in the desert in the fifth and sixth centuries was probably home remedies.

Chapter 5

Zooarchaeological Remains

Salima Ikram

During the 2001 Bir Umm Fawakhir study season, all the animal bones excavated during the 1999 season were studied. These totaled 4,148 (including teeth), of which the major categories are summarized in table 1. The bones came from three main contexts: Building 93 and its two associated middens and tabuns (clay ovens), Building 177, and Building 181.

Methodology

The bones were collected by hand, save for a few loci that were sieved (one or two from each area). It is noteworthy that the sieved samples did not show any difference in the species and anatomical elements represented in comparison with those found in the unsieved collections. All bones were examined and recorded. Information recorded for each bone included: taxon, element, portion, side, age (when possible, based on epiphysial fusion or tooth wear), butchery marks, work, gnawing, burn marks, erosion/weathering, gender (when possible), and breakage patterns. Fragments (measuring over 1.5 cm at least) of limb bones, ribs, and vertebrae that were identifiable only by mammal size were counted. The ageing systems for bones and teeth that were used were those of Silver (1963), Grant (1982), Schmid (1972), and Payne (1973).

Condition/Taphonomy

The bones were relatively well preserved, albeit eroded from their exposure to heat and sun (or possibly even during cooking) and their subsequent interment in dry sand. Some bones showed clear evidence of burning — possibly as they were used for fuel. The preservation was so good that in several instances fragments of cartilage, bits of meat, hide, and hair were still adhering to the bones. The keratin horn-sheaths of ovicaprids and gazelle were also recovered (Dump 2 in particular). Some bones had been burned and might have been used as fuel. There was surprisingly little gnawing on most of the bones: only a few bones bore gnaw marks, and only three of these were from rodents; the others seem to be the results of carnivore activity. This suggests that the faunal deposits were not accessible to predators who might gnaw them and leave them behind, and that rodents would have access to other, preferable, food sources.

The Fauna

The range of fauna was similar throughout all three contexts (table 1, fig. 43), with all parts of the animals being represented. This indicates that joints of preserved meat were not brought into the site, but that live animals were kept at Bir Umm Fawakhir and slaughtered as needed.

The most common type of domestic animal, as might be expected in such an arid environment, was goat (*Capra aegagrus* f. *hircus*), closely followed by sheep (*Ovis ammon* f. *aries*). At the time of work, universally accepted reliable methods for differentiation between the species were limited (Boessneck 1969), thus a large number of bones (738) are simply labeled as ovicaprid. In any case, these species remain the favored

Table 1. Zooarchaeological remains

	Bldg. 93, Room A	Bldg. 93, Room B	Bldg. 93, Room C	Bldg. 93, Room D	Bldg. 93, Room E	Dump 1	Dump 2	Bldg. 177	Bldg. 181	**Total**
Goat	38	3	2	2	1	29	37	31	1	**144**
Sheep	8	4	0	0	0	15	14	11	0	**52**
Sheep/Goat	144	26	42	6	4	130	176	200	10	**738**
Cow	5	4	5	4	0	67	43	14	0	**142**
Water Buffalo?	0	0	0	0	0	0	0	6	0	**6**
Camel	0	0	0	0	0	2	0	0	0	**2**
Gazelle	0	0	0	0	0	0	1	1	0	**2**
Gazelle?	0	0	0	1	0	4	4	3	0	**12**
Donkey	0	0	0	0	0	0	0	1	0	**1**
Silky Jird	1	0	0	0	0	61	0	0	0	**62**
Pig	0	0	0	0	0	3	0	0	0	**3**
Bird	0	0	0	0	0	0	0	2	0	**2**
*Cowrie**	2	0	0	0	0	0	0	0	0	**2**
Fish	0	0	0	0	0	0	0	0	1	**1**
Snail Shell	1	0	0	1	0	0	0	0	0	**2**
Turtle	0	0	5	0	0	0	1	0	0	**6**
Lg. Mammal	27	21	44	14	0	210	145	67	1	**529**
Med-Lg. Mam.	14	7	12	0	0	37	13	40	4	**127**
Med. Mammal	261	85	156	62	27	318	569	809	28	**2,315**
Total	**501**	**150**	**266**	**90**	**32**	**876**	**1,003**	**1,185**	**45**	**4,148**

*The remaining five cowries are tabulated in Appendix D. A worked cowrie shell with its top sliced off is discussed in the sections on "Dump 1" and "Jewelry" in *Chapters 2* and *7*.

animals of the Bedouin today (Hobbs 1990). It is noteworthy, however, that the site of Mons Claudianus had relatively few bones from these animals (Hamilton-Dyer 2001, pp. 270–73), although they were more common at Berenice (van Neer and Ervynck 1998, 1999; van Neer and Lentacker 1996).

Cattle (*Bos taurus*) were the next most common animals represented at the site, with six possible water buffalo/*gamoosa* (*Bubalus bubalis*) bones coming from Building 177; the identification was based on morphology and size. It is possible that these are intrusive, but one cannot ignore the possibility that these animals were part of the economy in the Roman period. The number of cattle bones at Bir Umm Fawakhir is in marked contrast to the number found at Mons Claudianus, where only six bones were found (Hamilton-Dyer 2001, pp. 273–74), and Quseir al-Qadim (Wattenmaker 1982); at Berenice they are slightly more numerous (van Neer and Ervynck 1998, 1999).

A few bone fragments were identified as belonging to camel (*Camelus dromedarius*). During a site visit a few more camel bones were found lying on and near midden areas, at surface level — these might be part of the original deposit, or later discards made by the Bedouin. It is surprising that more camel bones were not found, as these animals were increasingly common during the Roman era and are an ideal beast of burden in the desert. Of course, it is possible that if they were only acting as beasts of burden and not regularly consumed, they were disposed of outside of the settlement. Sites such as Mons Claudianus (Hamilton-Dyer 2001, p. 264) and Berenice (van Neer and Ervynck 1999, 1998) also had a surprisingly few camel bones.[29]

[29] See also Osypińska 2011, p. 73.

A small number of pig (*Sus scrofa domestica*) bones were recovered from Dump 1. Possibly these bones (two parts of an ulna and one of a femur) indicate preserved meats being brought in, as these animals are ill suited to life in an arid environment and are fairly dependent on water and mud for survival. Interestingly, despite similar environmental conditions, pigs are the "second most frequent category of mammal remains" at Mons Claudianus (Hamilton-Dyer 2001, p. 267).

Equids were not represented save for a single probable donkey (*Equus asinus*) incisor. Equids are excellent beasts of burden, particularly mules and donkeys, and one would have expected a significant number at the site. It is possible that they were deposited elsewhere, as has been suggested for the camels. Certainly the faunal remains from the not very distant Mons Claudianus were dominated by equids (Hamilton-Dyer 2001, pp. 255–62), where they were consumed as well as used for transportation. On the other hand, Berenice, like Bir Umm Fawakhir, has yielded very few (van Neer and Ervynck 1999; Osypińska 2011, p. 73), as has Didymoi, which was occupied from the late first to early third century (Leguilloux 2011, pp. 171–72). Recent excavations at Roman-period Myos Hormos (Quseir al-Qadim) reported a low percentage of equid, cattle, and camel bones, but a high percentage (15.7%) of cattle/equid-size bone (Hamilton-Dyer 2011, p. 246), so the situation there is less clear.

Wild animals were represented by a few gazelle (*Gazella* sp.) bones and the keratin from a horn core. No bones that clearly belonged to ibex (*Capra ibex*) were identified, although they are known to exist in the area, as attested by the fine pair of horns that we saw over the door of a hut near the site. Neither were any bones of Barbary sheep (*Ammotragus lervia ornatus*), common until at least the 1950s (Hobbs 1990, p. 100), identified,

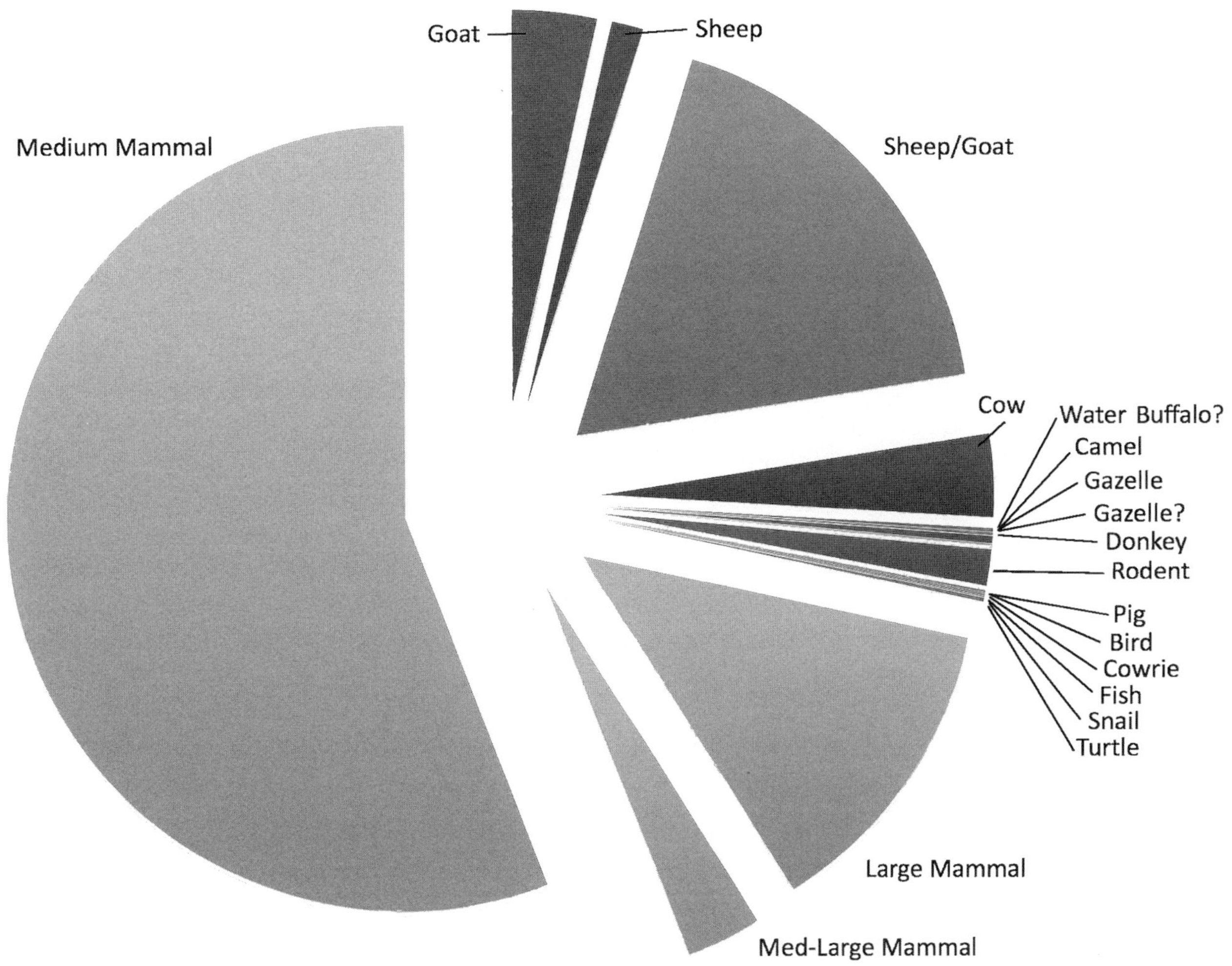

Figure 43. Distribution of animals at Bir Umm Fawakhir

although one distal radius of a juvenile ovicaprid might be assigned to this species. Both gazelles and ibex remain common in the region today, and a fleeting glimpse of the former was afforded during a site visit.

Only one fish bone was found during sieving soil samples from Building 181 — none of the other sieved samples yielded any fish bone. As it was a fragmentary vertebra measuring 1.5 mm, it is impossible to identify the species. This stands in stark contrast with the findings at Mons Claudianus (Hamilton-Dyer 2001, pp. 283 ff.), and of course from the sea port of Berenice (van Neer and Ervynck 1999, 1998), which also had evidence for Nile fish, some of which were brought in live (Cuvigny 2005, p. 12).

Fragments of the carapace of a marine turtle were also recorded; it might have served as food or been part of an object, such as a musical instrument. Similar finds are reported from Berenice (van Neer and Ervynck 1999, 1998). Bir Umm Fawakhir can boast the remains of two cowrie shells from the Red Sea, probably used in jewelry. (The rest of the seashells are discussed in *Chapter 4* and tabulated in *Appendix D*.) One snail shell (*Helix* sp.) was also noted. Perhaps it was brought in from the Nile valley, or it might attest to wet phases at the site — certainly such shells have been found far in the Western Desert (pers. obs.). It should be noted that some forms of this snail, *Helix pomatia*, originate from the Mediterranean. Examples have been found in Berenice and Mons Claudianus in the Roman period (van Neer and Ervynck 1999, p. 339) and were imported into the site (Hamilton-Dyer 2001; van Neer and Ervynck 1999).

Two fragmentary bird bones were also found. The fragments are from small birds and are unfortunately insufficiently preserved to identify the species.

Rodent bones were not well attested at the site, save for one entire silky jird (see table 1 and below), and a femur of another individual. The sites of Berenice and Mons Claudianus curiously have many more rodent remains, including bones from the jirds as well as rats and mice.

Discussion

As only three areas of this vast site were excavated, it is difficult to completely reconstruct ancient diet or range of fauna with total confidence. As mentioned above, a site visit on our day off showed scatters of camel bone, as well as donkey bone. This clearly indicates that although the excavated remains provided a good sample, further work should be carried out, especially in the very rich midden areas, if one is to get a more representative assemblage. However, the bones that were examined provided some interesting results.

The residents of Bir Umm Fawakhir were raising goats, sheep, and cattle. All portions of these animals were well represented in the excavated sample, which argues convincingly against the importation of special cuts from the Nile valley. It can be safely assumed that all these animals were used as meat, a conclusion that is supported by the butchery marks found on several of the bones. There was a notable abundance of metapodials, carpals, tarsals, and phalanges, elements that are often discarded during the course of butchery, and whose presence is indicative of on-site meat production. This also suggests that the inhabitants of the site were well provided with meat, as in meat-poor areas the flesh from the metapodials is used, and the bones can also be used for soup. The good preservation of the bones and relative absence of gnaw marks on the bones suggest that there was a minimal canine population at the site. Quite possibly if dogs existed at the site (no canid bones were found, in contrast with Berenice, Quseir, and Mons Claudianus; van Neer and Lentacker 1996; van Neer and Ervynck 1998, 1999; Watternmaker 1982; Hamilton-Dyer 2001), they were well cared for and might have acted as herd dogs for the flocks of sheep and goats.

Pork was rare at Bir Umm Fawakhir and was probably brought there in a preserved state. This practice was particularly common in the Roman era (Curtis 1991, p. 75), and evidence for this is attested at the Roman fort at Abu Shaʾar (van Neer and Lentacker 1996, p. 348). If the majority of the population was Egyptian rather than the Roman soldiers who lived at the fort sites, pork might not have been as desirable as mutton, goat, or beef — possibly a holdover from the Pharaonic era (Ikram 1995).

The cattle, sheep, and goats would also be used for their dairy products. Pottery finds further support an active dairy industry (note the possible cheese-making vessels). In fact, cheese would be a good way to extend the life of milk in the heat of the desert. Due to the stresses of desert environment, animals such as sheep and cattle would probably not provide as much milk as they would in the Nile valley. Goats are more adaptable and would be much more useful as a stable milk/dairy source, as can be seen today in Bedouin camps in the Eastern Desert, and would explain the larger percentage of goats in comparison to sheep.

Wool and hair from the sheep and goats could have easily been used for weaving, just as it is today. Perhaps weaving was a domestic activity, or even a second economic activity at the site. Certainly the residents' own textile needs would have been more than met by the number of animals they seem to have had at their disposal. Further excavation might reveal some spinning or weaving tools. Cowhide, of which fragments were recovered from middens together with goatskin, could also have been used for leather products such as those recorded at Didymoi (Leguilloux 2006) and Mons Claudianus (Winterbottom 2001).

The presence of sheep and goat bones is not surprising, as these animals, especially goats, flourish in the rather stark desert environment. However, the presence of cattle at the site is unexpected. Cattle tend to be more successful in slightly cooler and wetter environments, and, most importantly, their fodder requirements are higher than those of ovicaprids. Goats and sheep can forage with relative ease in the Eastern Desert; this, however, is harder for cattle. Was fodder brought in from the Nile valley for these animals, or was the area much greener in antiquity? Cattle are ill adapted to desert life, thus it is surprising that they appear in such great numbers in the zooarchaeological record at Bir Umm Fawakhir. In general, and especially in the desert, they are not effective as pack animals, although they can be used to drag wagons and so on. However, unlike Mons Claudianus and Mons Porphyrites, there is little evidence of solid pathways on the site.

The abundance of cattle bones contrasts oddly with the paucity of camel bones; camels are much better suited to life in the desert and like cattle can provide meat and milk, as well as being used as draft animals. Certainly they were being used for both in Mons Claudianus (Hamilton-Dyer 2001). The dearth of camel bones suggests that these animals were used primarily for transport, rather than for meat or milk. No doubt they were used to transport the gold from the site to the Nile valley and to bring in whatever was needed for the residents of the town. However, as the site visit showed, there might be more camel bones at Bir Umm Fawakhir than hitherto suspected, which might alter the current interpretation of the material and activities at the site.

The almost total absence of donkey bones in the assemblage studied is surprising, especially given their preponderance at Mons Claudianus (Hamilton-Dyer 2001). One would expect donkeys to be kept at the site, as they are quite hardy and very useful as pack animals, especially in hilly environments such as that surrounding the town. The houses that lie farther away from the wells would need to have water supplied to them in some volume, which would be more easily accomplished by using donkeys, as was done at the Workmen's Village at Tell el-Amarna some 1,700 years earlier (Kemp 1984; Fenwick 2004, 2005), than by people. Furthermore, the miners would no doubt have used pack animals to carry ore from the mines. Further research might possibly reveal donkey bones (one was seen during the site visit) at Bir Umm Fawakhir. However, it is also possible that a few camels were kept on site to carry water. Camels would be less effective than donkeys for the miners as they do not move over the rocky slopes with as much aptitude as donkeys do, but they could certainly be used to provide water to the town residents living at some distance from the wells.

Hunting was carried out, albeit infrequently and rather more for sport and recreation than to obtain food, if one is to judge by the paucity of bones of wild animals excavated here. Despite the fact that the area supported gazelle, ibex, and Barbary sheep, only a few gazelle remains were recovered. Gazelles and ibex have long frequented the hills and wadis of the Eastern Desert and would probably have been attracted to the water source at the site in antiquity, just as they are today, which is why it is surprising that their bones do not form a larger part of the assemblage. Notably, this pattern is also found at other Eastern Desert Roman sites such as Mons Porphyrites (Cuvigny 2011, p. 119), Mons Claudianus (Hamilton-Dyer 2001), Berenice (van Neer and Lentacker 1996; van Neer and Ervynck 1999, 1998; Osypińska 2011, p. 76), and Roman-period Quseir al-Qadim (Hamilton-Dyer 2011, p. 250). Clearly these settlements depended on more stable food sources — perhaps provisions supplied by the state.

Unlike some other Eastern Desert sites, such as Mons Claudianus (Hamilton-Dyer 2001, pp. 283ff.) and Mons Porphyrites, almost no fish remains from either Nile or Red Sea fish were found, despite sieving. Only one tiny, fragmentary vertebra was found during sieving a soil sample from Building 181. Sadly, it is unidentifiable to species. If dessicated (salted) fish were brought in, then the bones might have been eaten or destroyed during cooking, as they do not appear in the assemblage from the limited excavations carried out at the site thus far. The dearth of freshwater fish is surprising given the greater proximity of this site to the Nile than Berenice, which had evidence for Nile fish (Cuvigny 2005, p. 12; van Neer and Ervynck 1999, 1998).

The only bird remains are fragmentary, and of small, wild birds, although eggshells of unidentified birds were recorded from two loci (RN 99/190). Domestic fowl are known from other desert sites, such as Mons Claudianus, although it is clear that the animal economy there was quite different from that of Bir Umm Fawakhir.

Thus, from the evidence currently available, it seems that the diet of the residents of Bir Umm Fawakhir was rich in meat from cattle, sheep, and goats, as well as being well supplied with dairy products. It is more than possible that the inhabitants of the site were consuming more meat-based protein than the peasants in the Nile valley. The fact that they were successfully raising animals at the site would argue for a plentiful water supply, and a possible secondary economic activity in the form of weaving. It would be rewarding to further excavate the site in order to determine the types of draft animals that might have been used, as well as to identify the areas where cattle might have been penned.

Addendum

Carol Meyer

The skeleton (RN 99/235) of a small animal thought to be a rodent was excavated from Dump 1, locus 17, the lowest level reached and the site of the "cheese factory." The bones were tentatively identified as those of a silky jird in 2001, but lacking references in Quft, confirmation had to wait for library research in Chicago. Judging from the skulls illustrated in Osborne and Helmy 1980 (pp. 192–93), the skeleton is indeed a silky jird, *Meriones crassus* (pl. 19).

Jirds are small, soft-furred mammals somewhat akin to gerbils and jerboas, but unlike these they have a long tail with a black brush at the tip (Osborn and Helmy 1980, p. 191; Osborne 1998, pp. 50–51), and unlike the latter, their hind legs are not adapted for jumping. Silky jirds are reported from the Eastern Desert, including the Fawakhir mines (Osborne and Helmy 1980, p. 202). Jirds dig burrows

> "where there is vegetation or human habitation or past activity. Burrows may be in barren, stony, gravelly, or mud terraces around or beneath buildings or tents; under trash heaps and straw piles, but not always in the immediate vicinity of a food source." (Osborne and Helmy 1980, p. 198)

Jirds eat fruits or seeds, including acacia, camel thorn (*Zilla spinosa*), and bitter colocynth (*Citrullus colocynthis*) (Osborne and Helmy 1980, pp. 200–01), which occur at Bir Umm Fawakhir, though jirds might prefer dropped wheat grains, if available.

At Bir Umm Fawakhir site, silky jirds could explain the presence of animal holes in some of the baulks, for example, Building 93, Room E (pl. 26a), and part of the dearth of cereal grain, for which problem see *Chapter 6*. Since jirds do not seem to burrow very deeply, the remains of the jird near the bottom of Dump 1 suggests that they inhabited the site while it was occupied or shortly after it was abandoned, but before the level in question was buried in sand.

It should be noted that examples of such animals, both in bone form and as natural mummies, were also recorded at Mons Claudianus (Hamilton-Dyer 2001, p. 276).

Chapter 6

The Floral Remains

Wendy Smith

Goals

Archaeobotanical sampling was carried out during the 1999 excavations at Bir Umm Fawakhir in order to establish:

- What was the nature of diet at Bir Umm Fawakhir?
- Where were foodstuffs acquired? From the Nile Valley? From the Red Sea? From both areas?
- What wild foodstuffs, fodder, or fuel were collected from the immediate area?
- What fuels were in use?
- Could certain crops have been grown immediately at the site?

Method

Archaeobotanical sampling was undertaken without following a particular sampling strategy. As a result, there is a clear bias in the areas sampled for archaeobotanical material, with the majority of archaeobotanical samples collected from Building 93 and Dumps 1 and 2. In addition, the volume of soil sampled was usually 1 liter or less (in several cases < 100 ml) in volume, which meant that in most cases the sampling size was too small to produce results of interpretable value.

Samples were dry sieved over a 500 µm mesh sieve, and the > 500 µm fraction was sorted for plant remains. Both the unsorted < 500 µm fraction and the sorted > 500 µm fraction were retained. Identifications were made using a low-power binocular microscope at magnifications between ×10 and ×50. All the taxa were identified without consultation to a reference collection; however, modern reference material was acquired to confirm identifications of certain material (especially material that the author had not encountered archaeologically before, that is, dom palm fruit kernels). In the vast majority of cases, the plant remains identified were well-known, commonly encountered crops and weeds from Late Antique Egypt, which did not require reference material to identify.

Results

During the 1999 field season fifty-eight samples of hand-picked items identified as seeds, four contexts where seeds were included with other collected material (i.e., animal bone, wood, or charcoal), and twenty-three soil samples were collected for analysis. Tables 2–9 present the quantified results for this material, and figure 44 summarizes the overall proportions of plant remains recovered. Nomenclature follows Zohary and Hopf 1993 for economic plants and Täckholm 1974 for indigenous plants. In total, 1,297 identifications of plant remains have been made. Figure 44 summarizes the proportion of crops, wood/scrub, and other weed/wild plants identified for the entire assemblage. Food plants identified in the assemblage include barley (*Hordeum*

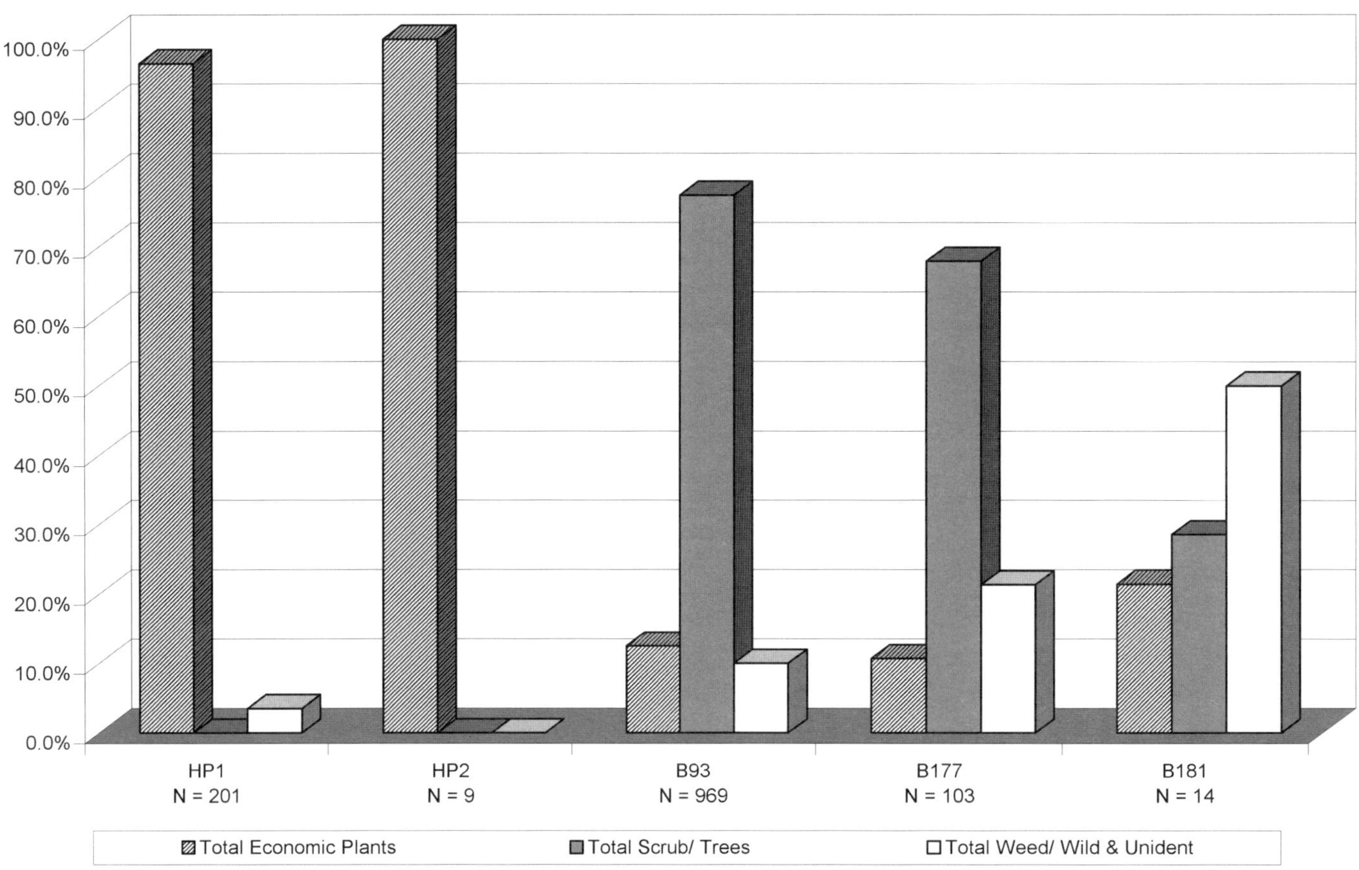

Figure 44. Proportion of plant remains recovered in hand-picked material and soil samples from Buildings 93, 177, and 181

sp.), bottle gourd (*Lagenaria siceraria*),[30] date (*Phoenix dactylifera*), dom palm (*Hyphaene thebaica*), grape (*Vitis vinifera*), olive (*Olea europea*), and wheat (*Triticum* sp.). In addition, unidentified large pulses (*Acacia* sp./*Vicia* sp./*Pisum* sp.) and pod fragments and seeds of Nile acacia (*Acacia nilotica*), both of which were most likely used for animal fodder, were also recovered. All these plants are typical crops of the Nile valley. The remainder of the assemblage is made up of seeds of weed/wild plants, many of which are typical of the vegetation (especially scrub) in the Bir Umm Fawakhir wadi today.[31]

The Bir Umm Fawakhir assemblage is not as rich or diverse as other Eastern Desert/Red Sea sites, such as Mons Claudianus (van der Veen 1996, 1998; van der Veen and Hamilton-Dyer 1998) or Berenice/Shenshef (Cappers 1996, 1998a, 1998b). However, the plant remains recovered at Bir Umm Fawakhir have also been identified at these sites.[32]

---

[30] Bottle gourd or calabash can be eaten as a vegetable, the seeds are oily, and the mature shell can be used for ladles or containers (van der Veen 2011, p. 165). (CAM)

[31] *Buglossoides* sp. specimens were recovered from several loci but are apparently unattested at other Eastern Desert sites. It is a weedy annual found along the Mediterranean coast, and one species on the Sinai peninsula, so perhaps the seeds reached Bir Umm Fawakhir as a contaminant with cereal grains. (CAM)

[32] On a presence/absence basis, all the plant remains (except perhaps *Buglossoides*) are found at other Eastern Desert sites. At Berenice and Shenshef, in addition to the references cited above, see also Cappers 1999a, pp. 299–305, and 1999b, pp. 419–26. At least sixty-eight cultivated plants have been recovered from Berenice (Cappers 2000, p. 305), many of them imported from Africa or India. In the earlier periods of occupation at Berenice (mid-first to mid-second century), the same plants as at Bir Umm Fawakhir may be noted, except that emmer wheat (*Triticum dicoccum*) rather than hard wheat (*T. durum*) is present (Zieliński 2011, p. 60).

Plant remains from Didymoi, occupied from the late first through early third century, include six-row barley (*Hordeum vulgare* subsp. *Hexastichium*), hard wheat (*Triticum durum*), peas (*Pisum sativum*), dates (*Phoenix dactylifera*), dom palm (*Hyphaene thebaica*), grape pips (*Vitis vinifera*), and olive pits (*Olea europaea*) (Tengberg 2011, pp. 206–09).

Roman-period (first to early third century) plant matter from Myos Hormos (Quseir al-Qadim) includes hulled barley (*Hordeum vulgare*) and hard wheat (*Triticum durum*) as the primary cereal grains, and all the other edible or utilitarian species recovered at Bir Umm Fawakhir were identified at Myos Hormos, as well as a large variety of other Egyptian or imported plants (van der Veen 2011, pp. 39–72, 221, 234; van der Veen, Cox, and Morales

Because of the limited nature of sampling, as well as the small sampling size, it is not possible to draw further comparisons. The assemblage from the soil samples is clearly biased toward charred plant remains. Not only are the majority of samples associated with oven installations, but as figure 44 demonstrates, the majority of identifications from Building 93 and Building 177 are of charred seeds of scrub/trees. The most likely interpretation is that this assemblage is dominated by material that was used as fuel on site.

Preservation of Plant Remains

The majority of the plant remains recovered from soil samples are charred. Not only are desiccated plant remains scarce in the Bir Umm Fawakhir samples, but when desiccated material is recovered, it usually is quite poorly preserved. The hand-picked plant remains, however, do not appear to follow this pattern. The majority of hand-picked material collected was desiccated (preservation varied from good to poor).

One possible explanation for the recovery of so much desiccated material in hand-picked samples may be the robust nature of date stones, which dominate the hand-picked plant remains recovered (i.e., 200 date stones were identified out of a total of 210 identified hand-picked plant remains). Since the majority of samples collected are from Building 93, Dumps 1 and 2, and in close proximity to oven installations, it is perhaps understandable that charred plant remains dominate the assemblages. However, at other Late Antique-period sites in Egypt, such as Kom el-Nana (Smith 1998), both charred and desiccated plant remains have been found in association with oven contexts. As a result, it may be possible that the desiccated plant remains do not survive in the area for some currently unknown taphonomic reason. Certainly at Quseir al-Qadim, Wetterstrom (1982, p. 355) observed that Roman-period desiccated plant remains were quite damaged by salt deposits, and it may be possible that similar problems affected the plant remains at Bir Umm Fawakhir.[33]

Evidence for Non-wood Fuels

The richest samples recovered from the Bir Umm Fawakhir 1999 sampling program are all in association with fuel use. Only two samples (both from Building 93, Dump 1, locus 2 and locus 12) were sufficiently rich to be of interpretable value. In both cases, seeds belonging to low-growing bushes, which typically form the scrub in the wadi today, dominated the assemblages. In most of the ash/oven contexts, mixtures of plant remains (often indicative of scrub), charred/desiccated twigs, charcoal, and charred/ desiccated dung were recovered.

It seems likely that the fuel supply for the Byzantine occupants of Bir Umm Fawakhir was a combination of such materials — all of which are fairly easily available in an environment with limited or possibly no trees. The project attempted to collect all the dung from Building 93, Dump 1, locus 2 (inside tabun 2),

---

2011, p. 230). For lack of time, however, weed or wild plant matter was not analyzed (van der Veen 2001, p. 15).

The plant remains from the Roman-period fort at Mons Claudianus include *Hordeum vulgare* as the most abundant cereal, *Triticum durum*, and a lot of chaff from both the barley and the wheat (van der Veen 2001, p. 180), the last probably imported from the Nile valley (ibid., p. 188) as animal fodder. Date palms, dom palms, grapes, olives, colocynth, bottle gourds, peas (*Pisum sativum*), fava beans (*Vicia faba*), camel thorn, acacia (ibid., p. 180), *Cornulaca monacantha*, *Coronopus niloticus*, *Raphanus raphanistrum*, *Avena fatua/sterilis* (ibid., p. 202), and *Chenopodium murale* (ibid., p. 203) are all reported, as well as many other species. *Triticum durum* or hard wheat is the prevalent kind of wheat; there is only a little bread wheat (T. *aestivum*) and less emmer (T. *dicoccum*) (ibid., p. 184).

The difficult-to-reach imperial porphyry quarries at Mons Porphyrites were worked mainly in two periods, early first to early third century and fourth to early fifth century (van der Veen and Tabinor 2007, p. 112). All the plant species at Bir Umm Fawakhir are also reported at Mons Porphyrites in the earlier period, minus some of the weeds (*Raphanus raphanistrum*, *Echinum* sp., *Avena* sp., *Cornulaca*, *Medicago*, and *Buglossoides*), plus many other edible plants (ibid., pp. 88–89). The later period, fourth to early fifth century, is not quite as well provisioned; among other plants, bottle gourd is not attested (ibid., p. 113). Some of the green vegetables may have been grown in small garden plots, probably near Badia and the main fort (ibid., p. 113) where the best wells were. (CAM)

[33] On the other hand, recent excavations at Quseir al-Qadim — at different parts of the site — recovered so much botanical material, especially from sebakh/middens, that it can be called "amongst the richest in the world" (van der Veen 2011, p. 2). For a summary of the non-weed plants, see table 6.2 in van der Veen 2011, p. 234. (CAM)

so a conservative estimate would be 80 percent of the contents of the tabun were available for analysis. In general, the charred dung contained highly broken-down plant matter that was not identifiable, but a few small grass seeds and tamarisk (*Tamarix* sp.) leaves were identified from a small sub-sample of ten droppings. During a visit to the site in the 2001 study season, we observed that such mixtures of dung, wood, and non-wood fuels are still in use, immediately on-site, by the local Bedouins.

Conclusion

It was not possible to fully address any of the aims for archaeobotanical analysis on the basis of the samples collected from the 1999 field season. In particular, the small sampling size has severely curtailed the interpretable value of the majority of samples studied. Nevertheless, it is clear that plant remains recovered are not atypical for sites dating to this period. The Bir Umm Fawakhir assemblage does provide good evidence for the regular use of mixtures of animal dung, wood, and non-wood fuels.

Table 2. Identifications of hand-picked "seeds"*

Area	Locus	Excavation Unit	Date	Phoenix dactylifera L.	Olea europea L.	Lagenaria siceraria L.	*Unidentified A (Unidentified pod)*	*Bark/wood (desiccated)*	*Sheep/goat dropping*	*Camel dropping*	*Gazelle dropping*	*Rodent dropping*	*Indeterminate dropping*
B93	—	Room C, NE quadrant, surface cleaning	ii-10-99	—	—	—	—	—	6	—	—	—	—
B93	—	Room D, surface silt	ii-14-99	—	—	—	—	—	2	1	—	—	—
Dump 1	?	—	ii-9-99	1	—	—	—	—	—	—	—	—	—
Dump 1	2/4/5	Clean-up	—	3	—	—	—	—	—	—	—	—	—
Dump 2	1	Wadi wash and surface	ii-14-99	3	—	—	—	—	—	—	—	—	—
B93	1	Room D	ii-23-99	—	—	—	—	—	1/ 1?	—	—	—	—
B93	1	Room D, east end	ii-25-99	—	—	—	—	—	1	—	—	—	—
B93	2	Room D	ii-13-99	1	—	—	—	—	—	—	—	—	—
Dump 2	2	—	ii-14-99	1	—	—	—	—	—	—	—	—	—
Dump 2	2	—	ii-15-99	10	—	—	1	—	—	—	—	—	—
B93	2	Room D	ii-24-99	—	—	—	—	—	3	—	—	—	—
Dump 1	2	—	ii-9-99	—	2	—	—	—	—	—	—	—	—
B93	3	Room D3, east end	—	—	—	—	—	—	1	—	—	—	—
Dump 1	3	—	ii-10-99	2	—	—	—	—	—	—	—	—	—
Dump 2	3	—	ii-14-99	9	—	1	—	—	—	—	—	—	—
Dump 2	3	Clean-up	ii-15-99	1	—	—	—	—	—	—	—	—	—
B93	3	Room D	ii-24-99	—	—	—	—	—	1	—	—	—	—
B93	4	Room C, NE quadrant	ii-13-99	—	—	—	—	—	—	—	—	—	yes
Dump 2	4	Middle strip	ii-15-99	1	—	—	1	—	—	—	—	—	—
Dump 2	4	—	ii-15-99	49	—	—	—	—	—	—	—	—	—
B93	4	Room A	ii-15-99	—	—	—	—	—	11	1	1	—	—
B93	4	Room A	ii-17-99	4	—	—	—	—	12	—	—	—	yes
Dump 1	4	—	ii-9-99	22	—	—	1	—	—	—	—	—	—
B93	5	Room A	—	3	—	—	—	—	14	—	—	—	—
Dump 2	5	Middle strip	ii-16-99	—	—	—	—	—	1	—	—	—	—
Dump 2	5	Middle strip	ii-16-99	—	—	—	—	—	1	—	—	—	yes
Dump 2	5	West strip	ii-16-99	2	—	—	—	—	1	—	—	—	—
Dump 2	5	Middle strip	ii-17-99	2	—	—	—	—	—	—	—	—	—
Dump 2	6	Middle strip	ii-17-99	1	—	—	—	—	—	—	—	—	—
B93	6	Room A	ii-17-99	9	1	—	—	—	7	—	—	—	—
Dump 1	7	Clean-up	—	1	—	—	—	2	—	—	—	—	—
Dump 1	7	Cleaning	ii-10-99	1	—	—	1	—	—	—	—	—	—
Dump 2	8	Around SW tabun	ii-16-99	1	—	—	—	—	3	—	—	—	—
Dump 1	9	—	ii-11-99	11	—	—	—	—	—	—	—	—	—
Dump 2	11	Tabun external excavation	—	1	—	—	—	—	1	—	—	—	—
Dump 1	11	—	ii-11-99	2	—	—	—	—	—	—	—	—	yes
Dump 1	11	—	ii-11-99	2	—	—	—	—	—	—	—	—	—
Dump 1	11	Tabun interior excavation	ii-20-99	3	—	—	—	—	9	—	—	1	—

* A total of 58 hand-picked samples were collected. All the plant remains listed are desiccated.

Table 2. Identifications of hand-picked "seeds" (*cont.*)

Area	*Locus*	*Excavation Unit*	*Date*	Phoenix dactylifera L.	Olea europea L.	Lagenaria siceraria L.	*Unidentified A (Unidentified pod)*	*Bark/wood (desiccated)*	*Sheep/goat dropping*	*Camel dropping*	*Gazelle dropping*	*Rodent dropping*	*Indeterminate dropping*
Dump 2	11	Tabun interior excavation	ii-21-99	15	—	—	3	—	—	—	—	—	—
Dump 1	12	—	—	3	—	—	—	—	—	—	—	—	—
B93	12	Room C, NE quadrant	ii-15-99	1	—	—	—	—	—	1	—	—	yes
Dump 2	12	Deep organic layer	ii-17-99	2	—	—	—	—	—	—	—	—	—
B93	13	Room C, NE quadrant	ii-15-99	—	—	—	—	—	1	—	—	—	—
Dump 1	15	Ash pit	ii-13-99	3	—	—	—	—	—	—	—	—	—
Dump 1	16	—	ii-13-99	1	—	—	—	—	—	—	—	—	—
B93	16	Room C, NW quadrant	ii-17-99	—	—	—	—	—	4	—	—	—	—
B177	3/5	Room A, clean-up	ii-29-99	—	—	—	—	—	26	—	1	1	yes
B177	1	Room C, east	—	—	—	—	—	—	—	—	—	—	yes
B177	2	Room D, west	—	—	—	—	—	1	2	—	—	—	—
B177	2	Room C, east	—	10	—	—	—	—	2	—	—	—	—
B177	3	Room D, west	—	—	—	—	—	—	4	1	—	1	yes
B177	3	Room A, SW quadrant	ii-22-99	—	—	—	—	—	—	—	—	—	—
B177	8	Room C west	—	4	—	—	—	2	—	—	—	—	yes
B177	9	Room C east	—	1	—	—	—	—	—	—	—	—	—
B177	11	Room A	ii-22-99	2	—	—	—	—	—	—	—	—	—
B177	12	Room A	ii-22-99	1	—	—	—	—	—	—	—	—	—
B177	12	Room A, SE quadrant	ii-24-99	1	—	—	—	—	—	—	—	—	—
		Total Identifications	**(n = 329**)**	**190**	**3**	**1**	**7**	**5**	**114**	**4**	**2**	**3**	**—**

** Out of the 329 identifications made, 201 were seeds. yes = probably present but no counted.

Table 3. Plant remains incorporated with other remains (animal bone, wood, charcoal, etc.)

Building	93		177	
Room	A	B East	A	
Locus	4	7	3	5
*Plant Remains Observed**				
Lagenaria siceraria L. (bottle gourd seed)	1	—	—	—
Phoenix dactylifera L. (date stone)	6	1	—	—
Hyphaene thebaica (L.) Mart. (dom palm fruit kernel)	—	—	—	1
Unidentified A (unidentified seed pod)	—	—	1	—

* All plant remains were desiccated.

Table 4. Plant remains recovered from Dump 1, loci 2, 12, 13

Locus	2				12		13	
Sample Volume	2.25 L		50 ml*		1.79 L		1 L**	
Volume >500 μm Fraction †	850 ml		20 ml		750 ml		850 ml	
Volume <500 μm Fraction	1.4 L		30 ml		1.04 L		150 ml	
Preservation	CARB	DESC	CARB	DESC	CARB	DESC	CARB	DESC
Economic Plants								
Triticum durum Desf. (hard wheat rachis internode)	–	–	–	–	–	–	–	–
Triticum durum Desf. (hard wheat basal rachis internode)	1	–	–	–	–	–	–	–
Triticum sp. (free-threshing wheat grain)	–	–	–	–	5	–	–	–
Triticum sp. (wheat glume)	–	1	–	–	–	–	–	–
Triticum sp. (wheat rachis internode)	–	–	–	–	–	–	–	–
cf. *Triticum* sp. (? wheat grain)	–	–	–	–	2	–	–	–
Hordeum vulgare L. (six-rowed barley rachis internode)	1	–	–	–	4	–	–	–
Hordeum sp. – hulled barley grain	1	–	–	–	13	–	–	–
Hordeum sp. – barley grain	4	–	–	–	–	–	–	–
Hordeum sp. – barley rachis internode	–	–	–	–	–	–	–	–
Hordeum sp. – barley basal rachis internode	–	–	–	–	1	–	–	–
Indeterminate cereal lemma	–	–	–	–	–	1	–	–
Indeterminate cereal rachis internode	–	–	–	–	1	–	–	–
Indeterminate cereal basal rachis internode	–	–	–	–	–	–	–	–
Indeterminate cereal grain/ Large grass	20	–	–	–	30	–	–	–
Indeterminate cereal/ large grass – detached embryo	–	–	–	–	–	–	–	–
Cereal / large grass culm node	–	–	–	–	–	1	–	–
Phoenix dactylifera L. – date stone	–	–	–	–	4	–	–	–
Vitis vinifera L. – grape pip	–	–	–	–	–	–	–	2
Weed/Wild Plants (seeds, unless otherwise indicated)								
cf. *Beta vulgaris* L.	–	–	–	–	2	–	–	–
Chenopodium murale L.	–	–	–	–	1	–	–	–
cf. *Coronopus* sp.	–	–	–	–	–	1	–	–
Cornulaca cf. *monacanatha* Del.	–	–	–	–	–	–	–	–
Zilla spinosa (Turra) Prantl	4	1	–	–	17	–	–	–
cf. *Zilla spinosa* (Turra) Prantl	–	–	–	–	1	–	–	–
Raphanus raphanistrum L. - capsule fragment	–	–	–	–	–	–	–	–
cf. *Raphanus raphanistrum* L. - capsule fragment	–	–	–	–	–	1	–	–
Acacia nilotica L.	–	–	–	–	–	–	–	–
cf. *Acacia nilotica* L.	–	–	–	–	–	–	–	–
Acacia sp. / *Vicia* sp. / *Pisum* sp.	–	–	–	–	–	–	–	–
Medicago sp. / *Melilotus* sp. / *Trifolium* sp.	–	–	–	–	–	–	–	–
Vicia sp. / *Pisum* sp.	1	–	–	–	–	–	–	–
Buglossoides sp.	586	–	–	–	5	–	–	–
Echium sp.	22	–	–	–	–	–	–	–

Key: + = <20 items, ++ = 20–50 items, +++ = >50 items.

† The results presented here are based of the plant remains recovered in the >500 μm fraction.

* The second (50 ml) sample was a "soil sample" collected for geological purposes, specifically, for its mica.

** A 1 L sub-sample of a 5 L sample was studied. Because sample was so poor, no further work was carried out.

CARB = charred; DESC = desiccated.

Table 4. Plant remains recovered from Dump 1, loci 2, 12, 13 (*cont.*)

Locus	2				12		13	
Sample Volume	2.25 L		50 ml*		1.79 L		1 L**	
Volume >500 µm Fraction †	850 ml		20 ml		750 ml		850 ml	
Volume <500 µm Fraction	1.4 L		30 ml		1.04 L		150 ml	
Preservation	CARB	DESC	CARB	DESC	CARB	DESC	CARB	DESC
Avena sp. – awn	—	—	—	—	1	—	—	—
Unidentified – bud	—	—	—	—	—	—	—	—
Unidentified – root	—	—	—	—	—	—	1	—
Unidentified – spine	1	—	—	—	—	—	—	—
Unidentified, amorphous charred plant/ food	++	—	—	—	—	—	—	—
Unidentified	1	1	—	—	—	—	—	—
Indeterminate	—	—	—	—	22	2	—	—
Total	**642**	**3**	**0**	**0**	**109**	**6**	**1**	**2**
OTHER MATERIAL OBSERVED								
Rodent pellet	—	—	—	—	—	—	—	—
Insects - modern appearance	—	—	—	—	—	—	—	—

Table 5. Plant remains recovered from Dump 1, locus 13, tabun

Depth	26 cm		31 cm		39 cm		44 cm	
Sample volume	50 ml		25 ml		100 ml		75 ml	
Volume >500 µm fraction	20 ml		15 ml		75 ml		40 ml	
Volume <500 µm fraction	30 ml		10 ml		25 ml		35 ml	
Preservation	CARB	DESC	CARB	DESC	CARB	DESC	CARB	DESC
ECONOMIC PLANTS								
Triticum durum Desf. (hard wheat rachis internode)	—	—	—	—	—	—	—	—
Triticum durum Desf. (hard wheat basal rachis internode)	—	—	—	—	—	—	—	—
Triticum sp. (free-threshing wheat grain)	—	—	—	—	—	—	—	—
Triticum sp. (wheat glume)	—	—	—	—	—	—	—	—
Triticum sp. (wheat rachis internode)	—	—	—	—	—	—	—	—
cf. *Triticum* sp. (? wheat grain)	—	—	—	—	—	—	—	—
Hordeum vulgare L. (six-rowed barley rachis internode)	—	—	—	—	—	—	1	—
Hordeum sp. – hulled barley grain	—	—	—	—	—	—	—	—
Hordeum sp. – barley grain	—	—	—	—	—	—	—	—
Hordeum sp. – barley rachis internode	—	—	—	—	—	—	—	—
Hordeum sp. – barley basal rachis internode	—	—	—	—	—	—	—	—
Indeterminate cereal lemma	—	—	—	—	—	—	—	—
Indeterminate cereal rachis internode	—	—	—	—	—	—	—	—
Indeterminate cereal basal rachis internode	—	—	—	—	—	—	—	—
Indeterminate cereal grain/ Large grass	—	—	—	—	—	—	1	—
Indeterminate cereal/ large grass - detached embryo	—	—	—	—	—	—	—	—
Cereal / large grass culm node	—	—	—	—	—	—	—	—
Phoenix dactylifera L. – date stone	—	—	—	—	—	—	—	—
Vitis vinifera L. – grape pip	—	—	—	—	—	—	—	—

Table 5. Plant remains recovered from Dump 1, locus 13, tabun (*cont.*)

Depth	26 cm		31 cm		39 cm		44 cm	
Sample volume	50 ml		25 ml		100 ml		75 ml	
Volume >500 µm fraction	20 ml		15 ml		75 ml		40 ml	
Volume <500 µm fraction	30 ml		10 ml		25 ml		35 ml	
Preservation	CARB	DESC	CARB	DESC	CARB	DESC	CARB	DESC
WEED/WILD PLANTS (seeds, unless otherwise indicated)								
cf. *Beta vulgaris* L.	–	–	–	–	–	–	–	–
Chenopodium murale L.	–	–	–	–	–	–	–	–
cf. *Coronopus* sp.	–	–	–	–	–	–	–	–
Cornulaca cf. *monacanatha* Del.	–	–	–	–	–	–	–	–
Zilla spinosa (Turra) Prantl	–	–	–	–	–	–	3	–
cf. *Zilla spinosa* (Turra) Prantl	–	–	–	–	–	–	–	–
Raphanus raphanistrum L. - capsule fragment	–	–	–	–	–	–	–	–
cf. *Raphanus raphanistrum* L. - capsule fragment	–	–	–	–	–	–	–	–
Acacia nilotica L.	–	–	–	–	–	–	–	–
cf. *Acacia nilotica* L.	–	–	–	–	–	–	–	–
Acacia sp. / *Vicia* sp. / *Pisum* sp.	–	–	–	–	–	–	–	–
Medicago sp. / *Melilotus* sp. / *Trifolium* sp.	–	–	–	–	–	–	–	–
Vicia sp. / *Pisum* sp.	–	–	–	–	–	–	–	–
Buglossoides sp.	–	–	–	–	–	–	1	–
Echium sp.	–	–	–	–	–	–	–	–
Avena sp. – awn	–	–	–	–	–	–	–	–
Unidentified – bud	–	–	–	–	–	–	–	–
Unidentified – root	–	–	–	–	–	–	–	–
Unidentified – spine	–	–	–	–	–	–	–	–
Unidentified, amorphous charred plant/ food	–	–	–	–	–	–	–	–
Unidentified	–	–	–	–	–	–	–	–
Indeterminate	–	–	–	–	–	–	3	–
Total	**0**	**0**	**0**	**0**	**0**	**0**	**9**	**0**
OTHER MATERIAL OBSERVED								
Rodent pellet	–	–	–	1	–	–	–	–
Insects – modern appearance	–	–	–	–	–	–	–	–

Table 6. Plant remains recovered from Dumps 1 and 2

Excavation Unit	Dump 1				Dump 2			
Locus	13		17		4		10	
Depth	Tabun, 49 cm		—		—		—	
Sample Volume	175 ml		2 L		800 ml		100 ml	
Volume >500 µm Fraction	50 ml		900 ml		400 ml		50 ml	
Volume <500 µm Fraction	125 ml		1.1 L		400 ml		50 ml	
Preservation	CARB	DESC	CARB	DESC	CARB	DESC	CARB	DESC
ECONOMIC PLANTS								
Triticum durum Desf. (hard wheat rachis internode)	3	—	—	—	—	—	—	—
Triticum durum Desf. (hard wheat basal rachis internode)	—	—	—	—	—	—	—	—
Triticum sp. (free-threshing wheat grain)	—	—	—	—	—	—	—	—
Triticum sp. (wheat glume)	—	—	—	—	—	—	—	—
Triticum sp. (wheat rachis internode)	—	—	—	—	—	—	—	—
cf. *Triticum* sp. (? wheat grain)	—	—	—	—	—	—	—	—
Hordeum vulgare L. (six-rowed barley rachis internode)	—	—	—	—	—	—	—	—
Hordeum sp. – hulled barley grain	—	—	—	—	—	—	—	—
Hordeum sp. – barley grain	2	—	—	—	—	—	—	—
Hordeum sp. – barley rachis internode	2	—	—	—	—	—	—	—
Hordeum sp. – barley basal rachis internode	—	—	—	—	—	—	—	—
Indeterminate cereal lemma	—	—	—	—	—	—	—	—
Indeterminate cereal rachis internode	—	—	—	—	—	—	—	—
Indeterminate cereal basal rachis internode	1	—	—	—	—	—	—	—
Indeterminate cereal grain/ Large grass	1	—	—	—	—	—	—	—
Indeterminate cereal/ large grass - detached embryo	—	—	—	—	—	—	1	—
Cereal / large grass culm node	—	—	—	—	—	—	—	—
Phoenix dactylifera L. – date stone	—	—	—	—	—	2	—	—
Vitis vinifera L. – grape pip	—	—	—	—	—	—	—	—
WEED/WILD PLANTS (seeds, unless otherwise indicated)								
cf. *Beta vulgaris* L.	—	—	—	—	—	—	—	—
Chenopodium murale L.	—	—	—	—	—	—	—	—
cf. *Coronopus* sp.	—	—	—	—	—	—	—	—
Cornulaca cf. *monacanatha* Del.	—	—	—	—	—	—	—	—
Zilla spinosa (Turra) Prantl	7	—	—	—	1	1	—	—
cf. *Zilla spinosa* (Turra) Prantl	—	—	—	—	—	—	—	—
Raphanus raphanistrum L. - capsule fragment	—	—	—	—	—	1	1	—
cf. *Raphanus raphanistrum* L. - capsule fragment	—	—	—	—	—	—	—	—
Acacia nilotica L.	2	—	—	—	—	—	1	—
cf. *Acacia nilotica* L.	3	—	—	—	—	1	—	—
Acacia sp. / *Vicia* sp. / *Pisum* sp.	—	—	—	—	3	—	—	—
Medicago sp. / *Melilotus* sp. / *Trifolium* sp.	1	—	—	—	1	1	—	—
Vicia sp. / *Pisum* sp.	—	—	—	—	—	—	1	—
Buglossoides sp.	9	—	—	—	38	—	7	—
Echium sp.	4	—	—	—	—	3	—	—
Avena sp. – awn	—	—	—	—	—	—	—	—

Table 6. Plant remains recovered from Dumps 1 and 2 (*cont.*)

Excavation Unit	Dump 1				Dump 2			
Locus	13		17		4		10	
Depth	Tabun, 49 cm		—		—		—	
Sample Volume	175 ml		2 L		800 ml		100 ml	
Volume >500 µm Fraction	50 ml		900 ml		400 ml		50 ml	
Volume <500 µm Fraction	125 ml		1.1 L		400 ml		50 ml	
Preservation	CARB	DESC	CARB	DESC	CARB	DESC	CARB	DESC
Unidentified - bud	—	—	—	—	2	—	—	—
Unidentified - root	—	—	—	—	—	—	—	—
Unidentified - spine	—	—	—	—	—	—	—	—
Unidentified, amorphous charred plant/ food	—	—	—	—	—	—	—	—
Unidentified	—	—	—	—	3	—	—	—
Indeterminate	10	—	—	—	—	—	5	—
Total	**45**	**0**	**0**	**0**	**48**	**9**	**16**	**0**
OTHER MATERIAL OBSERVED								
Rodent pellet	—	—	—	—	—	—	—	—
Insects - modern appearance	—	—	—	yes	—	—	—	—

Table 7. Plant remains recovered from Dump 2 and Building 93, Rooms B, C, E

Excavation Unit	Dump 2		Room B West		Room C Northwest		Room E	
Locus	12		3		18		3	
Sample Volume	25 ml		2.53 L		20 ml		175 ml	
Volume >500 µm Fraction	5 ml		1 L		15 ml		50 ml	
Volume <500 µm Fraction	20 ml		1.53 L		5 ml		125 ml	
Preservation	CARB	DESC	CARB	DESC	CARB	DESC	CARB	DESC
ECONOMIC PLANTS								
Triticum durum Desf. (hard wheat rachis internode)	—	—	—	—	—	—	—	—
Triticum durum Desf. (hard wheat basal rachis internode)	—	—	1	—	—	—	—	—
Triticum sp. (free-threshing wheat grain)	—	—	6	—	—	—	—	—
Triticum sp. (wheat glume)	—	—	—	—	—	—	—	—
Triticum sp. (wheat rachis internode)	—	—	1	—	—	—	—	—
cf. *Triticum* sp. (? wheat grain)	—	—	—	—	—	—	—	—
Hordeum vulgare L. (six-rowed barley rachis internode)	—	—	—	—	—	—	—	—
Hordeum sp. - hulled barley grain	—	—	3	—	—	—	—	—
Hordeum sp. - barley grain	—	—	—	—	—	—	—	—
Hordeum sp. - barley rachis internode	—	—	—	—	—	—	—	—
Hordeum sp. - barley basal rachis internode	—	—	—	—	—	—	—	—
Indeterminate cereal lemma	—	—	—	—	—	—	—	—
Indeterminate cereal rachis internode	—	—	—	—	—	—	—	—
Indeterminate cereal basal rachis internode	—	—	—	—	—	—	—	—
Indeterminate cereal grain/ Large grass	—	—	3	—	—	—	—	—
Indeterminate cereal/ large grass - detached embryo	—	—	—	—	—	—	—	—
Cereal / large grass culm node	—	—	1	—	—	—	—	—

Table 7. Plant remains recovered from Dump 2 and Building 93, Rooms B, C, E (*cont.*)

Excavation Unit	Dump 2		Room B West		Room C Northwest		Room E	
Locus	12		3		18		3	
Sample Volume	25 ml		2.53 L		20 ml		175 ml	
Volume >500 µm Fraction	5 ml		1 L		15 ml		50 ml	
Volume <500 µm Fraction	20 ml		1.53 L		5 ml		125 ml	
Preservation	CARB	DESC	CARB	DESC	CARB	DESC	CARB	DESC
Phoenix dactylifera L. – date stone	—	—	—	—	—	—	—	—
Vitis vinifera L. – grape pip	—	—	—	—	—	—	—	—
WEED/WILD PLANTS (seeds, unless otherwise indicated)								
cf. *Beta vulgaris* L.	—	—	—	—	—	—	—	—
Chenopodium murale L.	—	—	—	—	—	—	—	—
cf. *Coronopus* sp.	—	—	1	—	—	—	—	—
Cornulaca cf. *monacanatha* Del.	—	—	7	—	—	—	—	—
Zilla spinosa (Turra) Prantl	—	—	3	1	—	—	11	1
cf. *Zilla spinosa* (Turra) Prantl	—	—	—	—	—	—	—	—
Raphanus raphanistrum L. - capsule fragment	—	—	—	—	—	—	—	—
cf. *Raphanus raphanistrum* L. - capsule fragment	—	—	—	—	—	—	—	—
Acacia nilotica L.	—	—	—	—	—	—	—	—
cf. *Acacia nilotica* L.	—	—	—	—	—	—	—	—
Acacia sp. / *Vicia* sp. / *Pisum* sp.	—	—	5	—	—	—	—	—
Medicago sp. / *Melilotus* sp. / *Trifolium* sp.	—	—	1	—	—	—	—	—
Vicia sp. / *Pisum* sp.	—	—	—	—	—	—	—	—
Buglossoides sp.	1	—	10	—	—	—	—	—
Echium sp.	—	—	—	—	—	—	—	—
Avena sp. – awn	—	—	—	—	—	—	—	—
Unidentified – bud	—	—	—	—	—	—	—	—
Unidentified – root	—	—	7	—	—	—	—	—
Unidentified – spine	—	—	—	—	—	—	—	—
Unidentified, amorphous charred plant/ food	—	—	—	—	—	—	—	—
Unidentified	1	—	5	—	—	—	1	—
Indeterminate	—	—	9	—	—	—	—	—
Total	**2**	**0**	**63**	**1**	**0**	**0**	**12**	**1**
OTHER MATERIAL OBSERVED								
Rodent pellet	—	—	—	—	—	—	—	—
Insects - modern appearance	—	—	—	—	—	—	—	—

Table 8. Archaeobotanical results from Building 177

Excavation Unit	Room A								Room D East	
Locus	3		13		15		16		8	
Sample Volume	600 ml		350 ml		350 ml		245 ml		15 ml	
Volume >500 µm Fraction	250 ml		175 ml		230 ml		150 ml		5 ml	
Volume <500 µm Fraction	350 ml		175 ml		120 ml		95 ml		10 ml	
Preservation	CARB	DESC	CARB	DESC	CARB	DESC	CARB	DESC	CARB	DESC
Economic Plants										
Triticum durum Desf. (hard wheat rachis internode)	–	–	1	–	–	–	–	–	–	–
Triticum sp. (free-threshing wheat grain)	–	–	1	–	–	–	–	–	–	–
Triticum sp. (wheat grain)	–	–	–	–	–	–	1	–	–	–
Hordeum sp. (hulled barley grain)	–	–	–	–	1	–	–	–	–	–
Hordeum vulgare L. (six-rowed barley rachis internode)	–	–	–	–	–	–	–	–	–	–
Hordeum sp. (barley basal rachis internode)	–	–	–	–	–	–	–	–	–	–
cf. *Hordeum* sp. (? barley rachis internode)	–	–	–	–	1	–	–	–	–	–
Indeterminate cereal lemma	–	–	–	–	–	–	–	–	–	–
Indeterminate cereal rachis internode	–	–	–	–	–	–	–	–	–	–
Indeterminate Cereal grain / large grass	–	–	2	–	2	–	2	–	–	–
Cereal / Large grass culm node	–	–	–	–	–	–	–	–	–	–
Phoenix dactylifera L. stone	–	–	–	–	–	–	–	–	–	–
Vitis vinifera L. pip	–	–	–	–	–	–	–	–	–	–
Weed/Wild Plants (seeds, unless otherwise indicated)										
cf. *Beta vulgaris* L.	–	–	–	–	–	–	–	–	–	–
Chenopodium murale L.	–	–	–	–	–	–	–	–	–	–
cf. *Coronopus* sp.	–	–	–	–	–	–	–	–	–	–
Cornulaca cf. *monacantha* Del.	–	–	–	–	3	–	7	–	–	–
Zilla spinosa (Turra) Prantl	–	2	1	–	2	–	1	2	–	–
cf. *Zilla spinosa* (Turra) Prantl	–	–	–	–	–	–	–	–	–	–
cf. *Raphanus raphanistrum* L. – capsule fragment	–	–	–	–	–	–	–	–	–	–
Acacia nilotica L. – pod segment	–	–	–	–	–	–	1	–	–	–
Acacia sp. / *Vicia* sp. / *Pisum* sp.	–	–	1	–	1	–	–	–	–	–
Medicago sp. / *Melilotus* sp. / *Trifolium* sp.	–	–	–	–	–	–	1	–	–	–
Buglossoides sp.	–	–	4	1	17	–	29	–	–	–
Avena sp. – awn	–	–	–	–	–	–	–	–	–	–
Unidentified	–	–	6	–	1	–	5	–	–	–
Indeterminate	–	–	–	–	–	–	7	–	–	–
Total	**0**	**2**	**16**	**1**	**28**	**0**	**54**	**2**	**0**	**0**
Other Material Observed										
Sheep/goat dropping	–	1	–	–	–	–	–	–	–	–
Charcoal	–	–	yes	–	–	–	yes	–	–	–
Twine	–	–	1	–	–	–	–	–	–	–

Table 9. Archaeobotanical results from Building 181, Locus 2

Depth	at 71 cm		at 80 cm	
Sample Volume	450 ml		475 ml	
Volume >500 µm Fraction	225 ml		100 ml	
Volume <500 µm Fraction	225 ml		375 ml	
Preservation	CARB	DESC	CARB	DESC
ECONOMIC PLANTS				
Triticum sp. (wheat grain)	1	—	—	—
Phoenix dactylifera L. (date stone)	—	—	1	—
Vitis vinifera L. (grape pip)	—	1	—	—
WEED/WILD PLANTS (seeds, unless otherwise indicated)				
Zilla spinosa (Turra) Prantl	—	—	—	1
Buglossoides sp.	—	1	2	—
Indeterminate leaf / petal / stem	—	1	—	1
Indeterminate stem	—	1	—	—
Indeterminate root	—	1	—	—
Unidentified	—	—	—	—
Indeterminate	—	1	—	2
Total	**1**	**6**	**3**	**4**

Chapter 7

Object Conservation

Richard L. Jaeschke

Introduction

Conservation work for the Bir Umm Fawakhir 1999 season actually started several months before excavation of the site began. Since no excavation had been undertaken in previous seasons, the range, size, quantity, and condition of artifacts likely to be uncovered could only be estimated. In order to allow for as many contingencies as possible, a wide range of materials and equipment was amassed in the United Kingdom. Further purchases were made in Cairo and Luxor of useful local materials and equipment and bulky or dangerous items that could not easily be brought by air, such as organic solvents. In addition, some appropriate articles were obtained from the stores of the previous Bir Umm Fawakhir seasons, and some were made available from early Quseir al-Qadim expeditions, courtesy of Janet Johnson and Donald Whitcomb.

On the day after arrival at the site, a work area in the dig house was designated for the conservation laboratory, and facilities were set up. Stock solutions were mixed, and some surface finds from previous seasons were laid out for immediate attention. As the season progressed, work was divided between conservation in the field, as various delicate items were discovered, and work in the laboratory on finds that could be transported back to the dig house.

Conservation on Site

Iron Ladle

Almost as soon as the first excavation work began, a delicate object was found that required treatment in situ. An iron ladle (RN 99/228) in an extremely fragile state was uncovered inside Building 93, Room B (pl. 36). It was left in place by the excavators, to be lifted by the conservator. First, the remaining overlying sand and grit were gently blown away with a photographic puffer/blower (a small tool used to clean camera lenses) to expose the upper surface. Any contact with brushes or dental picks threatened to disturb the iron, flakes of which were loose and detaching. The object and a small amount of the surrounding matrix were consolidated by pipetting a consolidating solution gently into the area, making sure that the action of the liquid did not disturb the object or its substrate. The first application was of a 10 percent weight/volume solution of Paraloid B72 (an acrylic copolymer resin of ethyl methacrylate and methyl acrylate) in acetone for maximum penetration and saturation of the area, followed by a 25 percent solution, also applied by pipette, to give further structural strength and support to the gaps in the fabric of the iron and to hold the loose flakes in place. The Paraloid resin hardened fairly rapidly in the open air, and the ladle with the adjoining soil block was lifted onto a plastic lid as a support and subsequently placed in a plastic box within about one hour. It was then taken to the laboratory for subsequent conservation treatment (pls. 36).

Tabuns

During excavation, several small ceramic ovens or tabuns were discovered, which needed to be excavated with some care and often required conservation treatment to allow work to proceed.

Dump 1, "Tabun" 1

The first tabun or *dolium*, described as "tabun" 1 in Dump 1 (locus 13 inside and locus 14 outside), consisted of a coarse ceramic jar, about 33–37 cm in diameter at the rim, with a slightly elliptical shape. The upper layers of debris were initially cleared to reveal the entire top rim of the completely buried tabun (or *dolium*). It was immediately observed that the upper levels were layered with sherds forming a double wall, the inner being the intact ceramic of the tabun, the outer being a secondary wall built up from a mosaic of potsherds stacked edge to edge and lying next to the inner wall with no space between (fig. 45). The area outside the layered tabun, described as locus 14, was itself enclosed in a drystone wall surround. The interior of the tabun was carefully excavated. The coarse ceramic of the inner tabun had fractured into roughly rectangular fragments ranging from 4 × 6 cm to 6 × 8 cm. Several large fragments at or near the top rim were removed. The edge surfaces were cleaned, and the fragments were reattached using a viscous solution of Paraloid B72 in acetone. Some very friable ceramic was consolidated by pipetting a 10–15 percent solution of Paraloid B72 in acetone. Much of the contents (locus 13) consisted of granite fragments approximately 2–3 mm in length with occasional potsherds and small fragments of bone. As the interior was excavated, part of a compacted clay floor was found, approximately 26 cm below the rim level, running around approximately two-fifths of the internal circumference of the pot and extending in toward the center as much as 15 cm. Several subsequent floor levels of varying size were found at 31 cm, 39 cm, and 44 cm below the rim level. Samples were taken from each of these floor levels as well as a sample of the granite chips and a sample of the ash found at 49 cm below the rim level. The widest external diameter of the ceramic tabun was estimated at 55 cm near the base.

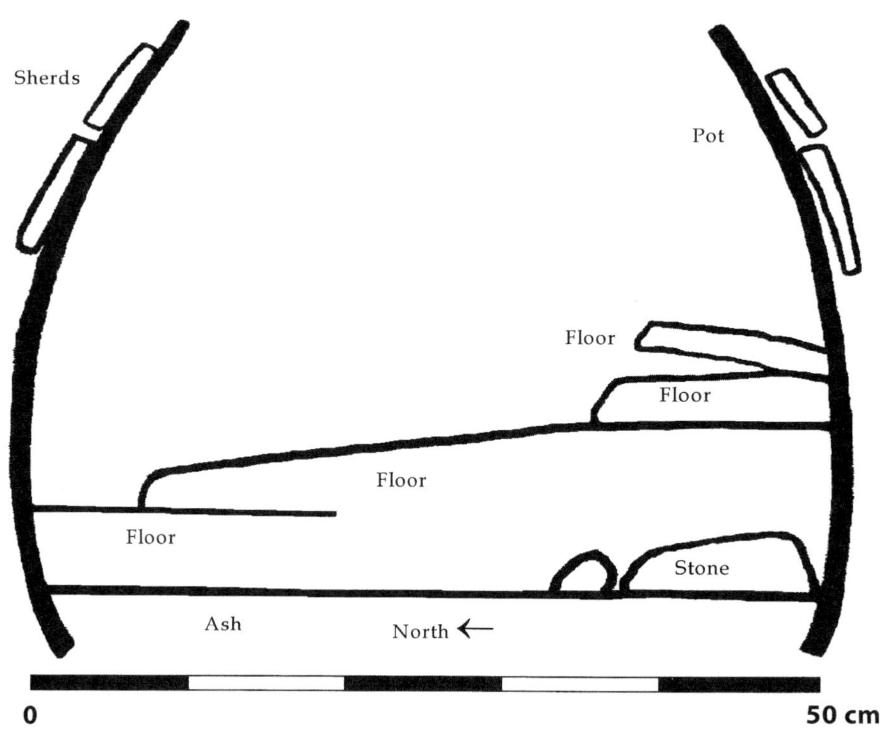

Figure 45. Schematic cross section of Dump 1, "tabun" 1

The outside of the tabun, the area between the outer surface of the ceramic lining and the drystone wall (locus 14), was then excavated. A possible floor level was found at 25 cm below the top of the tabun. The fill above the 25 cm level consisted of mixed soils, ash, sherds, bone, and charcoal with some fiber and dung. The fill below this 25 cm level was of a more uniform, lighter "fly ash" with larger sherds embedded in it. As the soil level was reduced to approximately 28 cm below rim level, starting on the east side, the overhanging ceramic of the tabun began to collapse inward. The fragments of the tabun were found to be slightly displaced with gaps between and a lacuna beneath. This area did not have sufficient bearing surfaces to support its own weight. The collapsed fragments were moved and consolidated with a 10 percent solution of Paraloid B72 in acetone applied by pipette, as was the inside surface and the break edges of the remaining ceramic in the ground.

The detached fragments from the tabun wall were joined in two sections using a viscous solution of Paraloid B48 (an acrylic copolymer of ethyl methacrylate and methyl acrylate with a larger polymer size than the B72 grade) in acetone as adhesive, further strengthened with layers of glass-fiber tissue applied to the interior face with a 10 percent solution of Paraloid B72 in acetone. The edges of the laminating tissue were left protruding beyond the edges of the sherds to assist with reattachment. The two major sections were reattached to the tabun using a viscous solution of Paraloid B48 in acetone as adhesive and held in place with the overlapping glass-fiber laminate joined with a 10 percent solution of Paraloid B72 in acetone (pl. 37a). More glass fiber tissue was stretched over the cracks and used to bridge small gaps between the edges. This was attached using a 10 percent solution of Paraloid B72 in acetone. Once the replaced sections were set, but while the adhesive was still flexible, adjustments were made and the whole structure supported in place until the resin was completely hardened. Excess Paraloid was then removed by brushing with acetone.

Dump 2, "Pot 2"

"Pot 2" in Dump 2 ("pot smash," locus 11) proved to be an upturned amphora neck with dipinto (RN 99/224; fig. 37a) and was excavated in a similar manner to "tabun" 1 in Dump 1. The amphora neck installation was approximately 25 cm in diameter at ground level and had some potsherds in association as a double wall. On this occasion a few centimeters of space had been left between the inner and outer walls. Excavating the interior, tiny sherds mixed with ash and a few large stones were found. One large potsherd at the base of the amphora proved to be acting as a stopper in the inside of the neck of the upturned vessel. A sample was taken of the fill directly beneath this large sherd. A small copper-alloy fragment was found in the interior and was treated in the laboratory. The amphora was completely removed for further study.

Dump 2, "Pot 1"

"Pot 1" in Dump 2 (locus 9) proved to be a very fragile ceramic vessel, approximately 19 cm in diameter at the rim (fig. 13, pl. 37b, 38a). The outer surface and rim were consolidated with a 10 percent solution of Paraloid B72 in acetone applied by pipette. Excavating the interior revealed an unremarkable sandy uniform fill with very few inclusions until 30 cm below the rim. Below this level, small sherds, charcoal, and bone were present, and an ash level was present near the bottom at the 33 cm level. It was observed that the bottom of this pot had been broken out before the pot was set on the floor within this enclosed space. The exterior was excavated, and again lining sherds were discovered, packed around the body, starting at approximately 18 cm below the rim. In the upper areas some disturbed sherds were found that might have been the upper part of the liner.

Dump 2, "SW Tabun"

Locus 10 in Dump 2 contained a very thick, coarse, and fragile ceramic vessel, 2.5 cm thick, measuring 43 cm in diameter at rim (another "tabun" or *dolium*; see fig. 13). The exposed areas of the outer surface of the rim and some of the inner surface were consolidated with a 10 percent solution of Paraloid B72 in acetone applied by pipette. The interior of the tabun when first cleared revealed a layer of textile and fiber almost at the surface, approximately 10 cm from the highest point of the rim (pl. 38b). This layer lay over several large, rounded stones, with hair, fiber, and bone associated. Some glass fragments, wood, and seeds were found, and samples were taken. A portion of this fill was lifted intact for further examination in the laboratory. Internal excavations continued, revealing mixed debris of soil, ash, small sherds, and further glass fragments. At the 32–34 cm level, a mixture of fiber, textile, twigs, and leaves was found at a "floor" of large stones (cloth, fibers shown on pl. 39b). The lower edges of the coarse ceramic tabun pot could be seen at this level, and excavation stopped. Portions of the coarse ceramic in the body were as much as 4 cm thick. Excavating the exterior revealed relatively uniform layers of considerable amounts of ash and charcoal with some sherds and bone, quite well mixed. At about 25 cm below the rim, the walls of the tabun were very fragile, only being held in place by large stones stacked up around the base. Removal of one stone resulted in the lower part of the ceramic wall beginning to disintegrate, and since the base edges of the pot could be seen at this level, excavation stopped at this point (pl. 39a).

Later, two intact jars with contents were removed from locus 17 of Dump 1 by the conservator, to be excavated later in the laboratory.

In-house Conservation

Conservation was performed in-house on an interior table with some natural light and artificial light (when available) and also on the open-sided veranda. A selection of basic materials and supplies was available, including hand tools and a stereo microscope of ×20 magnification. Objects undergoing full conservation treatment were examined and photographed before and after treatment. Each was assigned a lab sheet and a lab treatment number and cross-referenced with the dig registration numbers and Antiquities Service numbers. The following objects were treated:

1. Orange Ceramic Plate

Registration Number: RN 99/233

Illustration: fig. 1814, pl. 31a

Provenance: Dump behind Building 181, surface

Treatment: This orange plate was cleaned by light brushing with a soft natural-bristle brush. A glass-bristle brush was used on the break edges to remove concretions of dirt and facilitate rejoining. The fragments were rejoined using a viscous solution of Paraloid B72 in acetone. Several joins were made forming three major sections that unfortunately did not interconnect.

2. Orange Ceramic Plate

Registration Number: RN 99/221

Illustration: —

Provenance: Dump behind Building 228, surface

Treatment: This plate had been previously treated[34] with an acetone-soluble adhesive (perhaps Duco polyvinyl acetate). Since the old joins were not sufficiently accurate, they were taken down with acetone applied by brush. The break edges were further cleaned by brushing. The fragments were rejoined using a viscous solution of Paraloid B72 in acetone. The edges of the remaining gaps were protected with a coating of a 25 percent solution of Paraloid B72 in acetone. The gaps were then filled with Polyfilla, a commercial blend of plaster of Paris containing cellulose. When hardened this was carved to shape and in-painted with Rowney acrylic inks.

[34] The sherds were found during the 1997 season and published in Meyer and Heidorn 2011, p. 32, fig. 38:175.

3. Deep Bowl or "Krater"

Registration Number: RN 99/218

Illustration: fig. 27:104, pl. 32a

Provenance: Surface find

Treatment: This ceramic jar had a buff-colored slip around the rim. The surface was cleaned by light brushing with a soft brush. The fragments were joined using a viscous solution of Paraloid B72 in acetone. A complete profile could be formed, but because much of the body was missing, the vessel was reconstructed as a half pot. The edges of the remaining gaps were protected with a coating of a 25 percent solution of Paraloid B72 in acetone. The gaps were then filled with Polyfilla, a commercial blend of plaster of Paris containing cellulose. When hardened this was carved to shape and in-painted with Rowney acrylic inks.

4. Red Ceramic Jar with Red Slip and Black Paint

Registration Number: RN 99/234

Illustration: fig. 34:138, pl. 32b

Provenance: Surface behind Building 61

Treatment: The fragments of this jar were joined using a viscous solution of Paraloid B72 in acetone. Some fragments formed larger associations allowing the design to be seen.

5. Iron Ladle

Registration Number: RN 99/228

Illustration: pls. 34e, 36

Provenance: Building 93, Room B, locus 6

Treatment: This iron ladle was lifted in the field, as described above. In the laboratory it was first mechanically cleaned to remove the sand and grit. Acetone was pipetted onto the surface as required to soften the consolidant, allowing further sand and grit to be detached using the tip of a fine bamboo stick. The iron was mechanically cleaned using a polished scalpel under a binocular microscope. As the corrosion was removed, many small pieces that had been held by the corrosion, some in incorrect positions, were freed. These were reattached in the correct position using a viscous solution of Paraloid B48 in acetone. A separate fragment found in the surrounding debris was also attached using a viscous solution of Paraloid B48 in acetone. The ladle was mostly cleaned but was too fragile for complete cleaning in the time available. Any excess Paraloid B72 from the field consolidation was removed with acetone. When the remaining consolidant had thoroughly hardened again, a protective coating of microcrystalline wax (Cornelissen MCW) in white spirit was applied by brush.

6. Textile and Fiber Collection

Registration Number: RN 99/217

Illustration: pl. 39b

Provenance: Dump 2, locus 4

Treatment: Several small fragments of textile and loose fibers were brought to the laboratory for treatment. Some trial cleaning was attempted using distilled water containing a few drops of Synperonic non-ionic detergent and a few crystals of sodium hexametaphosphate. Some cleaning and lightening of the samples was observed (pl. 39b), but it was not necessary or desirable to proceed further at this stage.

7. Amphora

Registration Number: —

Illustration: fig. 35:150, pl. 40a

Provenance: Surface find

Treatment: Many fragments were found that were originally thought to be part of one vessel. These proved to belong to several amphoras. The fragments were joined, forming larger assemblages but no complete vessels, using a viscous solution of Paraloid B48 in acetone.

8. Orange Ceramic Plate, Stamped

Registration Number: RN 99/226

Illustration: fig. 18:16

Provenance: Surface find

Treatment: This plate was cleaned by swabbing with distilled water containing a few drops of Synperonic non-ionic detergent and a few crystals of sodium hexametaphosphate. This was followed by light brushing with a soft brush.

9. Intact Jar with Contents

Registration Number: RN 99/220

Illustration: fig. 33:135, pls. 7, 14

Provenance: Dump 1, locus 17

Treatment: The contents of this jar were excavated in the laboratory and proved to be mostly coarse sand and soil containing stones, a few bone fragments, some sherds, and charcoal. Five deliberate holes had been made in the bottom of the jar at the time of manufacture by pushing from the outside to the inside. These holes had clean edges with excess clay removed. It was conjectured that the jar might have been used for cheese making, the holes allowing the whey to drain.

10. Complete Jar (not intact) with Contents

Registration Number: RN 99/219

Illustration: fig. 32:129, pls. 7, 13b

Provenance: Dump 1, locus 17

Treatment: This jar was of red ware with black markings. It was cracked, with part of the rim missing and part detached. The contents were excavated and were found to be mostly coarse sandy grit containing very little charcoal and one vertebra, possibly from a sheep. There were three very small holes, 1.5–2.0 mm in diameter, in the base of jar, which may not penetrate completely. A large triangular potsherd was found inside on the bottom of the jar, covering the holes. This was intrusive and was not a fragment from the jar. Again, it is conjectured that this jar might have been used for cheese making. Detached fragments found in proximity were joined using a viscous solution of Paraloid B72 in acetone. The surface was cleaned by light brushing with a soft brush.

11. Copper-alloy Coin

Registration Number: 99/237

Illustration: fig. 40a

Provenance: Building B93, Room C northwest, locus 18

Treatment: This coin was mechanically cleaned to remove corrosion products and reveal the original surface level, using a polished scalpel under a binocular microscope, followed by brushing with a glass-bristle brush. It was degreased by immersion in acetone, then stabilized by immersion in a 3 percent solution of benzotriazole in industrial methylated spirits (IMS) overnight. It was rinsed in IMS and allowed to dry. The surface was then protected with three coats of a 5 percent solution of Paraloid B72 in acetone containing a small amount of Qcell (fumed silica) used as a matting agent.

12. Copper-alloy Coin

Registration Number: RN 99/237

Illustration: fig. 40b

Provenance: Building 93, Room C northwest, locus 18

Treatment: This coin was mechanically cleaned to remove corrosion products and reveal the original surface level, using a polished scalpel under a binocular microscope, followed by brushing with a glass-bristle brush. It was degreased by immersion in acetone, then stabilized by immersion in a 3 percent solution of benzotriazole in IMS overnight. It was rinsed in industrial methylated spirits (IMS) and allowed to dry. The surface was then protected with three coats of a 5 percent solution of Paraloid B72 in acetone containing a small amount of Qcell (fumed silica) used as a matting agent.

13. Copper-alloy Ornament

Registration Number: RN 99/240

Illustration: fig. 41b, pl. 34a

Provenance: Building 93, Room C northwest, locus 18

Treatment: This object was mechanically cleaned to remove corrosion products and reveal the original surface level, using a polished scalpel under a binocular microscope, followed by brushing with a glass-bristle brush. It was degreased by immersion in acetone, then stabilized by immersion in a 3 percent solution of benzotriazole in IMS overnight. It was rinsed in industrial methylated spirits (IMS) and allowed to dry. The surface was then protected with three coats of a 5 percent solution of Paraloid B72 in acetone containing a small amount of Qcell (fumed silica) used as a matting agent. The object was found to be a small amulet, probably of Bes.

14. Copper-alloy Coin

Registration Number: RN 99/237

Illustration: fig. 40c

Provenance: Building 177, Room A, locus 3

Treatment: This coin was mechanically cleaned to remove corrosion products and reveal the original surface level, using a polished scalpel under a binocular microscope, followed by brushing with a glass-bristle brush. It was degreased by immersion in acetone, then stabilized by immersion in a 3 percent solution of benzotriazole in industrial methylated spirits (IMS) overnight. It was rinsed in IMS and allowed to dry. The surface was then protected with three coats of a 5 percent solution of Paraloid B72 in acetone containing a small amount of Qcell (fumed silica) used as a matting agent.

15. Iron Strap

Registration Number: RN 99/231

Illustration: —

Provenance: Building 177, Room A, locus 7

Treatment: This object was a small iron strap with a loop fitting on one end. It could have formed part of a delicate piece of machinery or even part of an item of jewelry such as a fibula. It was mechanically cleaned to remove corrosion, using a polished scalpel under a binocular microscope. The surface was then given a protective coating of microcrystalline wax in white spirit, applied by brush.

16. Copper-alloy Coin

Registration Number: RN 99/237

Illustration: fig. 40e

Provenance: Building 177, Room C west, locus 2

Treatment: This coin was mechanically cleaned to remove corrosion products and reveal the original surface level, using a polished scalpel under a binocular microscope, followed by brushing with a glass-bristle brush. It was degreased by immersion in acetone, then stabilized by immersion in a 3 percent solution of benzotriazole in industrial methylated spirits (IMS) overnight. It was rinsed in industrial methylated spirits (IMS) and allowed to dry. The surface was then protected with three coats of a 5 percent solution of Paraloid B72 in acetone containing a small amount of Qcell (fumed silica) used as a matting agent.

17. Copper-alloy Strap

Registration Number: RN 99/238

Illustration: –

Provenance: Dump 2, locus 5, north end, middle strip

Treatment: The strap was mechanically cleaned to remove corrosion products and reveal the original surface level, using a polished scalpel under a binocular microscope, followed by brushing with a glass-bristle brush. It was degreased by immersion in acetone, then stabilized by immersion in a 3 percent solution of benzotriazole in industrial methylated spirits (IMS) overnight. It was rinsed in industrial methylated spirits (IMS) and allowed to dry. The surface was then protected with three coats of a 5 percent solution of Paraloid B72 in acetone containing a small amount of Qcell (fumed silica) used as a matting agent.

18. Metal-alloy Bracelet

Registration Number: RN 99/230

Illustration: fig. 41a, pl. 33b

Provenance: Building 93, Room A, locus 6

Treatment: This item is probably a gold alloy, with copper preferentially corroded on the surface. The original surface is a soft yellow metal. It was mechanically cleaned using a polished scalpel under a binocular microscope followed by very light glass-bristle brushing. The surface was finally polished with using Solvol Autosol (a commercial chrome polish containing fine abrasives in a white spirit-soluble base) to reduce cuprite overlay. A fragile tag at one end was secured in place more firmly using a viscous solution of Paraloid B48 in acetone.

19. Copper-alloy Weight

Registration Number: RN 99/239

Illustration: fig. 41c, pl. 35b

Provenance: Building 177, Room A southwest, locus 3

Treatment: This object, possibly an assay weight, was mechanically cleaned to remove corrosion products and reveal the original surface level, using a polished scalpel under a binocular microscope, followed by brushing with a glass-bristle brush. It was degreased by immersion in acetone, then stabilized by immersion in a 3 percent solution of benzotriazole in IMS overnight. It was rinsed in industrial methylated spirits (IMS) and allowed to dry. The surface was then protected with three coats of a 5 percent solution of Paraloid B72 in acetone containing a small amount of Qcell (fumed silica) used as a matting agent. A small inscription was revealed on one side, a deeply impressed "NB" with a small circle over the N.

20. Copper-alloy Coin

Registration Number: RN 99/237

Illustration: fig. 40f

Provenance: Building 177, Room C west, locus 7

Treatment: This coin was mechanically cleaned to remove corrosion products and reveal the original surface level, using a polished scalpel under a binocular microscope, followed by brushing with a glass-bristle brush. It was degreased by immersion in acetone, then stabilized by immersion in a 3 percent solution of benzotriazole in IMS overnight. It was rinsed in industrial methylated spirits (IMS) and allowed to dry. The surface was then protected with three coats of a 5 percent solution of Paraloid B72 in acetone containing a small amount of Qcell (fumed silica) used as a matting agent.

21. Stone Fragment

Registration Number: —

Illustration: —

Provenance: Building 177, Room C west, locus 9

Treatment: This small, greenish fragment was originally thought to be copper alloy. It was mechanically probed and found to be a fragment of a greenish stone.

22. Ceramic Plate, Stamped Impression

Registration Number: RN 99/236

Illustration: fig. 18:15

Provenance: Building 177, Room A, locus 12

Treatment: This plate was very fragmentary, with severe salt deterioration and a heavy dirt encrustation. The sherds were consolidated by immersion in an 8 percent solution of Paraloid B72 in acetone for 1.5 hours. The fragments were then drained and allowed to dry slowly in a sealed container with the acetone fumes to increase penetration and prevent surface darkening. The top surface only was cleaned by swabbing first with acetone, then with a mixture of equal parts of acetone and distilled water containing a few drops of Synperonic non-ionic detergent and a few crystals of sodium hexametaphosphate. The sherds were then joined using a viscous solution of Paraloid B48 in acetone.

23. Possible Incense Burner, Limestone

Registration Number: RN 99/227

Illustration: fig. 41e, pl. 15c

Provenance: Building 177, Room A, locus 9

Treatment: This object had a very fragile texture. Some fragments were attached using a viscous solution of Paraloid B48 in acetone. It was gently cleaned by light brushing with a soft brush.

24. Copper-alloy Strap

Registration Number: RN 99/241

Illustration: fig. 41d

Provenance: Dump 1, locus 12

Treatment: This object was mechanically cleaned to remove corrosion products and reveal the original surface level, using a polished scalpel under a binocular microscope, followed by brushing with a glass-bristle brush. It was degreased by immersion in acetone, then stabilized by immersion in a 3 percent solution of benzotriazole in IMS overnight. It was rinsed in industrial methylated spirits (IMS) and allowed to dry. The surface was then protected with three coats of a 5 percent solution of Paraloid B72 in acetone containing a small amount of Qcell (fumed silica) used as a matting agent. The metal seemed to be almost pure copper and was redder and softer than bronze.

25. Copper-alloy Coin

Registration Number: RN 99/237

Illustration: fig. 40d

Provenance: Building 177, Room A, locus 15, stone circle

Treatment: This coin was mechanically cleaned to remove corrosion products and reveal the original surface level, using a polished scalpel under a binocular microscope, followed by brushing with a glass-bristle brush. It was degreased by immersion in acetone, then stabilized by immersion in a 3 percent solution of benzotriazole in IMS overnight. It was rinsed in industrial methylated spirits (IMS) and allowed to dry. The surface was then protected with three coats of a 5 percent solution of Paraloid B72 in acetone containing a small amount of Qcell (fumed silica) used as a matting agent.

26. Lead Ring

Registration Number: RN 99/241

Illustration: —

Provenance: Dump 1, locus 16, baulk cleaning

Treatment: The object was mechanically cleaned using a polished scalpel under a binocular microscope followed by very gently brushing with a glass-bristle stick. The surface was then given a protective coating of microcrystalline wax in white spirit, applied by brush.

27. Iron Wedge

Registration Number: RN 99/241

Illustration: pl. 35a

Provenance: Room B west, locus 5

Treatment: The object was mechanically cleaned using a polished scalpel under a binocular microscope followed by very gently brushing with a glass-bristle stick. The surface was then given a protective coating of microcrystalline wax in white spirit, applied by brush.

28. Copper-alloy Fragment

Registration Number: RN 99/241

Illustration: —

Provenance: Building 177, Room A, locus 3

Treatment: This object was partly cleaned using a polished scalpel under a binocular microscope. It proved to be a very small fragment, approximately 5 × 8 mm. It was covered with hard corrosion, and contained no core and very little metal. The object broke easily and no detail could be seen on the surface. The fragments were joined using a viscous solution of Paraloid B72 in acetone. No further cleaning was undertaken.

Packing and Storage

The excavated objects that had been conserved were to be stored in the official storage magazines at Quft. They were wrapped in acid-free tissue and placed in the purpose-built wooden boxes, which were to be pad locked and sealed in accordance with Supreme Council of Antiquities specifications. The most fragile items were placed in polythene boxes for greater support and protection before packing into the wooden boxes. More substantial small items were placed in zip-lock polythene bags that were then packed in the boxes. The zip-lock bags were not completely sealed, to prevent the possible build-up of moisture and the formation of deleterious micro-climates. Small bags of silica gel were not included, partly because the atmosphere is likely to be dry rather than damp and because there is no reliable opportunity for the silica gel to be checked and changed in the next few years. Wood is usually avoided for the manufacture of storage containers for archaeological material because it can give off acidic vapors. Since there was no alternative, as much acid-free tissue as possible was included in the packing to provide some buffering.

General Observations

The ceramic material, although frequently found broken, was not very eroded. There was surprisingly little salt damage in general, although there were some exceptions. The presence of completely intact pots seemed to be as much a factor of the remoteness of the site and its more or less single occupation and abandonment than any superior conditions of preservation.

Organic materials, including wood, textiles, and bone were quite well preserved. The metals present were generally quite corroded, but the lack of detail on surfaces seemed to be more a result of use and wear than the burial conditions.

Backfilling

To identify the squares excavated and to mark the extent of the excavation, plastic rope was laid across the excavation before in-filling began. The excavated areas were backfilled with the sieved dirt from the excavation. Once filled, the tops of the ropes were cut off flush with the ground level. This will mark the excavations for future archaeologists, but will not identify digging activities to casual visitors.

Safety

Hazards

The main hazards when conserving in the field on such a site are dust, biological agents, solvent fumes, and toxic reagents, as well as physical factors such as lack of adequate lighting or benching. The conservator is more likely to have to lift and carry heavy loads without the aids commonly relied on in conservation laboratories such as trolleys. Care must be taken to plan maneuvers in advance to minimize risk to conservator and object. Corrosion products (especially from lead and copper-alloy objects) are also hazardous, and care must be taken during their removal and disposal.

Protection

Masks and gloves are generally needed. Masks should be rated to cope with organic vapors, since a fume cupboard is rarely available. Opening up a site may expose material containing biological hazards, including anaerobic bacteria and human and animal wastes and remains. In addition, since the living accommodation and conservation area are often adjoined (and sometimes shared), great care must be taken to avoid transfers between the two. Food residues must not be allowed to enter the conservation area, and traces of excavated materials must not be transferred to the living areas.

Benzotriazole

Although this is the subject of some debate, benzotriazole is still considered a suspect carcinogen. The dry powder and solutions must be handled while gloved and masked, and great care must be taken to dispose of them properly. Copper-alloy items that have been treated are safe to handle once they have received a protective coating.

Disposal

Care must always be taken when disposing of conservation wastes, including solvents, used solutions, and residues. Extra forethought is needed when disposing of materials in a remote site such as Bir Umm Fawakhir to prevent the wastes causing damage to the environment or to people or wildlife that may subsequently be in the area. Items such as broken scalpel blades may be wrapped in masking tape to prevent them cutting and disposed of with the household waste. Solvent solutions that do not contain toxic substances may be poured on an area of sand well away from habitation and allowed to evaporate. It is best to pour solutions out early in the morning so that they are not exposed to hot ground surfaces. Solutions with obnoxious residues (such as resins) may be better disposed of by controlled burning and must be carefully supervised until completely extinguished. Solutions with toxic properties must be brought back to an area where they can be disposed of safely. The same principles should be applied to wastes (such as cotton wool or paper towel) that have been used with these solutions. Glassware that is washed out must be thoroughly rinsed and sufficient wash water used to ensure a safe dilution of any traces of reagents. Wash water must be disposed of carefully, since residues may concentrate upon evaporation. Several good handbooks for hikers and campers are available on disposing of wastes in wilderness areas that contain much useful information.

Chapter 8

Site Conservation Report

Thomas C. Roby

Introduction

In response to previously documented damage to the architectural remains of the ancient Byzantine mining settlement site of Bir Umm Fawakhir due to vehicular traffic (pl. 20a), the construction of a barrier was proposed that would prevent vehicles from entering the site in the future. Several different barrier proposals were made, but the simplest, least obtrusive, and lowest-maintenance proposal was to lay boulders across the entrance to the wadi where the principal settlement is located. Once the proposal was approved by the Egyptian Antiquities Project of the American Research Center in Egypt (ARCE), a local building contractor, Girgis Samwel, of Luxor, was hired to carry out the operation during one week, and I was contracted by Carol Meyer to supervise the barricade's construction.

Selection of Boulders

Care was taken in the selection of boulders for use in the barricade to make sure that they were not removed from an area of archaeological remains, as evidenced by surface finds and worked stone. Once the area was judged not to be archaeological, each boulder selected for removal was also inspected to make sure it was not worked in any way. Boulders approximately 1–2 square meters in size were selected and removed from four separate locations along the main Quft–Quseir road opposite the old mining camp in the Wadi el-Sid, 3–4 kilometers to the south of the site, where the excavation team was housed (fig. 46). Several different locations were used for boulder removal in order to minimize the change to the natural landscape. The boulders were chosen to be of the same type and color of stone as the rock cliffs surrounding the site so that the barricade would blend in with the site's landscape. The size of the boulders to be used was based on the criteria that they be large enough not to allow re-positioning by hand by several people after placement, nor to be quickly covered over by windblown sand, but not too large to risk damaging the machinery employed for lifting and transportation of the boulders by the contractor. The boulders were selected from those that had fallen from the cliff faces along the edge of the road, so there was no need to excavate them out of the ground or from the cliff face.

Transportation and Placement of Boulders

A large front-loader lifted the boulders from the side of the road and placed them in a truck, which then transported them north up the road to the wadi entrance of the main settlement, where they were dumped in separate piles (pls. 20b–21a). Approximately six truckloads of boulders were transported to the site. The same front-loader was then used to lift the boulders from the piles and drop them across the wadi. The narrowest part of the wadi entrance was chosen as the location of the barricade for reasons of economy and minimum intervention. The barricade extends from a very large boulder already in situ on the east side of the wadi to a small boulder in situ just behind the modern house ruins on the west side of the wadi (see fig. 3a). In the interest of creating a barricade that would be less likely to act as a dam for out-flowing water

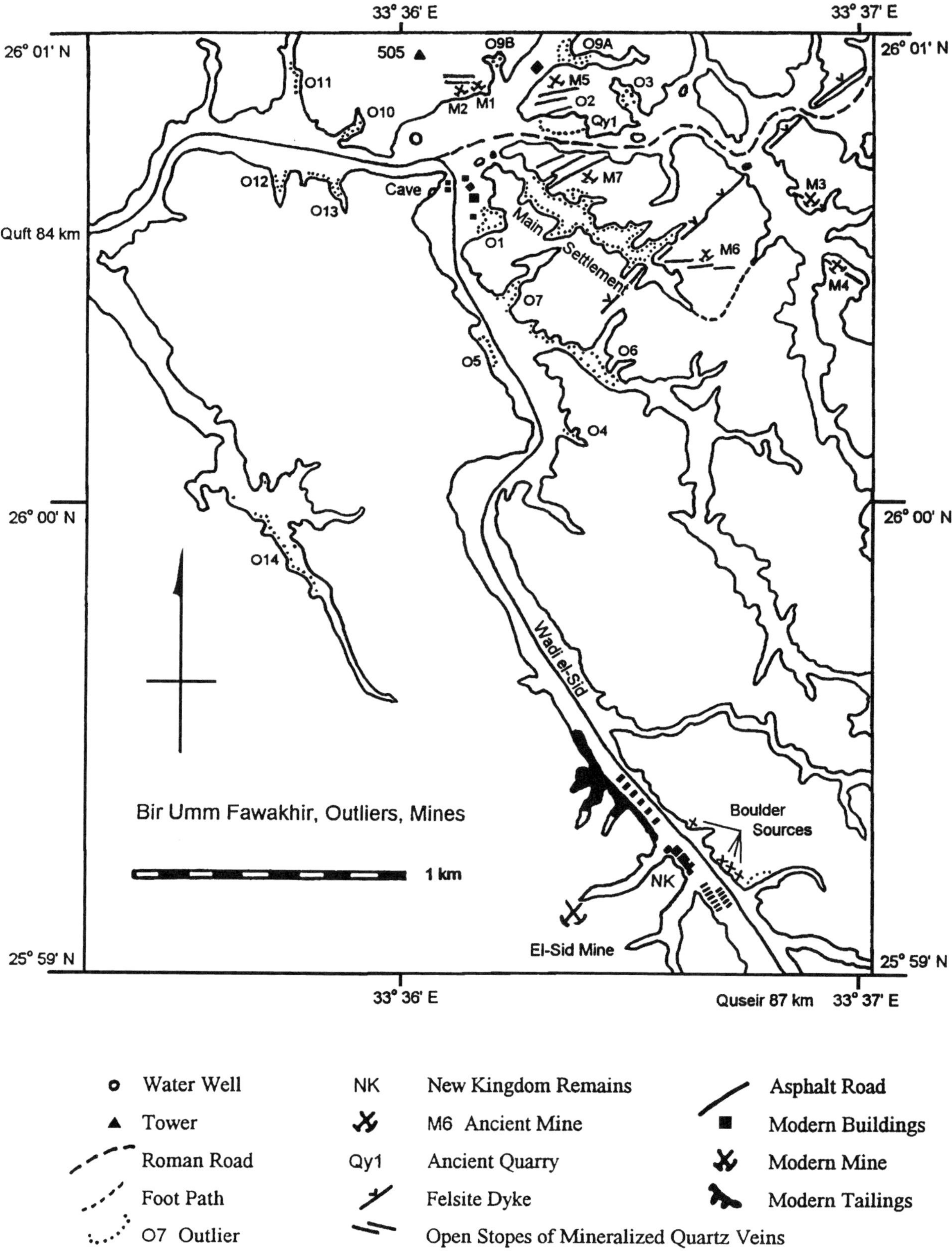

Figure 46. Map of boulder selection areas

during rains, and would not be too evident as a modern construction, the boulders were placed in a slightly arched line across the wadi, bowing away from the site.

The boulders were placed about one-half meter apart to allow water and sand to pass between them during the rare heavy rains and the more common sandstorms and to permit pedestrians to enter. The largest boulders were placed in a row first, then a second row of smaller ones were placed behind them in the gaps between the larger boulders (pl. 21 and fig. 3a top). The second row of boulders acts to make the re-positioning of a boulder for passage of a vehicle a considerably more difficult task, while making the eventual sanding over of the barrier by wind or water flow a much longer process. The spacing between the two rows should not impede sand from passing through. After adjusting the placement of the two rows of boulders with both the front-loader and by hand, the excess boulders were placed back on the truck and carried away from the site, while some were left on the east side of the wadi for possible future use in maintaining the barricade.

During and after the barricade construction, photographic documentation was carried out by the excavation photographer, Henry Cowherd, while the graphic documentation was carried out the following day with the help of the project geologist, Mohamed Omar. The barricade was first sketched at 1:100, then surveyed, and then drawn on a site plan (1:200).

Project Evaluation

The major threat to the long-term success of the barricade project is the possible future covering over of the boulders by windblown and rain-washed sand. The configuration of the barricade should prevent this, but for how much time is difficult to estimate. Larger boulders could have been used, but the contractor did not want to risk damaging his machinery with heavier loads. Some degree of maintenance of the barricade may be required in the future to periodically remove sand that collects around the boulders.

The placement of the boulders could have been more precise and regular, and the clean-up afterward should have been better, but the contractor was intent on leaving the site well before nightfall. The addition of a smaller front-loader or other lifting equipment would have allowed for better and easier positioning of the boulders. The one front-loader was too big for certain tasks, while others were beyond the capabilities of manual labor. The late arrival of the contractor on site at the end of the week meant that the work was carried out in less time than planned and not completed in as orderly a fashion as would have been preferred.

Site Conservation Assessment

An inspection of the architectural remains of the site during my week at Bir Umm Fawakhir revealed that the walls were constructed of dry-laid granite rubble, generally two stones in width, with small pieces of felsite and pottery used as chinkers to fill the gaps between the granite cobbles. The walls were laid either on the granite bedrock or on the silty sand of the wadi. Larger granite cobbles were often used for the bases of the walls, but they had no true foundations. The walls are preserved in some cases to a height of more than a meter, and initial excavation of several buildings in 1999 revealed that they generally continue at least one-half meter below ground level. According to the Bir Umm Fawakhir geologist, the local granite has a high mica content, which accounts for the highly weathered rough surface and friable nature of the stone, both when used as a building material and as found naturally as bedrock. There is no evidence yet of any wall surface protection or decoration layer, nor any floor construction. There is also no evidence yet of how the structures were roofed. The excavation did uncover a number of ceramic ovens, a stone-lined hearth, and other stone features within the buildings. One of the ovens required stabilization during excavation, which was carried out by the objects' conservator using a facing of fiberglass adhered to the interior walls of the oven with and acrylic resin in solution (Paraloid B48) to reinforce the oven walls and prevent its collapse (see *Chapter 7*).

The constituent materials and construction technique of the ancient buildings leave very few feasible conservation treatment options to stabilize or protect the walls. Repointing or capping of walls with mortar would be inappropriate treatment since mortar was not used originally to bind the rubble masonry. Consolidation treatment of each individual stone would be prohibitively expensive unless it was done on a very limited scale. As a result, the preservation of the site remains, which are already to a large extent present above ground before excavation, can best be accomplished by carrying out preventive conservation measures that lessen future damage to the buildings, rather than by directly treating the walls. Such measures are discussed below.

Control of Visitor Access

While the barricade construction project described above will prevent a major source of damage to the architectural remains of the site in the future — namely, vehicle entry — the fragile nature of the dry-wall construction of the several hundred granite rubble structures makes them very susceptible to damage by visitors climbing over them. The best way to prevent this activity would be to encourage visitors to view the site from a distance on a cliff above, easily reached from the entrance to the wadi. A descriptive panel could be placed near the barricade that indicates the viewing location, provides information about the site, and encourages visitors not to walk on the walls if they do enter the site, as they can easily be damaged, and one can be injured falling from them. There are several guards already posted at the site, so they could be instructed to enforce this policy when visitors are present, particularly until an information panel is installed at the site. If any part of the excavated site is eventually to be presented to the public, it would be advisable to select several of the ancient buildings near the entrance to the site and prepare and display them as examples for visitors. They should be structures that can be easily maintained and visitation to them controlled.

Control of Erosion

Natural causes of deterioration are also a threat to the site's preservation, but they are far more difficult to prevent. Depending on the location and configuration of walls at the site, wind and rainwater flow could help protect the walls by burying them deeper in the sand, or could further erode the walls. The potential damage to some structures from flash-flooding could be prevented by directing water away from structures along the wadi edges, where rainwater flows down preferentially. However, the presumed rareness of flooding, and the degree of intervention required on the landscape of the site to control it, do not make flood control a desirable preventive measure of site protection. The effects of wind erosion on the unexcavated site would be even more problematic to prevent.

Wind and flash-flood erosion of structures are a particular threat after a building or room has been excavated, but post-excavation damage can simply be prevented. The walls often rest only on very silty sand, which can quickly be eroded away and eventually cause their collapse. For this reason it is particularly important that excavated walls and all squares in general be backfilled at the end of each season. This was in fact done at the end of the 1999 season. Plastic mesh screen was advised for use as a horizon marker before carrying out backfilling, but, as it was unavailable, plastic rope, already on hand on site, was laid down in the bottom of the excavation squares and up to the baulks before reburial. Special care was taken to refill the ovens and hearth with sieved sand, which was executed by the excavation conservator. Similar careful reburial should be followed at the end of each excavation season in the future, unless there is a plan and funding to immediately stabilize and eventually present a building to the public.

Control of Refuse

An additional cause of damage to the site is the presence of windblown trash, which is deposited on the site from a modern settlement near the Quft–Quseir road at the entrance to the wadi, in particular from the rest house. While this damage is of an aesthetic nature, the site's remoteness and its natural setting are significant parts of its appeal to visitors, which is greatly diminished by the presence of food wrappers, containers, and plastic bags among the building remains and within the wadi vegetation. Efforts should be made to improve the proper removal of trash near the site by providing a closed trash receptacle for use by the local residents and customers of the roadside cafeteria. This issue affects the local community as well; apart from burning there are no means of trash disposal whatsoever.

Conclusions

The Bir Umm Fawakhir site has the potential to be a significant object of tourist visitation given its location on the road between Luxor and Quseir on the Red Sea, and its proximity to other nearby sites of archaeological interest, such as the rock hieroglyphic inscriptions of Wadi Hammamat and the various Roman forts along this road. An important first step in preventing damage to the site has now been taken by constructing a barricade to keep vehicles from entering the site. However, particularly if tourist visitation of the site is to be encouraged in the future, visitor access will need to be controlled to prevent damage to walls from people climbing over them. If excavation of the site continues in the future, reburial immediately after excavation and documentation should be continued as a general policy. The silty sand underneath many of the walls, once exposed, is very susceptible to wind and water erosion, and could lead to wall collapses if excavation squares are not reburied at least to the level of the bottom of the walls. Ideally, an architectural conservator should also be part of any future excavation team, in addition to an objects conservator, in order to carry out any necessary wall (or other architectural feature) stabilization treatments, and to supervise reburial operations. If any part of the site is to be eventually presented to the public, a specific observation plan should be drawn up for the selected area and adequate funding sought to carry it out.

Acknowledgments

I am grateful to Carol Meyer, director of the Bir Umm Fawakhir project, and the other staff archaeologist, Clare Leader, photographer Henry Cowherd, conservator Richard Jaeschke, geologist Mohamed Omar, and the driver Abdu, for their hospitality and assistance during my stay on site. In Luxor, I am indebted to the staff of Chicago House, particularly Epigraphic Survey director Ray Johnson and administrator Ahmed Harfoush, for their hospitality and generous use of a computer for preparing this report.

Chapter 9

Life at Ancient Bir Umm Fawakhir

Carol Meyer

We can assume that the setting of ancient Bir Umm Fawakhir was much as it is now, hyperarid desert (van der Veen 2001, p. 203; Maxfield 2001, p. 143; Sidebotham 2011, pp. 8–9). The long, two- or three-day march from the Nile valley abruptly left the green fields, rose to a flat and nearly featureless desert, broken primarily by the oasis at Phoinicon (modern Laqeita). About the third day, however, travelers would just as abruptly have met the rusty brown basalts and charcoal gray granites forming the rugged mountains of the central Eastern Desert. A few deep clefts or wadis eroded in the mountains permit passage from west to east and hence to the Red Sea coast. Our travelers to ancient Bir Umm Fawakhir followed one of the most ancient and most traveled of these routes, the one through the Wadi Hammamat. During the first and second centuries A.D., the route all the way to the major port at Myos Hormos (Quseir al-Qadim) was heavily utilized to supply the Red Sea merchants sailing to Aden, India, and East Africa for incense, spices, ivory, slaves, and other rich and exotic treasures. The route was supported by about ten fortified *praesidia*, all of which had deep cisterns, though almost all of them were abandoned by the early third century when Myos Hormos itself faded (Brun 2003b, pp. 201–02). The fort at Krokodilô (Wadi Mweh), however, saw some reuse in the fifth and sixth centuries (Brun 2003b, p. 204), and the station at Phoenicon is a question mark. It has a good water source and even palm trees, but it has never been extensively investigated archaeologically and now has a rapidly growing population. It is also the point at which the road from Coptos (Quft) branches south toward Berenice, a major port site very much in use into the sixth century. Certainly the imperial Roman *praesidia*, a few of which are still impressive, would have been most imposing in the fifth century, and any surviving wells or cisterns would have been welcome. At Bir Umm Fawakhir, we have to assume that the deep and abundant wells were either functional or quickly restored in order to support the mining community.

We know that the area around Bir Umm Fawakhir had been mined for gold and silver as early as the Twentieth Dynasty, as demonstrated by the Turin gold-mining papyrus (Harrell and Brown 1992) and by traces in the Wadi el-Sid and Shemkhiya (Meyer 2011, pp. 7–19), though by the fifth century A.D. these remains would have seemed ancient indeed. The Ptolemaic and Roman-period remains would have been more obvious than they are now. In particular, the Ptolemy III shrine to Min still stood fairly close to the wells of Bir Umm Fawakhir, and there are a few Ptolemaic and Roman-period potsherds and small finds from the Wadi el-Sid (Meyer 2011, pp. 20–29). Bir Umm Fawakhir itself yielded a handful of Roman-period potsherds, particularly amphora sherds around the small granite quarries, and a few bits of glass. The graffiti in the cave behind the modern tea house are mostly first to third century in date (Wilfong 1995). In addition to the wells, there might still, in the fifth century A.D., have been remains of a Roman-period *praesidium* like the others on the Wadi Hammamat route. It is hard to believe that the Roman military and merchants would have ignored so good a source of water in the desert. The ostraca published by Guéraud (1942) and revisited by Cuvigny (2003, pp. 284–85) seem to pertain to military activity in the desert and refer to other posts along the road. Unfortunately, whatever Roman structures may have existed at Bir Umm Fawakhir have long been destroyed by flash floods raging through the Wadi Hammamat[35] or by twentieth-century mining. In short, the Wadi el-Sid and Bir Umm Fawakhir area may still have been known in the fifth century as a mining zone.

[35] Flash floods between 1980 and 1982 washed away the asphalt road just east of the Wadi Hammamat and another segment just before reaching modern Quseir on the Red Sea (pers. obs.).

We also know that the ores at the Wadi el-Sid were much richer than those at Bir Umm Fawakhir.[36] Certainly the first miners extracted the easiest and richest ores first. We assume, however, that by the fifth century the much-worked-over lodes in the Wadi el-Sid had been exhausted by ancient techniques; it was not possible to drive deeper into the mountainside with existing Roman-era technology. We do know that if ever there were enough free gold to wash out by simple panning, by the time of the New Kingdom miners were already resorting to cut, opencast trenches in the mountainsides. For the gold at Bir Umm Fawakhir and Wadi el-Sid is not free. It occurs as metallic minerals in quartz veins injected into granite. The granite is fractured and jointed and at the surface may be rotten, but the quartz is tough, Mohs hardness 8. It demands hard-rock mining techniques, not simply panning.

Hard-rock mining requires a large, organized labor force, heavy capitalization, and, in the case of a remote mine such as Bir Umm Fawakhir, a reliable supply of tools, food, and other essentials. In Egypt, however, these problems had long been solved; one of the most famous rock inscriptions in the Wadi Hammamat recounts an expedition of ten thousand soldiers, scribes, and overseers to quarry stone for Mentuhotep IV of the Eleventh Dynasty (ca. 2055–1985 B.C.) (Breasted 1906, p. 213, no. 442; Shaw 1998). It is also true, however, that the government had to control and allocate sufficient supplies of labor and grain to send expeditions into the desert for mining or quarrying what were essentially sumptuary products, a vast expense that not all rulers could command.[37] By the fifth century A.D., the chief city of Egypt was Alexandria. Upper Egyptian cities such as Coptos (Quft) and Diospolis (Luxor) still existed, and at least the latter had a military garrison, but documentary and archaeological evidence is sparse. A *comes sacrarum largitionum* was responsible for supervising mines and certifying the purity of gold (Kaegi 2000, p. 4), but we do not know where his office was located, much less his connection, if any, to Bir Umm Fawakhir. We do know that the gold requirements of the Byzantine government in Constantinople and in Egypt were staggering. The imperial government required gold for paying soldiers, wars, military and ecclesiastical construction, trade, ransoming hostages, and supporting the glittering splendor of the court. The Egyptians needed gold for taxes and personal consumption such as jewelry, though gold coins were minted at Alexandria seldom or not at all. An edict of Justinian I dated to A.D. 559 refers to the problem of lightweight solidi circulating in Alexandria (Kaegi 2000, p. 4), which suggests a problem in acquiring sufficient gold. Diocletian abandoned the Dodekaschoinos, the Nile valley south of Aswan and the First Cataract, in A.D. 298 (Priese 1997, p. 216). Thus any direct control over the gold supplies from Nubia was lost. There were other potential sources of gold in the fifth and sixth centuries A.D., such as Armenia, the Balkans, the Urals, or the Caucasus (Kaegi 2000, p. 3), and imports from outside the empire, but it does seem that gold sources within the shrinking boundaries of the empire would have become more valuable than ever. Given our estimate of a thousand or so souls living at Bir Umm Fawakhir (Meyer et al. 2000, pp. 15–17), it is hard to see who apart from the government could have capitalized the mining operations, and, given the urgent need for gold, even the marginally productive mines at Bir Umm Fawakhir would at times have seemed worthwhile. Despite the existence of Byzantine-period coinage and exchange systems, we do not think the mines at Bir Umm Fawakhir were "economic" in the modern sense of the word, which is to say, producing gold equal to or in excess of the value of capital expended. This may be one of the reasons for the excellent preservation of the site: its mines have not been worth exploiting since their abandonment at some time in the sixth century.

We do not know where the miners were recruited, but they almost certainly came from villages in the Nile valley. It is hard to see where else so many workmen could have originated. The masses of Aswan pink, marl, Nile silt, and amphora sherds are not only comparable to Nile pottery corpora, but they must have come from the Nile valley, and likewise small finds such as glass, coins, the Bes amulet, the weight, and the pottery figurine fragment (Meyer et al. 2000, p. 23, fig. 51:a). We also think that the workmen were paid miners and not captives or prisoners of war. We base this conclusion on the sprawling, unregimented layout of the main settlement of Bir Umm Fawakhir and its outliers, the lack of fortifications to keep people in or out, the silos in Outlier 2 that look like household granaries (Meyer 2011, pls. 60, 61a), and the surprisingly

---

[36] Ancient mining and ore reduction at Bir Umm Fawakhir as well as subsequent smelting operations are treated more extensively in Meyer et al. 2005.

[37] For a discussion of the efforts required to maintain the Roman-period stone quarries, especially Mons Porphyrites and Mons Claudianus, see Maxfield 2001.

rich finds from even limited excavations (part of a copper/gold bracelet, an agate gemstone, coins, emeralds). At the somewhat earlier first- and second-century A.D. quarrying site of Mons Claudianus, a wealth of ostraca attests to relatively high salaries for all workmen, plus grain and wine rations (Cuvigny 1996). Despite some ancient authors such as Aristides, recent work at Mons Porphyrites, which was exploited into the fifth century, has found no evidence of convict labor there, and much more for free workers (Maxfield 2001, pp. 154, 165). Not even Agatharcides or Diodorus Siculus called the Egyptian miners slaves, and the results of archaeological survey and excavation at Bir Umm Fawakhir do not agree with their descriptions of the miners as prisoners, criminals, or war captives (Meyer and Heidorn 1998, p. 207). The raw emeralds (green beryl) are interesting in this context. The emerald mines at Mons Smaragdus/Sikait to the south were exploited at this time. The emeralds at Bir Umm Fawakhir are raw, sometimes still embedded in matrix, which speaks for contact with the emerald mines. The stones could have belonged to miners who worked in both places as needed and hired, they could have been picked up and transported by nomads, or they could have passed from hand to hand by some less direct route. We do not know whether the Byzantine government attempted to monopolize the trade in emeralds — the Eastern Desert was the only known source within the empire — but if so, they failed.

There was a nomadic population in the Eastern Desert in Late Antiquity, just as there is now. The ostraca from the *praesidia* on the Roman-period Coptos-to-Myos Hormos road mention "Arabs," "barbarians," and occasionally "brigands" from the desert. Sometimes the contacts were economic, such as supplying "topazes," and sometimes the contacts were hostile. One very long ostracon from Krokodilô (Wadi Mweh) recounts an attack in A.D. 118 by sixty "barbarians" on a *praesidium* far to the south. The attackers carried off a woman and two children. A second section of the same ostracon contains orders to the curatores (headmen) of the *praesidia* to protect travelers on the road from attacks by "barbarians" (Cuvigny 2003, pp. 351–52). A sizeable corpus of handmade pottery now called "Eastern Desert Ware" has been attributed to nomads and dated primarily to the fourth through sixth centuries (Barnard 2008a, 2008b), and a handful of Eastern Desert Ware sherds has been recovered from Bir Umm Fawakhir (see *Chapter 3*). The lifestyle of the Eastern Desert nomads in the fifth and sixth centuries, however, is still very poorly known. Most likely they depended on herds of goats and sheep, and they might have at times supplied meat, milk products, wool or goat hair, leather, or hides to the occupants of ancient Bir Umm Fawakhir. By this time the Eastern Desert nomads may have relied more on camels than on donkeys for transportation; horses if any would have been a luxury because of the shortage of fodder. The nomads might on occasion have served as guides, couriers, or escorts, or they might have turned about and raided a settlement or caravan. With such hazy information, we hesitate to attach a name such as "Blemmyes" or anything else to the nomadic groups that shared the desert with the Bir Umm Fawakhir miners. Certainly we have no reason to think that the nomads were a significant source of labor for the mines.

We do not know what the first groups of miners found when they reached the vicinity of Bir Umm Fawakhir. We have only a rough estimate of when the first Byzantine/Coptic-period mines were opened, sometime during the fifth century. We do not know whether advance parties scouted out the mines in order to tell people where to camp and where to start mining, though this seems a logical first step. Certainly the wells at Bir Umm Fawakhir would have been a desirable starting point. If any attempt was made to re-open the older Roman mines in the Wadi el-Sid, it was short-lived. There are virtually no Coptic/Byzantine-period sherds there,[38] and the only remains of the period that are close by are the huts in Outlier 8, which is not extensive (Meyer 2011, pp. 106–07). At Bir Umm Fawakhir, however, the miners and their overseers would have found water, the Ptolemaic Min temple, and possibly the remains Roman-period structures of some sort.

We assume that the miners quickly set to work building shelter; at the very least shade from the blazing sun and shelter from the wind would have been desirable. Judging from the sprawling layout of the town (see figs. 3–4), there was no central planning. The sandy wadi bottom was kept clear to serve as the main street, but apart from that houses were laid out on either side in clusters or up the lower slopes of the wadi walls.

[38] Only three Coptic/Byzantine-period sherds were identified, nos. 59, 60, and 66 in Meyer 2011 (pp. 22–25).

Sometimes strings of houses roughly encircle a central area or "plaza." While it would have been convenient for the residents around a "plaza" to coordinate certain activities such as trash dumping, we cannot prove any particular relationship between the occupants of the houses. The basic house unit is two or three interconnecting rooms, occasionally more, or sometimes external doorways set side by side so the rooms could function together. All the houses at Bir Umm Fawakhir have a similar style of construction. Walls have no special footings or foundations, though in places they rest on granite bedrock. The walls consist of inner and outer faces of rough granite cobbles with small stones, or occasionally potsherds, filling in between the faces. The builders simply utilized handy pieces of granite, of which there is any amount at Bir Umm Fawakhir. On the other hand, burnt or mudbricks are so rare we marked them individually on the base map. Only two of the chinking sherds collected proved datable, and they were amphora toes (nos. 102 and 103 in Meyer 2011, pp. 118–19, fig. 31). Floors were sandy soil or perhaps mats, judging from the layers of brownish organic matter. Windows were rare at best, but many rooms had built-in features such as benches or storage niches, and both the excavated houses, Buildings 93 and 177, had small hearths or potstands in one or more rooms. Large, neat, flat stones formed the bottoms, sides, and tops of niches, and larger stones were sometimes set upright for door posts or thresholds, but none of the stones seems to have been deliberately shaped. Note the neat threshold between Rooms A and B of Building 93. Some of the buildings in Outlier 2 have a step or two down from the outside or from one room to the next. Also in Outlier 2, some houses are so well preserved that the walls seem to stand to their original height. This is now only 140 to 150 cm above the current surface, but both the interior and exterior of the buildings in question are sanded up (Meyer 2011, p. 83, pl. 59b). Still, ceilings seem to have been low. Roofing would have been a problem. We have no evidence for granite roof beams such as those at Mons Claudianus, and if wooden beams were employed, they must have been hauled in from the Nile valley. Wood is also so valuable in the desert that it would have been one of the first things removed by travelers or nomads for tools or firewood. Usually, small branches, twigs, or mats are laid over the primary roof beams and then a layer of mud. At Bir Umm Fawakhir, however, we have no evidence for mud roofs, no chunks of clay with twig or mat impressions, so it is possible that the miners contented themselves with mats weighted down by stones. Coarse cloth or tent fabric lashed down with ropes is another possibility.[39] Rain is not a problem, and if one of the rare flash floods hit, the safest place would have been out, away, and up on the hillsides, not indoors. We have no evidence whatsoever for second stories,[40] though some of the houses are built on such steep slopes that they are split level. Many of the houses have small circular or rounded rooms "hooked on." Their walls seem thinner than usual, so it is possible that they were intended only to hold matting in place to enclose secondary storage space. Judging from the admittedly limited excavations, cooking took place outdoors, and if roofing consisted of mats, hides, or similar materials, cooking indoors would have been all the more risky. Building 93 had two kitchen areas on either side. Building 177 had no similar kitchen area, but there is so little free space around the building it is hard even to walk around it. The kitchen area, if any, might have been on an unexcavated part of the Hillock. Courtyards, a common feature of Near Eastern architecture, are surprisingly rare, though quite a few groups of houses seem to circle and open onto a common, central space or "plaza" (Meyer 2011, p. 50, figs. 15–16). Scattered around the houses were a number of one-room outbuildings. They could have been added at any time during the occupation of the site, and we do not know whether they were used for storage, animals, workshops, or if they had several uses over time. A few located high on the cliffs overlooking the main settlement seem to be guardposts (Buildings 75 and 236) (Meyer et al. 2000, p. 11, fig. 7; Meyer 2011, p.

[39] A series of Late Roman (mainly fifth–sixth century) remote, short-lived settlements in the Eastern Desert consisted of loose groups of huts with wall construction like that at Bir Umm Fawakhir, but apparently no higher than ca. 1.2 m. It is suggested that the upper part of the wall was a wooden framework and the structure as a whole was covered with cloth, hides, or mats (Sidebotham, Barnard, and Pyke 2002, p. 189). The Biʾr Minayh publication includes some reconstructions of possible roofing methods for one-room houses or huts (Luft 2010, p. 17). The version with a simple flat roof of branches seems the most feasible; the version with a lashed-down tent-like covering would not work very well for the rambling, multi-room agglomerated buildings so common at Bir Umm Fawakhir. But the miners may well have used whatever came to hand.

[40] Two-story houses with well-built stairways are well attested in Late Roman Berenice (Sidebotham and Wendrich 2007, pp. 109–12), but this was far the most important port and town in the Eastern Desert in this period.

72, fig. 23:a), and some very small ones look like latrines, but the only outbuilding excavated, Building 181, offered no evidence for that or for any other particular usage.

Judging from the stratigraphy of Building 93, Room C and Dump 1, the site may have been abandoned, or nearly so, and reoccupied twice. The gap between occupations need not have been long; one good sandstorm can deposit a lot of sand, especially if it is trapped within uncovered but walled spaces.[41] The miners who came to re-open the mines probably did not have to rebuild all their shelters from scratch. Many buildings would have had standing walls, and if needed, stones for repair or reworking would have been readily available. Roofing material was another question, however.

On the other hand, we can reconstruct a great deal about the mines and mining.[42] The hills and cliffs around ancient Bir Umm Fawakhir and its outliers are riddled and trenched with opencast and underground mines. The most basic are the opencast mines, trenches cut down from the surface to follow a quartz vein. The veins are generally narrow, 50 cm or so, down to fine veinlets. The part richest in metallic minerals is the contact zone between the quartz and the granite country rock. The contact zone often looks stained reddish or grayish against the pure white quartz, and this may have been the visual clue the ancient miners were seeking. A wide range of metallic minerals including iron pyrite (fool's gold) and chalcopyrite have been detected at Bir Umm Fawakhir and Wadi el-Sid, but the gold itself is not visible. The miners had to hack out chunks of white and stained quartz from the granite. At the surface, where the granite is rotten, this is not so hard, but following a vein underground would have been much harder, even in places where the granite was fractured and jointed. The iron wedge from Building 93 (pl. 35a) is the only tool found that could have been used in such work. Once the quartz was hacked out, someone right at the edge of the cut would have inspected the chunks or cracked them in order to pick out the pieces worth the considerable effort of further reduction. We have good evidence for the preliminary sorting at Mine 4, a deep cut across a mountainside. Right next to the cutting is a large, flat stone with a pecked depression, chunks of quartz ore all around it except for a gap where the workman presumably squatted to sort ore. A whitish sheet of discarded quartz spills down the mountainside below (Meyer et al. 2005, figs. 17–18; Meyer 2011, pp. 168–69, pl. 94a).

The next step was to crunch the selected ore, to "the size of a pea," according to Agatharcides. For this stage we have scores and scores of dimple stones.[43] These are chunks of basalt, granite, or porphyry hewn to 15 cm or so across. One face is smooth with a pounded depression in the middle. The dimple stones are used by putting a chunk of ore on a lower, flat, or shallowly concave stone, pounding down with the dimple stone, and grinding around. When the dimple gets too deep to crush ore to the desired size, it is discarded. Thus many of the dimple stones recovered at Bir Umm Fawakhir are in secondary context, built into walls or set on a slope as steps. We have fewer of the flattish lower stones, but they may have lasted longer. The last stage in grinding is attested by the many rotary grinding stones or querns on the site. The lower stone is a massive block, usually of granite, with a more or less deep circular depression in the middle. A thinner, disk-like upper stone rotates in the depression in the lower stone. The upper stone is turned by a stick in a hole near the edge, and the two stones are further aligned by a knob in the center of the lower stone that fits into a hole in the center of the upper one. Such rotary grinding stones can be used for other materials of course, notably grain, but they are abundant at Bir Umm Fawakhir, and this kind of ore does have to be ground to powder to release as much gold as possible. Grinding and crushing stones are in fact the second most common type of artifact at Bir Umm Fawakhir after potsherds. The next stage, washing the powdered ore, requires more skilled labor. We suspect that ore washing took place close to the wells as a generous supply of water is needed. We do not know whether rough boards and sponges were used, as Agatharcides describes, or sheepskins, or other washing techniques, but the result probably was not visible gold but a dark, sparkly, heavy residue. Since the metal ores at Bir Umm Fawakhir are all sulphides, they would have required a multi-stage smelting operation with cupellation. We have no evidence for smelting at ancient

[41] On a visit on Friday, March 13, 1987, we experienced such a severe sandstorm that visibility was limited, eyes, nose, and ears were filled with sand, and eating or drinking was impossible.

[42] For a fuller discussion of mines, mining, and smelting Bir Umm Fawakhir ores, see Meyer et al. 2005.

[43] The various kinds of crushing and grinding stones are discussed and illustrated in Meyer 2011, p. 153, pls. 94–100.

Bir Umm Fawakhir, though we looked for it. Smelting is very, very fuel intensive, and fuel is precious in the desert. Therefore we suspect that the washed, concentrated "head" was sent back to the valley, where fuel and skilled smelters were available. Shipping sacks of washed ore rather than gold or gold dust across the desert would have significantly reduced the threat of brigands as well.

A well-organized project takes care of first things first: infrastructure and basic support for start-up operations. (In a poorly organized project anything can happen.) Judging from the extent of the mine cuttings, the size of the main settlement, and the sheer abundance of potsherds, organization, labor force, and materials were sufficient to meet the goal of the project: mine gold ore. Unfortunately, we know almost nothing about the administration of the mine. We suspect that the offices[44] and dwellings of the overseers and clerks may have been situated in the most desirable part of Bir Umm Fawakhir, close to the wells, precisely the area most damaged by flash floods and modern mining.[45] We suspect that there were warehouses for valuable iron tools and smithies to keep them sharp, but so far we have not located any such structures. There were probably areas set aside for pack animals to rest, water, and load or unload, but these would leave little archaeological trace. The name applied to the area and wells of Bir Umm Fawakhir in the Roman period, "Persou," may still have been in use. If not, we do not even know the ancient name of the site. We have every reason to think that from the very outset lists of workmen, days of work, and pay were kept. Surely all supplies from the valley were tallied and cross-checked. Above all, the washed gold or concentrated ore, the whole purpose of the mining operations, must have been recorded. Unfortunately, no ostraca or texts have been recovered from the Nile valley that refer to desert mines, and our search for ostraca or other texts at Bir Umm Fawakhir was unsuccessful. We have only several score of nearly illegible dipinti scrawled on wine amphoras. Either our limited excavations of two house dumps was too small a sample, or written materials were discarded closer to their place of use in long-lost administrative buildings, or the writing materials were perishable. If flammable[46] they could have been used used for tinder when no longer needed. The situation at Berenice seems to have been similar. After years of excavation, Late Roman (mid-fourth to mid-sixth century) Berenice yielded almost nothing in the way of texts, apart from dedications carved in stone (Sidebotham 2011, pp. 260–61).

Curiously, we do not even know what religion the workmen acknowledged, whether a flavor of Christianity or whether they still held to the old gods. The fifth and sixth centuries A.D. are well into the Christian era, but in Upper Egypt the picture is not so clear; Christianity or paganism seems to have been a village-by-village decision (Frankfurter 1998). The port town at Berenice certainly tolerated a range of cults: Christianity, Isis, Serapis, the Palmyrene Yarhibol, and perhaps Mithras (Sidebotham, Hense, and Nouwens 2008, pp. 135–48; Sidebotham 2011, pp. 262, 264–68; Sidebotham and Wendrich 2007, p. 370). At Bir Umm Fawakhir we have traces both of paganism in the surviving Ptolemy III shrine to Min and a little Bes amulet, and of Christianity in symbols stamped on plates and XP monograms scrawled on wine jars, but nothing that looks like a church. The little "incense burners" remain enigmatic. If nothing else, the religion of the miners makes a difference to their work week, holidays, and feast calendar.

One thing the mine administration, both in the Nile valley and at Bir Umm Fawakhir, seems to have done quite well is feed the work force. The prime item, bread, is, however, the most poorly attested. Grains of wheat and barley were surprisingly uncommon (*Chapter 6*). At Berenice and Shenshef, six-row hulled barley was a staple, perhaps for bread (though even better for beer) and at least at times as camel fodder (Cappers 2006, p. 90). Most of the wheat remains were durum wheat, which is excellent for pasta but too stiff to make good bread (Cappers 2006, pp. 130–31).[47] At Bir Umm Fawakhir we have to consider the possibility that bread

---

[44] The puzzling Complex 26 in Outlier 6 (Meyer 2011, pp. 94–95) is not particularly large, but it does have unusually thick walls, and it was walled off in a corner of the wadi. It is, however, so secluded and remote from the main settlement that it seems an unlikely candidate for day-to-day business functions.

[45] Nor do we have any hint of a bath in any of the hundreds of structures investigated so far, though there were small baths at Mons Claudianus, Didymoi (Brun and Reddé 2011, pp. 24–25), and a few other Roman-period desert sites.

[46] One of the Roman-period ostraca from Fawakhir includes a request for letter paper (Guéraud 1942, pp. 171–72), presumably papyrus.

[47] In earlier periods at Berenice (mid-first to mid-second century), however, emmer wheat (*Triticum dicoccum*) rather than hard wheat (*T. durum*) seems to have been prevalent (Zieliński 2011, p. 60). The Nicanor archive of ostraca (18 B.C. to A.D. 69) records large numbers of shipments of modest amounts of wheat to Myos Hormos and Berenice, some barley, and a little bread,

was sometimes shipped to the town as loaves. On the one hand, it would quickly have stiffened to hardtack, but on the other, it would have saved a considerable amount of precious fuel. The silos in Outlier 2 (Meyer 2011, fig. 27, pls. 60–61) speak for grain storage, but it is possible that they could not always be filled as hoped, or that they pertain only to the latest phase of occupation. A couple of the "tabuns" in Dumps 1 and 2 might have been a kind of homemade *dolium* for grain storage. We do know that earlier, first- and second-century A.D. ostraca attest to bread as well as grain supplies to other Eastern Desert sites. Barley,[48] bread, oil, vinegar, fennel seeds, and non-comestibles were sent to Myos Hormos and Berenice (Cuvigny 2003, p. 275); "35 pairs of bread" were listed on an ostracon from Krokodilô (K599, Cuvigny 2003, p. 409), and another twenty-five "pairs" of baked bread were priced at four drachmas (K553, Bülow-Jacobsen 2003, p. 423). Grain may have been preferred, as indicated by an ostracon from Maximianon, "if the horseman is able to take 3 *matia* of grain, I shall send it to you, if not (I shall send) 5 pairs of loaves" (M725, Cuvigny 2003, p. 417). Baked bread was often sent from Krokodilô to Persou (Fawakhir) because there was a problem with the oven there (Bülow-Jacobsen 2003, p. 420), conceivably a shortage of fuel. The Roman-period Fawakhir ostraca also mention bread: fifteen and six (loaves of?) bread on one occasion and salt for bread-making on another (Guéraud 1942, p. 153–56).[49] Even at Roman-period Myos Hormos (first to third century), a possible communal bakery in trench 8 was so well supplied with spices and grinding stones but not cereal grains that it is suggested that flour was brought in (van der Veen 2011, p. 193). Mons Claudianus and Mons Porphyrites seem to have had communal bake ovens as well (van der Veen and Tabinor 2007, p. 116), which would have saved labor and fuel.[50] Thus there may have been several ways to supply the ancient Fawakhiris with their daily bread: grain carried to the town, ground there and baked by a household or community oven, flour shipped in and baked on site somewhere, or bread or hardtack sent in. Bread made from freshly ground grain may have been preferred, but bringing in flour is another possibility, and we do have many attestations of baked bread sent to Persou and other Eastern Desert sites in the first and second centuries, the only relevant period for which we have documentary evidence.

In addition to the hard wheat (*Triticum durum*), other wheat (*Triticum* sp.), six-row barley (*Hordeum vulgare*), and other barley (*Hordeum* sp.) grains reported in *Chapter 6*, edible plants attested at Bir Umm Fawakhir include dates (*Phoenix dactylifera*), olives (*Olea europea*), bottle gourd (*Lagenaria siceraria*), dom palm (*Hyphaene thebaica*), and one lone grape pip (*Vitis vinifera*). Subsistence agriculture, in the sense of supplying all plant food for an entire household or village over a period of years or generations, has not succeeded in this hyperarid desert at any point in history or prehistory, but the basic grains and staples carried in from the Nile valley may have been supplemented by locally grown vegetables.[51] Again referring to the Roman-period ostraca from Persou, Maximianon, and Krokodilô, a number of vegetables and condiments are listed as sent from Persou to other desert stations: asparagus (or fresh shoots of young vegetables), turnips (very good pickled), lettuce, cabbage, leeks, radishes, beets, beans, purslane (good cooked with meat), pennyroyal, endive/chicory, dill-seed, basil, and apparently even saffron (Bülow-Jacobsen 2003, pp. 420–21).[52] Didymoi, on the Berenice road, seems to have obtained vegetables from kitchen gardens at Phoinikon (Laqeita) (Cuvigny 2012, p. 34). At Berenice itself and at Shenshef, about four dozen kinds of edible seeds, nuts, fruits, herbs, and

among an array of other items (Casson 1989, pp. 13–14), but of course does not specify "emmer" versus "hard" wheat.

[48] Speaking of Didymoi, Cuvigny (2012, p. 35) says that barley was used mainly as food for donkeys and horses, which were rare, and occasionally for brewing beer.

[49] The quarry workers at Mons Claudianus, who were well supplied and paid, sent notes (*entolai*) to agents in the Nile valley with instructions as to how to spend their salary. Part of a workman's wheat allocation might be given to a female relative to be baked into bread and then sent to the desert, or some of the drachmas could be used to buy oil, lentils, onions, dates, or other foods (van der Veen 2001, p. 218; Cuvigny 1996).

[50] Stacks of unleavened bread piled in a corner of granary A411 at Karanis (Gazda 1983, p. 28) were simply abandoned, but they look like a generous supply for many households for many days.

[51] In modern times, kitchen gardens are fairly common in Eastern Desert settlements where water is available, and even small gardens may be surprisingly productive (Cappers 2006, pp. 45–46), though cereal grain cultivation is generally opportunistic and small scale (ibid., p. 47).

[52] Persou in the Roman period seems to have been a very active place, due in part to its generous and reliable wells. In addition to a manned station serving the Coptos-to-Myos Hormos road, there was some mining activity a few kilometers farther along the track at Wadi ed-Sid, and evidently vegetable gardens extensive enough to supply other *praesidia*. Looking at a map (see fig. 2) of the rather restricted flat space at Bir Umm Fawakhir, the only good place for gardens would be right around the wells, a space that looks even more restricted if there were a *praesidium* comparable in size to the one at Krokodilô or Maximianon.

spices are attested, though many occurred in tiny quantities and some were obviously exotic, like coconut (Cappers 2006, pp. 55–135). The ancient occupants of Berenice may have had their gardens as well (ibid., pp. 140–43), and the range of leafy vegetables recovered from Roman-period Myos Hormos (Quseir al-Qadim) is extensive enough to suggest garden plots there, despite the scarcity of fresh water (van der Veen 2001, p. 161). There is evidence for some gardening at Mons Claudianus, which was occupied intermittently from the first to third century A.D. (van der Veen 1998, pp. 228–34), and some green vegetables may have been grown even at Mons Porphyrites (van der Veen and Tabinor 2007, p. 113). Oil was another important food item that we have to assume was supplied to the Bir Umm Fawakhir workmen, even though we have as yet no direct evidence for it.

Wine was a staple, and the abundance of amphora sherds at Bir Umm Fawakhir gives the impression of an ample supply. Unfortunately, the numerous dipinti from Bir Umm Fawakhir do not give us much help in determining where the amphoras and their contents came from. We do know, however, that wine was a major product of the Delta region, and, closer to the jumping-off point at Coptos, Antinoopolis seems to have produced some wine as well (Guidotti 2008, p. 353; mention of vine-dressers, Pintaudi 2008, pp. 11, 548). Furthermore, the Late Roman 1 amphoras from Antinoopolis were used exclusively for wine (Fournet and Pieri 2008, p. 184), and not, say, garum. Fourth-century texts from Oxyrhynchus, on the Bahr Yusuf south of the Fayyum, indicate that in this case the average ration per man per day was a relatively generous 1.4 kilos of bread, a *sextarius* of wine (half a liter), and a half a Roman pound (163 grams) of meat (Leguilloux 2003, p. 551). At Mons Claudianus in the first half of the second century A.D., one class of workmen was paid 47 drachmas per month plus wheat and wine rations. The ostracon cited specified one amphora of wine for the month, though whether this was always the case is less certain (Cuvigny 1996, pp. 139–40). At the much smaller first- and second-century site of Didymoi, Cuvigny (2012, p. 32) remarks on the masses of amphoras and hundreds of thousands of liters of wine supplied to the inhabitants, and also how little evidence of that supply was to be found in the thousands of ostraca. The texts from Wadi Sarga are somewhat later than Bir Umm Fawakhir (seventh century), but they attest to whole camel caravans of wine carried to the monastery on the desert edge (Crum and Bell 1922). If we estimate the maximum population of ancient Bir Umm Fawakhir at about 1,000, or roughly four people per household, then the quartermasters would have to supply at least 200 amphoras of wine per month, a fair-sized caravan. It seems to have been done. Had it not, there might have been trouble with the workforce; there are few enough necessities, much less luxuries, in the desert.[53]

Figure 47. Wine consumption

[53] In the reconstruction (fig. 47), the central figure's tunic is based on Cannuyer 2001, pp. 56–57, the pottery on vessels in *Chapter 3*, and the ladle on the one from Building 93, Room B, pls. 76, 81–82. Matting is well attested at Berenice.

We have no evidence for contact with the contemporaneous pre-Islamic peoples of the Arabian peninsula on the other side of the Red Sea, and there is no Coptic/Byzantine-period tradition of poetry like the famous *qasida*, but the latter do attest to the far-flung distribution of wine in the Arabian desert, and to the popularity of gambling (Sells 1989).

Another thing that seems to have been maintained remarkably well is the meat supply. Not only the expected sheep and goat bones were found, but also an unusually high proportion of cattle bones (see *Chapter* 5). The bones suggest that the animals were butchered on site. The sheep and goats could have been driven in from the Nile valley and could have been maintained at Bir Umm Fawakhir at least for a while, though forage in the immediate area would have been rapidly used up. (It also raises the question of who, in a mining town, could have been spared to tend the flocks.) Alternatively, some sheep and goats could have been obtained from pastoral nomads, though this might have been a less predictable source. Judging from the "cheese factory" excavated at the bottom of Dump 1, milk seems to have been processed into cheese, a good solution for keeping dairy products in a very hot climate. The cattle, however, are another question, especially as there was so little fodder for them and no grass at all. The best solution may have been to march them to the site and butcher them shortly after arrival.[54] This practice is attested much, much earlier in quarrying expeditions sent to the Wadi Hammamat in the Middle Kingdom. A group of famous rock inscriptions there records an expedition carried out in the reign of Mentuhotep IV under the supervision of his vizier, Amenemhet. An army of 10,000, including miners, quarrymen, stonecutters, draftsmen, and other skilled workers, is said to have quarried a massive sarcophagus of *bekhen*-stone without loss of life, not even that of an ass. On completion, cattle and goats were slaughtered and incense offered up (Breasted 1906, pp. 212–16; Couyat and Montet 1912, pp. 98–100).

Which brings us to the problem of fuel for cooking and heating in the desert. Climatic conditions in the Eastern Desert seem to have been the same in the first half of the first millennium as now, though it is possible that there were more trees (van der Veen 2001, p. 203; Maxfield 2001, p. 143; van der Veen and Tabinor 2007, p. 84; Sidebotham 2011, pp. 8–9). What is certain is that trees are now so rare they can be marked individually on maps. The Bedouin tribes north and south of the Wadi Hammamat usually insist on burning only dead branches. Floyer (1893) reported that certain tribes were much criticized by their neighbors for cutting trees for charcoal to sell in the Nile valley because once a tree is killed, there is virtually no chance of rooting a new one. The kitchen areas in Dump 1 of Building 93 were dense with fine ash, but the only fuel found in the small tabun was dung. Our experiments (see *Chapter 2*, n. 11) show that this does indeed burn to a fine, light ash, but dung also soots a vessel placed over it. Sooting is surprisingly uncommon on Bir Umm Fawakhir cooking pots, which suggests that cooks used something like a stove rather than placing pots directly over a fire. The little hearth in Room A of Building 177, presumably for heating, contained only remnants of small twigs; indeed, most of the wood remains from the site as a whole are only small branches or twigs.[55] Even such scrappy bits of vegetable matter must have been valuable for cooking or for feeding animals. How best to use it? Food or fuel? Camels could eat camel thorn in the desert, sheep and especially goats can forage widely for whatever desert vegetation may be available, but cattle must have grass or fodder. Allowing the animals as much vegetation as possible and then collecting animal dung for fuel may have been very necessary. Still, supplementary fodder and fuel may have been added to the burdens of protesting camels trudging from the Nile valley, and if this and local fuel supplies did not suffice even to cook bread, then pleas for bread may have gone out to the Nile valley or perhaps an intermediate station, as happened in the earlier Roman period. Humble as it sounds, fuel for cooking food and vegetation for feeding animals may have been perpetual headaches for the mine authorities.

Regular or not, the supply trains to Bir Umm Fawakhir were sufficient to maintain the workforce not only in food but also tools, clothing,[56] and a staggering abundance of pottery. The arrival of a caravan with supplies, other items such as oral or written communications, and new people must have been a most welcome

[54] Cattle bones were very rare at Roman-period sites in the Eastern Desert. Only one fragment per site is reported from Didymoi, Maximianon, and Abu Shaʾar, and at Krokodilô and Mons Claudianus, cattle bones compose 0.5 and 0.07 percent, respectively, of the faunal material (Leguilloux 2011, pp. 174–75).

[55] At Mons Porphyrites, chaff and wood from desert plants seem to have been preferred for domestic uses, and the acacia wood charcoal brought in from the Nile valley was reserved for special purposes such as use in smithies (van der Veen and Tabinor 2007, p. 115).

[56] It is a pity that only a few fragile scraps of cloth were recovered from the excavations. The Coptic-period textiles are one of the glories of the age. Miners and their families may not have possessed many elaborate fabrics, much less have worn them often, but the snippets of colored cloth (RN 99/217) found suggest that there was at least some decorated material.

event. As the work progressed at the mines, additional miners might have been called for, and it seems likely that if the miners' families did not come right at first, they arrived as soon as they could have been fed, sheltered, and employed. In addition to hauling water, preparing food, and perhaps gardening, women may have carried out the fine-grinding of the ore. Agatharcides describes rotary grinding stones set in a row with two or three women to each quern to grind crushed ore to the fineness of flour. In addition, he says that young boys were employed to carry ore from the mine face to men who took it to the ore crushers (Burstein, trans. 1989, pp. 62–63). We cannot prove either occupation at Bir Umm Fawakhir, but they are possible. If there were herds of sheep and goats to tend, this too is often a chore for children, not to mention running errands or carrying messages between the village and the mines. Collecting dung and twigs may well have been another daily chore for women and children. And then there is sex. Mining settlements are often short of women, and the newer and more remote the mining camp the higher the ratio of men to women tends to be (cf. Dolly's Creek in Australia; Lawrence 1998, pp. 46–48). Prostitutes in the Eastern Desert are quite well documented. The famous Coptos Tariff of A.D. 90 charged a whopping 108 drachmae for prostitutes versus twenty for wives of soldiers and two obols for a donkey (Bernand 1984, pp. 200–01). In the second-century A.D. ostraca from the *praesidia* on the Coptos-to-Myos Hormos road, women are attested as residents engaged in spinning, weaving, drawing water, and above all as prostitutes (Cuvigny 2003, pp. 374–94). The last are quite well documented, perhaps because they were so expensive. At Bir Umm Fawakhir we have to admit that we have little evidence for women and children, even though we think there must have been some. The beads, the copper/gold bracelet, and other bits of jewelry are suggestive, but spindle whorls would have been even more indicative. Cloth and leather were poorly preserved or scarce in the two middens sampled, and hence evidence such as children's clothing or shoes is as yet lacking. On the other hand, there probably would not have been very many old or sick people, not if there were a home village in the Nile valley to which they could return. Supplying a non-working body in the desert is not optimal. Furthermore, mining can be a dangerous occupation, especially underground. Sprains, broken bones, burns (especially if lamps were used underground), heat stroke, scorpion stings, and falling rock are risks over and above the hazards of life in a large community possessed of poor sanitation, little more than folk medicines, and limited means of food preservation. We can only hope that the plague that started in Egypt in the 540s did not reach ancient Bir Umm Fawakhir, but it takes only one rat.

At its height, ancient Bir Umm Fawakhir must have been a lively place. In winter work would have started at sunrise and stopped at sunset, but during the long days of summer, work would best have been broken by a long siesta in the flaming heat of midday. Such women and children as there were presumably had the customary perpetual chores of hauling water from the wells, scavenging fuel, cooking in the outdoor kitchens, tending animals in and out of the wadis, and perhaps a little gardening. In addition, women may have been employed grinding ore; there is little evidence for women's work in the form of spindle whorls, needles, or the like. Households without women would have had to add the basic chores of hauling water, cooking, and washing to the daily mining routine. We do not know what the work "week" was or what the holiday or feast routine may have been, but even if there were no births, marriages, or holy days, there were funerals.

Some of the ancient Fawakhiris stayed in the desert long enough to die. Regrettably, we did not have the time to explore the many cemeteries on the ridges around the main settlement. So far as we could tell, however, all the burials had been looted and the bones crushed and scattered. One infant burial would have spoken volumes, but these are the most fragile bones of all. Many of the graves were merely clefts in the granite bedrock covered over with rough rock cairns. All the clefts or graves noted were so small the body must have been flexed, and grave goods, if any, are long gone. What did remain, however, was a significant scatter of large sherds around the graves, especially pieces of amphoras. Since the last are far too large to fit in a grave, they suggest a funeral or memorial meal, feast, or offering.[57]

We do not know exactly how long the site of Bir Umm Fawakhir was occupied, though the excavation of Building 93 and its middens suggest at least three phases of occupation, abandonment, and reuse. The

---

[57] For what we can say about the cemeteries, see Meyer 2011, pp. 109–14.

decision to open the mines and expend significant resources to hire, organize, and supply the miners in a remote desert was a matter for officials in the Nile valley, Alexandria, or even Constantinople. When resources or demand was low, it is unlikely the mining operations could have been maintained. The output of the Bir Umm Fawakhir mines seems to have been marginal, at least by comparison to the yield of the older mines in the Wadi el-Sid. And all mines play out. After a point, current mining technology cannot efficiently produce any more useable ore (though new techniques often lead to reworking old mines). Finally, at the end of the sixth century and the beginning of the seventh, the Byzantine empire and Egypt were under severe stress. The end of occupation of an archaeological site is seldom easy to date, but it seems likely that toward the end of the sixth century, resources to support the mines and miners were no longer available. The miners, their families if any, the clerks, and anyone else packed up what they could carry and returned to the Nile valley and to a turbulent situation.[58] The Sasanians conquered Alexandria and Egypt in 619. Heraclius established himself as emperor (ruled 610–641); defeated or negotiated with Slavs, Avars, Caucasian tribes, and other enemies; and in 627 conquered the Persian army and regained Syria, Palestine, and Egypt, but not for long. In 639 Babylon (now Old Cairo) fell to the Islamic army under ʿAmr, and in 642 Alexandria itself was conquered. In the following centuries, nomads, merchants, and pilgrim caravans most certainly did cross the Eastern Desert, but the mineral resources of the Bir Umm Fawakhir, Wadi Hammamat, and Wadi el-Sid area saw little further exploration, much less exploitation, until the nineteenth century.

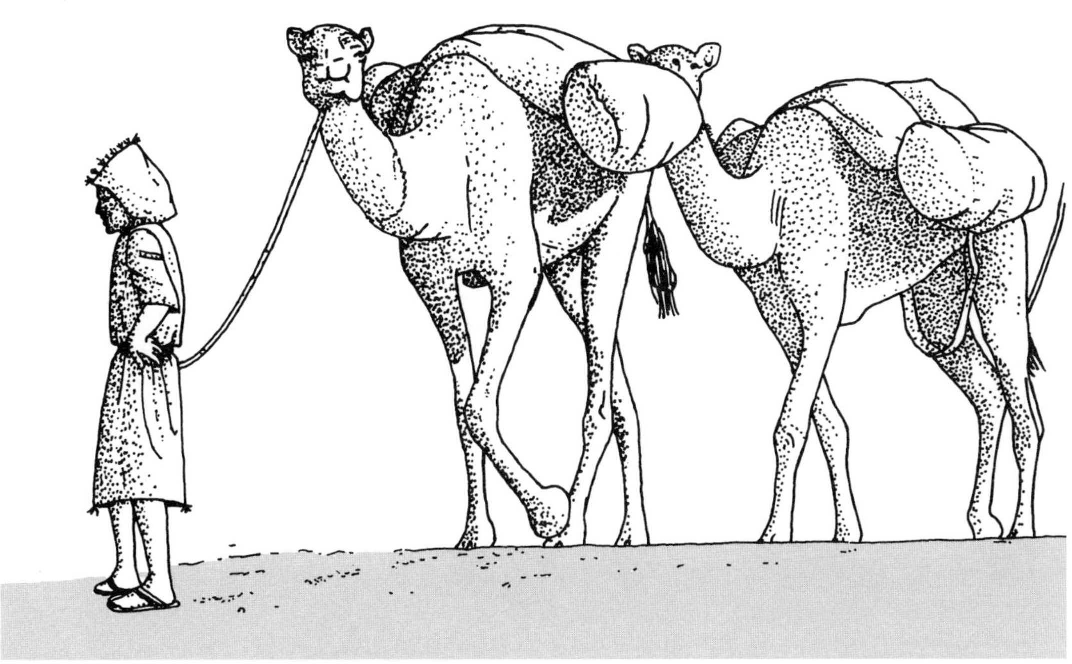

Figure 48. Reconstruction of head of camel train

[58] In figure 48, the camel driver's hooded, tasseled tunic is based on Cannuyer 2001, p. 56; his sandals, on Russo 2008, p. 449; camels, courtesy of Saudi Aramco World.

Appendix A

Locus Descriptions

Building 93, Room A

Locus	*Description*
1	Surface fill over whole room, a few sherds, bone, small bit of glass
2	East half of room, ca. 3.5 × 1.5 m, loose, silty sand
3	Below locus 2, darker brown, silty sand, more granular; sherds, charcoal, bone, glass, bit of wood, bits of black woven matting, some ash
4	North half of trench, dark brown organic-rich sandy layer below locus 3; gray ash in spots, clumps of hair, bits of woven material, sherds, bone (including hoof), charcoal, glass, sticks and twigs, matting, pestle (RN 99/207). Top 98.538, bottom 98.288 to 98.188 m (same as locus 5)
5	Same as locus 4, south half of trench
6	Below loci 4 and 5, much organic matter, bone (including vertebrae), sherds, hair, charcoal, "mano," shell, glass, copper/gold-alloy bracelet (RN 99/230). Top 98.288, bottom ca. 98.180 m

Building 93, Room B

Locus	*Description*
1	East side of room, top 3 to 12 cm, loose, silty sand on surface (same as locus 4)
2	East side of room, coarse, gravelly sand with lenses of fine silty sand (same as locus 5)
3	East side of room, sandy to silty to gravelly fill over granite, pockets in bedrock
4	West side of room, top layer, loose silty sand (same as locus 1)
5	West side of room, slightly more compact sand, to top of potstand (same as locus 2)
6	West side of room, sandy to silty to gravelly fill, many finds: animal teeth and bones, sherds, charcoal, eggshell, a tiny amount of blue glazed faience and glass, a rectangular piece of talc chlorite schist, a small, crude serpentinite bowl (RN 99/205)
7	East side of room, scraping rotten granite to bedrock
8	West side of room, cleaning rotten granite to bedrock, pockets in granite

Building 93, Room C

Locus	*Description*
1	Top, loose surface in northwest quadrant; thin
2	Northeast quadrant, loose, silty sand on surface; sherds, bone, charcoal, organic matter, raw emerald (RN 99/232), coin (RN 99/237), two dimple stones (close to north wall)
3	Northeast quadrant, below locus 2; slightly more granular silty sand, down to more ashy locus 5; ash in spots, bone
4	Under locus 3, top of bin fill; porphyry dimple stone in inner partition
5	Northeast quadrant, below locus 3; ashy layer and fill down to floor; potstand in situ
6	Bin fill, below locus 4; soft, powdery silty sand fill at "door" of bin; few sherds, some ash and charcoal
7	Bin fill, western half, below locus 4; fine, silty, powdery sand, very compact, laminated so it flakes; ash, charcoal, a few bones, raw emerald (RN 99/232), coin (RN 99/237)
8	Bin, outside vertical slab, below locus 4; more granular sand; many small bits felsite
9	Northwest quadrant; sandy fill down to level of locus 5 floor; ash, broken vessel, metal fragment (RN 99/241)
10	Northeast quadrant; ash, bone, broken pottery from floor and depression
11	(number skipped)
12	Northeast quadrant, below loci 5 and 10; granular, silty sand, some grayish patches with bits of burnt earth and charcoal, patch of brown silt at southeast corner of quadrant; sherds, bone, glass, "plaster," organic matter (same as locus 13)
13	North half northeast quadrant; gravelly silt; sherds, bone, charcoal, glass fragment, dung(?), emerald (RN 99/232) (same as locus 12)
14	Northeast quadrant, below locus 13; large granite rocks
15	Northwest quadrant, below locus 9; much ash and charcoal, emeralds in matrix (RN 99/232)
16	Northwest quadrant, below loci 9 and 15; silty sand down to possible floor; much charcoal, sherds, some bone, glass, organic matter
17	Northwest quadrant, possible floor or surface; bone, sherds, charcoal, ash
18	Northwest quadrant, under locus 17; granular, silty sand, patches of ash, patch of red-brown soil by south baulk; much ash, charcoal, sherds, some bone, intact upside-down krater (RN 99/222), two coins (RN 99/237), agate gemstone (RN 99/203), Bes amulet (RN 99/240)
19	Northwest quadrant, floor or surface on which pot rested
20	Northeast quadrant; sandy fill, attempt to reach approximate level of locus 19

Building 93, Room D

Locus	Description
1	Surface silt over whole room, ca. 25–40 cm deep, down to compact surface; one bead, a little bone, a grinding stone
2	Southwest corner, 1.8 × 1.9 m. Compact, fine, silty sand (possibly windblown), pinkish and reddish patches; many rocks, probably wall fall; much pottery, some charcoal, a little bone and shell, a few seeds and fragments of glass;
3	Below locus 2, around stone feature; more granular, including rotten granite, compact and silty; a few tiny roots; bottle plug, some ash
4	Inside rock circle and below locus 3; fine silty to fine sand, fine gravel toward bottom; charcoal, a little bone and ash, many sherds, bits of plaster(?) and wood, insect casings
5	Below locus 3; hard, reddish, silty fill

Building 93, Room E (northeast quadrant)

Locus	Description
1	Fine windblown surface silt, virtually no finds
2	Thick layer (42 cm deep) of sandy and silty laminated layers down to packed silt layer 3; animal holes; two beads RN 95/195, a little glass, but few finds
3	Very fine silty layer, charcoal patch and lenses, down to rocky tumble (locus 4)
4	Brownish laminated silt (A pot partly buried under rocks was left in situ)

Dump 1

Locus	*Description*
1	Top 10–30 cm, sandy to powdery windblown soil, some ash, heavy sherds, four dipinti, two quartzite pounding stones, a cowrie shell cut to make an ornament (RN 99/201; pl. 18a), a thick basalt stone disk, and a very coarse plate stamped "XP" (RN 99/226)
2	Thin ashy layer, bone, one horn, organic material (twine, charcoal, cloth fibers, wood, twigs, date pits, dung), decorated glass, and two dipinti
3	Thick ash layer in southeast corner, much bone, burnt bone, organic matter, one burnt brick, wooden peg (RN 99/208)
4	Sandy fill 18–25 cm thick, many ash lenses
5	Black ash around tabun 2
6	Thin, tough, ashy, hard layer
7	Thick layer of very fine ash in southeast corner, between vertical stone, tabun 1, and corner of trench
8	Inside potstand (originally called "tabun" 3), sandy, a little bone
9	Floor or working surface, packed sandy soil (thought to be "gebel" at first); some organic matter, bone, a horn, iron, one dipinto
10	Interior of tabun 2, upper layer; sandy, a little charcoal, some burnt bone (seeds, bone, sherds, fiber possibly from baulk)
11	Interior of tabun 2, lower layer, bottom at 99.867 m; dark, ashy, much dung, fine ash
12	Thick layer with many lenses of ash, organic material; much bone, also cloth, seeds, wood, charcoal, twine, bits of fiber, leather, copper-alloy strap
13	Interior of "tabun" 1 (or *dolium*), granite fragments, a little bone and sherds down 26 cm to clay floor)
14	Exterior of "tabun" 1, between inner ceramic wall of tabun and outer stone rim. Top 25 cm: mixed soil, ash, sherds, bone, charcoal, some fiber and dung; bottom 3 cm: fine ash with sherds
15	Burning place in angle of stones; ashy
16	Packed sandy silt below loci 12 and 15, ca. 8–10 cm thick, lead ring RN 99/241
17	Fine, fairly soft, silty sand, 25–30 cm thick, possibly windblown; jars 129 and 135 (RN 99/219 and 220) on "floor"

Dump 2

Locus	*Description*
1	Top 4–25 cm, over whole trench; sandy wash from cliff; heavy sherds, some bone, a little ash; thin ash on bottom
2	Over whole trench; sandy, darker than locus 1; abundant sherds, glass
3	Ash pit near middle of trench with much organic debris
4	Western two-thirds of trench; softer, sandier than locus 2; down to thick ash layer locus 5; much organic debris northwest corner including cloth, fiber, seeds, twine, charcoal, dung, glass
5	Ash layer below locus 4, thick in places; down to tops of tabun and pots
6	Sandy, gritty, outside pot 1 in northwest corner, equivalent of layers 5 and 8 in southwest part of trench; yellow bead
7	Black ashy fill of "bin" between pots 1 and 2
8	Sand and ash lenses, blue cloth, sherds, organic matter; down to hard packed surface in northwest corner

9	Pure ash inside rim of stones around pot 1
10	Ash between "SW tabun" and surrounding wall; layers of ash, charcoal, some sherds and bone
11	Pot 2 and surrounding ash
12	Lower part of pit, below locus 3, deep organic pocket, brownish soil; much bone, also hoof, skin, cloth, fiber, and dung
13	Inside "SW tabun" (or *dolium*), mixed debris, fiber, textile, twigs, leaves, large stones at bottom

Building 177, Room A

Locus	*Description*
0	Fine, soft surface silt
1	Packed, fine silt over almost whole room, ca. 2.3 × 3.0 m to tumble at south wall
2	Pit cut into layers 1 and 3; laminated silt with pockets of pure silt and a few rocks, white specks
3	Brown with white flecks, under locus 1, north and west part of room, ca. 2.3 × 3.0 m plus ca. 50 cm toward southwest corner; stopped by locus 7 tumble; much organic matter, some dung, bronze weight, coin, decorated glass, fibers, twine, glass beads, pounding stone; smashed sherds on bottom
4	Brown patch east of hearth [locus 13], lump with locus 3
5	Brown patch south of hearth [locus 13], lump with locus 3
6	Pit in locus 3, pale, silty fill; circle of stones lies below top of pit
7	Tumble from south wall (originally thought to be a bench), mostly rocks and fill; under surface silt, over locus 1; modern trash but also a baked brick, an "incense burner," sherds, bone, glass, dimpled crushing stone
8	Sherdy patch under locus 3, by west wall in locus 9
9	Rough sandy and soft silty sand layer under locus 3; many sherds, bones, two stone "incense burners," steatite bead, small finds (emerald and dipinto)
10	Ashy patch in southwest corner, under locus 7; lamp nozzle
11	Fine sand under locus 10; dipinto
12	Mostly sand, some sherds and bone; under locus 9, three dipinti, stamped plate, hoof, dung
13	Inside hearth in west corner, much ash and charcoal, some splintery sherds
14	Sandy, below locus 12; ash lens, some sherds and bone, dung
15	Circle of stones with charcoal underneath; over locus 3
16	Small shallow pit with charcoal, black soil, a little wood

Building 177, Room B

Locus	Description
1	Fine, soft surface silt
2	Packed silt, two ashy patches, little charcoal
3	Thin ash layer over bedrock
4	Ashy, silty sand in crevice in granite; grinding stone, little pottery and bone

Building 177, Room C

Locus	Description
1	Fine, soft, silty sand, east half of room; some pottery, bone, charcoal, bead, glass
2	Brown fill, silty sand; organic matter, seeds, wood, charcoal, pottery, bone, hair, matting, bead, glass
3	Small patch of lighter fill under locus 2, in depression in granite
4	South end, to bedrock
5	West half of Room C, same as locus 1; pieces of three grinding stones
6	West half of Room C, same as locus 2, brown patches
7	West half of Room C, under locus 2/6; ashy, silty sand; much charcoal, some bone and pottery, coin, bead, glass
8	Northwest corner of Room C, brown fill, burnt bone
9	West half of Room C, along west wall and at door; silty sand over bedrock

Building 177, Room D

Locus	Description
1	Loose, fine, silty sand; little ash, grinding stone, pottery, bone, charcoal, beads
2	Compact silty surface, reaches granite bedrock on east; patch of ash and burnt bone, two brown patches
3	Ashy and brown sandy area on west side of trench, over bedrock; much bone, some charcoal and pottery, a few seeds
4	Depression in bedrock
5	Depression in bedrock; bead, a little pottery, bone, charcoal
6	West half of trench; loose, silty surface sand; beads, glass, little other material
7	West half of trench; granular, silty sand over bedrock
8	West half of trench, depression in granite bedrock with compact silty surface; fill of reddish silt

Building 181

Locus	Description
1	Fine, silty sand, top 3–5 cm; some pottery, glass, bone, a little charcoal
2	More compact fill, alternates between fine silty sand and coarser sand with bits of rock, layers are flat and perhaps water-laid; small bits of pottery, bone, some charcoal, shell, beads, “mano”
3	Fill below slightly more compact sand (locus 2) and a large sherd (40 cm below surface) in doorway; coarse sand with bits of granite, to bedrock

Appendix B

Registered Objects

Registration No.	Provenance	Sub No.	Description	Material	Remarks	Registration Date	Illustration
99/138	Dump 1		1 bag bone	Bone	—	II-8-99	—
99/139	Dump 1, locus 1, ashy		1 bag bone	Bone	—	II-9-99	—
99/140	Dump 1, locus 2		4 bags bone	Bone	—	II-99	—
99/141	Dump 1, locus 3		1 bag bone	Bone	—	II-9-99	—
99/142	Dump 1, loci 2, 4–5, clean-up		3 bags bone	Bone	—	II-99	—
99/143	Dump 1, loci 6–7		4 bags bone	Bone	—	II-10-99	—
99/144	Dump 1, loci 8–11		4 bags bone	Bone	—	II-99	—
99/145	Dump 1, loci 12, 16, clean-up		4 bags bone	Bone	—	II-99	—
99/146	Dump 1, loci 3–5, and clean-up		4 bags wood fragments	Wood	—	II-99	—
99/147	Dump 1, loci 6, 9, 11		3 bags wood fragments	Wood	—	II-99	—
99/148	Dump 1, loci 12, 16, clean-up		3 bags wood fragments	Wood	—	II-99	—
99/149	Dump 1, loci 1–5		5 bags charcoal	Charcoal	—	II-99	—
99/150	Dump 1, loci 6, 9–11		4 bags charcoal	Charcoal	—	II-99	—
99/151	Dump 1, loci 12, 15–17		5 bags charcoal	Charcoal	—	II-99	—
99/152	B93, Room B, locus 3		2 bags wood fragments	Wood	—	II-10-99	—
99/153	B93, Room B, locus 8; Dump 2, loci 1–3, 5		7 bags wood fragments	Wood	—	II-99	—
99/154	Dump 2, loci 4–6, 8		5 bags wood fragments	Wood	—	II-99	—
99/155	Dump 1, loci 15, 17		2 bags bone	Bone	—	II-99	—
99/156	Dump 2, loci 1–2		4 bags bone	Bone	—	II-99	—
99/157	Dump 2, locus 4		3 bags bone	Bone	—	II-99	—
99/158	Dump 2, locus 5		4 bags bone	Bone	—	II-99	—
99/159	Dump 2, loci 6–8, 10		5 bags bone	Bone	—	II-99	—
99/160	Dump 2, loci 5, 10–12, clean-up		7 bags bone	Bone	—	II-99	—
99/161	B93, Room A, all loci		14 bags bone, little teeth	Bone	—	II-99	—
99/162	B93, Room A, surface, unexcavated west end		1 bag bone	Bone	—	II-15-99	—
99/163	B93, Room B, loci 1–3		7 bags bone, little teeth, shell?	Bone	—	II-99	—
99/164	B93, Room B, loci 4, 7–8		4 bags bone	Bone	—	II-99	—
99/165	B93, Room C, loci 3–10, 12		11 bags bone	Bone	—	II-99	—
99/166	B93, Room C, loci 12–15		5 bags bone	Bone	—	II-99	—

* Sub numbers: d- = dipinto number, st- = stamped sherd number, lab- = conservator's lab number (see *Chapter 7*)

Registration No.	Provenance	Sub No.	Description	Material	Remarks	Registration Date	Illustration
99/167	B93, Room C, loci 16–18, 20		7 bags bone	Bone	—	II-99	—
99/168	B93, Room D, all loci		11 bags bone	Bone	—	II-99	—
99/169	B93, Room E, loci 1–3		4 bags bone	Bone	—	II-99	—
99/170	B177, Room A, loci 0–2		8 bags bone	Bone	—	II-99	—
99/171	B177, Room A, loci 3–5, 7–8		18 bags bone	Bone	—	II-99	—
99/172	B177, Room A, loci 9–12, 14–15		13 bags bone	Bone	—	II-99	—
99/173	B177, Room B, all loci		4 bags bone	Bone	—	II-20-99	—
99/174	B177, Room C, all loci		12 bags bone	Bone	—	II-99	—
99/175	B177, Room D, all loci		8 bags bone	Bone	—	II-99	—
99/176	B181, loci 1–2		2 bags bone	Bone	—	II-99	—
99/177	Dump 2, loci 4, 11		2 bags hair fragments	Hair	—	II-99	—
99/178	B181, locus 3		1 bag bone	Bone	—	II-23-99	—
99/178	B93, Room A, loci 4–6; Room C, locus 12		5 bags hair fragments	Hair	—	II-99	—
99/179	B177, Room A, loci 3, 5; Room D, locus 3		3 bags hair fragments	Hair	—	II-99	—
99/180	B93, Rooms A, C, D; Dumps 1 and 2, misc. loci		24 bags fibers	Fiber	—	II-99	—
99/181	B93, Room A, Dumps 1 and 2; B177, Room A, misc. loci		9 bags rope or twine	Rope/twine	—	II-99	—
99/182	B93, B177, Dump 1, Dump 2 all loci		34 bags dung	Dung	—	II-99	—
99/183	B93, Rooms D, E, all loci; Dump 1, loci 2, 4–5; Dump 2, loci 1–8, 10–12		39 bags charcoal fragments	Charcoal	—	II-99	—
99/184	B93, Rooms A, B, C, all loci		43 bags charcoal fragments	Charcoal	—	II-99	—
99/185	B177, Rooms A, B, C, D, all loci; B181, all loci		59 bags charcoal fragments	Charcoal	—	II-99	—
99/186	Dump 1, loci 2, 4		2 bags hair and cloth	Hair and cloth	—	II-99	—
99/187	Dump 1, locus 2		1 bag bone	Bone	—	II-9-99	—
99/187	B93, Room E, screen		1 bag bone	Bone	—	II-27-99	—
99/188	Dump 1, locus 12; Dump 2, locus 12		2 bags, 3 dung beetles total	Insects	—	II-99	—
99/189	Dump 1, loci 2, 9		2 bags organic residue, on sherds	Organic	—	II-99	—
99/190	B93, Room B, locus 3; B177, Room C, locus 8		2 bags eggshell	Eggshell	—	II-99	—
99/190	B93, Dump 1, locus 4		Ochre	Ochre	—	II-22-99	—
99/191	B93, Rooms C, D; Dump 2; B177, Room A, misc. loci		4 bags insects	Insects	—	II-99	—
99/192	B93, Rooms A, B, C, D, E; Dumps 1 and 2; B177, Rooms A, C, D; B181, misc. loci		69 bags wood fragments	Wood	—	II-99	—
99/193	B93, Rooms A, B, C, D; Dumps 1 and 2; B177, Rooms A, C, D, misc. loci		58 bags seeds	Seeds	—	II-99	—

Registration No.	Provenance	Sub No.	Description	Material	Remarks	Registration Date	Illustration
99/194	B93, Rooms A, B, C, D, E; Dumps 1 and 2; B177, Rooms A, C, D; B181, misc. loci		32 bags seashells	Shells	See *Appendix D* for details	II-99	–
99/195	B93, B177, Dump 1, Dump 2, all loci		72 bags glass fragments	Glass	See *Appendix C* for details	II-99	–
99/196	B93, Room A, locus 4		2 bags hair, skin, hoof	Hair, skin	–	II-15-99	–
99/196	B93, Room A, surface, Dump 1, locus 12; Dump 2, locus 12; B177, Room A locus 3		4 bags leather/ skin	Leather	–	II-99	–
99/196	Dump 1, locus 4		Sheep skin	Skin	–	II-9-99	–
99/197	B177, Room D, locus 2 west		Sherd with painted "XM" inscription	Ceramic	–	II-21-99	fig. 39k
99/198	Dump 2, locus 1 (surface)		Stone bowl; small fragment of very large, polished white calcite bowl	Stone	–	II-14-99	fig. 42a
99/199	B177, Room A, locus 4		Bead, date-pit shape	Stone	–	II-15-99	fig. 40q, pl. 15a
99/199	B177, Room C west, locus 8		Steatite bead, flower-like	Stone	–	II-22-99	fig. 40r, pl. 15b
99/199	B177, Room C west, locus 1		Stone pendant, oblong, incised "X," 1.4 cm long	Stone	–	II-21-99	fig. 40t
99/199	B177, Room A, locus 9		Soapstone pendant, trapezoid?, ca. 1.5 × 0.6 cm, broken	Stone	–	II-22-99	fig. 40s
99/199	B177, Room D, locus 5 west		Stone pendant, tiny, "potted plant" shape, 1.0 cm	Stone	–	II-21-99	fig. 40u
99/200	Dump 2, locus 9 "pot circle"		"Game piece," ca. 2.4 cm dia.	Ceramic	–	II-17-99	fig. 42t
99/200	B177, Room A, locus 3		"Game piece," ca. 2.5 cm dia.	Ceramic	–	II-20-99	fig. 42s
99/200	B177, Room A, locus 9		2 "game pieces," each ca. 4 cm dia.	Ceramic	–	II-22-99	fig. 42r, one not illustrated
99/201	Dump 1, locus 1, top		Cowrie shell, sliced, mouth only, 1.8 cm long	Shell	–	II-8-99	pl. 18a
99/202	B93, Room B, locus 3		Plug?, ca. 2.0 × 2.5 cm	Plaster	–	II-10-99	–
99/202	B93, Room D, locus 3		Bottle plug?, ca. 3 × 2 cm dia.	Plaster	–	II-25-99	–
99/202	B93, Room D, locus 4		Plug?, small bit	Plaster	–	II-25-99	–
99/202	B177, Room A, locus 3		Plug, ca. 2 cm dia.	Mud?	–	II-20-99	–
99/203	B93, Room C northwest, locus 18		Red and black agate oval gemstone 11 x 9 x 3	Stone	–	II-18-99	pl. 33c

Registration No.	Provenance	Sub No.	Description	Material	Remarks	Registration Date	Illustration
99/204	B177, Room A, locus 7, wall tumble		"Incense burner"(?), ca. 11 × 9 × 5.5 cm	Brick	—	II-20-99	pl. 16b
99/205	B93, Room B west, locus 6		Very crude serpentinite bowl, dia. ca. 9 cm	Stone	—	II-9-99	pl. 17a
99/206	B93, Room B, locus 5		Amphora fragments, potstand	Ceramic	—	II-10-99	—
99/207	B93, Room A, locus 4		Pestle, square cross section ca. 3 × 8 cm, broken	Stone	—	II-15-99	pl. 17b
99/208	Dump 1, locus 3		Peg, ca. 14 cm long	Wood	—	II-10-99	pl. 18b
99/209	B177, Room C west, locus 9		Blank disk, soapstone, ca. 1 cm dia.	Stone	—	II-22-99	—
99/210	B177, Room A southwest, locus 3		Bead, elongated, polygonal, broken, greenish	Glass (see Appendix C for details)	—	II-22-99	fig. 40o
99/211	Dump 2, locus 11 (pot 2)		Bowl(?), very flaring rim, three grooves, decayed	Faience	—	II-21-99	fig. 42p
99/212	B177, Room A, locus 7		Worked stone, unfinished whorl?	Stone	—	II-21-99	—
99/213	B177, Room A, locus 10 (surface silt)		Lamp(?) nozzle fragment(?), burnt	Ceramic	—	II-21-99	pl. 35d
99/214	Dump 2, locus 12 (rich organic)		Plug, dia. ca. 3.5 cm	Mud	—	II-17-99	fig. 42q
99/215	Dump 2, locus 3		Small cup or bowl with incised "+H"	Ceramic	—	II-14-99	fig. 22:64, pl. 31b
99/216	Dump 2		Many fragments of cloth and bone	Cloth, bone	—	II-20-99	—
99/217	Dump 2, locus 4	lab-6	Cloth, many bits, some colored	Cloth	—	II-9-99	pl. 39b
99/218	Surface	lab-3	Deep bowl or "krater"	Ceramic	—	II-99	fig. 27:104, pl. 32a
99/219	Dump 1, locus 17	lab-10	Wide-mouth, globular jar, for milk?	Ceramic	Found with vessel no. 135 (RN 99/220)	II-13-99	fig. 32:129, pls. 7, 13b
99/220	Dump 1, locus 17	lab-9	Jar with 5 holes in bottom, for cheese-making?	Ceramic	Found with vessel no. 129 (RN 99/219)	II-13-99	fig. 33:135, pls. 7, 14
99/221	Dump behind B228, surface	lab-2	Plate, nearly complete	Ceramic	—	II-99	—
99/222	B93, Room C, locus 18		Pot or "krater," cracked, 27.9–29.7 cm, at rim	Ceramic	—	II-18-99	fig. 28:109, pls. 13a, 24c

Registration No.	Provenance	Sub No.	Description	Material	Remarks	Registration Date	Illustration
99/223	High on hill behind B93, surface	d-8	Dipinto, large inscription	Ceramic	–	II-99	fig. 38e
99/223	Path above Outlier 7, north bay, surface	d-12	Dipinto, small inscription, "enk..." or "enn..." ?	Ceramic	–	II-99	fig. 39d
99/223	Dump below B177, surface	d-14	Dipinto, four lines of small inscription, "tetra"	Ceramic	–	II-99	fig. 39f, pl. 33a
99/223	Area below B236, surface	d-15	Dipinto, two lines of small inscription	Ceramic	–	II-99	fig. 39g
99/223	Dump behind B214, surface	d-16	Dipinto, bit of large inscription	Ceramic	Fabric: exterior (slip?) 10YR 8/2, interior 2.5YR 7/6; coarse,sandy temper, gritty; very abundant black bits, abundant medium-size red and quartz bits, very large red bit (unlevigated clay?)	II-99	fig. 38i
99/223	Above "plaza," surface	d-17	Dipinto, curl of large inscription	Ceramic	Fabric like d-16	II-99	–
99/223	Dump east of B206, surface	d-18	Dipinto, part of large, worn inscription	Ceramic	Fabric like d-16	II-99	–
99/223	Dump below B183, surface	d-19	Dipinto, two bits of large inscription on amphora neck	Ceramic	Orangey pink fabric with whitish exterior, gritty, like d-16	II-99	–
99/223	Dump behind B104, surface	d-20	Dipinto, large, faded inscription	Ceramic	Gritty, like d-16	II-99	–
99/223	Dump west of B200, surface	d-21	Dipinto, bit of large inscription	Ceramic	–		–
99/223	Near B233	d-22	Dipinto, bit of large inscription	Ceramic	Gritty, like d-16	II-99	–
99/223	Path between Outlier 7 and main settlement, surface	d-23	Dipinto, two bits of large inscription on neck	Ceramic	Gritty, like d-16	II-99	–
99/223	Dump beside B214	d-24	Dipinto, very faint large inscription	Ceramic	–	II-99	–
99/223	Above (to west) path to Outlier 7, surface	d-25	Dipinto, 2 bits of large inscription, faint	Ceramic	Gritty, like d-16	II-99	–
99/223	On mountain above and behind B33, close to d-27	d-26	Dipinto; rim, neck, part of handles and shoulder with top of large inscription	Ceramic	Gritty; 10YR 8/4 to 7.5YR 8/4 surface and fabric; very abundant medium-size black bits, abundant medium-size red and white bits	II-99	fig. 37b

Registration No.	Provenance	Sub No.	Description	Material	Remarks	Registration Date	Illustration
99/223	On mountain above and behind B33, close to d-26	d-27	Dipinto, bit of large inscription	Ceramic	Gritty, like d-16		—
99/223	Hill above north bay 3, northeast of Hillock, surface	d-28	Dipinto, three lines of small inscription	Ceramic	Much of amphora shoulder and handle found, only one small dipinto; gritty, like d-16	II-99	fig. 39e
99/223	Dump behind B104	d-29	Dipinto, amphora rim and neck with top of large inscription	Ceramic	Fabric like d-16	II-99	fig. 37c
99/223	Around B177, surface	d-30	Dipinto, 2 bits of large inscription	Ceramic	Fabric and surface like d-16	II-99	—
99/223	Around B177, surface	d-31	Dipinto, bit of large, clear inscription	Ceramic	Fabric and surface like d-16	II-99	—
99/223	Around B177, surface	d-32	Dipinto, bit of small inscription	Ceramic	Fabric like d-16	II-99	—
99/223	Around B177, surface	d-33	Dipinto, piece of large inscription near handle scar	Ceramic	Fabric like d-16	II-99	—
99/223	Around B177, surface	d-34	Dipinto, piece of large, faint inscription	Ceramic	Fabric and surface like d-16	II-99	fig. 38h
99/223	Around B177, surface	d-35	Dipinto, loop of large inscription	Ceramic	Fabric like d-16	II-99	—
99/223	Around B177, surface	d-36	Dipinto, curl of large inscription	Ceramic	Interior and exterior surface and fabric 10YR 8/4; very abundant black and red bits, a few white bits, a few large white quartz bits	II-99	—
99/223	Behind B13	d-37	Dipinto, curl of large inscription	Ceramic	Fabric like d-16	II-99	—
99/223	Above north bay 2, surface	d-38	Dipinto, bit of large inscription, worn	Ceramic	Fabric like d-16	II-99	—
99/223	Northeast of Hillock, high on slope	d-39	Dipinto; amphora rim, neck, part of handles & shoulder with bit of faint, small inscription, 10 sherds	Ceramic	Gritty; 2.5YR 7/6 to grayer 2.5YR 7/3 core, surface 10YR 8/4; abundant black, white, red, gray bits, a few large white and red bits	II-99	—
99/224	Dump 2, locus 11		Dipinto; large, faint inscription	Ceramic	"Pot 2" vessel; amphora neck, shoulders, handles, faint dipinto	II-20-99	fig. 37a
99/225	B177, Room A, locus 11	d-1	Dipinto, bit of large inscription	Ceramic	—	II-22-99	—

Registration No.	Provenance	Sub No.	Description	Material	Remarks	Registration Date	Illustration
99/225	B177, Room A, locus 9	d-2	Dipinto, large inscription	Ceramic	—	II-22-99	fig. 37d
99/225	B93, Room C northeast, locus 2,	d-3	Dipinto, large inscription	Ceramic	—	II-11-99	fig. 38a
99/225	Dump 1, locus 1 top	d-4	Dipinto, large inscription	Ceramic	—	II-8-99	fig. 38b
99/225	Dump 1, locus 1 top	d-5	Dipinto, small inscription at neck	Ceramic	—	II-8-99	fig. 39c
99/225	Dump 1, locus 1 top	d-6	Dipinto, parts of large and small inscriptions near handle	Ceramic	—	II-8-99	fig. 38c
99/225	Dump 1, locus 9	d-7	Dipinto, large inscription	Ceramic	—	II-11-99	fig. 38d
99/225?	Dump 2, locus 11, interior tabun	d-9	Dipinto, most of large inscription	Ceramic	—	II-21-99	fig. 38f
99/225	Dump 2, locus 4 (middle, north end)	d-10	Dipinto, piece of large inscription	Ceramic	—	II-16-99	—
99/225	Dump 2, locus 5 (middle strip)	d-13	Dipinto, piece of large inscription with "XP"	Ceramic	—	II-16-99	fig. 38g
99/225	Dump 2, locus 5 (middle strip)	d-40	Dipinto, bit of large inscription	Ceramic	Burnt interior, fabric probably like d-16	II-16-99	—
99/225	Dump 2, "discard" bag	d-41	Dipinto, piece of large, clear inscription	Ceramic	Sooted interior, fabric probably like d-16	II-99	fig. 39a
99/225	B93, Room A, locus 5	d-42	Dipinto, bit of large, faint inscription, utilized as scraper?	Ceramic	Fabric like d-16	II-16-99	—
99/225	B93, Room C northeast, locus 5	d-43	Dipinto, loop of large inscription (see also d-60)	Ceramic	Very gritty; 7.5YR 8/4 surface, 7.5YR 8/5 interior; very abundant black, white (quartz), and red medium-size bits	II-13-99	—
99/225	Dump 1, top 5 cm [= Locus 1]	d-44	Dipinto, piece of large inscription	Ceramic	Fabric and surface like d-16	II-8-99	—
99/225	B93, Room A, locus 4	d-45	Dipinto, 2 lines of small inscription	Ceramic	Fabric like d-16	II-15-99	fig. 39j
99/225	Dump 2	d-47	Dipinto, small bit of large inscription	Ceramic	White concretion on surface but fabric probably like d-16	II-99	—
99/225	Dump 2	d-48	Dipinto, small bit of large inscription	Ceramic	Gritty; 10YR 8/2 fabric and interior; surface dirty looking; very abundant medium-size black and red bits, a few large white (quartz) bits	II-99	—

Registration No.	Provenance	Sub No.	Description	Material	Remarks	Registration Date	Illustration
99/225	Dump 2, locus 6 (middle)	d-49	Dipinto, small bit of large inscription	Ceramic	Fabric like d-16	II-17-99	—
99/225	Dump 2, locus 6 (middle)	d-50	Dipinto, end of large inscription	Ceramic	Very worn but fabric probably like d-16	II-17-99	—
99/225	Dump 2, locus 12, rich organic	d-51	Dipinto, bit of large inscription	Ceramic	—	II-17-99	—
99/225	Dump 2, locus 1 (wadi wash)	d-52	Dipinto, large piece of large inscription	Ceramic	Fabric like d-16	II-14-99	fig. 39b
99/225	B93, Room D, locus 2	d-53	Dipinto, small bit of large inscription	Ceramic	Fabric like d-16	II-24-99	—
99/225	Dump 1, locus 2 (ash patch)	d-54	Dipinto, bit of large inscription	Ceramic	Fabric like d-16	II-8-99	—
99/225	Dump 2, locus 8	d-55	Dipinto, loop of large inscription	Ceramic	Fabric like d-16 but interior very rough and cracked	II-16-99	—
99/225	B181, locus 2	d-56	Dipinto, 2 lines of small inscription plus smear of large one	Ceramic	Fabric like d-16	II-23-99	fig. 39h
99/225	B177, Room A, locus 12	d-57	Dipinto, very faint	Ceramic	—	II-23-99	—
99/225	B177, Room A, locus 12	d-58	Dipinto, very faint, perhaps 1 line of small plus tail of large one	Ceramic	Fabric like d-16	II-23-99	fig. 39i
99/225	B177, Room A, locus 12	d-59	Dipinto, very faint	Ceramic	—	II-23-99	—
99/225	B93, Room C northeast, locus 5	d-60	Dipinto, "L" of large inscription (see also d-43)	Ceramic	Fabric like d-16	II-13-99	—
99/225	Dump 2, surface	d-61	Dipinto, bit of large, scrawly insription	Ceramic	—	II-14-99	—
99/225	Dump 2, surface	d-62	Dipinto, bit of large, faint inscription	Ceramic	Fabric like d-16	II-14-99	—
99/225	B93, Room A, locus 5		Dipinto, curl of large inscription	Ceramic	—	II-13-99	—
99/225	B93, Room C northwest, locus 15		Dipinto, bit of large inscription	Ceramic	—	II-16-99	—
99/225	Dump 1, locus 2 (ashy)		Dipinto, small bit, faint	Ceramic	—	II-9-99	—
99/226	Dump 1, locus 1	st-1	Stamped, very coarse plate, "XP"	Ceramic	—	II-8-99	fig. 18:18
99/226	Dump 1, surface cleaning	st-2	Stamped, plate, faint flowers	Ceramic	—	II-8-99	fig. 18:17

Registration No.	Provenance	Sub No.	Description	Material	Remarks	Registration Date	Illustration
99/226	Surface	st-3, lab-8	Stamped, "duck"	Ceramic	–	II-99	fig. 18:16
99/226	B13, surface		Stamped, African Red Slip flower	Ceramic	–	II-28-99	fig. 17:3
99/226	South of B177, surface	st-15	Stamped, flower	Ceramic	–	II-99	fig. 18:22
99/226	Dump south of B177, surface		Rouletted, African Red Slip	Ceramic	–	II-99	fig. 17:2
99/226	Dump behind B13	st-7	Stamped, cross	Ceramic	–	II-13-99	fig. 18:19
99/226	Dump 2, surface cleaning	st-8	Stamped, cross	Ceramic	–	II-14-99	fig. 18:20
99/226	South of B177, surface	st-9	Stamped, circles	Ceramic	Fabric like st-12	II-99	fig. 18:21
99/226	South of B177, surface	st-5	Stamped, part of rosette	Ceramic	–	II-99	–
99/226	South of B177, surface	st-16	Stamped, concentric circles with small circles like petals outside? very worn	Ceramic	Fabric hard-fired 10R 6/6, remnant 10R 6/8 orange slip; very fine red and black bits	II-99	fig. 18:25
99/226	South of B177, surface	st-12	Stamp, circles	Ceramic	Tough orange fabric 2.5YR 6/8, slip 10R 6/8; abundant small black bits, some medium-size black bits	II-99	–
99/226	South of B177, surface	st-10	Stamp, sunburst	Ceramic	–	II-99	–
99/226	B177, surface	st-14	Stamped, leaves	Ceramic	–	II-99	fig. 18:23
99/226	South of B177, surface	st-13	Stamped, flower	Ceramic	–	II-99	fig. 18:24
99/226	South of B177, surface	st-11	Stamped, very faint	Ceramic	–	II-99	–
99/227	B177, Room A, locus 9	lab-23	Two "Incense burners," one very soft stone (7.2 x 2.9 x 5.3 cm), carved arches, niches, column feet; simpler "incense burner" (6.2 x 5.3 x 4.0 cm), 4 feet, incised lines on side	Stone	–	II-22-99	fig. 41e–f, pls. 15c, 16a
99/228	B93, Room B, top of locus 6	lab-5	Iron ladle	Metal	25.4 cm long, 3.5 wide at bowl; handle ca. 1.2 sq. section	II-9-1999	pls. 34e, 36
99/229	Dump 1, locus 9		Iron fragment	Metal	–	II-11-99	–
99/229	B177, Room A, locus 9		Metal fragment	Metal	–	II-11-99	–
99/229	B177, Room D, locus 3		Metal fragment	Metal	–	II-11-99	–
99/230	B93, Room A, locus 6	lab-18	Ca. 1/2 copper/gold-alloy bracelet, narrow, with spatulate ends	Metal	Dia. ca. 4.5, max. width 0.5, thickness 0.1 cm	II-17-99	fig. 41a, pl. 33b

Registration No.	Provenance	Sub No.	Description	Material	Remarks	Registration Date	Illustration
99/231	B177, Room A, locus 7	lab-15	Iron strap, thin, ca. 5 cm	Metal	—	II-21-99	—
99/232	B93, Room A, locus 3		Two emeralds	Emerald/ beryl	—	II-14-99	—
99/232	B93, Room A, locus 4		Emerald	Emerald/ beryl	—	II-17-99	pl. 34d
99/232	B93, Room A, locus 5		Emerald	Emerald/ beryl	—	II-16-99	—
99/232	B93, Room C, locus 15		Emerald, large chunk with crystals	Emerald/ beryl	—	II-16-99	—
99/232	B93, Room C, locus 13		Emerald	Emerald/ beryl	—	II-15-99	—
99/232	Dump 2, locus 10, interior "fragile pot"		Emerald	Emerald/ beryl	—	II-20-99	—
99/232	B177, Room A, locus 9		Emerald	Emerald/ beryl	—	II-22-99	—
99/232	B177, Room C, locus 1 east		Emerald	Emerald/ beryl	—	II-20-99	—
99/232	B177, Room C, locus 2		Emerald	Emerald/ beryl	—	II-20-99	—
99/232	B177 Room C, locus 7 west		Emerald	Emerald/ beryl	—	II-22-99	—
99/233	Dump behind B181, surface	st-18, lab-1	Orange plate	Ceramic	—	II-99	fig. 18:14, pl. 31a
99/234	Dump behind B61, surface	lab-4	Jar with fancy painted zigzags	Ceramic	—	II-99	fig. 34:138, pl. 32b
99/235	Dump 1, locus 17		Silky jird skeleton	Bone	—	II-18-99	pl. 19
99/236	B177, Room A, locus 12	st-17, lab-22	Stamped plate, splintered	Ceramic	—	II-23-99	fig. 18:15
99/237	B93, Room C northwest, locus 18	lab-11	Copper-alloy coin, dia. 11.57 mm	Metal	—	II-18-99	fig. 40a
99/237	B93, Room C northwest, locus 18	lab-12	Copper-alloy coin, dia. 11.59 mm	Metal	—	II-18-99	fig. 40b
99/237	B177, Room A, locus 3	lab-14	Copper-alloy coin, dia. 9.56 mm	Metal	—	II-20-99	fig. 40c
99/237	B177, Room C west, locus 2	lab-16	Copper-alloy coin, max. dia. 9.51 mm	Metal	—	II-21-99	fig. 40e
99/237	B177, Room C west, locus 7	lab-20	Copper-alloy coin, dia. 8.47 mm	Metal	—	II-22-99	fig. 40f
99/237	B177, Room A, locus 15 (stone circle)	lab-25	Copper-alloy coin, max. dia. 9.56 mm	Metal	—	II-24-99	fig. 40d
99/238	Dump 2, locus 5 (north end, middle)	lab-17	Copper-alloy strap, very small, thin, curved	Metal	—	II-16-99	—
99/239	B177, Room A southwest, locus 3	lab-19	Copper-alloy weight, small, square, "NB" inscription	Metal	—	II-22-99	fig. 41c, pl. 35b

Registration No.	Provenance	Sub No.	Description	Material	Remarks	Registration Date	Illustration
99/240	B93, Room C northwest, locus 18	lab-13	Copper-alloy Bes amulet, 1.5 cm tall	Metal	Two	II-18-99	fig. 41b, pl. 34a
99/241	Dump 1, locus 16, baulk cleaning	lab-26	Lead, thin ring, dia. ca. 1.5 cm, broken	Metal	—	II-14-99	—
99/241	B93, Room B west, locus 5	lab-27	Iron wedge, ca. 4.7 long x 2.5 x 1.6 cm at head	Metal	Two	II-9-99	pl. 35a
99/241	B177, Room A, locus 3	lab-28	Copper-alloy fragment, 5 × 8 mm	Metal	—	II-24-99	—
99/241	B177, Room C, locus 9		Metal fragment	Metal	—	II-99	—
99/241	Dump 1, locus 12	lab-24	"Copper-alloy strap"	Metal	—	II-99	fig. 41d

Appendix C

Glass

Provenance	Date	Description	Size	Color	Fabric, etc.	Registration No.	Illustration
B93, Room A, locus 1	II-14-99	Body sherd	Tiny	Transparent	White weathering	–	–
B93, Room A, locus 2	II-14-99	Body sherd	Tiny chip	Transparent	White weathering	–	–
B93, Room A, locus 3	II-14-99	Body sherd	Small*	Blue-green tint	–	–	–
–	–	Looped-out, bent rim	Ca. 3.0 × 0.7 cm	Transparent	Bubbles, weathering	99/195	fig. 42e
B93, Room A, locus 4	II-14-99	Body sherd	Tiny chip	Light yellow-green	Bubbles	–	–
B93, Room A, locus 4	II-14-99	Body sherd	Chip	Transparent	–	–	–
–	–	Bead, bicone	Small	Very dark brown	–	99/195	fig. 40k
–	–	Bead	Tiny	Bright yellow	–	99/195	fig. 40g
B93, Room A, locus 4	II-15-99	Body sherd	Very small	Transparent	Thin	–	–
–	–	3 body sherds	Chips	Transparent	2 weathered	–	–
–	–	2 body sherds	Small	Transparent	Few bubbles, weathered	–	–
–	–	Body sherd	Ca. 2.3 × 2.3 cm	Dirty blue-green	Very bubbly, impurities	–	–
–	–	Body sherd	Small	Light blue-green	Bubbly, white weathering	–	–
–	–	Rolled rim(?)	Tiny	Transparent	–	–	–
–	–	Bottle neck	4.8 × 3.0 cm	Dirty green-olive	Very bubbly, impurities	99/195	fig. 42l
B93, Room A, locus 4	II-17-99	Body sherd	Tiny chip	Transparent	–	–	–
–	–	Body sherd	Very small	Transparent	White weathering	–	–
B93, Room A, locus 5	II-16-99	Body sherd	Very small	Cobalt	Very thick	–	–
B93, Room A, locus 6	II-17-99	2 body sherds	Small; very small	Transparent	Bubbles, white weathering	–	–
–	–	Body sherd	Small	Transparent	Slight weathering	–	–
–	–	Body sherd	Ca. 3.0 × 2.5 cm	Transparent	White weathering	–	–
–	–	Body sherd	Small	Transparent	Thick	–	–
–	–	Rim(?), simple	Tiny	Green	Translucent, very bubbly	–	–
–	–	Body sherd	Very small	Blue-green tinge	Slight weathering	–	–
–	–	Body sherd	Small	Dirty blue-green	Very bubbly	–	–

* Small = thumbnail size

Provenance	Date	Description	Size	Color	Fabric, etc.	Registration No.	Illustration
—	—	Body sherd	Small	Olive	Slight weathering, some bubbles	—	—
—	—	Body sherd	Very small	Cobalt	—	—	—
—	—	Body sherd, decorated	Very small	Cobalt with blue and white ruffle?	Slight weathering	99/195	—
—	—	Pedestal base, straw marks	ca. 2.3 × 1.0 cm	Yellow-green tinge	Thick, white weathering	99/195	—
B93, Room B west, locus 2	II-9-99	3 body sherds	Very small, 2 chips	Blue-green	Bubbly	—	—
B93, Room B west, locus 3	II-9-99	Body sherd	Small	Cobalt	Thick	—	
B93, Room B west, locus 3	II-10-99	Bead, hexagonal	Tiny	Turqoise	Translucent	99/195	fig. 40p
—	—	Bead, bicone	Small	Opaque white and transparent	Slight weathering	99/195	—
B93, Room B west, locus 3	II-10-99	2 body sherds	Small	Transparent	White weathering	—	—
—	—	Body sherd	ca. 4.3 × 3.0 cm	Transparent	Thick, white weathering	—	—
—	—	Body sherd	Small	Transparent	Thin, slight weathering	—	—
—	—	Body sherd? Decorated?	Very small	Turquoise	Opaque	99/195	—
—	—	Pedestal base, straw marks	Very small	Transparent	Thick	99/195	—
—	—	Knock-off rim	Tiny	Transparent	—	99/195	—
—	—	Knock-off rim	ca. 2.6 × 1.6 cm	Transparent	White weathering	99/195	fig. 42b
—	—	Bottle neck, thread decoration	Very small	Cobalt on light blue-green	Few bubbles	99/195	fig. 42k
—	—	Decorated?	Tiny chip	Cobalt	—	—	—
B93, Room C northeast, locus 5	II-14-99	Body sherd	ca. 3.0 × 1.5 cm	Transparent	Thick, weathered	—	—
—	—	Bead, bicone, wound	Small	Yellow and gray-green	Opaque	99/195	—
B93, Room C northeast, locus 9	II-14-99	Body sherd	Very small	Transparent	White weathering	—	—
B93, Room C northeast, locus 12	II-15-99	Body sherd	Very small	Transparent	Weathered	—	—
—	—	Body sherd	Very small	Light blue-green	Slight weathering	—	—
—	—	2 body sherds, ribbed, molded	Small and 6.3 × 3.0 cm	Transparent	White weathering	99/195	—
B93, Room C northeast, locus 13	II-16-99	Body sherd	Small	Olive	Bubbly	—	—
B93, Room C northeast, locus 14	II-16-99	2 body sherds	Small	Transparent?	Gray weathering	—	—
B93, Room C northwest, locus 15	II-16-99	Body sherd	Small	Transparent?	Weathered	—	—
—	—	Body sherd	Chip	Cobalt	—	—	—

Provenance	*Date*	*Description*	*Size*	*Color*	*Fabric, etc.*	*Registration No.*	*Illustration*
B93, Room C northwest, locus 16	II-16-99	Bead, bicone, wound	Small	Yellow and gray-green	Opaque	99/195	—
B93, Room C northwest, locus 16	II-17-99	Bead, bicone	Small	Green	Opaque, weathered	99/195	fig. 40j
—	—	Rim, thickened, decorated	Very small	Transparent(?) with white threads marvered in	Weathered	99/195	fig. 42h
B93, Room C northwest, locus 17	II-17-99	Body sherd	Chip	Transparent	—	—	—
B93, Room C northeast, locus 20	II-18-99	Bead	Small	Green	Translucent	99/195	—
B93, Room D, surface cleaning	II-13-99	Base? Thick, join at pedestal?	Small	Transparent	Very bubbly	—	—
—	—	Bead	Tiny	Green	Opaque	99/195	—
B93, Room D, locus 1	II-23-99	Bead, bicone	Small	Dark amber brown	Translucent	99/195	—
B93, Room D, locus 2	II-24-99	Body sherd	Tiny chip	Cobalt	Translucent	—	—
B93, Room D, locus 3	II-24-99	2 body sherds	Small	Transparent?	Tough gray weathering	—	—
B93, Room E, locus 2, silty, sandy	II-25-99	Body	Small	Transparent?	Thin, weathered	—	—
—	—	2 body sherds	Ca. 4.0 × 2.5 cm	Blue-green tinge	Very thin, few bubbles	—	—
—	—	Base, pedestal, straw marks	Very small	Transparent	Slight weathering	—	—
—	—	Bead	Small	Blue	Opaque	99/195	—
—	—	Bead, hexagonal	0.8 cm long	Deep blue-green	Translucent	99/195	—
B93, Room E, locus 3	II-25-99	Body sherd	Very small	Transparent	White weathering	—	—
B93, Room E, locus 3, silty (from screen)	II-27-99	Body sherd	Small	Transparent?	Thin, weathered	—	—
—		Base? Looped	Very small	Transparent?	Weathered	—	—
B177, Room A, locus 7, surface	II-21-99	Body sherd	Small	Light blue-green	Bubbly	—	—
—		Bead	Tiny	Turquoise	Opaque	99/195	—
B177, Room A, locus 0, surface silt	II-21-99	Beaker(?) rim	Very small	Light blue-green	Bubbly	99/195	—
B177, Room A, locus 0, surface silt	II-23-99	Body sherd	Tiny chip	Transparent with purple tip	Worn	—	—
B177, Room A, locus 0, surface silt	II-24-99	Body sherd	Very small	Yellow-green tint	Very thin, few bubbles	—	—
B177, Room A, locus 1	II-20-99	Body sherd	Very small	Transparent	Very thin	—	—
—	—	Bead, barrel	—	Blue-green	Opaque	99/195	—
—	—	Bead, fat cylinder	—	Red-orange on black	Opaque	99/195	—
—	—	Bead	Tiny	Green and yellow	Opaque	99/195	—
—	—	Bead	Tiny	Yellow millefiore	Opaque	99/195	—

Provenance	*Date*	*Description*	*Size*	*Color*	*Fabric, etc.*	*Registration No.*	*Illustration*
B177, Room A, locus 2 (pit)	II-20-99	Bead, wound bicone	Small	Yellow and greenish	Opaque	99/195	fig. 40m
B177, Room A, locus 2 (from screen)	II-21-99	Body sherd	Small	Transparent	Very bubbly	—	—
—	—	Body sherd	Small	Amber	—	—	—
—	—	Body sherd	Very small	Transparent	Bubbly	—	—
B177, Room A, locus 3	II-20-99	Body sherd	Very small	Very dark, cobalt	—	—	—
—	—	Kick-up base	Ca. 2 × 2 cm	Green tinge	Thick, pontil	99/195	—
B177, Room A southwest, locus 3	II-22-99	Body sherd	Very small	Light olive-amber	Thin	—	—
—	—	Body sherd	Tiny chip	Transparent	—	—	—
—	—	Body sherd	Very small	Transparent	Thick	—	—
—	—	2 body sherds	Ca. 2.0 × 1.5 cm	Transparent	Thin, weathered	—	—
—	—	Body sherd	Very small	Transparent and purple	Few bubbles	—	—
—	—	Body sherd	Very small	Transparent	Slight weathering	—	—
—	—	Body sherd	—	Translucent, light blue-green	Very bubbly, slight weathering	—	—
—	—	Body sherd, curve to base	Ca. 3.5 × 2.5 cm	Transparent	Bubbly, sLight weathering	—	—
—	—	Goblet, bowl stem? Slip of folded-in base	Ca. 3.0 × 2.5 cm	Transparent	Slight weathering	99/195	—
—	—	Bead	Tiny	Turquoise	Opaque	99/195	—
B177, Room A southwest, locus 3	II-22-99	Bead, slightly polygonal (originally called "faience")	Small	Blue-green	Opaque, white weathering	99/210	fig. 40o
B177, Room A southwest, locus 3 (clean-up)	II-22-99	2 body sherds	Tiny	Transparent	Slight weathering	—	—
—	—	Rolled rim	Tiny	Transparent	—	—	—
B177, Room A northeast, locus 3	II-23-99	Body sherd	Very small	Light blue-green	Very thin, few bubbles	—	—
B177, Room A southeast, locus 3	II-24-99	Bead	Tiny	Turquoise	Opaque	99/195	—
—	—	Bead	Small	Light blue	Opaque	99/195	—
—	—	Bead, hexagonal	Ca. 0.6 cm	Blue	Opaque	99/195	—
—	—	3 body sherds	Very small	Light amber	Very thin, few bubbles	—	—
—	—	Body sherd	Tiny chip	Blue-green tint	Very thin	—	—
—	—	Body sherd	Small	Transparent	Very thin, few bubbles	—	—
—	—	Body sherd	Very small	Light olive, blue blob	—	99/195	—
B177, Room A, locus 7	II-21-99	Body sherd	Ca. 2 × 2 cm	Light blue-green	Bubbly	—	—

Provenance	*Date*	*Description*	*Size*	*Color*	*Fabric, etc.*	*Registration No.*	*Illustration*
B177, Room A, locus 9	II-22-99	Body	Very small	Transparent	Thin, weathered	—	—
—	—	Curve to kick-up base?	Ca. 3.0 × 2.3 cm	Blue-green	Bubbly, slight weathering	—	—
—	—	Knocked-off rim	Small	Light olive	Few bubbles, slight weathering	99/195	fig. 42c
—	—	Half a bead	Ca. 0.9 cm	Black	Opaque	99/195	fig. 40i
B177, Room A, locus 12	II-22-99	Bead, bicone	Small	Very dark brown	Near opaque, gray	99/195	—
B177, Room A, locus 12	II-23-99	Bead	Small	Green	Opaque	99/195	—
—	—	Half a bead	Very small	Yellow	Opaque	99/195	—
—	—	Body sherd	Very small	Transparent	—	—	—
—	—	Kick-up base	Bottle?	Blue-green tint?	White and black weathering	—	—
B177, Room A southeast, locus 12	II-24-99	2 body sherds	Very small	Cobalt	—	—	—
B177, Room A, locus 15 (stone circle)	II-24-99	Body sherd	Very small	Light blue-green	Bubbly, weathered	—	—
B177, Room C east, locus 1	II-20-99	Body sherd	Very small	Transparent	Thin, weathered	—	—
—		Body sherd	Very small	Purple tint	—	—	—
—	—	Body sherd, looped bit?	Very small	Light blue-green	—	—	—
—	—	Bead, bicone	Small	Black	Opaque	99/195	—
B177, Room C, locus 1	II-21-99	Bead	Tiny	Black	Opaque	99/195	—
B177, Room C east, locus 2	II-20-99	Bead	Tiny	Black(?)	Opaque	99/195	—
B177, Room C, locus 2, west	II-21-99	Body sherd	Small	Transparent	Few bubbles	—	—
—	—	Body sherd	Very small	Transparent	Slight weathering	—	—
B177, Room C east, locus 3	II-20-99	3 body sherds	All small	Light olive	Very thin, white weathered	—	—
—	—	Body sherd	Tiny chip	Transparent	—	—	—
—	—	Body sherd	Tiny chip	Cobalt	—	—	—
B177, Room C east, locus 4	II-21-99	Bead, bicone	Tiny	Turquoise	Opaque	99/195	—
B177, Room C west, locus 7	II-22-99	Body sherd	Very small	Transparent	Slight weathering	—	—
—	—	Body sherd	Small	Transparent	Slight white weathering	—	—
—	—	Base angle	Ca. 4.8 × 0.7 cm	Transparent	Some bubbles, thick	99/195	—
—	—	Bead, wound bicone	Small	Yellow and gray-green	Opaque	99/195	—
B177, Room C, locus 8, west	II-22-99	Body sherd	Very small	Transparent	Thin, slight white weathering	—	—
—	—	Body sherd	Ca. 2 × 1.5	Transparent	Bubbly	—	—
—	—	3 body sherds	Ca. 2 × 1.5	Blue-green tinge	Very thin	—	—

Provenance	Date	Description	Size	Color	Fabric, etc.	Registration No.	Illustration
B177, Room C, locus 9, west	II-22-99	Body sherd	Very small	Transparent	White weathering	—	—
—	—	Body sherd	Very small	Transparent	Very thin, white weathering	—	—
—	—	2 body sherds	Tiny	Blue-green tint	White weathering	—	—
—	—	Body sherd	Very small	Blue-green	White weathering	—	—
—	—	Body sherd	Very small	Amber	Few bubbles	—	—
—	—	Body sherd	Very small	Cobalt blue	—	—	—
—	—	Body sherd	Tiny chip	Cobalt blue	Translucent	—	—
B177, Room D, locus 1, west half	II-21-99	Bead	Tiny	Bright green	Opaque	99/195	fig. 40h
—	—	Bead	Small, 1.4 cm long	Yellow and olive green	Opaque	99/195	fig. 40n, pl. 34b
B177, Room D, locus 2, west half	II-21-99	2 body sherds	Splinters	Transparent	Thin, slight weathering	—	—
—	—	Bead	Very tiny	Turquoise	Opaque	99/195	—
—	—	Bead	Small, bicone	Black?	Opaque	99/195	—
B177, Room D, locus 3, west half	II-21-99	Body sherd	Very small	Transparent	Bubbly, slight weathering	—	—
—		Body sherd	Small	Blue-green tint	Few bubbles	—	—
B177, Room D, locus 5, west half	II-21-99	Pedestal foot, straw marks	Ca. 2.0 × 1.5 cm	Transparent	Few bubbles	99/195	fig. 42j
B177, Room D, locus 6, east	II-22-99	Body sherd	Tiny	Light olive	Very thin	—	—
—		Rim, rolled	ca. 7 mm	Blue-green	Thick rim	—	—
—		Bead	Small, 4 x 5 mm	White opaque and translucent, yellowish stripes	—	99/195	fig. 40l, pl. 34c
—	—	Bead, bicone	0.7 cm	Black	Opaque	99/195	—
B181, surface	II-22-99	Body	Very small	Olive	Few bubbles	—	—
—	—	Kick-up base	Ca. 9 cm dia.	Blue-green tinge	Bubbly, slight weathering	—	—
B181, locus 1	II-22-99	2 body sherds, ribbed, molded?	ca. 3.5 × 5.5 cm total	Transparent	Large bubbles	—	—
—	—	Body sherd	Tiny chip	Light blue-green	[not visible]	—	—
B181, locus 2	II-23-99	2 beads	Tiny	Turquoise	Opaque	99/195	—
—	—	Bead	Small	Turquoise	Opaque	99/195	—
—	—	Bead	Small, polygonal	Black?	Opaque	99/195	—
—	—	Bead	Small	Yellow	Opaque	99/195	—
B181, locus 2	II-23-99	2 body sherds	Tiny	Blue-green tinge	Bubbly, thin	—	—
—	—	2 body sherds	Very small	Light olive	Some bubbles	—	—
—	—	Body sherd	Very small	Cobalt	Thin	—	—

Provenance	Date	Description	Size	Color	Fabric, etc.	Registration No.	Illustration
—	—	Bottle neck?	Ca. 3 cm dia.	Yellow-green	Medium thick, bubbly	—	—
—		Body, ribbed	Ca. 4.0 × 2.5 cm	Blue-green tinge	Few bubbles, slight weathering	99/195	—
Dump 1, locus 2, ash	II-8-99	Looped-out rim with ruffle decoration	Ca. 3.2 × 1.8 cm	Light green with light turqoise ruffle	Bubbles	99/195	fig. 42f
Dump 1, locus 2, ashy	II-9-99	Body sherd	Small	Green tinge	Very thick	—	—
Dump 1, locus 2 ash	II-9-99	Strap handle	Ca. 3 × 3 cm	Dirty blue-green	Very bubbly, impurities	99/195	fig. 42m
Dump 1, locus 4	II-10-99	Body sherd	Ca. 2.5 × 1.8 cm	Transparent	—	—	—
Dump 1, locus 10	II-11-99	Body sherd	Very small	Blue-green tinge	White weathering	—	—
Dump 1, locus 11	II-11-99	Body sherd	Ca. 3 × 2 cm	Transparent?	Weathered	—	—
Dump 2, locus uncertain	II-99	Body sherd, ribbed	Ca. 3.5 × 3.5 cm	Transparent	Bubbly	99/195	—
Dump 2, backfill	II-28-99	Bead	Small	Turquoise	Opaque	99/195	—
—	—	Bead	Ca. 0.7 cm	Turquoise	Opaque	99/195	—
Dump 2, locus 1, wadi wash	II-14-99	Kick-up base	Ca. 3 × 2 cm	Transparent	Bubbly, tough gray	99/195	—
Dump 2, locus 2	II-14-99	Body sherd (base?)	Ca. 2.0 × 1.6 cm	Transparent	Thick, few bubbles	—	—
Dump 2, locus 2	II-15-99	2 body sherds	Ca. 3 × 3 cm	Transparent	Thin, white weathered	—	—
—	—	Body sherd	Very small	Purple-brown	Bubbly	99/195	—
—	—	Base, looped	Ca. 2.7 × 2.4	Transparent	Bubbles, white weathering	99/195	fig. 42i
Dump 2, locus 2	—	Rim, bowl, Roman	Dia. ca. 16 cm	Red	Opaque	99/195	fig. 42o, pl. 35c
Dump 2, locus 2, middle	II-17-99	Body sherd	Very small	Light blue-green	Very thin, slight weathering	—	—
—	—	Bead, molded	1.5 cm	Yellow and brown striped	Opaque	99/195	—
Dump 2, locus 4	II-15-99	Body sherd	Very small	Transparent	Thick, white weathering	—	—
—	—	Body sherd	Very small	Green tinge	Thick, bubbles, slight weathering	—	—
—	—	Knock-off rim	Dia. 6 cm	Transparent	Few bubbles	99/195	fig. 42d
Dump 2, locus 4, middle strip	II-15-99	Strap handle	Ca. 4.3 × 2.0 cm	Blue-green	Bubbly	99/195	fig. 42n
Dump 2, locus 4, middle strip	II-16-99	Body, bottle neck?	Ca. 3 cm dia.	Purple-brown	Bubbly, white weathering	—	—
Dump 2, locus 5, middle	II-16-99	Body sherd	Ca. 4.0 × 1.5 cm	Transparent?	Tough gray weathering	—	—
—	—	Base, flat?	Ca. 14 cm dia.	Transparent	White weathering	—	—
—	—	Body sherd	Very small	Light blue-green	Very bubbly	—	—
Dump 2, locus 5, north end middle (ash)	II-16-99	Body sherd	Small	Transparent?	Tough gray weathering	—	—

Provenance	*Date*	*Description*	*Size*	*Color*	*Fabric, etc.*	*Registration No.*	*Illustration*
Dump 2, locus 5, middle	II-17-99	Beaker rim	10 cm dia.	Transparent	White weathering	99/195	fig. 42g
Dump 2 loci 5/10/11 (clean-up)	II-17-99	Body sherd	Small	Transparent	Bubbles, white weathering	—	—
Dump 2, locus 7, around "SW tabun"	II-16-99	Body sherd	Very small	Transparent	Slight weathering	—	—
—	—	Body sherd, bottle neck?	2.5 cm dia.	Olive	Slight weathering	—	—
Dump 2, locus 8, around "SW tabun"	II-16-99	Body sherd	Very small	Thick	—	—	—
Dump 2, locus 11 (tabun interior)	II-16-99	Body sherd	—	Olive tinge	Bubbly	—	—
Dump 2, locus 11 (tabun interior)	II-20-99	Body sherd	Chip	Transparent	—	—	—
Dump 2, locus 11 (tabun interior)	II-21-99	Body sherd	Small	Transparent	Few bubbles	—	—
—	—	Pedestal foot?	Ca. 3.0 × 1.6 cm	Blue-green	Bubbles, impurities	—	—
Dump 2, locus 12	II-13-99	Body sherd	Very small	Transparent	Thick	—	—
B176, surface, dump downslope	II-99	Body sherd	Ca. 3.5 × 1.5 cm	Transparent and purple	Thick, very bubbly	—	—

Appendix D
Shell

Provenance	*Date*	*Quantity*	*Preliminary Identification*
B93, Room A, locus 1	II-14-99	1 bit	Tiny turritella
B93, Room A, locus 5	II-16-99	1 bit	Spotted cowrie
B93, Room A, locus 6	II-17-99	3 bits	Pearly, large, flat; trochus?
B93, Room B west, locus 5	II-9-99	2 bits	Small cowrie, worn bit of univalve
B93, Room B west, locus 4	II-10-99	1 shell	Tiny turritella
B93, Room B west, locus 4	II-12-99	1 bit	"Tooth shell"
B93, Room B west, locus 8	II-14-99	3 shells	2 tiny turritellas
B93, Room C northwest, locus 18	II-18-99	2 shells	Ring cowrie, tiny turritella
B93, Room C northeast, locus 20	II-18-99	1 shell	Tiny turritella
B93, Room D, locus 2	II-24-99	4 shells, 1 bit	4 tiny turritellas, 1 fragment of conch(?) shell
B93, Room D east end, locus 2	II-25-99	1 piece	Large fragment of conch shell
B93, Room D, locus 3	II-24-99	1 shell	Tiny turritella
B93, Room D, east end, locus 3	II-27-99	1 shell	Tiny turritella
B93, Room D, locus 4	II-25-99	1 shell	Bleeding tooth, top cut off
B93, Room D, locus 4	II-25-99	1 piece	Conch core
B93, Room E, locus 2	II-25-99	1 shell, 1 bit	2 tiny turritellas
B93, Room E, locus 3	II-27-99	1 shell	Tiny turritella
Dump 1	II-11-99	1 piece	Spotted cowrie
Dump 1, locus 4	II-9-99	1 shell	Bleeding tooth, top cut off
Dump 1, locus 5	II-10-99	1 piece	Pearly trochus?
Dump 1, locus 12	II-13-99	1 piece	Tridacna?
Dump 1, locus 16	II-18-99	1 shell	Tiny turritella
Dump 2, locus 2	II-15-99	1 piece	Pearly trochus
Dump 2, locus 5, middle strip	II-16-99	1 shell	Tiny turritella
Dump 2, locus 11	II-17-99	1 shell	Striped univalve (like bonnet shell, small)
B177, Room A southwest, locus 0	II-21-99	1 shell	Knobbed?
B177, Room A southwest, locus 3/9	II-23-99	1 shell, 1 bit	Small cowrie, striped univalve?
B177, Room A, locus 12	II-22-99	1 shell	Small turritella
B177, Room C east, locus 2	II-20-99	1 piece	Small cowrie
B177, Room D east, locus 7	II-22-99	1 bead	unknown
B181, locus 1	II-22-99	2 shells, 1 bit	Bit of "tooth shell," tiny olive, conus
B181, locus 2	II-23-00	1 piece	Pearly, piece of trochus?

Index

a

b

(*a*) Building 93 at upper left, Building 97 on right, Dump 1 in between; (*b*) Building 93 before excavation: Room B at lower left, Room A at upper left, Room C with meter sticks, Room D at upper right (long scale = 1 m)

a

b

Building 93, (*a*) view through door from Room A into Room B showing threshold, step down, and bedrock floor of Room B; (*b*) view of Room B (long scale = 1 m)

a

b

Building 93, Room C, (*a*) before excavation and (*b*) upper floor (long scale = 1 m)

a

b

Building 93, Room C, (*a*) bin with rim of stones and (*b*) bin bottom (long scale = 1 m)

a

b

Building 93, (*a*) Room D before excavation and (*b*) Room E before excavation (upper left) (long scale = 1 m)

a

b

Building 93, Dump 1, upper level with cooking installations, (*a*) looking south; (*b*) looking east (long scale = 1 m)

a

b

Building 93, Dump 1, large stones in middle level, in situ vessels 129 and 135 in lower level, (*a*) looking south; (*b*) looking north (north arrow = 50 cm)

a

b

(*a*) Building 93, Dump 2, cooking installations (long scale = 1 m);
(*b*) main settlement, Hillock in center

a

b

(*a*) Building 177 before excavation;
(*b*) Building 177, Room A, after excavation (north arrow = 50 cm)

a

b

(*a*) Building 177, Room A, hearth;
(*b*) Building 177, Room B, after excavation (long scale = 1 m)

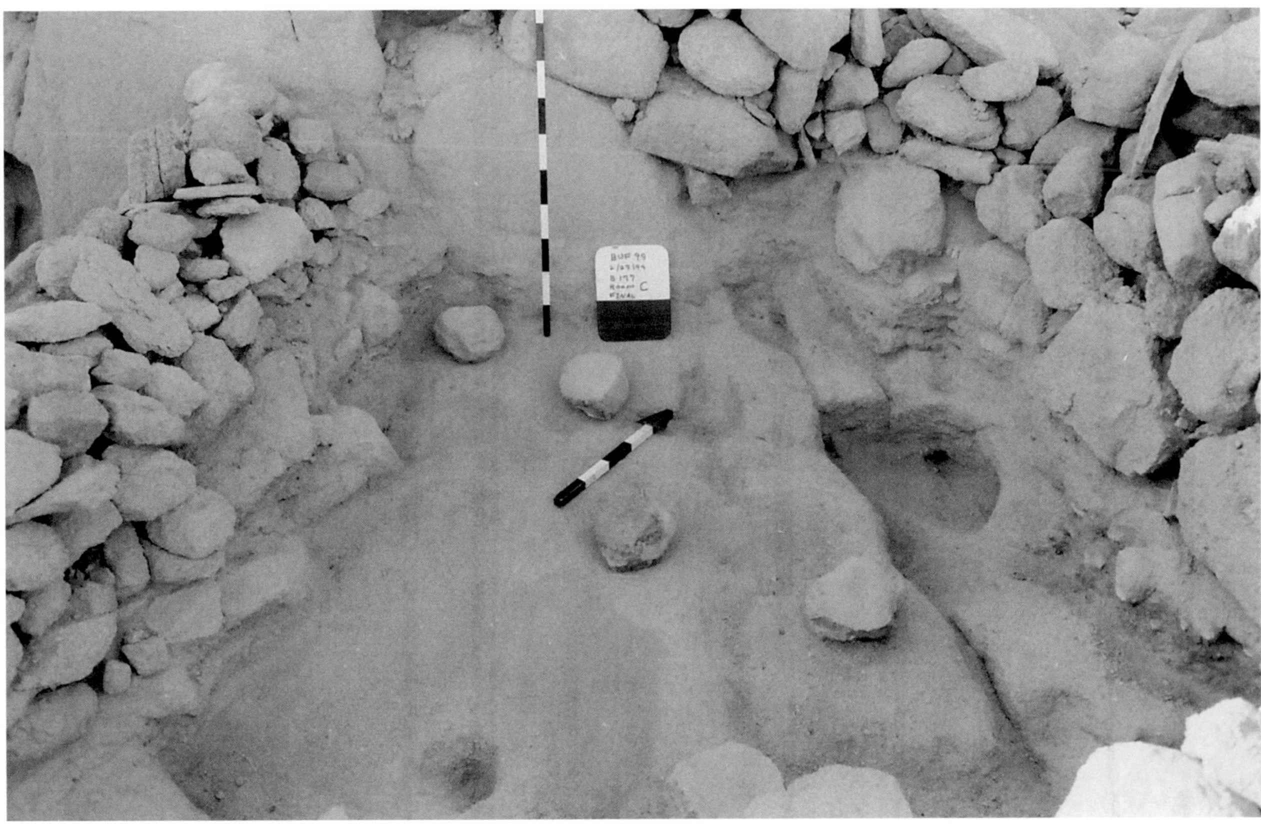

a

b

(*a*) Building 177, Room C, after excavation;
(*b*) Building 177, Room D, after excavation (long scale = 1 m)

a

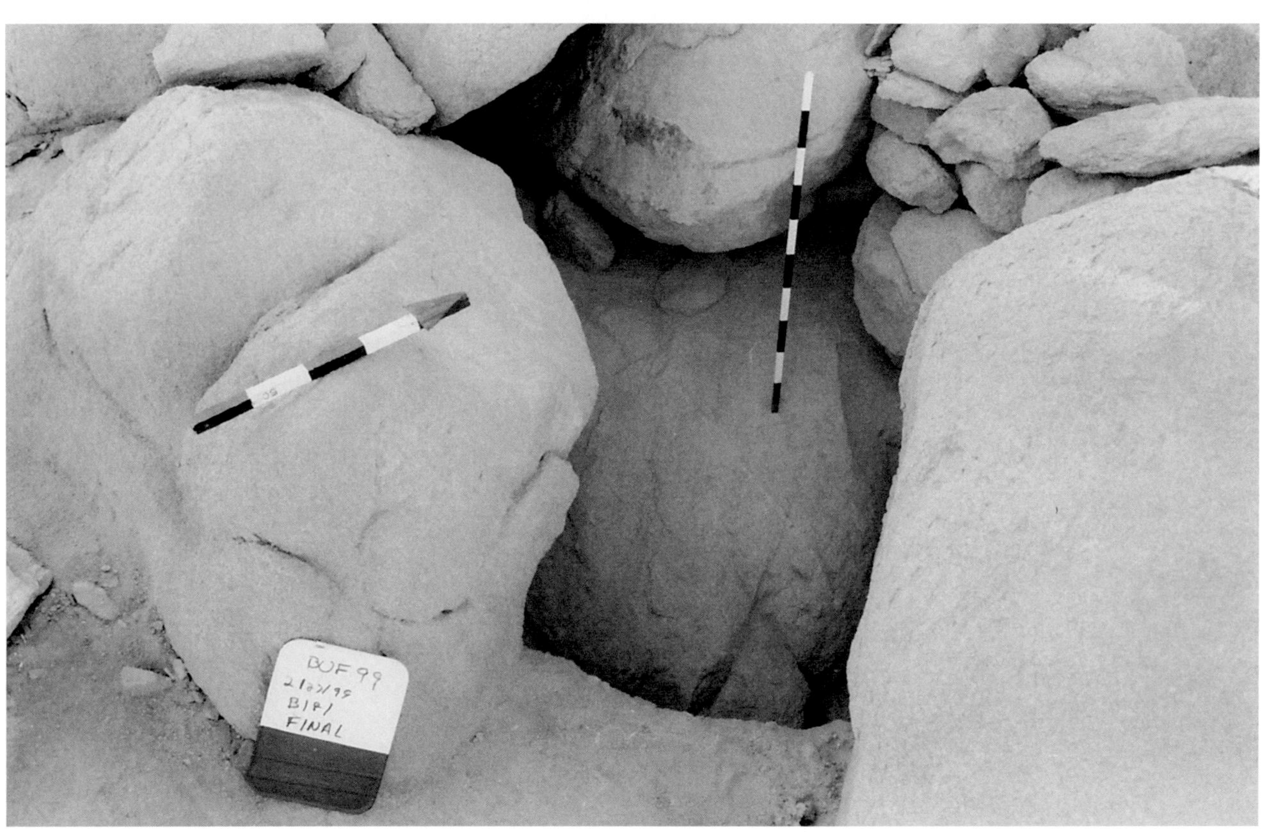

b

(*a*) Building 181 (in boulders), Building 178 (in center);
(*b*) Building 181, excavation to bedrock (north arrow = 50 cm)

a

b

(*a*) Silt "krater" 109 (RN 99/222);
(*b*) silt jar 129, possibly for milk (RN 99/219) (scale in decimeters)

a

b

(*a*) Silt jar 135, possibly for cheese-making (RN 99/220); (*b*) five holes in the bottom of silt jar 135

c

0
5 cm

(*a*) Date pit-shaped soapstone bead (RN 99/199);
(*b*) flower-shaped steatite bead (RN 99/199);
(*c*) stone "incense burner" with arches and legs (RN 99/227)

a

b

(*a*) Stone "incense burner" with feet (RN 99/227);
(*b*) brick "incense burner" (RN 99/204)

a

b

(*a*) Crude serpentinite bowl (RN 99/205);
(*b*) stone pestle (RN 99/207)

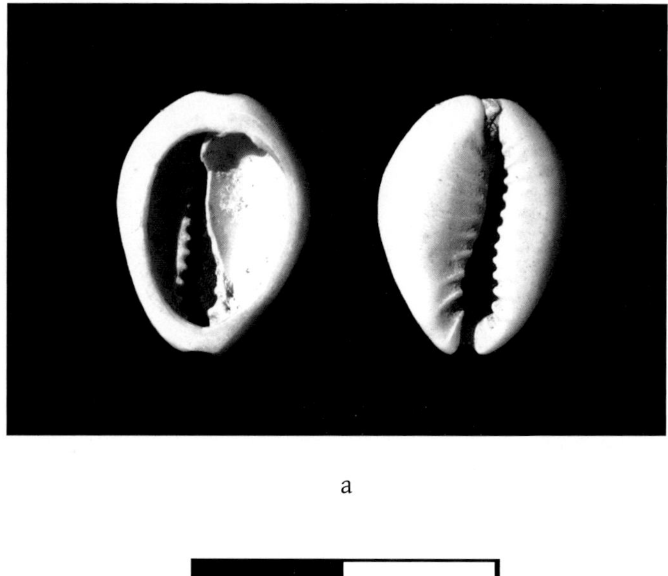

a

0 2 cm

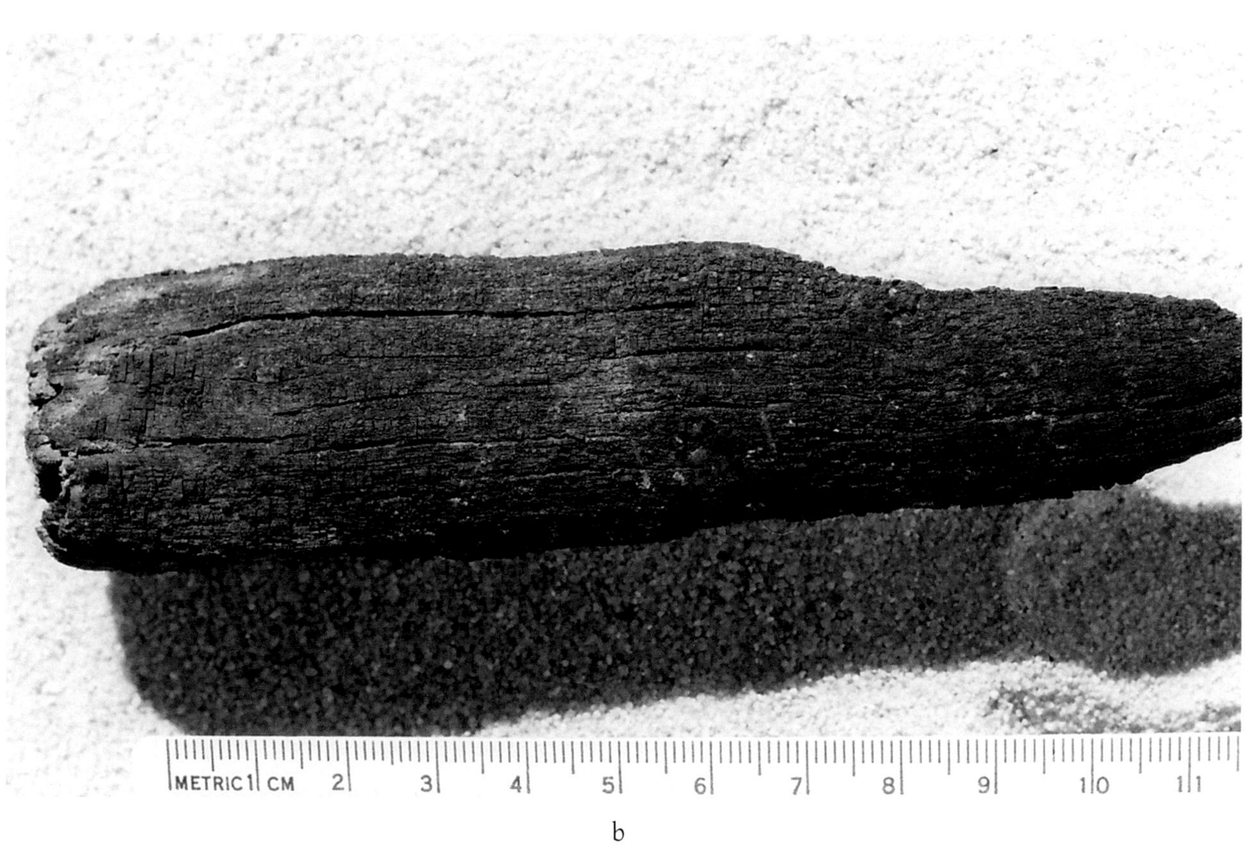

b

(*a*) Sliced cowrie shell (RN 99/201), top and bottom;
(*b*) wooden peg (RN 99/208)

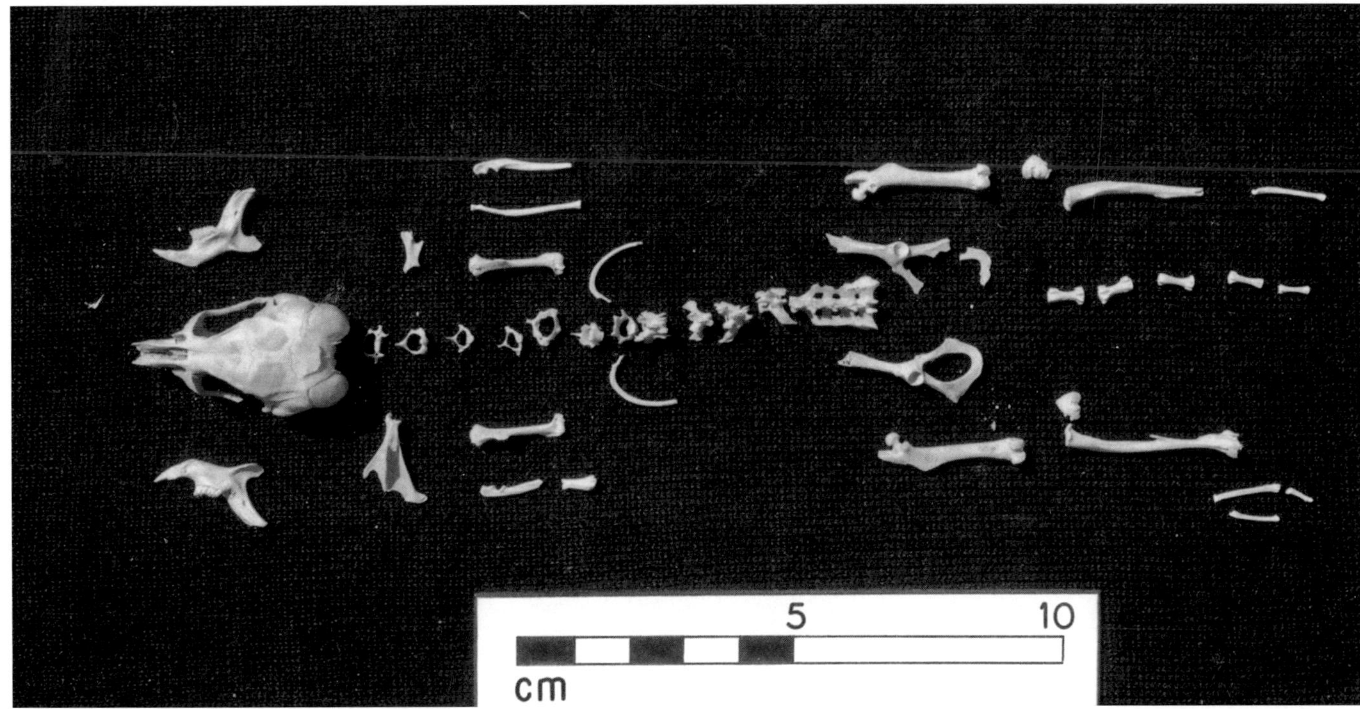

a

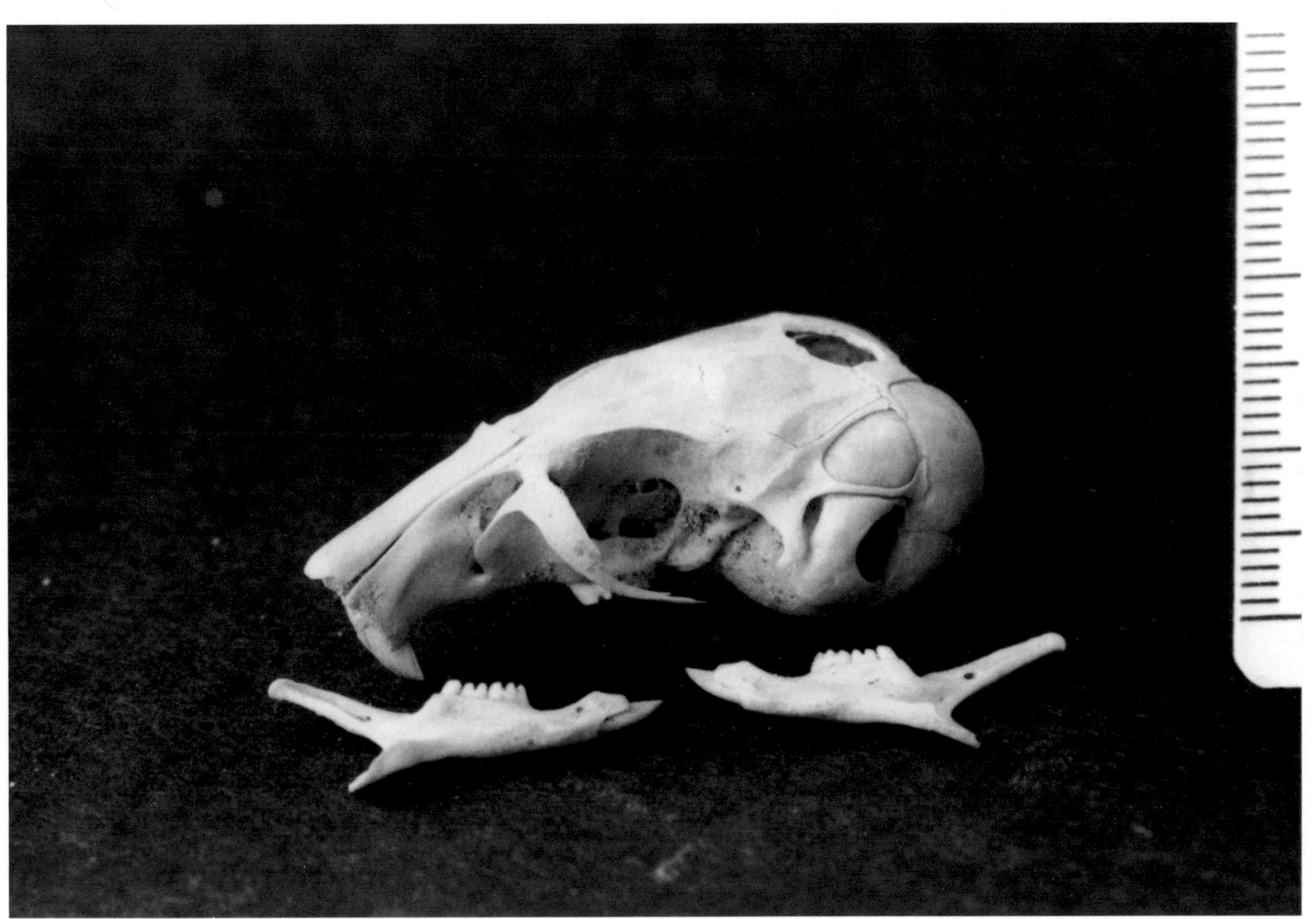

b

Silky jird (99/235) (*a*) skeleton and (*b*) skull

a

b

(*a*) Main settlement, tire tracks down wadi "street";
(*b*) truck dumping boulders for barricade

a

b

(*a*) Front-loader moving boulders into place;
(*b*) aligning first row of boulders for barricade

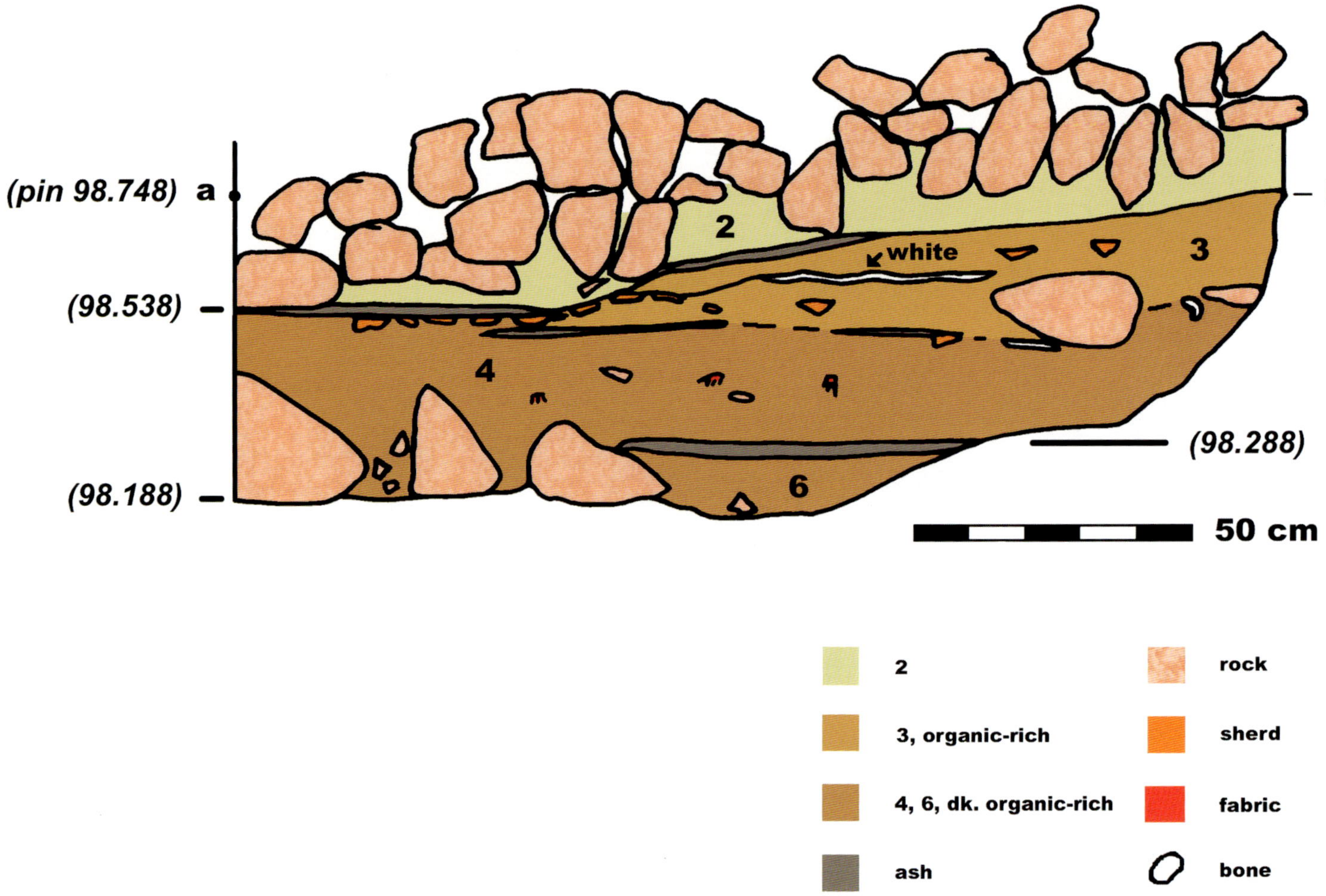

(pin 98.748) a
b
2
white
3
(98.538)
4
(98.288)
(98.188)
6
50 cm

2
rock
3, organic-rich
sherd
4, 6, dk. organic-rich
fabric
ash
bone

a. Building 93, Room A, section a–b

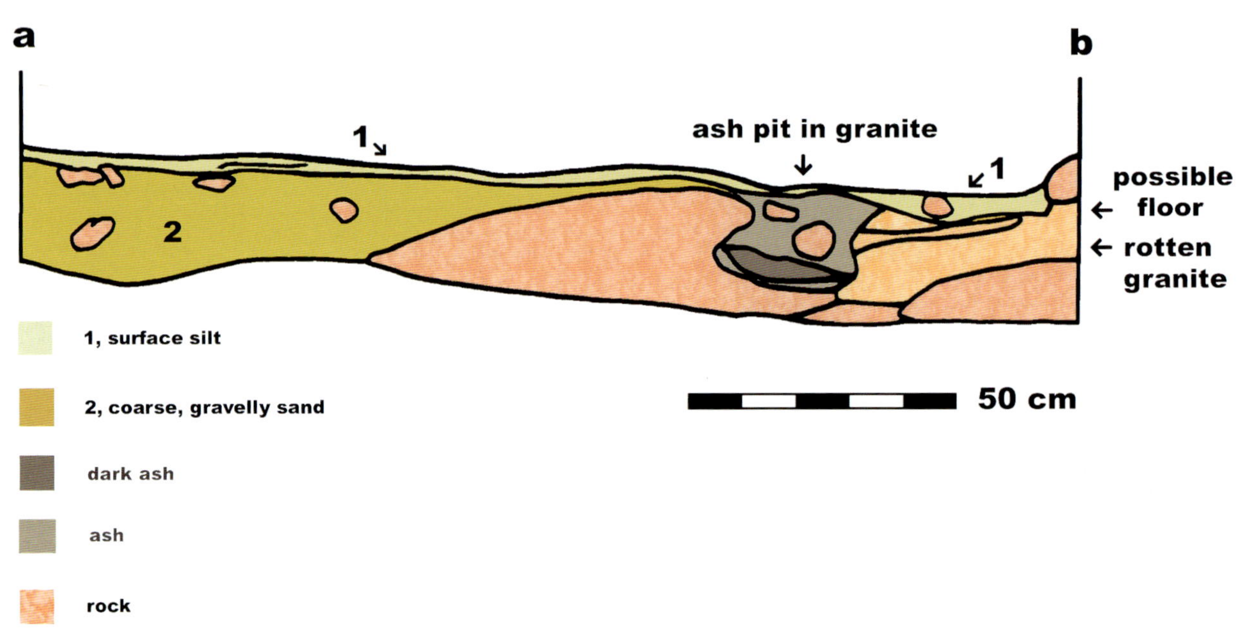

b. Building 93, Room B, section a–b (east baulk)

c
d
2
2, sandy fill
coarse sandy lenses
rock
50 cm

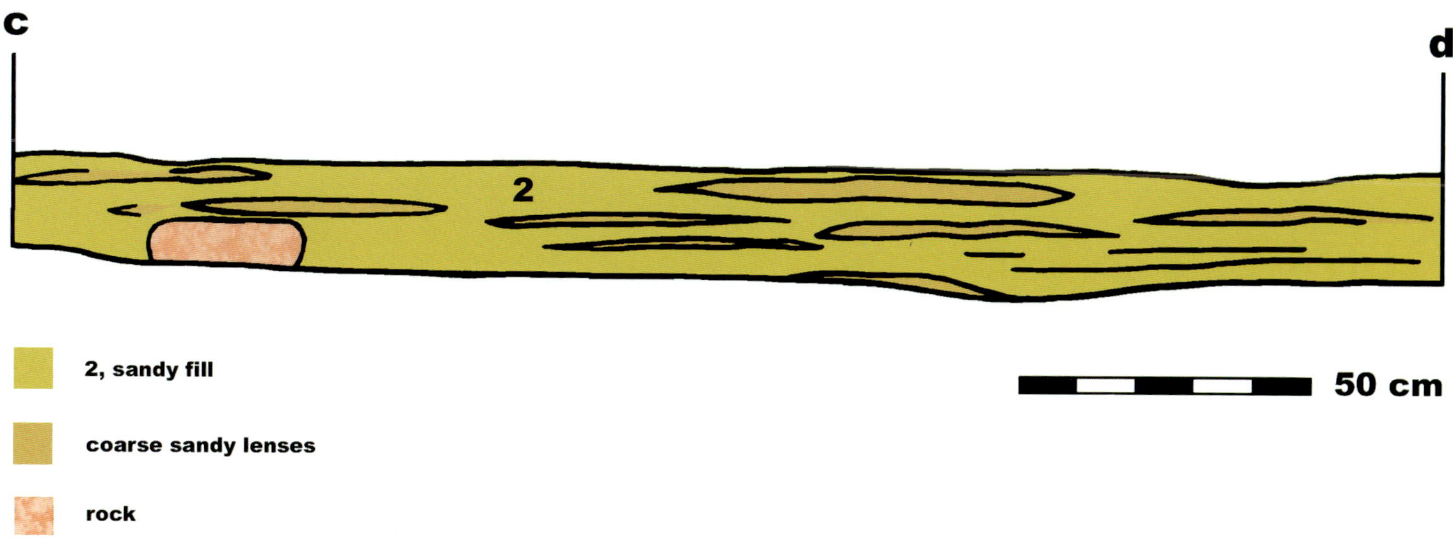

a. Building 93, Room B, section c–d (west [middle] baulk)

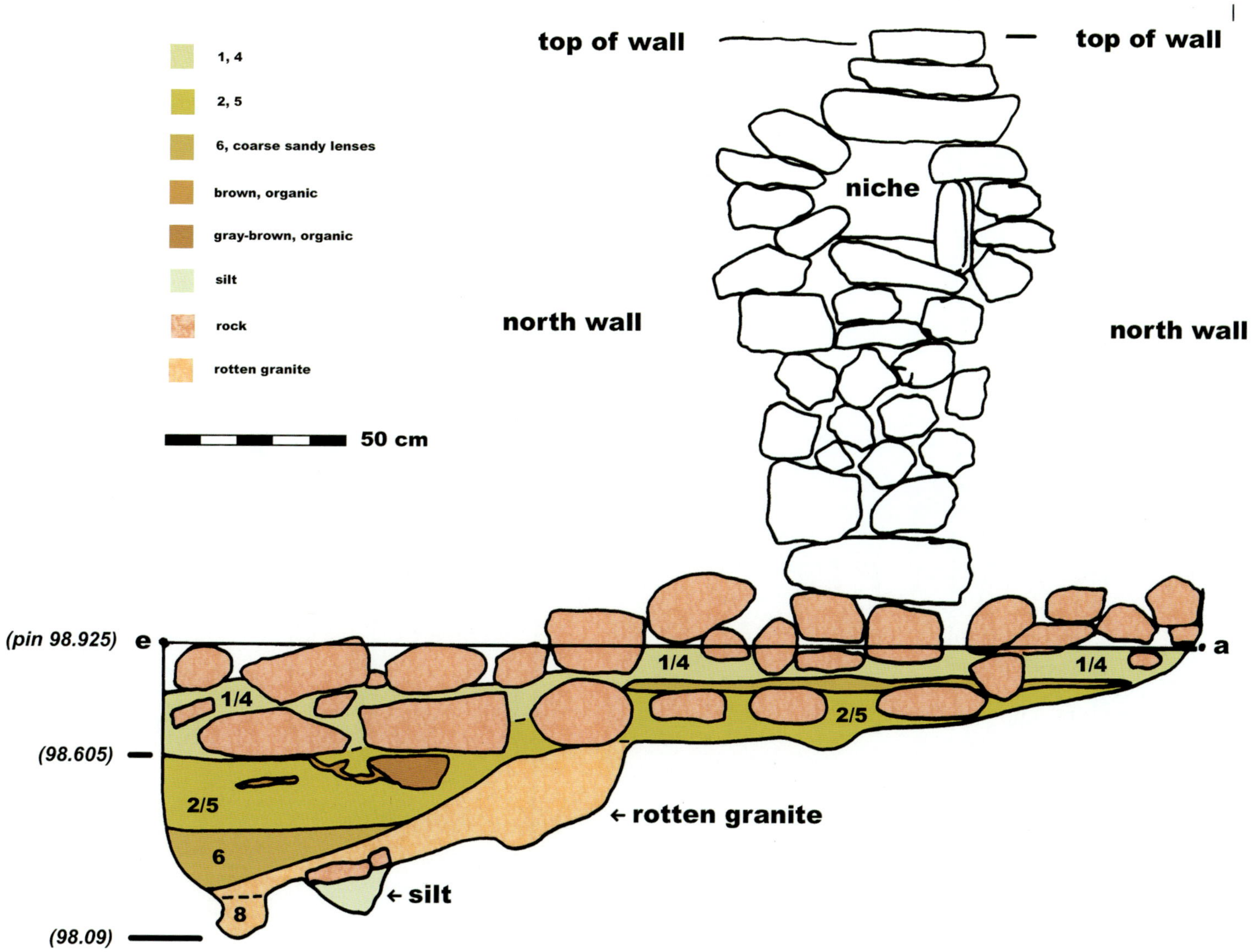

1, 4
2, 5
6, coarse sandy lenses
brown, organic
gray-brown, organic
silt
rock
rotten granite
50 cm
top of wall
top of wall
niche
north wall
north wall
(pin 98.925) e
a
1/4
1/4
1/4
2/5
(98.605)
2/5
6
8
← rotten granite
← silt
(98.09)

b. Building 93, Room B, section e–a (north baulk)

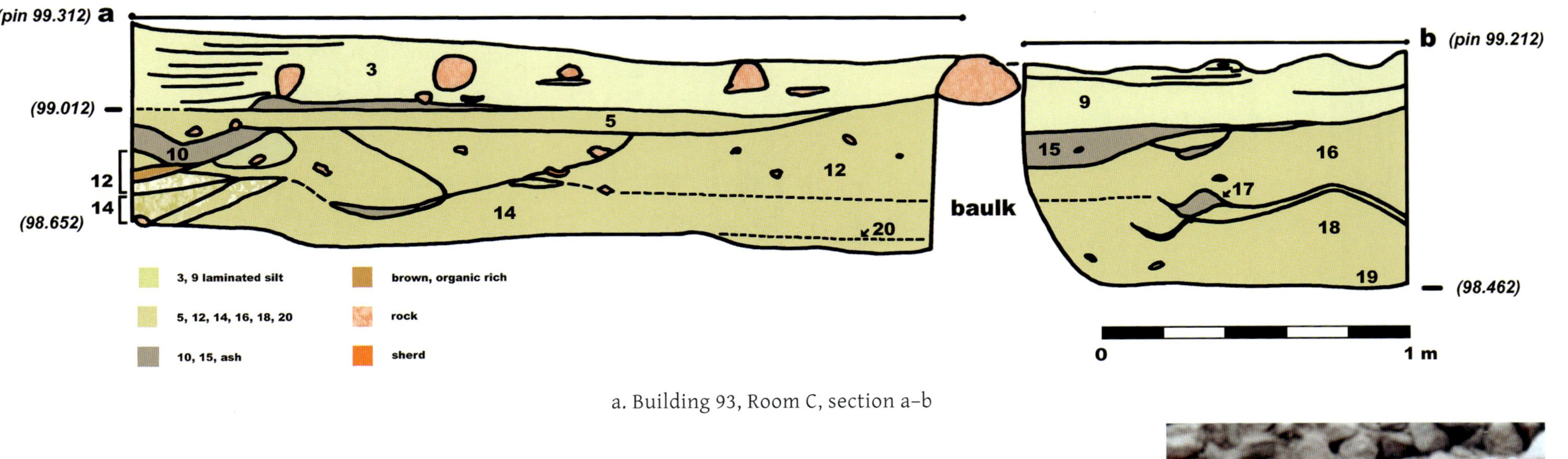

a. Building 93, Room C, section a–b

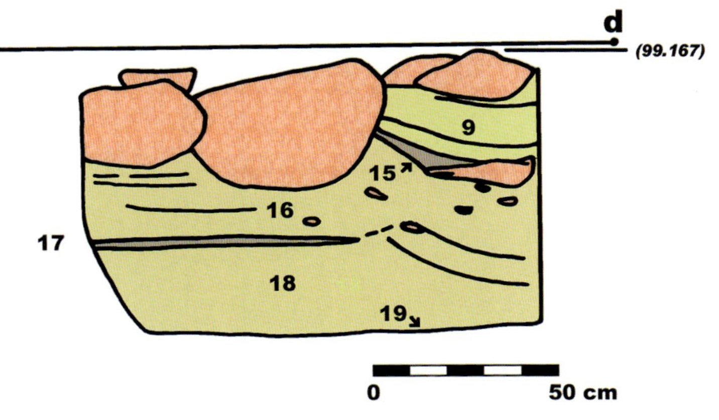

b. Building 93, Room C, section c–d

c. Building 93, Room C, "krater" (RN 99/222) in locus 18 fill, upside-down on floor

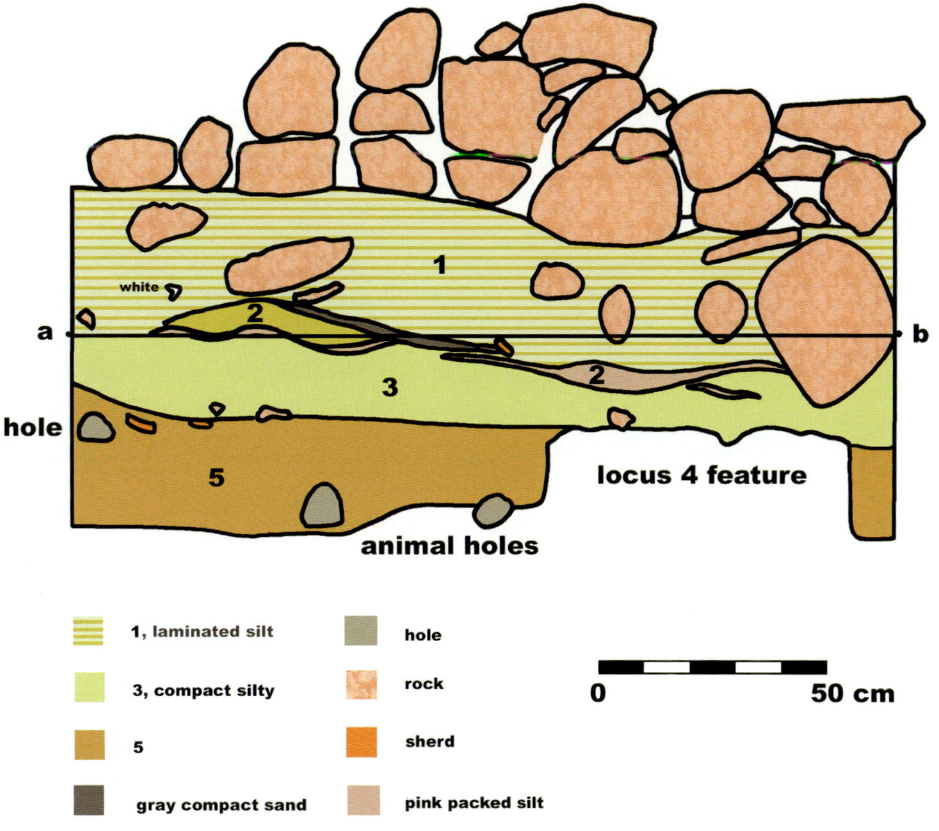

a. Building 93, Room D, section a–b

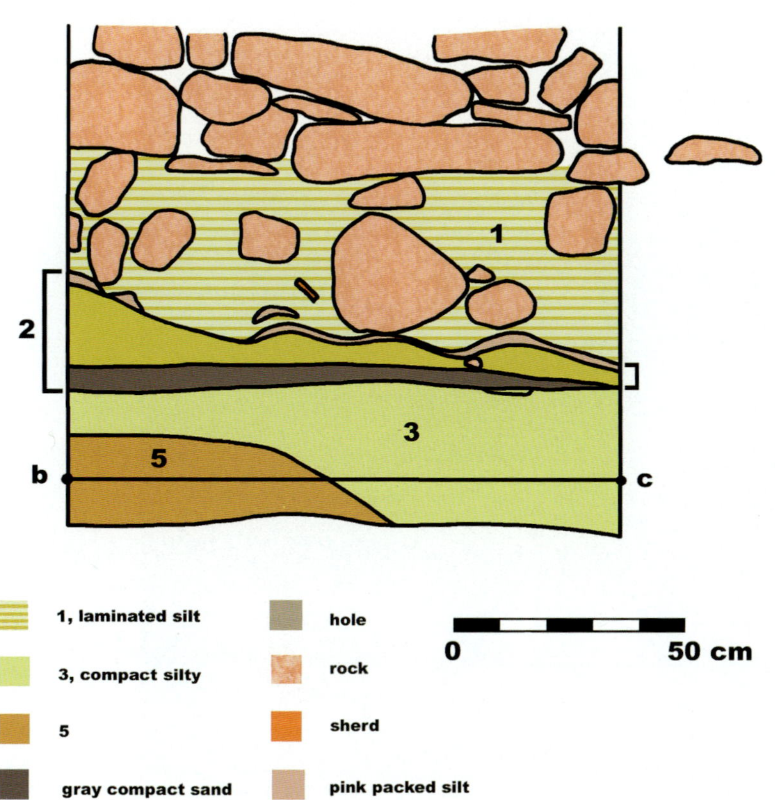

b. Building 93, Room D, section b–c

c. Building 93, Room D, circular feature (locus 3) (north arrow = 50 cm)

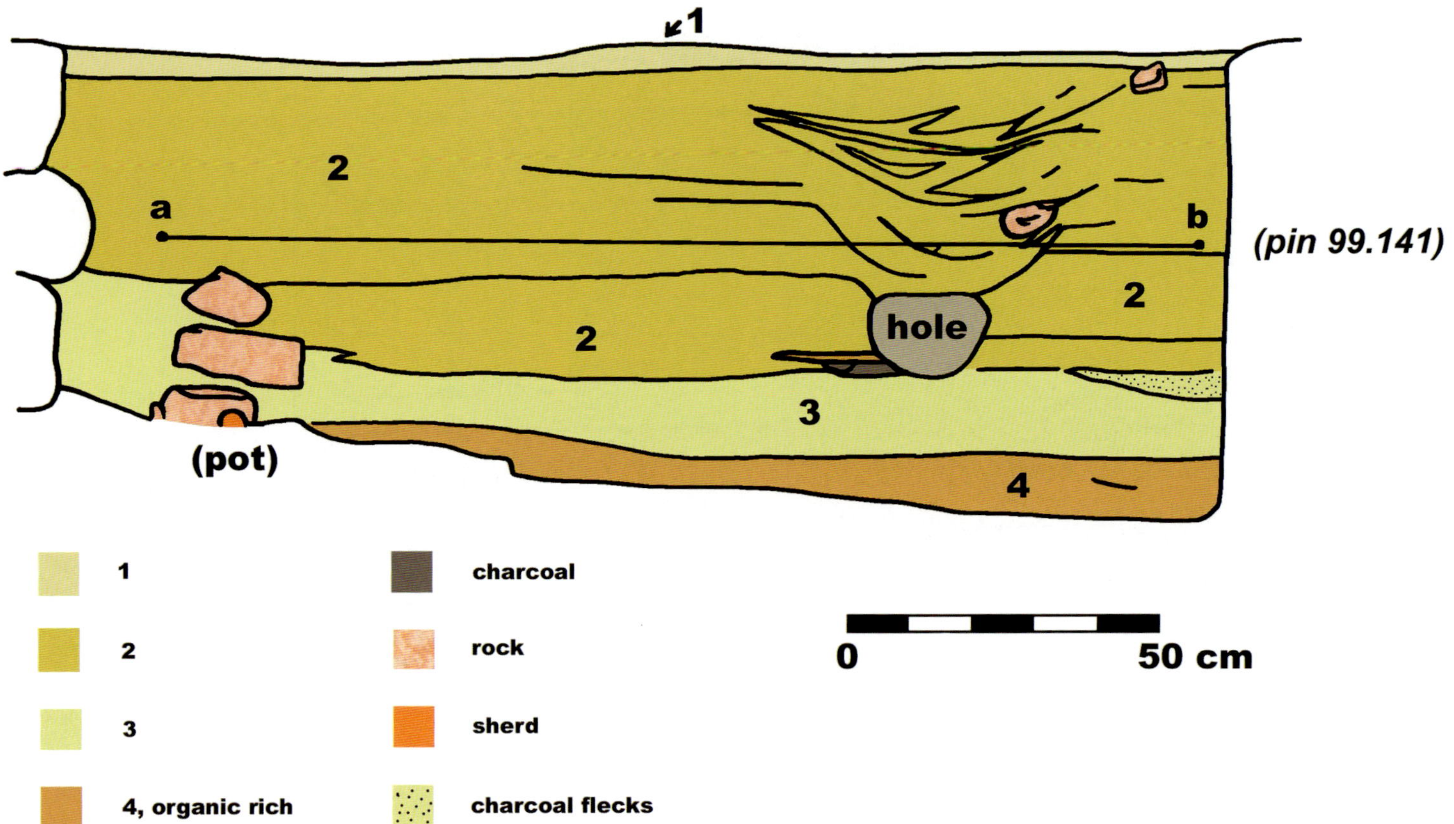

a. Building 93, Room E, section a–b (south baulk)

b. Building 93, Room E, pot in south baulk (north arrow = 50 cm)

a. Dump 1, before excavation

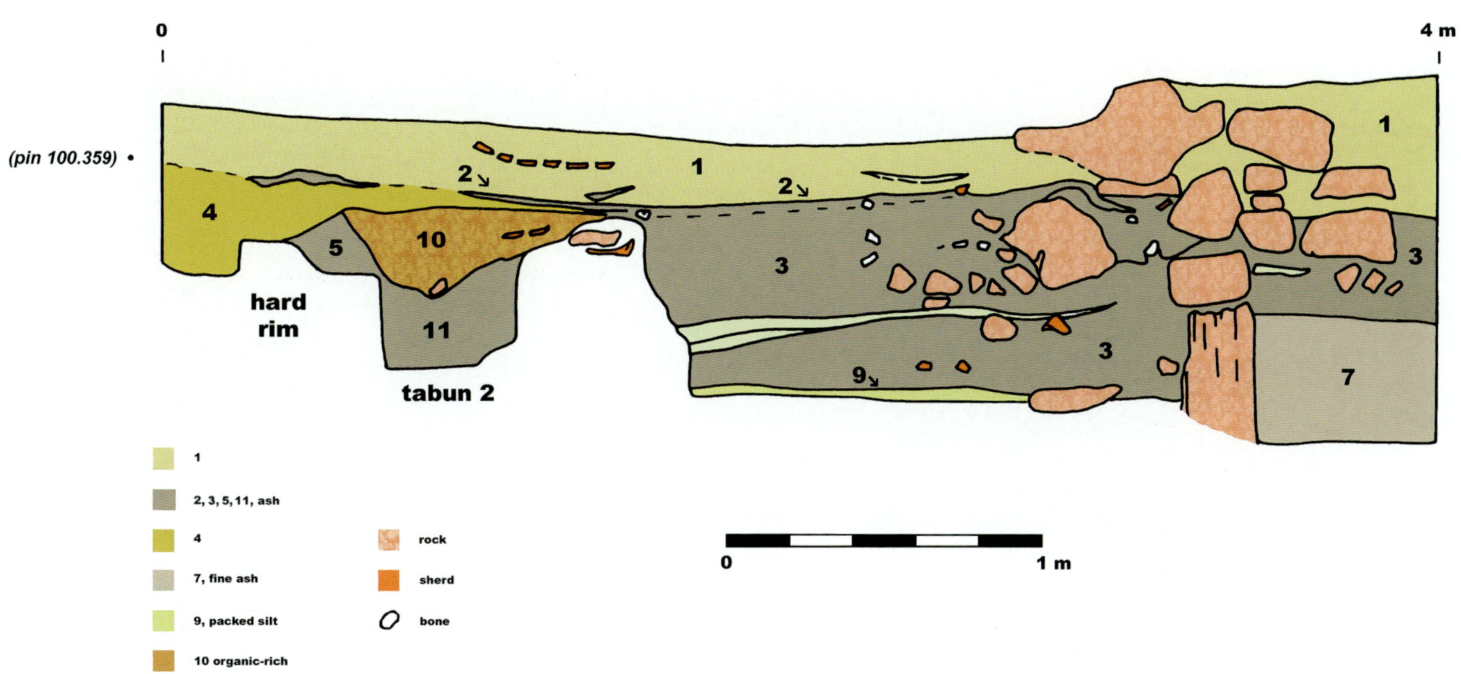

b. Dump 1, east baulk

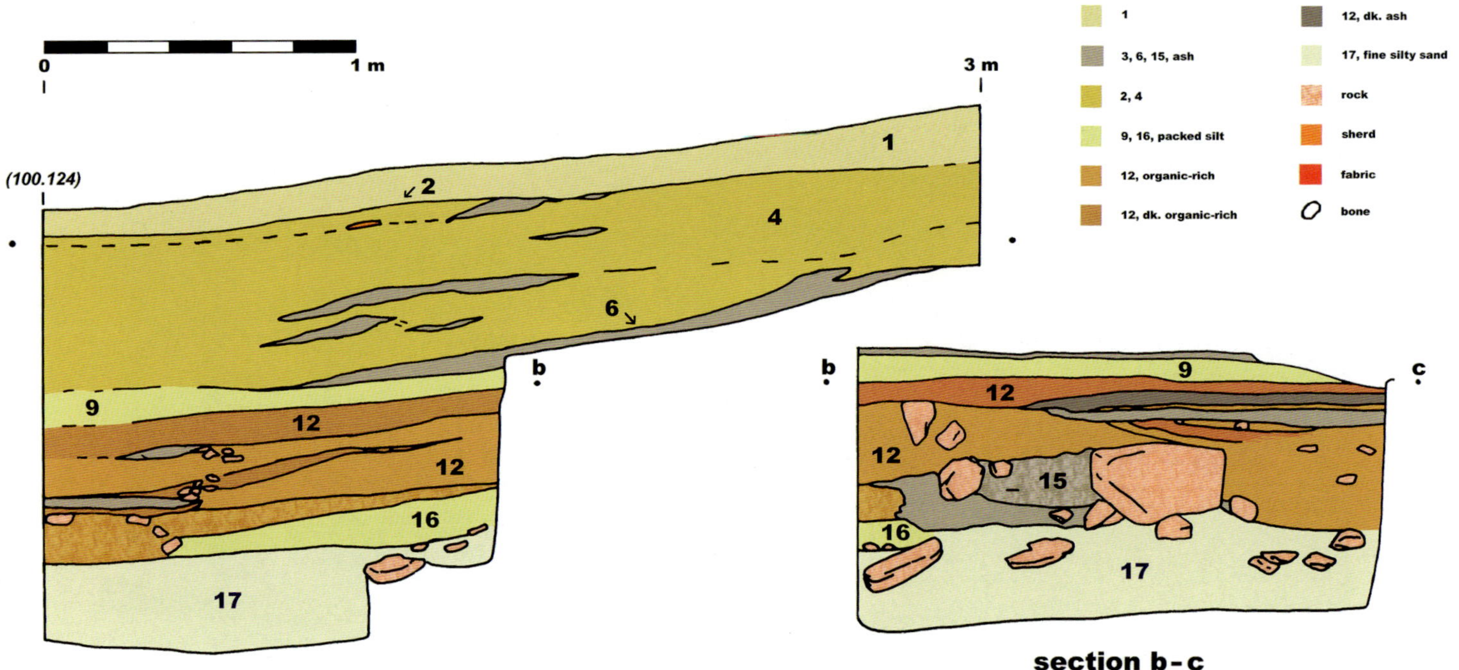

a. Dump 1, north baulk (and east baulk of deep cut)

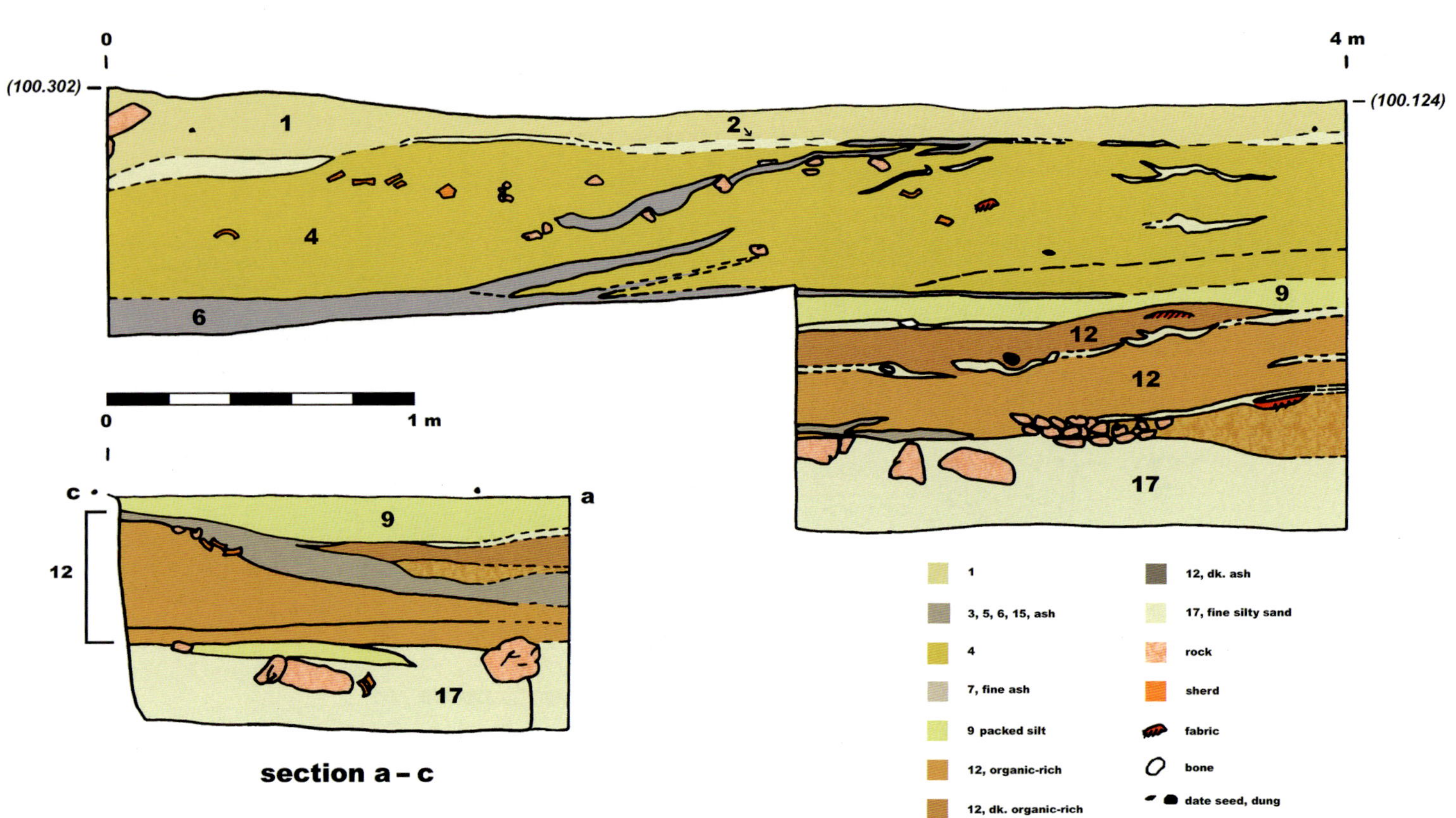

b. Dump 1, west baulk (and south baulk of deep cut)

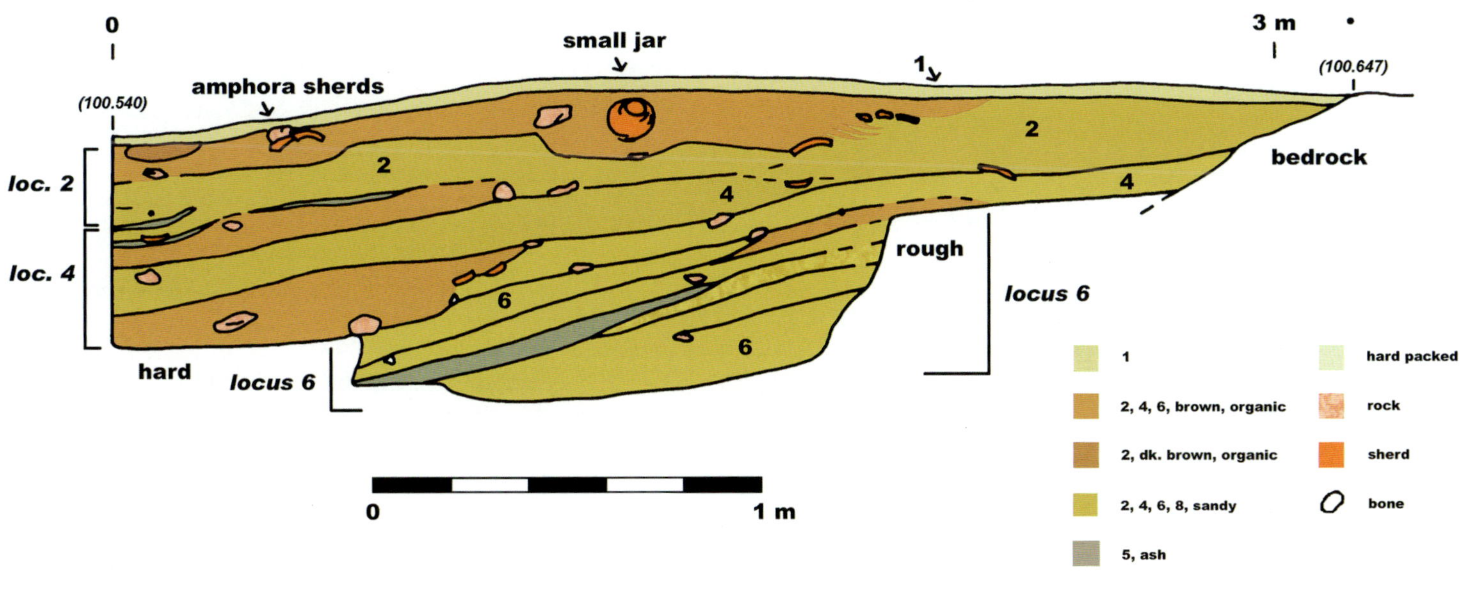

a. Dump 2, north baulk

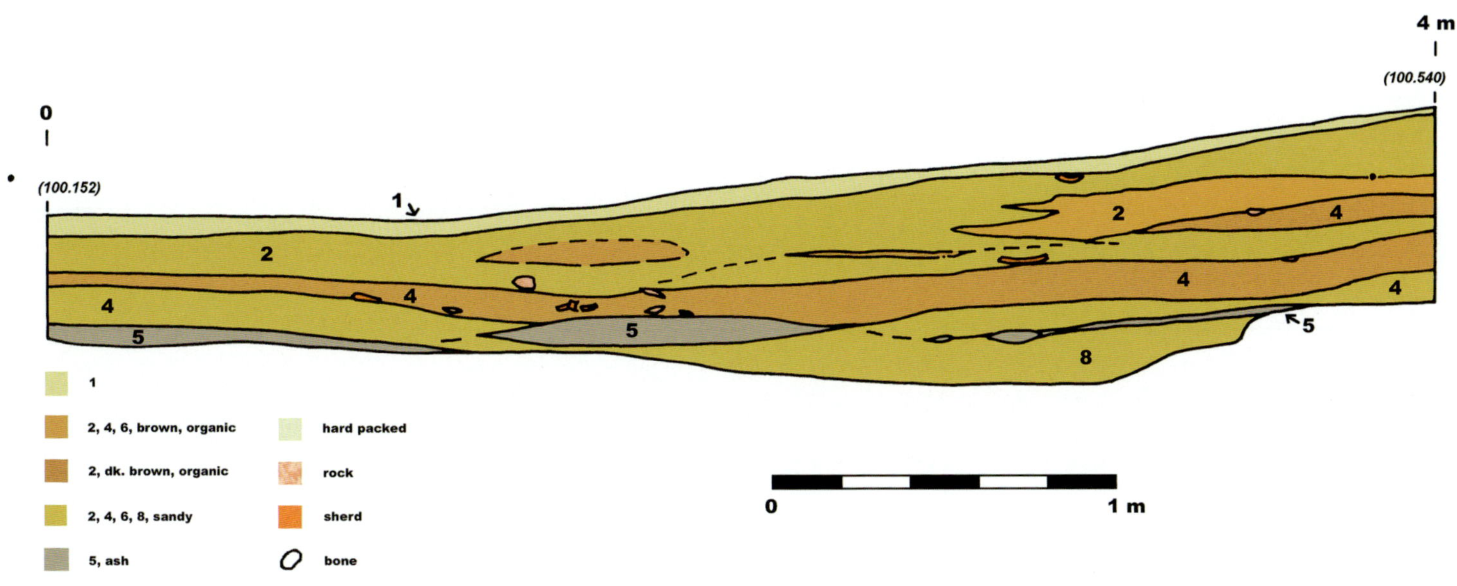

b. Dump 2, west baulk

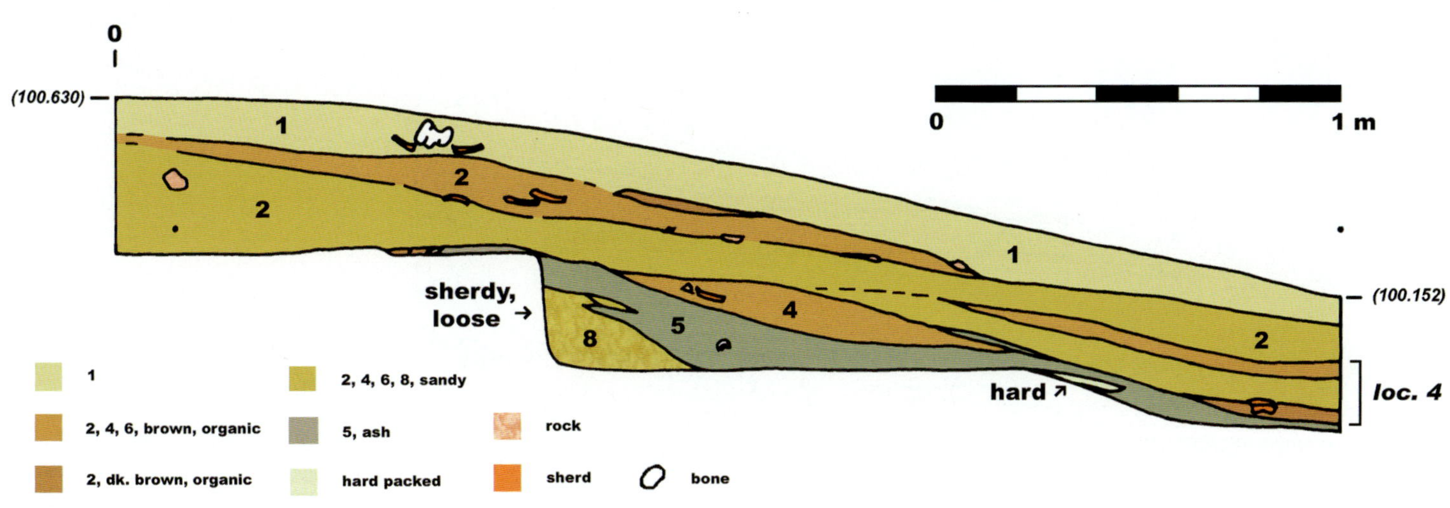

c. Dump 2, south baulk

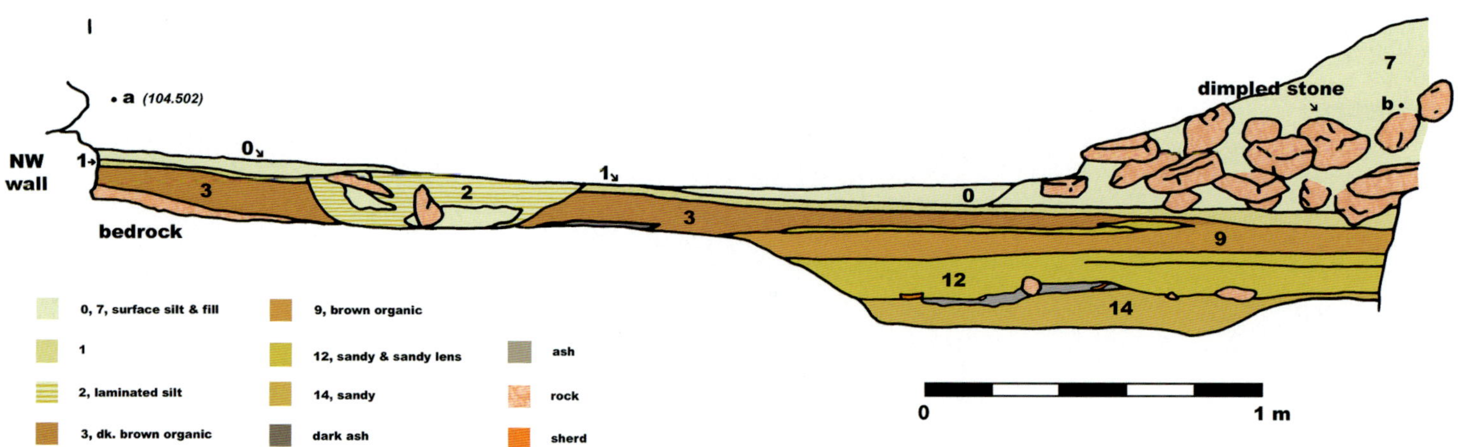

a. Building 177, Room A, section a–b

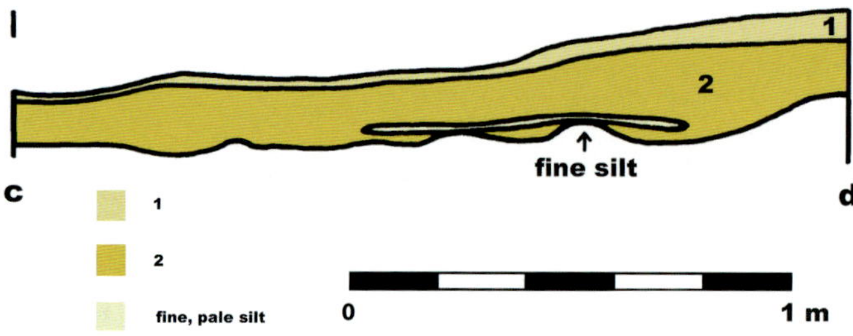

b. Building 177, Room C, section c–d

a

b

(*a*) Stamped plate 14 (RN 99/233);
(*b*) Small cup or bowl 64 with incised marks (RN/215)

a

b

(*a*) Deep bowl 104 (RN 99/218); (*b*) painted jar 138 (RN 99/234)

a

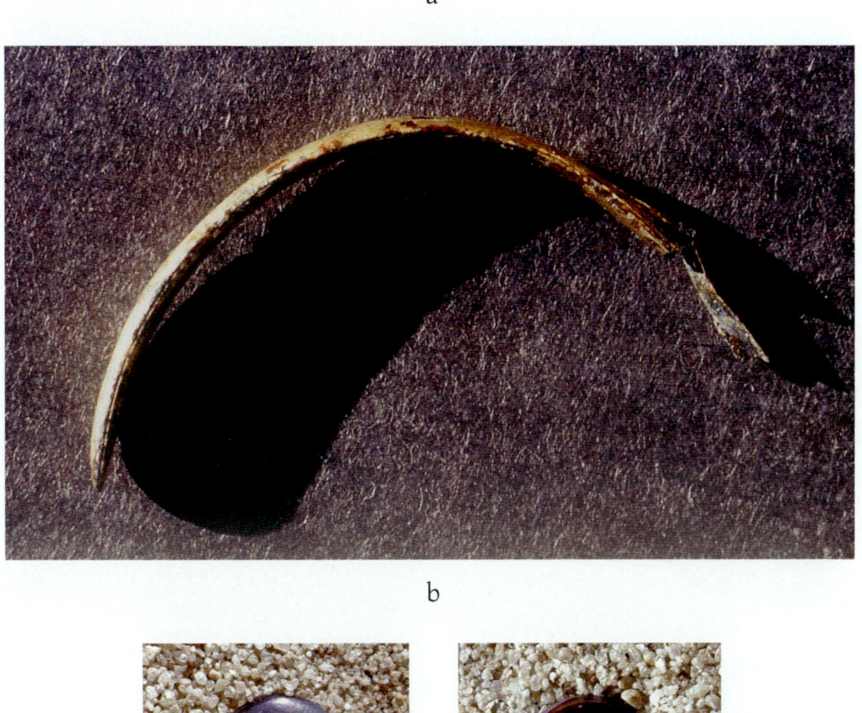

b

c

0 2 cm

(*a*) Dipinto with "tetra" inscription; (*b*) Copper/gold-alloy bracelet (RN 99/230); (*c*) Agate bezel (RN 99/203), top and bottom

(*a*) Copper-alloy Bes amulet (RN 99/240); (*b*) green and yellow wound glass bead; (*c*) striped biconical glass bead; (*d*) six of the eleven raw emeralds/green beryls (RN 99/232); (*e*) Iron ladle (RN 99/228), top and bottom

(*a*) Iron wedge or spike RN 99/241, top and side; (*b*) Copper/bronze weight (RN 99/239); (*c*) rim sherd of Roman-period red glass bowl (RN 99/195); (*d*) burnt lamp nozzle (RN 99/213)

a

b

Iron ladle (RN 99/228) (*a*) in situ and (*b*) after conservation, side view

a

b

(*a*) Dump 1, "tabun" 1 or *dolium*, after conservation; (*b*) Dump 2, pot 1 cooking installation with reused amphora

a

b

Dump 2, pot 1 (*a*) reused amphora after clearance and conservation; (*b*) Dump 2, "SW tabun," contents

a

b

Dump 2, "SW tabun," (*a*) after excavation; (*b*) cloth, twine, and fiber from Dump 2

a

b

(*a*) Late Roman Amphora 7 segment after conservation; (*b*) Building 93 under excavation by team of workers near end of 1999 season. Dump 2 (left) and Dump 1 (right) flank Building 93. Bir Umm Fawakhir. Photo by Henry Cowherd